D0236279

Currency Wars

Books by John K. Cooley

Baal, Christ and Mohammed: Religion and Revolution in North Africa
(1965)

East Wind Over Africa: Red China's African Offensive
(1966)

Green March, Black September: The Story of the Palestinian Arabs
(1973)

Libyan Sandstorm: The Complete Story of Qaddafi's Revolution
(1982)

Payback: America's Long War in the Middle East
(1991)

Unholy Wars: Afghanistan, America and International Terrorism
(1999, 2000, 2002)

An Alliance Against Babylon: the US, Israel and Iraq
(2005)

Currency Wars

Forging Money to Break Economies

John K. Cooley

CONSTABLE • LONDON

To Vania, Alexander and Katherine Anne

Constable & Robinson Ltd
3 The Lanchesters
162 Fulham Palace Road
London W6 9ER
www.constablerobinson.com

This edition published by Constable,
an imprint of Constable & Robinson, 2008

A copy of the British Library Cataloguing in Publication Data is available from the British Library

ISBN: 978-1-84529-369-7

Printed and bound in the EU

1 3 5 7 9 10 8 6 4 2

Contents

Cartoon by Sydney 'George' Strube, *Daily Express*, 19 September 1924. A number of forged Russian banknotes had been found in circulation in London.

Acknowledgements

This book could have never seen the light of day without the research, help and encouragement of many people. The editor, Mitchell Albert, was meticulous in his work on the manuscript, correcting flaws of all sorts and greatly improving the flow of several chapters. Constable & Robinson's managing editor, Eleanor Dryden, played a paramount role in preparations for publication, and she and Jan Chamier, the director of Constable, showed great patience as illness kept me from meeting several deadlines.

Inspiration, as work progressed, came from friends and colleagues, particularly those of my past Middle East reporting years and most especially from my friend and mentor, the late ABC News chief correspondent, editor and anchorman Peter Jennings. Before Peter's untimely death from lung cancer in August 2007, he had encouraged me in the research and discoveries of the 1990s, as the plague of counterfeit dollar 'Supernotes' swept through the world. Peter supported this and earlier books, and was always eager to help in any way.

The perceptive chief of ABC News' investigative 'I' Team, Chris Isham, reinforced Peter's inspiration with thoughtful assignments and rigorous guidance in my reporting for the network. The late Pierre Salinger, once US President John F. Kennedy's press secretary, was both a prescient guide and a loyal friend and colleague during his tenure as chief of the Paris and London bureaus of ABC News and the network's chief foreign correspondent. Friends and colleagues such as Eric Rouleau, former Middle East editor of *Le Monde* and French ambassador to Tunisia and Turkey, often offered his expertise; I benefited greatly from his instinct for deciphering the coded currents behind Middle East enigmas. In the more distant past, between 1965 and 1981 I was fortunate enough to have worked in the Middle East for Geoffrey Godsell, the legendary overseas news editor of my then employer, *The Christian Science Monitor*.

Author Loretta Napoleoni, a specialist in the murky political and financial background of international terrorism, introduced me to contacts that made publication of this book possible.

In Germany, my friend and colleague Wilhelm Dietl collaborated with several ABC News projects in the 1980s and 1990s, including the Supernotes story. Willi also kept me supplied with a flow of important German-language media stories about counterfeiting during the long research for this book. Susanne Härpfer provided useful research on hyperinflation and counterfeiting during Germany's Weimar Republic (1919–33).

In London, researcher Sabine Goodwin provided indispensable and highly professional help and advice in researching the chapter on First World War British covert operations.

Robert Miller, the publisher of Enigma Books and the author of a forthcoming new volume on the Nazi forgery operations, gave valuable counsel. He kindly authorized citations and quotes from SS officer Bernhard Krüger's unpublished German-language manuscript, to which Mr Miller holds the rights.

I owe my start in the investigative process into the Supernotes story to the two senior officers of the Cyprus forensic police, named in the text.

My friend Wes Johnson, who served at a number of US embassies from Kabul to Athens before beginning a new career as a journalist and author, has constantly encouraged me to plod on with my research. My wife, Vania Katelani Cooley, a Greek novelist, poet and painter, gives me constant encouragement and scrutinized my draft chapters of this and earlier books. Equal encouragement comes from our son, Alexander Cooley, a professor of political science at Columbia University, and my daughter by a previous marriage, Katherine Anne Cooley, an anchorwoman on a French TV news channel in Paris.

Interviews with authoritative people in several countries were of great assistance. Those who can be named are cited in the text and notes. Others, who will know who they are, must remain anonymous both for their protection and that of others. To all of them I owe recognition and gratitude.

List of Illustrations

Weimar Republic, 1922–3. Classroom poster published by Koester & Co., Munich, in the 1950s showing the effects of extraordinary inflation, where a stolen wheelbarrow is worth more than the banknotes it contained.

Introduction

First shown at the March 2007 Berlin International Film Festival, Stefan Ruzowitzky's *Die Fälscher* (*The Counterfeiters* in the English-language version) enabled viewers to witness the unfolding, if only through the medium of fiction, of Adolf Hitler's huge Second World War economic warfare operations. The title scarcely does justice to the magnitude and daring of the operation it portrays: the largest wholesale counterfeiting in history.

Between 1942 and 1945, Hitler forged Britain's pound sterling and America's dollar with the aim of undermining and ultimately destroying the currencies and hence the war efforts of his Allied opponents. The scene of the biggest Nazi covert operation of the war was Block 18 and 19 of Sachsenhausen concentration camp, on the outskirts of Berlin. (These were quite faithfully reproduced in Austrian filmmaker Ruzowitzky's studios in Babelsberg, Germany.) Subject to maximum security precautions and the tight supervision of a small group of dedicated Nazi SS officers, over a hundred Jewish master artists, engravers, printers and specialists in security papers and inks were enlisted. A few of them had past careers as criminal forgers of counterfeit paper money. Selected and collected by the SS from the rank-and-file prisoners incarcerated in Sachsenhausen, Auschwitz and several other Nazi death camps, the counterfeiters were given special food, regular work hours and time off for exercise. (To add authenticity to his film, Ruzowitzky even reproduced their Ping-Pong table, despite the disapproval of the two nonagenarian survivors.) The Jewish techno-slaves worked under the imperative that failure to produce perfect forgeries in sufficient quantities would mean death.

This book explores the far-reaching consequences of this huge covert operation as well as others like it throughout modern history. Although the largest and best known, this is only one example of the currency assaults that have characterized and at times dictated the political climate of the twentieth century. Efforts in war or peacetime to undermine the economies, societies and governments of adversaries by falsifying their money have proliferated since ancient times. The practice was widespread in the Greek city-states by the third century BC. In our own time, as with the efforts of revolutionary Iran, Saddam Hussein's fallen Iraqi dictatorship and the communist 'hermit state' of North Korea, politically motivated currency counterfeiting is often intricately related to massive criminal enterprises motivated by sheer greed.

Currency Wars examines, for instance, how some of the first European colonists in the New World bilked the native 'Indians' of everything from food supplies to their treasures of silver and gold with counterfeit wampum, the shells and beads used by the natives as their currency. It shows how the massive forgery of the first dollar banknotes, or 'Continentals', by British occupying forces in the rebelling American colonies resulted in widespread poverty, bankruptcy among the merchant and professional classes supporting the revolution, and huge difficulties for General George Washington's rebel patriot forces.

When revolution erupted in the 1780s in France (the best ally of the now victorious and independent Americans), Great Britain supported the royalist cause of Louis XVI and Marie Antoinette. King George III's men watched benignly as royalist exiles tried the same tactics the British had employed against the Americans: they counterfeited huge quantities of the French revolutionaries' paper banknotes, the *assignats*. In nineteenth-century Europe, Napoleon and his adversaries employed money forgery in their own wars.

In the United States, currency chaos reigned for decades before the Civil War of 1861–65. A bewildering array of banknotes and coins, issued by thousands of state and private banks and even by individuals, accompanied westward exploration and expansion, and complicated the growing struggles between free and slave-holding states and territories. After the terrible war between North and South began in 1861, Confederate President Jefferson Davis decreed the creation of the dollar of the Confederate States of America. Counterfeiters naturally had a field day. Union couriers, spies and soldiers spread phoney Confederate notes as far south as Mobile, Alabama and New Orleans. The resulting loss of confidence in an already shaky currency further debased it and undermined the South's slave and cotton-dependent economy. By 1863, despite the South's early military successes, hyperinflation had begun slowly to strangle the Confederacy. A combination of General Robert E. Lee's military defeat, President Jefferson Davis' acknowledgement of political failure, demoralization of the devastated Southern populace and economic collapse all finally, as the current popular song put it, 'drove Old Dixie down'.

In 1863 President Lincoln put an end to the pre-war currency chaos by creating the new federally issued dollar or 'greenback'. On the day of his murder in 1865, Lincoln had also signed into law the creation of the US Secret Service to protect the greenback from forgery. The same Secret Service was later given its daunting and not always successful mission of guarding presidents from assassination.

This book recounts how British covert warriors during the First World War secretly forged German imperial reichsmarks and smuggled them on to the Continent to undermine Kaiser Wilhelm. The operation, details of which still remain under tight official secrecy wraps, was a significant cause of the hyperinflation experienced in the defeated Germany in the 1920s. By its highest point in 1923, a *trillion* Weimar Republic marks were worth roughly one US dollar. It took a wheelbarrow full of the banknotes to buy a loaf of bread, and a lot more – if they could even be found – to purchase butter or sausages.

Under the terms of the peace treaties at the end of the First World War, French and Belgian occupation armies exacted vengeful reparations against defeated Germany and Austria-Hungary. Germany's Ruhr was stripped of much of its industry, and even its railroad tracks and telephone poles were seized. As early as the mid-1920s, amid the strikes and passive resistance of the destitute population, a secret operation was run by the intelligence branch of General von Seeckt's Reichswehr in the Weimar Republic. Counterfeited French and Belgian francs were produced to meet the forced reparation payments and to undermine the economies of the republics' ex-enemies. Anti-counterfeiting operations indirectly gave rise to the International Criminal Police Commission, which has survived as today's Interpol, quartered in Lyon, France. Fighting the plague of currency counterfeiting in Europe quickly became one of Interpol's main tasks.

In the 1920s, Germany was gradually rescued from hyperinflation, joblessness and acute poverty by drastic currency reform and by the Dawes Plan, conceived by American bankers with the help of Dr Hjalmar Schacht, a German banker who had served his Kaiser by overseeing the forgery of Belgium's currency during the German occupation of 1914–18. Schacht called in the mountains of paper marks and nearly worthless coin. However, Germany's return to more stable times, still shadowed by continuing unemployment and a growing gap between rich and poor, did not prevent Hitler's election to power as Chancellor in 1933.

One of this book's central themes is the link between economic warfare, including the currency manipulation and forgery rife in the twentieth century, and the rise of political totalitarianism. This is clear in the case of Fascist Italy under Benito Mussolini. Il Duce fiercely defended against devaluation of the Italian lira and its counterfeiting by the Mafia. The dictators of the 1930s understood the crucial importance of protecting the integrity of their national monetary systems.

Bestselling thriller author Eric Ambler was envious of the true story behind the greatest financial scandal in twentieth-century Europe. 'I wish I had invented the whole thing,' he wrote.[1] In 1924, the Portuguese master forger Arturo Alves Reis began successfully counterfeiting Portugal's national currency, the escudo. This jolted Portugal with the force of an earthquake and ruined Sir William Waterlow, Lord Mayor of London and Waterlow & Co., the proud printing firm that had worked for MI6 against Germany in 1914–18. The forgery scheme helped to destroy Portugal's imperial economy and its ties to its once profitable African colony of Angola. Most crucially, Alves Reis' criminal enterprise led to the empowerment in 1932 of Europe's most enduring fascist dictator, António de Oliveira Salazar.

After Lenin's death in the 1920s, Soviet dictator Josef Stalin entrusted AMTORG, the Soviet trade mission in New York, with the twin tasks of stealing as many American economic and industrial secrets as possible and purchasing as cheaply as it could the goods needed for the USSR's economic survival. Stalin also put the GRU (Soviet military intelligence) in charge of an ambitious programme to forge and so debase the American dollar. The GRU enlisted a private bank in Berlin to produce and distribute nearly perfect $100 forgeries. They even tried to involve at least one major gangster of America's 'roaring twenties', Arnold Rothstein. Ultimately the scheme failed to weaken the dollar and subvert the local capitalist systems. By 1931 the agents involved who had not managed to flee were doing time in federal prisons. Trying to warm relations with Stalin sufficiently to coax Congress into accepting full diplomatic relations with Moscow (which came to pass in 1934), President Franklin Delano Roosevelt discouraged publicity about this and other Soviet covert operations in the US.

Despite its magnitude and expert technical execution, the largest counterfeit operation of the 1940s – the Nazis' 'Operation Bernhard', depicted in Ruzowitzky's *The Counterfeiters* – was only a partial success. This was due less to Allied countermeasures than to decisions by Hitler's economic aides, who feared it would destabilize German control of the occupied countries and, more importantly, the currency systems in neutral lands such as Sweden and Switzerland. Although most sterling notes circulating after the war were recalled and replaced by the Bank of England as a precaution, the repercussions of Operation Bernhard on British and Allied economies have never been fully evaluated.

As Europe lay in ruins in the wake of the Second World War, the Allies moved to revalue and stabilize local currencies in occupied Germany and Austria, and to protect them from counterfeiters. In 1948, the successful creation of the deutsche mark became a pillar of West German recovery and prosperity.

American experience, gained in its efforts to destroy the Japanese economy during the Second World War, was utilized in the anti-communist wars in Indo-China of the 1960s and 1970s. In Vietnam, Laos and North Korea, the CIA and US Army Psychological Warfare (PSYOPS) units printed and scattered millions of counterfeit local currency banknotes, often with detachable propaganda messages, to undermine enemy economies. The CIA carried out similar operations against Fidel Castro's Cuban peso, especially during the failed Bay of Pigs invasion by CIA mercenaries in 1961.

Since the euro's introduction in 2002, the European Central Bank (ECB) in Frankfurt, Germany, has striven to protect the currency whenever its integrity is threatened. The ECB, Interpol and Europol use the same level of secrecy to safeguard confidence in the euro as is employed by the US Treasury and Secret Service in their battle to maintain confidence in the US dollar as the world's reserve currency.

Today's proliferation of counterfeit euros and dollars, which flow from workshops in Russia, Ukraine, Bulgaria and other eastern states, was preceded and sometimes paralleled by a huge flow of dollar counterfeits (of medium to superior quality) from Iran and the nascent nuclear state of North Korea. Bush's stigmatic 'Axis of Evil' slogan might have been fairly applied to the capitals Pyongyang, Tehran and Baghdad. This book examines the relationship between counterfeiting and terrorism. British and other foreign intelligence units have uncovered evidence of collaboration between state and quasi-state money forgers in Iran and North Korea and groups like Hizbullah and the Irish Republican Army (IRA), which are accused of hiring agents or collaborating to fund arms purchases or to pay militants with Supernotes. My own investigations into Iranian counterfeiting for ABC News revealed unresolved questions such as whether communist East Germany's Ministry of State Security was the secret accomplice of Khomeini's Iran in trying to flood the West with counterfeit dollars. The story of Iranian and North Korean 'Supernotes', the near-perfect $100 forgeries that even Federal Reserve experts failed to detect, is a subject this book explores in all its fascinating detail.

The most momentous consequence of the Supernote era was the US Treasury's massive currency design reform. As part of a policy to preserve worldwide confidence in the almighty dollar, older bills – even the much-counterfeited 'Series 1991 $100 Federal Reserve' note – have never been withdrawn. Since 1995, however, the

Treasury began making major security improvements in the $50 and $100 denominations. They also redesigned the $20 and $10. Emulating European banknote printers, the Treasury began using coloured inks to frustrate forgers, especially the thousands of petty operators using colour copiers and laser printers. In 2004 the Bush administration transferred the Secret Service from the Treasury's jurisdiction to that of his Bureau of Homeland Security. The Treasury's intelligence and currency experts continue to guide both enforcement and design efforts, in the ongoing battle against counterfeiting.

I have made every effort to verify information in this book in both public and, where accessible, private or government domains. Perhaps inevitably, some of my research has produced what an oilman might call 'dry holes'. In any case, I alone am responsible for the selection of the data and for any resulting errors.

John K. Cooley
Athens, November 2007

Cartoon by 'Giles', *Sunday Express*, 28 November 1971. On 27 November the Amsterdam public prosecutor decided there was not sufficient evidence to press charges against three Londoners arrested in connection with £100,000 in forged £5 notes found in Amsterdam.

One

Royal Charm, Smoking Dragon

Make money, money, honestly if you can, but
If not, by any means at all, make money!
Horace (Quintus Horatius Flaccus, 65 BC–8 BC), Epistles

As your hydrofoil from Hong Kong glides into the dock at Macao, at the delta of the Pearl River on China's south coast, you can't miss the grandiose façade of the Lisboa Hotel and gambling casino. It is a baroque cakemaker's dream of ornate, seventeenth-century elegance. It recalls Portugal's past colonial heritage, accumulated over the 442 years of Portuguese rule of the 95-square-mile enclave and its two islands before the communist regime of the People's Republic of China recovered it for the motherland on 20 December 1999.

This temple and newer competitors, some transferred from Las Vegas, are dedicated to cards, roulette, dice and slots for the hundreds of thousands of Chinese and foreign tourists and gambling addicts who visit them each month. They are living monuments to the massive money power concentrated in Macao, as well as to Communist China's colossal latter-day love affair with capitalism. Visitors since the Chinese takeover confirm what I myself saw on the seafront in 1976, during the final generation of Portuguese rule: eager gamblers from Hong Kong, the Chinese mainland or abroad. Now there are well-dressed, opulent Russian and Asian visitors eager for places at the gaming tables.[1] Presiding over the fortunes of the Lisboa operation and Macao's other older casinos, the territory's main industry and source of revenues, is an octogenarian Chinese multimillionaire. Many of Macao's 520,000 permanent residents, with respect, affection or awe, depending on their own financial and social status, call him 'Dr Ho'.

He is Stanley Ho. For the past half-century he has held a monopoly over gaming through his Sociedade de Turismo e Diversões de Macau, the Portuguese name of the umbrella firm he created to manage his lucrative Macao financial empire, which enjoys a daily cash flow in the millions of dollars. Since the turn of the century, new competitors have moved in, such as Sheldon Adelson, boss of the Venetian gambling and pleasure complex in Las Vegas, and Steve Wynn, another big casino operator from Vegas.

A few blocks from Macao's gaming district is the Banco Delta Asia, an edifice far less prepossessing than the casinos. According to US Treasury and other Bush administration officials, the bank is or was a vital branch, if not a centre, of global distribution for premium-quality counterfeit US $50 and $100 bills printed under government auspices in Kim Jong Il's hermetic dictatorship in North Korea. In September 2005 the Treasury temporarily crippled Banco Delta Asia by designating it as a 'primary money-laundering concern'. The Treasury, acting (as it had to) in concert with the Chinese authorities, froze some key accounts of members of North Korea's top rulers. Among specific offences alleged were accepting 'large deposits of cash including counterfeit US currency' from North Korea and 'agreeing to place that currency into circulation'.[2]

Long complacent, if not supportive, in North Korea's irregular financial activities and other international misdeeds, China soon after this cracked down on parallel activities by the official Bank of China's Macao branch. Pyongyang sought new accomplices: it opened fresh accounts in new banks from Asia to Europe and used its nuclear capability as a bargaining chip (as detailed below).

The Early Macao–Pyongyang Partnerships

At the time of Macao's separation from Portugal, gambling taxes provided an officially reported 30 per cent of its revenue.[3] The huge profits from gambling acted as a magnet for loan sharking; laundering of drug trafficking profits and counterfeit money, especially US dollars and Chinese yuan; prostitution and other sorts of organized crime.

North Korea's printing and distribution of forged US dollars dates back to the 1970s and can be linked to its other alleged criminal activities, such as drug trafficking and counterfeiting of merchandise like cigarettes and watches. The 'Great Leader' Kim Il Sung's cohorts first acquired the means to print bogus American money in 1973. North Korean emissaries purchased from the Swiss-based firm of De la Rue Giori an intaglio colour-8 printing system. It was identical with the system used by the US Treasury's Bureau of Printing and Engraving to produce the billions of dollars in genuine greenbacks that the US prints each year. In 1998 Kim Jong Il, the 'Dear Leader' in Pyongyang's official propaganda, succeeded his departed father. He continued to build criminal networks on the foundations Kim Il Sung had laid.

As long ago as the 1970s the US government has known about North Korea's production of superb-quality bogus $100 and $50 bills whose paper, inks and security devices are indistinguishable from authentic currency. Washington kept dollar counterfeiting in North Korea and elsewhere a secret to avoid undermining public confidence in the dollar as the world's main reserve currency. This secrecy ended at least temporarily, however, after two separate but connected sting operations by US federal agents and cooperating agencies against criminal activities originating in North Korea. Designated by the Feds and publicized as 'Royal Charm' and 'Smoking Dragon', the operations involved patient and laborious sleuthing, and penetration of the organized crime syndicates used by the North Koreans and their allies. These most publicly visible successes of the US Secret Service, the FBI and other police and intelligence organs of the US government began to appear after 2 October 2004.

On that date, the container ship *Ever Unique*, sailing under a Panamanian flag of convenience from Yantai, China, unloaded its freight containers at the Port of Newark, New Jersey. One of the containers was quickly trucked to a warehouse where federal agents were waiting. They opened it to find, buried under plastic toys, forged $100 bills of superb quality – called 'Supernotes' by law enforcement officials and by the media. Another $3 million in Supernotes arrived by sea in Newark in December. During the months that followed, more of the same began reaching the Pacific coast, beginning with a $700,000 shipment seized at Long Beach, California, in May 2005.[4]

There was nothing new about quantities of Supernotes showing up in the United States. During the eighties and nineties, Chinese organized crime syndicates called 'triads' had helped to import the bogus $100 and $50 bills into Canada. There they were often laundered, first in casinos in Toronto and elsewhere, then in the US. Las Vegas and other casinos from New York to Miami were soon encountering the forgeries. Many were distributed by a striking female Chinese gang leader as well as by a gang called the 'Big Circle Boys', first spotted by Hong Kong and Royal Canadian Mounted Police (RCMP).

Quantities of Supernotes had begun to flood into Europe and eventually the United States from 1989 onwards. These emerged from Iran, Syria and Lebanon, and they caused one of the major but better-hidden crises of the Clinton administration. Along with currency forgery of major proportions in and around Iraq both before and after the US–British invasion of March 2003, the Iranian and North Korean counterfeiting campaigns were important.

Links to Terror and Organized Crime

Since the final decades of the twentieth century, the intelligence services of the West and of the State of Israel have been discovering the strong ties between local and global terrorism and the counterfeiting of money by governments and organized crime – more often than not in tandem.

One major US intelligence operation provided the West with incentive to pay attention to presumed Macao and China-centred links with terrorism in Europe. In May of 1997 a US Air Force Boeing RC-135 took off from Kadena Air Base in Japan. The intelligence-gathering jet was equipped with a small forest of antennas and other spy equipment capable of separating individual conversations from the cacophony of telephone talk in China and recording them. It flew parallel to China's coast at a distance of about fifty miles. Such missions are capable of listening as far inland in

China as the distant western province of Xinjiang, where Chinese nuclear and missile tests have been conducted. The RC-135's sweep of the airwaves lasted nine hours and was unchallenged by Chinese interceptors.

Intelligence analysts, probably working at the secret National Security Agency (NSA) at Fort Meade, Maryland, surfed through the volume of data gathered by the plane. They are believed to have discovered that Sean Garland, a prominent Irish film producer and businessman, had apparently met with Cao Xiaobing, a female senior official in the ruling Chinese Communist Party's Central Committee. Their agenda included 'unidentified business opportunities'. Garland at the time was managing director of a Dublin firm called GKG Comms International Ltd. He was well known to British and US intelligence agencies as a veteran senior Irish Republican Army (IRA) officer, most recently in the breakaway faction called the Official IRA. This faction dissented with mainstream IRA and Sinn Fein tactics to downplay or renounce terrorist violence in the perennial struggle to unite British-ruled Northern Ireland with the Irish Republic. The American analysts were interested in Garland's role as general secretary of the Workers Party of Ireland, which was classed in police and intelligence files in the US and UK as a communist organization. Soviet archives reportedly disclosed a letter Garland had sent to the secretary of the Soviet Communist Party dated 15 September 1986, addressing the secretary as 'Dear comrade' and asking for £1 million (close to $2 million) to finance Workers Party programmes 'to benefit the world struggle for Peace, Freedom and Socialism'.

According to a book by *Washington Post* correspondent Bill Gertz, the Cao–Garland meeting helped US analysts to confirm China's role as 'ideological leader of what was left of the world communist movement'. Though probably in error, they regarded official Beijing as supporting criminal activities by international communists, including those producing and distributing the forged $100 bills. Gertz claims that 'unwelcome' news about Far Eastern crime, including counterfeiting, was deliberately suppressed by the Clinton–Gore administration. This supposed suppression was said to be part of a policy of hiding negative stories that might work against Clinton's pro-China foreign policy, which favoured opening China's vast market to American investors and vendors. Conniving in the cover-up, according to Gertz, were White House National Security Adviser Sandy Berger and Secretary of State Madeleine Albright.[5] Clinton's conservative political foes made much of Canadian intelligence reports claiming that Macao's Stanley Ho was the leader of a triad operating in mainland China, Hong Kong and Macao, and involved in a variety of crimes, from prostitution, migrant smuggling, drugs and money laundering to counterfeiting of American, Chinese and other currencies. At a 1997 White House reception to fund the Franklin D. Roosevelt Memorial (which occurred after the flight of the RC-135), Stanley Ho personally handed Clinton a cheque for $250,000, ostensibly for this charitable venture.

An RCMP intelligence file was said to identify 'Ho Sung Sun, alias Stanley Ho, born in Hong Kong November 25, 1921' as a 'member/leader' of the Kung Kok criminal triad, assigning him the 'gang file number' 89–1170. A book co-authored by former US congressional investigator Edward Timberlake, *The Year of the Rat* (which quoted the file above), exposed alleged funding of the Clinton–Gore election campaign by Chinese interests and its presumed effects on US national security decision making. Although other allegations of Stanley Ho's alleged criminal connections and activities surfaced in the Philippines and elsewhere, no proof was published and no charges have been filed against the Macao tycoon at the time of writing.

Matters were quite different in the investigation of Sean Garland's ties to North Korean production and distribution of Supernotes, which were apparently linked to the Royal Charm and Smoking Dragon operations. Public exposure began on 22 August 2005 when the US Justice Department, FBI and regional law-enforcement officers from several states held a news conference. Royal Charm, they disclosed, was an elegant sting operation: over a hundred guests, mostly foreigners and a few American suspects living abroad, reportedly including associates of Sean Garland, received invitations to a wedding aboard a yacht named the *Royal Charm* docked near the resort of Atlantic City, New Jersey. The reputed bride and groom were actually undercover US federal agents. They had infiltrated a gang of alleged smugglers of bogus dollars, bootleg cigarettes packaged with phoney Newport and Marlboro brand labels, and drugs. These were hidden in the cargoes that contained $4.4 million in Supernotes like the ones that had arrived earlier in Newark and Long Beach, California.

The Smoking Dragon operation targeted similar cargoes and forged money shipped to the West Coast. Few details emerged, but the operation was evidently activated by long and patient detective work in the US and overseas. Of the fifty-nine people arrested over the weekend of 20 to 21 August in eleven US and Canadian cities, eight were dressed in their best. They bore wedding gifts and were en route to the supposed bash aboard the yacht at Atlantic City.

Indictments were returned against eighty-seven Asians and US citizens on charges of smuggling counterfeit money, drugs and cigarettes into the United States. The Feds' haul also included $700,000 in forged US postage stamps; counterfeit goods including watches valued at a total of $42 million; and ecstasy, metamphetamine and Viagra worth hundreds of thousands of dollars. The first trials were supposed to open in the autumn and winter of 2007 and 2008.

On 7 October 2005 British police in Northern Ireland, acting on a warrant for Sean Garland's arrest and extradition to the United States, raided a Belfast pub. They detained Garland as he made merry with friends, some of whom were attending the Irish Labour Party's annual conference with him. In court next day, Garland was informed that a US federal grand jury in Washington, DC, had indicted him and six other defendants, all of them outside the US. They were charged with violating US federal laws against conspiracy, counterfeit acts committed against the United States and dealing in counterfeit obligations or securities. The slowly grinding wheels of justice had not secured a British warrant for Garland's arrest until 19 May. Its execution had been delayed for nearly five months.

The secret US indictment was unsealed and released in Washington after Garland's arrest. Garland and his lawyer denied all the charges, and continued to deny them at this writing. Belfast

Judge Tom Burgess released Garland on bail on 8 October. He required three sureties of £10,000 each to be lodged with the court and that Garland reside with a 'lifelong friend', as his lawyer put it, in Northern Ireland's County Down. It was understood that US authorities had forty-five days to file extradition papers. However, by mid-November Garland had gone home to the Irish Republic and was living there under a low profile. The US made new extradition overtures to the Dublin government. Garland's prominence and popularity as an old IRA fighter and successful film producer, and his wide circle of friends and sympathizers who actively lobbied for him, pressured the Eire authorities to block his extradition. As time went on, publicity and the Justice Department's fervour grew faint, perhaps due to efforts at political accommodation of North Korea on the nuclear issue.

According to the old US indictment, Garland and the six named co-conspirators connived to distribute Supernotes

> manufactured in, and under auspices of the government of, the Democratic People's Republic of Korea [North Korea] . . . Individuals, including North Korean nationals acting as ostensible government officials, engaged in the worldwide transportation, delivery and sale of quantities of Supernotes.[6]

Commentaries by US officials simultaneously charged that Pyongyang was flooding the world with bogus $100 bills in order to earn hard currency to continue its nuclear programme. They alleged that North Korea, like other belligerent governments in the past, was aiming to destabilize the US currency and, by extension, the US economy and its capitalist system.

Persistent US and British inquiries had preceded Garland's indictment. In July 2002 three men, one of them a former Soviet KGB agent from Armenia, were convicted by a British court of conspiring to import and distribute counterfeit $100 bills. Trial evidence linked them to Garland and a worldwide network that probably included many suspects busted in the Royal Charm and Smoking Dragon operations, though this has not been publicly confirmed. Consisting of contacts in the Czech Republic, Germany, Poland and Belarus, the group was believed to have used Moscow contacts to organized crime gangs established earlier by David Levin, one of the indicted co-conspirators. (Levin's aliases listed in the US indictment were David Batikovitch Batikian, Gediminas Gotautas, 'Russian Dave', and 'The Doctor'.)

The US indictment reviewed some of the history of the appearance of Supernotes in the global economy, beginning in the early 1990s. After the US Treasury's redesign of the $100 note with new security features to foil counterfeiters, new and correspondingly redesigned Supernotes began to appear in the late 1990s. The indictment alleged that between December 1997 and July 2000 Garland and associates in the United Kingdom and elsewhere used vehicles and other facilities belonging to the Workers Party for 'travelling, communicating and meeting with persons, including North Koreans, engaged in . . . selling "Supernotes", and arranging the purchase, transportation and resale of Supernotes in quantities up to $1 million'. Garland was said to have preserved the secrecy of the notes' source by letting his associates believe they were from Russia.

According to Judge John Cavell, the British magistrate in the 2002 case, the counterfeit notes handled by the three defendants he convicted and sent to prison 'were of such exceptional quality that even banks were deceived by them'.[7] The *Daily Ireland* newspaper published an unconfirmed report that Garland's so-called Official IRA collected its first $1 million in forged bills in 1989 The bills first appeared at the North Korean Embassy in Moscow and were then sent to 'a popular holiday destination in Eastern Europe', where they were handed over to 'mostly married couples and pensioners' to avoid suspicion, then transferred to Ireland. The newspaper further reported:

> Just before the group returned, an Official IRA representative in Moscow was involved in a shoot-out with the Russian mafia. This led to the Official IRA losing $100,000 in fake notes that were also bound for Ireland.[8]

The US federal indictment claimed that the North Korean counterfeits began appearing in Ireland in the early 1990s along with other forged notes believed by the Washington-trained Cypriot forensic police and the US Secret Service to have originated in Iran.

In June 2004 the BBC programme *Panorama* broadcast an exposé called 'The Super Dollar'. They reported:

> The police investigation is producing a detailed picture of an international counterfeiting cartel. The surveillance shows that it's all run by a tightly knit group of criminals. They're getting their hands on the Superdollars in Moscow. The counterfeit cash is then smuggled to Dublin. From Ireland it's taken to Birmingham [England] and distributed in the criminal underworld. Much of it is then bought in bulk by one man.

The US indictment identified four of Garland's alleged co-conspirators – David Levin, Terence Silcock, Mark Adderley and Alan Jones – as Birmingham residents. At the 2002 trial in Worcester Crown Court, Levin was jailed for nine years. The Court of Appeal in London rejected his appeal against confiscation of £789,000 after hearing that his profits from handling Supernotes were over £1 million. Silcock was given six years after he admitted distributing the forged notes.

Panorama interviewed Russian Interior Minister General Vladimir Uskov, whose men apparently shadowed Sean Garland when he visited North Korea's Moscow embassy. 'We registered his contacts with the North Korean Embassy,' Uskov affirmed. 'He visited the embassy several times. The fact [that] he went to the North Korean Embassy, our information was that people there might have been involved in the transportation of counterfeit dollars.'[9]

A speculative British newspaper report added more about the Russian connection: together with cooperative communist agents, some Official IRA members working in Dublin moved to Eastern Europe in the 1980s. However, the American FBI and US Secret Service bases established to fight transnational Russian mafia crime in post-Soviet Moscow caused them to move 'initially to Denmark and eventually to North Korea'. (It is also possible that Iranians involved in producing Supernotes also moved operations to Russia and eventually elsewhere during the same period, following warnings by the Clinton administration around 1984.) The newspaper story continued:

> Former KGB agents who moved into organized crime took over control of the operation and used their networks in Europe and abroad to spread the notes . . . while friends in . . . North Korea were providing the counterfeiters with a foolproof exit route from Russia by using diplomatic bags.[10]

Supernotes and the North Korean Bomb

The US Treasury's formal accusations in 2005 that North Korea forged US cash had less formal precedents. One notable example was a report by Deputy Assistant Treasury Director Bruce Townsend in Chicago to the International Association of Financial Crimes Investigators. Townsend identified a family of 'sophisticated' counterfeit notes 'emanating from North Korea' as 'evidence of a well-funded, ongoing criminal enterprise, with a significant scientific and technical component'.[11]

Once the Sean Garland, Smoking Dragon and Royal Charm affairs had helped to precipitate the October 2005 US Treasury charges against Kim Jong Il's regime, the Bush administration announced the sanctions against Macao's Banco Delta Asia. The bank had been under scrutiny since Supernotes were first traced to it in 1994, and the sanctions were imposed under the US Patriot Act enacted by the Bush administration to fight global terrorism. In early 2006 Banco Delta claimed that it had halted all business with North Korea and was taking measures to block money laundering; Washington ignored the claim.

Also in October 2005, the US Treasury named eight North Korean companies it said were involved in the proliferation of weapons of mass destruction and their delivery vehicles (presumably missiles sold to Iran, Syria, Libya and possibly others). Three North Korean companies in the Far East were affected, along with five others in Syria and Iran the following June. Symbolically the action froze any of the firms' assets under US jurisdiction – they had few, if any, assets in the United States – and forbade US citizens from doing business with them. This was intended to deny the companies access to the international banking system (some were evidently suspected of dealing in counterfeit money or securities) by threatening to hit any otherwise innocent foreign entities aiding them.

From 9 to 11 November 2005, the US, China, North Korea, South Korea, Japan and Russia held a fifth round of talks on how to wean North Korea from its self-declared nuclear weapons programme; the North Korean delegates reacted furiously. In December, the Pyongyang regime declared it would not attend any more such talks until the anti-counterfeiting and anti-black marketing sanctions were lifted. It was as good as its word.

Despite Banco Delta's protestations of innocence and its promises to cut ties with North Korea and its ruling elites, the US at first remained adamant about keeping the sanctions in place. Other banks around the world began to restrict business with North Korea in order to avoid US Treasury sanctions. On 25 January 2006, Daniel Glaser, the senior US Treasury official dealing with terrorist financing and financial crime, concluded an agreement with senior Japanese diplomat Akitaka Saiki to strengthen cooperation against North Korea's alleged counterfeiting and other illicit activities. Glaser had just visited Beijing, Macao, Hong Kong and Seoul, where he had discussed Macao's Delta Bank as a 'primary money-laundering concern'.[12]

Ever anxious to appease its tough and well-armed northern neighbour, South Korea's government publicly downplays counterfeiting allegations against the North when it can. In February 2006, the South Korean National Intelligence Service in Seoul claimed that North Korea was not 'currently' producing counterfeits, contradicting the US charges that Pyongyang had used as a pretext to freeze the six-nation nuclear talks. 'North Korea circulated counterfeit currency in the 1990s,' intelligence spokesman Choi Jae-keun told newsmen. Although it had no knowledge that this continued after 1998, 'the government has serious concerns regarding the issue of the North's counterfeiting and is closely following the situation', he added, perhaps with the US media in mind.[13]

An investigative book on the currency-printing industry, German journalist Klaus W. Bender's *Moneymakers, the Secret World of Banknote Printing* implied, without elaboration or proof, that the CIA might be fabricating Supernotes at a 'secret printing plant' near Washington, DC, in order to blame North Korea (or others). Perhaps taking a cue from Bender, North Korean police claimed on 20 April 2006 that there was 'shocking information' that the CIA hired counterfeit experts to produce fake currencies at American military bases around the world. 'They let these notes find their way to the DPRK and go out of it in the course of commercial transaction in a desperate bid to term it "a producer of counterfeit notes",' the North's Ministry of People's Security said.[14]

South Koreans sympathetic to the North, or if not to its government at least to its manifold economic distress, spoke out in March 2006. Working for better people-to-people relations with the North, the Seoul-based Good Friends organization affirmed that Pyongyang had called a halt to counterfeiting. The North's ruling Workers' Party, contended Good Friends spokesman Lee Seung-Yong, had ordered local party organizations on 26 March to 'come up with measures to get rid of the phenomenon of fake money being circulated'. The order covered 'dollars as well as fake Chinese and North Korean money', Mr Lee added.[15] But neither Bush administration sources nor South Korea's Unification Ministry, which deals with intra-Korean affairs, would discuss what might well have been an outburst of wishful thinking.

The authoritative London-based International Institute for Strategic Studies (IISS) identified serious disagreement inside the Bush administration on how the sanctions against the Delta Bank could, or should, relate to the suspended six-nation nuclear talks on nuclear matters. Vice President Dick Cheney and staffers in his office, like hardliners in the Pentagon, were highly sceptical about the future success of nuclear negotiations with North Korea. They believed that like the ruling mullahs supervising Iran's nuclear research Kim Jong Il would never give up the weapons option unless the regime was at stake. Instead of offering North Korea or Iran incentives, as many in South Korea, China and Europe (especially in the case of Iran) advocated, the hardliners regarded financial sanctions as a way to increase political pressure.

One by one, Western ties within the hermetic North Korean establishment were cut. Members of the World Food Programme (WFP) and other international food aid officials had left before the end of 2005. Pyongyang had demanded that they either leave or convert emergency programmes aimed at alleviating current famine to longer-term developmental projects. After its aid had fallen to one-tenth of its previous 500,000 to 700,000 tons, the WFP caved in to Pyongyang's demands, but without substantial increases in the aid package. The Pentagon's programme to recover the remains of US soldiers killed in the 1950s during the Korean War had also ended in mid-2005. The Bush administration had been concerned about North Korean corruption and interference, and also that the programme's American personnel could become hostages. In January 2006 the Korean Peninsula Energy Development Organization (KEDO) extracted its last few personnel from North Korea's light water reactor site at Kumho.

During the spring of 2006 Pyongyang showed further signs of its deep concern over the US Treasury sanctions and how to overcome them. In March, after debates inside the Washington Beltway over how to re-engage the North Koreans, Pyongyang sent an emissary to the US, hoping to parley. He was Li Gun, a senior delegate to the six-nation talks. In New York US Treasury officials briefed him on the sanctions and steps North Korea could take to get them removed. The Americans stressed to Li that they weren't negotiating; they were explaining. They rejected his proposal for the time-honoured non-solution of setting up a committee. It would be a mixed group to exchange financial data, including measures to cope with illicit activities and to assist international efforts against money laundering, Li insisted. He got nowhere with the US Treasury.

In late March, the US Treasury for the first time broadened application of sanctions to a Western company outside those states accused of nuclear proliferation. It froze all the assets of Kohas AG, a Swiss company selling industrial assets wholesale, and its president. US companies were forbidden to deal with Kohas. The

Treasury claimed that the company was half-owned by a North Korean firm designated for sanctions in October 2005 and that it had procured weapons-related goods for North Korea.

In April 2006 the main six-party negotiators met in Tokyo. Veteran US negotiator Christopher Hill refused bilateral encounters with his counterpart from Pyongyang. In May China sent a senior diplomat to try to coax North Korea back to the meetings. Kim Jong Il repeated, in person, that there was no way North Korea would return without the US first lifting the sanctions on Banco Delta Asia in Macao. Instead, during the summer of 2006, Washington pressured Pyongyang further by banning US citizens and US-based companies, including their subsidiaries, from owning, leasing or insuring any North Korean-registered ship.[16]

Despite these extensions of bilateral American sanctions, nuclear negotiators prevented a total break between Washington and Pyongyang. On 22 January 2007 the South Korean newspaper *Chosun Ilbo* was first to report, with obvious relief, that North Korea had agreed in principle to halt operations of the plutonium-producing reactor in Yongbyon and allow on-site monitoring by the International Atomic Energy Agency (IAEA), following North Korea's nuclear test explosion of 6 October, 2006. The top North Korean envoy Kim Kye Gwan and Christopher Hill agreed that the US would grant new economic and energy aid in return. They would also unfreeze the $24 million in North Korean accounts with the Banco Delta Asia in Macao. The accord was made more formal in talks on 13 February.

Details were painstakingly thrashed out during a series of further meetings during the first six months of 2007. The US concessions included the transfer of the funds from the blocked Macao accounts to other North Korean accounts. This seemed to satisfy the North's demand that the US start treating North Korea as part of the international banking system. The biggest obstacle, as it turned out, was getting the Banco Delta funds transferred to Pyongyang through a system that had been intimidated by US pressure not to deal with North Korea. It was Russia's Dalkombank that finally agreed to handle the transfer, and the funds were sent to the Foreign Trade Bank of North Korea.

Finally, as the *New York Times* recorded on 26 June 2007, North Korea said that the money problem had been resolved and that it would begin to carry out its promise to shut down the main reactor at Yongbyon, south of Pyongyang, and an adjacent fuel processing plant that had possibly been producing plutonium for as many as six bombs. In early July 2007, a visiting delegation of IAEA experts certified that the plant had indeed been shut down. No one seemed to know at the time what checks could be made to assure that promise would be kept.

Stability of the 'Almighty Dollar' Threatened?

What danger did North Korean counterfeiting operations pose to the dollar as the world's most stable and principal reserve currency? For generations economists, law-enforcement officials and especially bankers, traders and investors the world over had been puzzling over the real impact of forged money on the political and economic stability of the more affluent countries.

Polemics over the manifestly much more serious matter of North Korea's nuclear and missile capabilities aside, short-term estimates about the North Korean case tend to follow the public position of the US Treasury: the massive forgery of the dollar by North Korea and others has so far *not* critically affected its reputation for stability. While acknowledging that North Korea earned $15–25 million annually from spreading bogus dollars around the world, the US Congressional Research Service has asserted that this has not imperilled the dollar's solidity.[17]

There are, however, broader historical and psychological considerations, familiar to any Americans who spend much of their working lives overseas. In the twentieth century most Americans – and certainly many Europeans who survived the horrors of two world wars – faithfully believed that there was nothing as sound as the American dollar. American expatriates, from illustrious authors such as T. S. Eliot, Ernest Hemingway and Gertrude Stein living cheaply in Paris or London in the 1920s and 1930s, as well as thousands of other writers, artists, scholars, businesspeople and journalists who preferred life overseas, depended on payrolls, pensions or other dollar sums sent from home to finance their rent payments, food and their sessions of coffee klatsch at Europe's sidewalk cafes.

In July 1944, amid a massive Nazi effort to destabilize the world's older reserve currency (the pound sterling) through counterfeiting, an international conference at Bretton Woods, New Hampshire, solidified the dollar's paramount role in the global economy. During the final years of the Second World War, Western economic analysts believed that the weakening of major currencies during the inter-war years had been a major cause of world economic crises. Currencies, they reasoned, had to be convertible so that everyone could benefit from increased trade in the post-war world.

Historian Tony Judt identifies the distinguished British economist John Maynard Keynes as the prime mover and motivator of Bretton Woods. Keynes (who in 1920 had warned, 'There is no subtler, no surer means of overturning the existing basis of society than to debauch the currency') argued that the world deserved improvement of the inter-war global financial system. He said it should be looser and less deflationary than the old gold standard, which most nations including the US had abandoned during the 1930s. Keynes added, however, that it should be more reliable and sustaining over the years than a floating-rate currency system.

To achieve these goals, in 1944 Bretton Woods established the new World Bank and International Monetary Fund (IMF), using US capital for the latter. Constituting its first Executive Board were the future UN Security Council's Big Five: the US, UK, France, the USSR and mainland China. What later became the World Trade Organization (WTO) was also created. As Tony Judt points out, all of this amounted to 'an unprecedented degree of external interference in national practices'.[18]

Crucial to the establishment of a stable dollar as the main world reserve currency was the decision to give other currencies exchange rates pinned to the dollar. The US Federal Reserve Bank and the Western world's other central banks would defend rates at those parities. The price of gold was fixed at $35 an ounce. Only the new IMF could change parities, and then only in cases of major disruptions to monetary equilibrium. As the billions of dollars invested by the US to restore war-torn Europe in the Marshall Plan began to revive the Continent, the fixed exchange rates became more solid. The resulting international prosperity was to survive, despite periodic blips, for nearly thirty years.[19]

Since the 1970s, however, the dollar and other currencies have floated. Action taken by President Richard Nixon effectively ended the Bretton Woods regime of fixed exchange rates. Now traders in the financial markets buy and sell money like any other commodity.

In 2004, when the US Treasury first began publicly to express real concern about international counterfeiting, the dollar was falling against the new euro, the Japanese yen, the Swiss franc and others. US practices were causing or aggravating global financial strain: massive US government borrowing, furious spending and sparse saving by American consumers and a gigantic current account deficit that, as the *Economist* weekly observed on 2 December 2004, was 'big enough to have bankrupted any other country some time ago'. This made progessive depreciation, if not devaluation, of the dollar inevitable. The volume of cash printed by the US Treasury – and copied in significant quantities by the world's counterfeiters – tends to grow exponentially. When a central bank in Beijing, Moscow or elsewhere buys dollars in order to keep down the exchange rate of the local currency, that central bank prints more local money. This pushes up share prices and property values, producing bubbles in the prices of these assets.[20]

Peter G. Peterson, a lifelong Republican, chairman of the Blackstone Group and a former secretary of commerce under President Nixon, warned in his book *Running on Empty* (published during that same dangerous year, 2004) about the perils of

> printing money . . . the last recourse of governments throughout history. From Revolutionary France in the 1790s to Weimar Germany in the 1920s [cases examined later in this book], regimes under duress have made their ends meet by inflating their spending power ahead of their fixed obligations . . .

Inflation usually ends up destroying social trust and ruining the economy.[21]

Historically, currency counterfeiting has been perpetrated by governments seeking to destabilize enemy economies (as prescribed by Lenin and attempted unsuccessfully by Stalin against the US dollar in the 1920s). Money forgery has flourished during times of inflation, especially hyperinflation, such as the American and French Revolutions, the US Civil War, and in Weimar Germany before the rise of Hitler.

Of course, counterfeiting is only one cause, or potential cause, of instability. Peterson notes how under the Bush administration America, once the world's biggest creditor, became its largest debtor. The ten-year US budget, balanced when Bush first took office in 2001 and officially projected to be a surplus of $5.6 trillion, was eaten up by the end of the big stock market bubble late in the 1990s, Bush's tax cuts for wealthy Americans and the after-effects of 9/11 including the wars in Afghanistan and Iraq. By late 2006, the US public debt had reached and probably exceeded the legal limit of $11.6 trillion set by Congress. In addition, a trade deficit of over $500 billion and weak savings rates had made the US economy dependent on an intake of about $2 billion on each working day in loans from powers such as cash-wealthy China, which generate promises to pay vast amounts of future interest.

Peterson sums it up succinctly: 'America's twin deficits are now so large, and our savings rate so low, that *there is a real danger that investors around the world will simply lose faith in the dollar*.'[22] According to Peterson, multi-billionaire investor Warren Buffet began buying foreign currencies. At the annual World Economic Forum in Davos, Switzerland, and similar occasions, other moguls of world finance began speculating openly about how long the dollar could remain the world's reserve currency and whether a weakened dollar could cause the US economy to implode, possibly taking the global economy down with it.[23]

There will be more to say later in this book about dollar stability. Next, however, we need to examine how counterfeiting as a covert form of currency warfare by governments, sometimes allied with serious criminal elements, has progressed up to the era of the Supernote. We will also look at the forgery of what may be the next world reserve currency: the euro.

Two

Middle East Dimensions

> The destiny of a currency is, and always will be, the destiny of a nation.
>
> *Franz Pick, Austrian economist*

After a decade of basing in an often grey and murky London, flying into the Mediterranean island republic of Cyprus in November of 1990 brought welcome relief to my Greek wife, Vania, and me. From the window of our hotel room in Nicosia we could see bright sunshine and palm trees. Little did we know that we had arrived at a gateway for the most ambitious programme of covert financial warfare since Adolf Hitler's secret Second World War effort to ruin the economies of Britain, the United States and other opponents by counterfeiting their currencies. The drama of the nearly perfect $100 forgeries, the Supernotes, was well under way in the Far East. Now it was to be Europe's and America's turn.

Since 1979, there had been bad blood between the United States and Iran. The fall of Shah Muhammad Reza Pahlevi, America's main Middle East ally, had been followed by the clerical dictatorship of the Ayatollah Khomeini and his successors. Then there had been the drama of the American embassy hostages held in Tehran from November 1979, on President Jimmy Carter's watch, until their liberation half an hour after President Ronald Reagan's inauguration in January 1981. The ruinous 1980–88 Iran–Iraq war, in which the US had given Iraq's dictator, Saddam Hussein, financial, military and intelligence support, had compounded suspicion and mistrust between Washington and Tehran.

In the summer of 1985, and during the middle years of the Reagan era, Federal Reserve Chairman Paul Volcker had allowed the national money supply in the US to grow. Much of the increased dollar volume went into the financial markets. This drove up the stock market and brought about a huge rally on Wall Street. While financial traders grew rich, the 'real' national economy of production and consumption faltered, much as had occurred during the late 1920s in the run-up to the crash of 1929 and the following Great Depression.

In midsummer of 1987 – as Supernotes, perhaps coincidentally, began to appear here and there in the Far East – the US Federal Reserve acted as it had in the pre-crash summer of 1929. As veteran financial writer William Greider noted in a series of three articles in the *New Yorker* in November 1987, 'it began gradually to withdraw some of the excess liquidity that it had pumped into the private economy during the two previous years'.[1] As a result, while growth in the money supply declined, the stock market moved upwards. In order to reassure the bond market, the Federal Reserve tightened credit, raising the discount rate, with the intent of restraining the financial markets' speculation without panicking them: again a repetition of its 1929 tactics. The result, however, was similar to that in 1929.

Although the crash of October 1987 was far less catastrophic than that of 1929, it did cause losses of $500 billion on one trading day, 19 October. Markets in Asia and Europe soon saw global losses reaching several trillion dollars. Then under Alan Greenspan, the Fed responded by pouring billions of newly printed dollars into the US banking system and reducing interest rates to ease the shock.[2] The US and world markets recovered over the coming months. Dollar exchange rates fluctuated as they had ever since President Nixon effectively ended fixed parities in 1971. But the global volume of US dollars circulating, deposited and hoarded has tended to increase ever since, exceeding the trillion mark by the beginning of the twenty-first century.

At the end of the 1980s, patriotic certainties about the successful proxy war that the US and the CIA's Muslim mercenaries waged to rid Afghanistan of Soviet occupiers had waned. The relative prosperity of the 1980s gave way to a shakier economy, due in part to the expense of the 1991 war to expel Saddam Hussein from Kuwait. The US economy at this time presented a tempting target to those in Tehran and elsewhere who wished America ill. Destabilizing the US dollar may have looked to them, as it did to the North Korean regime in Pyongyang, like a sure way to create and increase economic mischief. It could also augment their power and that of some of their allies to buy arms, finance their development, and recruit and pay their favourite terrorists when and where they found it necessary.

By the mid-1990s, as bankers, law-enforcement officials and intelligence agencies around the world were awakening to the threat of currency counterfeiting in general and the Supernotes in particular, estimates of the amount of forged dollars circulating around the world varied from $100 million to $10 billion. Yet no one, including the US Secret Service, intelligence agencies or even the US Treasury's own intelligence branch, knew the real figures.

Supernotes in the Western World

In mid-1995, Steven Brine, a cashier at Thomas Cook Ltd in London, bent attentively over a US $100 bill that had crossed his desk earlier in the working day. The ink, the paper, the embossed effect produced by the ultra-high-pressure intaglio system used by the US Bureau of Engraving and Printing all seemed fine. But Brine had an uneasy feeling about it. He got out a powerful lens for a second look.

Peering through a lighted glass, Brine saw what was wrong: 'If you look at the first T in UNITED STATES OF AMERICA,' he told a television reporter later, showing the bill to the camera, 'the one in UNITED, the right-hand arm of the T is severed.' It was not connected to the letter's upright stem, although one needed a powerful magnifier to see this. 'What's more,' Brine observed, 'the O in OF is flattened at the top. Hence it's been dubbed the flat-top O.'[3]

Since the first detections of Supernotes in the Far East, which had been traced to North Korea, US Treasury agents had been helping Thomas Cook and many other bankers conduct courses in identifying counterfeit US money. What the Cook cashier had spotted on the otherwise near-perfect $100 banknote had been identified in 1983 in Singapore, then again in the Philippines in 1988. Like many of the bogus notes appearing in Macao, Hong Kong and elsewhere in the late 1980s and early 1990s, what became known to banking and law-enforcement insiders as the 'Singapore Supernote' was a sample of the best-quality American counterfeit money ever seen.

There had been variations with its reappearance in the Philippines in 1988, and then in growing quantities in the dying Soviet Union and the new post-Soviet Russia around 1989. Since the appearance of the severed T and the flat-top O, these versions were even harder to detect.

The discovery at Thomas Cook in London at first caused barely a ripple on the British or continental European scenes, even though bankers in the Middle East and nearby Cyprus had been keenly aware of the threat since the end of 1990. In Britain, counterfeit money, especially sterling but also middle- or low-quality dollar forgeries, had become common.

In the mid-1990s you could buy a counterfeit £50 note in London for about ten real pounds, a twenty for a fiver. A bartender in a south London nightclub, called 'Kevin' by the newspaper reporter who told his story, discovered that counterfeit £20 and £50 notes were current. Although by no means of the top quality produced by the massive Nazi operation during the Second World War, nevertheless they were good enough to fool the careless. In the nightclub, they were passed to pay for Ecstasy, cocaine and other drugs Kevin resold, or passed on to clients for change. They were made on either a colour photocopier in an office or a home, or by a night worker at a lithograph print shop doing a little nocturnal freelance work. The design was nearly perfect; the colour would fool all but the expert eye; and even the paper, always the trickiest step in identifying forgeries, usually felt genuine.[4] Thousands of amateur and would-be professional counterfeiters in the Americas and on other continents were trying their hands at 'making money' by the same method.

Although money forgery by amateurs was a commonplace in the West in the 1990s, the cunning and massive attacks on the dollar from North Korea and the Middle East were not. Some members and staffers of the US Congress were quick off the mark to denounce what they said was 'a joint Iran–Syria conspiracy to counterfeit US dollars, purportedly in order to strengthen Iran's economy and weaken the United States', to quote a US Information Agency (USIA) release issued in 1992. Apart from dutiful accounts on the inside pages of mainstream newspapers over a period of months, and reports on NBC television news and in *US News & World Report* magazine, congressional concern stirred scarcely any media attention during that hot and humid summer.

'The fact of the matter,' charged Representative Bill McCollum, a Republican from Florida, at a 1 July 1992 news conference, 'is that the Iranian government, in cooperation with Syria, has undertaken a massive counterfeiting campaign in order to alleviate their financial difficulties and pursue financial warfare against the West.'[5]

US Treasury and other officials of the Clinton administration reacted uneasily to such accusations. Wasn't it counterproductive, they wondered in closed meetings and private conversations, to air such grave allegations publicly? Iran indignantly denied the charges, adding them to the long list of controversies over frozen bank accounts, US military supplies ordered and paid for but never delivered due to embargoes since the Iran hostage crisis, and other explosive matters being thrashed out at US–Iranian talks in The Hague and elsewhere. And dollars, especially $100 but sometimes $50 bills, were being rejected by shops, restaurants and, most important, banks and other financial institutions outside the United States. The news had spread that even the US Federal Reserve analysts were often unable to detect the forgeries.

Citing the report by the House Task Force on Terrorism and Unconventional Warfare, which he chaired, Representative McCollum added that the

> origins of this strategy go back to Iran's efforts to rebuild its economy in the wake of the Iran–Iraq war. When it became apparent that Iran's exports could not meet its hard-currency needs the plan for a counterfeit operation was devised.[6]

Intelligence from American, British and Israeli agencies had supplied much of the information for the Task Force report. Iran, their reports showed, suffered from a chronic shortage of dollars following the eight-year war with Saddam Hussein's Iraq and the US trade embargo. The government of the ayatollahs needed cash to replenish stocks of arms, ammunition and medicine.

McCollum blustered: 'the Iranians . . . outraged me personally when they put in their official publication that this counterfeit money was being produced by the United States "intelligence community" and distributed over there. That's hogwash!' The Iranian charges foreshadowed those made by North Korea in 2005 that the CIA was faking the Supernotes attributed to them.

House Banking Committee Chairman Representative Henry Gonzalez and other sceptics later questioned whether the Task Force findings were based only on speculation. Much of the data reported was the work of one of its senior researchers, Yossef Bodansky, reputed to have excellent Israeli connections. At a congressional hearing held on 13 July 1994 on the prospective redesign of the US currency, beginning with the controversial $100 note, McCollum commented on later findings reinforcing his earlier charge: 'The Iranian responsibility for counterfeiting $100 bills by terrorist countries is a national security threat that we must not delay in addressing [and] . . . is not based on speculation.' Since the 1992 report, he added,

> the spread of high-quality counterfeit money has continued to rise. There is every indication the problem will grow as distributors adopt new methods and routes for smuggling this bogus cash. International organized crime is a key player in the increase of high-quality counterfeit $100 bills from Iran, Syria and Lebanon, the primary sources of printing and organized distribution into the West.[7]

Bob Leuver, former head of the US Treasury's Bureau of Engraving and Printing, which produces genuine American greenbacks, called the Supernote

> essentially an almost perfect example of our hundred-dollar

> bills . . . Everybody who has seen it, including those at the Federal Reserve, say it is close to being perfect; so good that it passes through detection machines at the Federal Reserve Banks.[8]

The Bureau of Engraving and Printing had been studying counterfeiting and how to fight it by redesigning the national currency.

The Forensic Challenge

The publicity Supernotes began to get in 1995 finally led ABC News and others to investigate it. At the time, my wife and I lived in the Greek-governed southern part of Cyprus, the most prosperous sector of the island. Since the Turkish invasion of July 1974 Cyprus has been partitioned between Greek Cypriots in the south and the northern one-third of the island held by a Turkish occupation army, mainland settlers and contract labourers. The Greek Cypriot police were alert and efficient when it came to tracking high-grade crime like counterfeiting, which threatened its prosperous merchants and banks.

In December of 1995, Inspector Andreas Nicolaides, chief of the forensic laboratories of the Cyprus national police, was tracking the counterfeiters closely, using the thorough training he had received with the US Secret Service in Washington, DC. In his cluttered office in Nicosia, over microscopes, computers and stacks of paper files, he gave me a crash course in detecting bogus dollars.

'What you look for,' said Nicolaides, 'are variations in printing. You compare the suspect bills with genuine ones. You determine whether the suspect ones are printed by offset, intaglio or some other process.' He showed me samples of some notes seized in Cyprus between 1992 and 1993. As Steven Brine had noted at Thomas Cook in London, the O in UNITED STATES OF AMERICA was a bit too high and slightly flattened against the upper border of one bill. On some bills, the Os also showed a faint tinge of orange ink. Also, the scrollwork at the sides of the reverse, black side of the greenback was not closed, as it should have been in the upper-left-hand corner. 'All in all,' the inspector told me, 'most of the forgeries we are seeing each have about thirty flaws, but many are so tiny that they are microscopic.' He added that no detection device is perfect. Even with the latest technology used by the Federal Reserve Banks in the US a genuine note is sometimes given a bad reading because of dirt, tearing or other acquired imperfections. Truly scientific detection is impossible.

How had Cyprus become one of the gateways to the West for the dollar forgers and money launderers in the East? From Nicolaides, Cyprus bankers and merchants, and some public media reporting, the answers slowly emerged.

Late in 1991, a Shi'ite Muslim mullah flew into Larnaca airport in Cyprus from Beirut. He was a cleric of the Iranian-oriented Shi'ites of Lebanon and either belonged to or supported Hizbullah, 'The Party of God' created in 1982 by Iranian Revolutionary Guards with the support of Syria to fight the Israeli attack on Lebanon and its numerous Palestinian 'guests'. He taxied to Limassol, the island's biggest and most commerce-oriented seaport, and checked into a hotel. Next morning, he appeared at a Limassol bank and tried to change two $100 bills. The teller had been trained by US Treasury agents in anti-counterfeiting seminars. Recognizing the two bills as excellent forgeries, he called the police. They detained the mullah, raided his hotel room and seized a suitcase containing $35,000 in Supernotes – a paltry quantity compared to seizures made from other couriers in the Far East, Russia and even New York at about the same time.

The mullah was charged in a Cypriot court, where a courageous judge sentenced him to several years in prison for distributing false money. Hizbullah in Lebanon sent several demands for his immediate release, coupled with threats. These were ignored at first. Six months went by. Finally, the president of Cyprus quietly ordered his release. Hizbullah was already notorious in Cyprus, as elsewhere, for taking American, British, German and other hostages during Lebanon's eighteen-year civil war. It had brought all kinds of pressure on the sentencing judge, including death threats, and on the Cypriot Ministry of Justice.

Inspector Nicolaides went on to tell me:

> After that, there were a good many other couriers, mostly Arabs until 1992. Then we got all kinds of nationalities, but especially Russians. One thing is certain: I've been dealing with false money of all descriptions throughout most of my twenty-five-year career. Your so-called Supernotes cannot be the work of small-time crooks. They have to have been produced by craftsmen with access to top-grade, official printing, reproduction and distribution facilities. *They must be the work of an organized government – or of an organization with government backing.*[9]

Journalists for publications such as *Reader's Digest*, *New Yorker* and Israel's *Haaretz* magazine were establishing that what US congressional investigators and the Cypriot police suspected was true. The massive counterfeiting of American currency had twin goals. The first was to destabilize the world's favourite currency and Western economies with it. That this goal had not come close to succeeding so far and that history since the ancient days of Mesopotamia and the Greek city-states had seen similar numerous failed attempts didn't deter the 'rogue states', as President Ronald Reagan had termed them. The second goal, based on the age-old human trait of greediness, was to turn as handsome a profit as possible. Throughout Clinton's two terms and the two terms of George W. Bush that followed, the twin instruments to achieve these goals remained the same: international organized crime and rogue elements protected by governments (as Irishman Sean Garland and his co-conspirators were alleged to be).

During the early 1990s, in the backwash of the Soviet Union's collapse, Russians, Ukrainians, Belorussians, Armenians and other ex-Soviet citizens arrived by the hundreds of thousands in Cyprus, London, Paris, Zurich and the other banking centres of the Western world. They carried suitcases and duffel bags full of dollars, many of them false. At first, they would buy up gold and jewellery in massive quantities and shuttle back and forth to Moscow, Kiev or Yerevan. There they would sell their booty for huge profits and then return to buy more. Later, taking advantage of liberal financial regimes such as the ones in Cyprus, Switzerland or Austria, they founded banks dedicated to large-scale money laundering. They bought up shops, homes and other real estate. Occasionally they murdered each other in gangland style. In Cyprus, some moved to the Turkish-occupied north, where illicit drug trafficking as well as counterfeiting and traffic in women exported from the East were profitable.

George Vassiliou, President of the Cyprus Republic from 1988 through 1993, resumed his role as a highly successful businessman after he left office. In 1995 he confirmed to me that there had indeed been a big influx of counterfeits ('and doubtless a large onward flow of them to the West') during his watch. Yes, he had initiated strong cooperation in fighting this with the US Treasury and Secret Service, but he felt that talk of serious damage to Middle East and world business had been exaggerated.

Like the executive branch of the Clinton administration in the US and most senior politicians in other countries faced with the problem, Vassiliou demurred on giving any judgement or estimate about the amount of the forgeries in circulation, or about their provenance and purpose.[10] This was left to a small, overworked staff of US Secret Service and some CIA officers and their aides. They crisscrossed first the Middle East and then the Far East, seeking to recruit more informants and collecting all of the samples of the fake dollars they could find. Most of the valid trails they were able to follow – and there were many false ones – pointed to printing and distribution operations in Iran, Syria and Lebanon. These in turn led back to intaglio printing presses in Tehran and other pipelines moving the false American notes outwards from similar presses in North Korea to China, Japan, Thailand, the Philippines and Indonesia. Counterfeit dollars of lesser quality were being produced in Lebanon, Syria, Russia, the Ukraine and Poland, and in Saddam Hussein's Iraq as a consequence of the invasion of Kuwait in August 1990 and of the huge, US-led Operation Desert Storm, the war to dislodge and destroy Saddam's forces in the winter of 1991.

Superdollars Buy Weapons

Some of the Middle Eastern money forgers worked with organized Mafia and Mafia-type groups outside the Middle East. Four main organized crime groups in Italy have been traditionally engaged in the trade, and still are today. There is Cosa Nostra, whose historical base has long been Palermo, Sicily. This is the group most familiar and most entrenched in the United States since the 1920s. The second main group is the Camorra, from Italy's Campagna region. The 'NDrangheta dominates the organized crime scene in the southern province of Calabria. A fourth organization, and a relative newcomer, is the United Holy Crown, a Roman and southern Italian phenomenon.

In counterfeiting US dollars, and more recently the euro, these groups have syndicated more and more with Russian and other eastern European organizations. They have extended operations into Central Asia and the Middle East. They have tried repeatedly to purchase nuclear material or weapons – and Usama bin Laden's central Al-Qaeda group is no exception. From the Italian Mafia, they receive both counterfeit currency and counterfeit merchandise, from fake Rolex watches to clothes with designer labels. Weapons, military electronic equipment and uranium, sometimes of the highly enriched, weapons-grade variety stolen from military stocks in Russia, the Ukraine or Kazakhstan, are in effect traded for the bogus cash and merchandise.[11] The whole story may never be known unless pertinent intelligence files are made public.

The US Probes the Supernotes Enigma

What was likely the most conclusive, and most publicized, investigation of the Supernotes phenomenon began in the spring of 1992. Two Lebanese-born drug traffickers, Gebran Hanna of Andover, Massachusetts and Peter Kattar of Ottawa, Canada, were caught red-handed by US Customs shipping into Boston over three tons of hashish from the Bekaa Valley in Lebanon. They avoided conviction and a mandatory three-year prison sentence by telling Paul Kelly, the Boston federal prosecutor who interrogated them, that they could help in the Supernotes investigation abroad. Hanna offered to send his brother to Lebanon for this purpose. Kelly agreed.

The brother returned to Boston's Logan Airport a few days later. He showed Kelly five bills, which Secret Service agents soon declared to be Supernotes. The same type had been circulating since about 1990, they told Kelly, and $2–3 billion worth had been produced during the previous two years. Printed by intaglio presses, they had the embossed effect produced by the etched printing plate being forced into the paper at high pressure. What was more, like that of Supernotes originating from North Korea, the paper was an extraordinary replica of currency paper produced exclusively for the US Treasury since 1879 by Crane & Company of Dalton, Massachusetts. Crane enjoyed a virtual monopoly on the trade and used a secret combination of linen and long-fibre cotton, with red and blue fibres embedded in it, produced on a French-patented machine. Until then, counterfeit notes using genuine paper had been imprinted on authentic US $1 bills. George Washington's likeness and the rest of the printing, green and black, had been bleached out. The blank paper was then printed with the likeness of Benjamin Franklin and all that went with him on the $100 bill. The most likely explanation for at least some of the 'genuine' paper was that the counterfeiters had somehow managed to find the secret mix of ingredients for the Crane paper. Subsequently, three different bankers insisted that the paper of the Supernotes they had seen looked and felt authentic. They believed it had to be real Crane currency paper.

The serial numbers on the Supernotes brought to Boston were sequential. The black ink on the black side of the $100 bills was authentic too; its magnetic properties meant it was made of ferrous oxide. The overall engineering of the bills was so precise that this type of Supernote had successfully passed through the Federal Reserve banks' testing machines. Even the quality of the metal plates used for printing the notes seemed to be improving.[12]

In 1991 persistent investigative work by Knut Royce, a Washington reporter of the Long Island, New York newspaper *Newsday*, had bypassed official denials and various apparent 'spin' stories by the US Treasury to show that a plate for printing the green face of thirty-two real $100 dollar bills was found missing from the Bureau of Engraving and Printing during an inventory check on 6 July 1990. Some of the government versions suggested that this was due to an 'accounting mishap' or that the plate had been mistakenly 'taken out with the garbage'.[13] One might conjecture, though without proof or evidence, that the missing plate could have been spirited abroad, perhaps in a diplomatic pouch, to Tehran or another centre of illicit printing such as East Berlin.

Paul Kelly's Lebanese informants told him that the forgeries had been circulating in Europe, the Far East, the Middle East and the former Soviet Union, something the Secret Service and top echelons of the US Treasury had long known but had been loath to publicize. According to official Treasury figures, in March 1995 about $360,831,314,979 (nearly $361 billion) were in world circulation. A Treasury spokeswoman added that it is generally assumed that two-thirds of that sum circulates outside the United States. Approximately $215 billion out of the grand total was in $100 bills.[14] These figures apparently failed to include an estimate of additional dollars being hoarded or in cash bank deposits abroad.

Circulars and brochures prepared for the public by the Federal Reserve often pointed out the dollar's popularity. Yet the fact that its popularity was fast waning in the mid-1990s was proven by numerous incidences of $100 and $50 notes, especially $100s of the oft-counterfeited series of 1991, being rejected. In hotels and restaurants in Beirut, Amman and Cairo, I often saw warning signs that old-style notes, printed before the anti-counterfeiting design changes that began in 1992 and 1996, were not accepted.

Unsuspecting American tourists arriving in Europe, including congressmen and at least one US senator, Patrick Leahy of Vermont, were shocked to find their $100 notes refused. The Ireland Tourist Board recommended that to avoid difficulties Americans arriving from the United States bring bills of denominations other than $100. When I arrived in Cyprus in November 1991 to live there, I had to sign photocopies of every $100 bill changed or deposited in a bank account, listing our ID or passport data, after each bill had been checked by detection devices.

Iranian Connections, Israeli Detections

In Nicosia I talked with George Sacavas, chief of the fraud and counterfeiting squad of the Cyprus National Police. Inspector Nicolaides' supervisor, Sacavas had also been trained by US agents, and had visited the US Treasury and Bureau of Printing and Engraving. He was liaising with Ronald Lusania, then the US Treasury representative at the American Embassy in Rome, whose territory included the east Mediterranean and Middle East. In the matter of the Supernotes, Sacavas strongly recommended that the US Secret Service open a sub-branch in Cyprus because of the problem's growth on the island. This was soon done. Interpol, based in Lyon, France, already had a Cyprus station and was working flat out to track the bogus bills, Sacavas said. He firmly believed that the thirty-two-bill plate missing from the Bureau of Engraving and Printing in Washington had indeed been stolen. He suggested that Israeli law enforcement was giving great attention to the subject and that he hoped Washington would concentrate on placing permanent personnel in Israel.[15]

In fact, Israel was one of the earliest states to recognize the problem. On 27 February 1992 NBC News veteran commentator Fred Francis broadcast a report including an interview with a senior Israeli forensic policeman, Amnon Shaltiel. The report quoted a US Secret Service source that Supernotes had already become 'a real national security concern'. The Israeli police contended that the bills were coming from Lebanon's Bekaa Valley and were being distributed by 'Hizbullah, the Iranian-backed terrorist group'. They argued that Iran had, in Francis' words,

> used the same tactics in Iraq, during the long war, flooding Baghdad with fake Iraqi dinars. So effective was the counterfeit campaign that large [dinar] bills are no longer used in trade . . . Many suspect that Iran is at it again. Israeli experts say the one-hundred-dollar bills are the kind of forgeries done on high-tech state-owned presses . . . with paper acquired only by governments.[16]

A few weeks later, at the beginning of June 1992, two senior US

Secret Service officers visited Israel. A US Embassy staffer met them at Ben Gurion International Airport and drove them directly to Israeli National Police Headquarters in Jerusalem. There they met with forensic researchers at the documents lab of the criminal identification division. After exchanging niceties, the Americans reminded their Israeli hosts that the Nazi counterfeiting effort in the Second World War had the

> specific purpose of undermining the British economy . . . We have grounds for believing that a similar scam is under way today, but this time it is directed against the United States. The Islamic Republic of Iran systematically produces counterfeit $100 notes of unprecedentedly high quality, distributing them, *inter alia*, as money for the financing of drug transactions and terrorist activities worldwide.[17]

Over the next few days, Americans and Israelis compared notes about the confiscated forged bills in the police lab's possession. One of the marks of forgery was the telltale letter O in the word DOLLAR, which Inspector Nicolaides had detected in Cyprus. Several months after this meeting, Jerusalem Police Headquarters received a message from the Secret Service:

> The mark we detected in the letter O has been leaked . . . The forgers have put right this error in their latest batches of counterfeit bills. Now all we have are three marks; enclosed you will find a new sample.[18]

Superintendent Avi Abulafia, the head of the documents lab at National Police Headquarters, and Sadek Gradieh, who was in charge of the counterfeits department at Interpol in Lyon, both confirmed that there had been a leak. Abulafia acknowledged that it had damaged the investigation. Gradieh responded, 'This is one of our toughest problems with this high level of forgery. We have not managed to discover the source of the leak.'

Gradieh told the Israelis that it was not Interpol policy to discuss the possible source of the forgeries: Interpol would not point the finger at Iran or anyone else. The central bank of Switzerland refused to respond to inquiries. Yossef Bodansky of Congresssman

McCollum's investigating team told Israel's *Haaretz* magazine that the US Treasury and Secret Service had pressured the team not to disclose the source.

When the Treasury replied negatively to these statements, Bodansky retorted, again to *Haaretz*, 'We are 100 per cent certain' of the Iranian origin of the forgeries. He continued:

> Iran is doing this primarily to balance its own budget, not to harm the United States. They are hitting hard at the dollar, and from their point of view it's an entirely logical thing to do. We stand fully behind what we have written. On the basis of the material that we have, the President or some leading official could inform the public that Iran has resorted to economic terrorism against the United States. The material in the reports is only the tip of the iceberg . . .[19]

The *Haaretz* report cited US congressional analyses of revolutionary (post-Shah) Iran's economic difficulties. These concluded that Tehran's decision to begin forging dollars was taken in 1989. Iran then had an external debt of $34 billion that was growing. Foreign borrowing was financing Iran's 'strategic national' projects, including purchases of nuclear programme components abroad, orders to upgrade and modernize its conventional forces and support for organizations like Hizbullah overseas. The mullah's regime, said the analyses, allocated an estimated $10 billion to these projects. Neither legitimate exports, mostly oil, nor credit on the world money market were adequate to staunch the outflow of hard foreign currency. So, the US and derivative Israeli analysts concluded, Iran and its allies began printing three grades of counterfeit bills, the highest standard being the Supernotes. They were said to be printed at a government plant on Tehran's Al-Shohada Street (the 'Street of the Martyrs') and at Keraj, about fifteen miles north of Tehran. Some or all of the printing was reportedly later transferred to a building near Mehrabad International Airport outside Tehran.

VEVAK (Vezarat-e Ettela'at va Amniat–e Keshvar), Iran's main external intelligence service run by the Ministry for Information and Security, is believed by Western agencies to have sent senior agents to western Europe to purchase machinery and equipment for its covert printing industry. In 1995 I began investigating a claim by an ex-agent of the Ministry of State Security (Stasi) that, beginning as early as 1983, the powerful former East German intelligence and security agency had mediated or even negotiated deals to sell Iran intaglio presses produced by the Polygraf AG state machine-building industry at Leipzig for $15 million each. East Germany was sorely in need of hard currency at the time, while Iran, despite its conflict then raging with Saddam Hussein's Iraq, had plenty of dollars from its oil revenues.[20]

We must next consider the background and the murky but probable details of the secretive East German regime's dealings with the Ayatollah Khomeini's Iran. These details appear to have been covered up by nearly all of the players concerned, each for different reasons: the former West German (pre-unification) government in Bonn, the new federal German government in Berlin, the Clinton and George W. Bush administrations in Washington, and possibly the Russian Federation government in Moscow after the fall and dissolution of the Soviet Union. It will be up to the reader and future historians to determine the truth.

Three

Eastern Forgers, Western Helpers

> Gresham's Law holds good in every field . . . and bad politics tends to drive out good politics just as bad money drives out good money.
>
> *Aldous Huxley, 1933*

The 1992 US congressional report on counterfeiting was scarcely noticed by the American public or people in the world at large. It was not only the focus on Iran that failed to make headlines; its implications for Iraq were largely missed too. In 1992 Saddam Hussein's Iraq was still regarded as an excellent market for American exports, especially high-tech ones, even though he was no longer seen as an ally against Ayatollah Khomeini's Iran – and even though America's chief Middle Eastern ally, Israel, was hatching plans to assassinate Saddam (something the CIA and Iraqi dissidents had also considered but failed to do). In any case, the report's unclassified version failed to mention the Iraqi dictator when it referred obliquely to suspected Iraqi covert operations in Baghdad.

The House Task Force on Terrorism and Unconventional Warfare report asserted that Supernotes had

> become a major instrument in facilitating the flow of militarily useful nuclear materials and equipment, military technologies, and various weapons systems to the radical states of the Middle East. Specifically, military goods originating in the former Soviet Union and Eastern Europe are shipped to the Middle East via Western/Central Europe, where arrangement for payment is

made through services provided by various organized crime operations.[1]

The guilty states, the Task Force report said, 'provide the Italian mafia with counterfeit dollars and drugs at a reduced price in payment for nuclear goods'. 'Guilty states' here could well refer to Iran as well as to Pakistan and Iraq, although in 1992 US intelligence was not fully aware of the clandestine nuclear marketing operations of the Pakistani nuclear physicist Abdul Qader Khan.

The report continued:

> The Italian mafia sells the drugs and launders the money through its international connections, with the Russian mafia playing an increasing role in these functions as well, and then diverts some of the profits to various financial centres, mainly Germany, as payment on behalf of their buyers.[2]

Storage points for the purchased goods were principally in Croatia, which in 1992 was locked in the wars between Serbia and the succession states of the former Yugoslav federation. From there, 'the Italian mafia took part in shipping the goods to Mid-eastern destinations'. Cash laundered in Russia and the ex-Soviet succession states included counterfeit $100 bills from Iran, of which 'there has been a significant increase in availability in Moscow and the [ex-Soviet states] as a whole'. By the end of 1992 'more than half the foreign currency in circulation' in Central Asia was estimated to be forged.[3]

The Task Force report found that the Italian Mafia was laundering money in the gambling establishments of Europe, mainly Germany and Monaco (Monte Carlo). It didn't mention Macao or other Far Eastern locations. It continues:

> Large sums in counterfeit $100 bills were being inserted into the winnings and deposits of big gamblers from the Third World or 'grey businesses.' The Mafiosi know that such individuals and groups take extreme measures to conceal their wealth and gambling activities and hence are not likely to complain if they discover counterfeit cash.[4]

In Cairo in 1998 I learned that the gambling casino of one of the big American chain hotels in Cairo was serving similarly as a laundry for Supernotes.

The story of how the Ayatollah Khomeini and his minions and successors in Iran obtained their main weapon for currency wars against the US dollar goes back to the 1970s. It is part of the history of the most successful banknote printing machine manufacturer in the world: the Italian entrepreneur Gualtiero Giori, whose main operations are installed on the shores of Lake Geneva in Lausanne, Switzerland.

In his book *Moneymakers, the Secret World of Banknote Printing*, German author Klaus Bender narrates the early history of the Giori family and how they came to exert such a powerful influence on the currencies, economies and futures of Iran, North Korea and the European Union. Gualtiero Giori's grandfather Dino Coen founded a successful security printing establishment in Milan in 1876. The firm received its first banknote order in 1939 from General Francisco Franco, 'el Caudillo', the victor of the Spanish Civil War of 1936–9 and dictator of Spain until his death in 1975.

At the very outset of the war, when Franco led his Moroccan suppletive troops from North Africa to launch his rebellion against the Spanish Republic, he ordered his new 'national' banknotes from Hitler's Germany, his best ally in the civil war that followed. The long-established and solid security printing firm of Giesecke & Devrient in Leipzig got his biggest order ever: it printed about 300 million-peseta notes for Franco until 1939. Franco or his financial advisers may have decided it was not politic to depend on a supplier in the state that was about to launch a new world war. So he switched to Mussolini's Italy and ordered the pesetas for the new Fascist Spain to be produced by Gualtiero Coen, who at twenty-six years old had yet to change his name to Giori. Gualtiero had the work done in Milan with machines manufactured by the French firm of Serge Beaune.

As Italian Jews and decidedly anti-fascist in sentiment, Gualtiero's family fled to Switzerland at the outbreak of war. Changing his family name from Coen to Giori, Gualtiero stayed behind in

Italy. Through his courage and cunning he lived partly underground and managed to protect the machinery and his printing business from the German occupiers.

As Bender recounts, a few private printers controlled banknote printing at the close of the Second World War. The big ones were the British high-security firm of Thomas de la Rue Company; Waterlow & Sons, also British; another UK firm, Wilkinson; United States Bank Note Corporation; and the British–American Banknote Company. In the 1920s and 1930s Waterlow & Sons had suffered a near-mortal blow when one of the partners was prosecuted for unwittingly printing millions in Portuguese escudo notes for a master Portuguese forger, using the original presses and paper the Portuguese Central Bank in Lisbon used to produce genuine notes.

Together with Serge Beaune, Giori conceived the idea of a huge innovation in banknote printing. Instead of using flatbed or other printing methods, they would build high-tech multicolour printing presses, capable of turning out several colours in a single press run. These could be sold to the many governments that lacked their own facilities to print money. Giori bought up Beaune's original patents for the intaglio process. With an expert team of Italians he built the first multicolour steel-plate engraving machine called 'Piloto' in 1947 in Alessandria, northern Italy. Another dictator facilitated the Giori business: Argentine strongman Juan Perón helped Giori's father sell the Piloto system to the Argentine state printing plant, Casa de Moneda, the 'House of Money', in Buenos Aires. Brazil, Chile, Colombia and several other Latin American governments also bought the Giori–Beaune technology.

In Europe, Bender explains, Siegfried Otto, managing director of the Giesecke & Devrient branch in Munich, put Giori in touch with Koenig & Bauer (KBA) in Würzburg, Germany, which Bender calls the 'oldest maker of printing machinery in the world'. Officially founded in London in 1817, KBA won fame as the successful printer of the venerable London *Times*. From KBA, Giori acquired more technology and components of his sheet-fed, colour intaglio printing system, and bought shares of KBA on the market. He set up his central plant in a mansion in Lausanne's up-market rue de la Paix.

The building was also the business office of the Société Industriel et Commercial des Produits Amon (SICPA), a manufacturer of the security ink that has since become a byword in banknote printing.[5] SICPA had long been Giori's partner, and it remains so today. When Gualtiero Giori's father, Rino Giori, moved from Italy to Switzerland, his cousin Albert Amon went with him. SICPA was Amon's company, producing food colourants and then branching into its present high-tech speciality in Switzerland.[6]

Giori operated other facilites for research and development and for demonstrations to prospective clients in two Lausanne suburbs, Sévelin and Le Mont respectively. By the late 1950s the Giori–KBA combine was marketing a sheet-fed, multicolour steel-plate printing system. This exerts about 80 metric tons of pressure, transferring the ink from the engraved depressions on the plates to the paper and producing the tangible, embossed or raised effect, which is a crucial characteristic of intaglio-printed banknotes and other security documents. The Dutch banknote printer Enschedé, and Giesecke & Devrient in Munich, acquired the first two Giori machines. Another was sold to the Austrian National Bank in Vienna. An arrangement was made with Maschinenfabrik Mödling near Vienna to manufacture the machines.

In the 1970s, the decade of Giori's sales of intaglio presses to both Iran and North Korea, the firm introduced new higher-performance presses. They were called the 'Super' series because of the extra-large sheets of paper used to print products, including banknotes. De la Rue, the UK banknote-printing giant, bought into Giori–KBA, changing the name to De la Rue–Giori during the time of the Iranian and North Korean transactions. In 2001 KBA bought full control of the firm, which since then has been officially named KBA–Giori. The new Giori machines print two sides of a banknote simultaneously in whatever colours are prescribed by the government central bank ordering them. By 2004 the 'Super Simultan', the trade name of a line of KBA–Giori offset presses (also needed in producing many kinds of security paper), was capable of printing ten colours. It was the first of its kind in the world.

After overcoming competition from the American Banknote

Company and difficulties stemming from the congressional 'Buy American' legislation, from the 1970s to the end of the 1990s Giori sold a whole series of intaglio printing systems, perhaps as many as eighty, to the Bureau of Engraving and Printing and was recognized by the US Treasury as 'sole source supplier'.[7]

With the world's leading reserve currency now rolling out of Giori presses, the world's most exacting counterfeiters had either to match the top standards of Giori or somehow acquire the same machines for themselves.

From the Shah to Khomeini

During the early and mid-1970s, before clouds of revolution drew darkly around Shah Muhammad Reza Pahlevi and ended his rule, the Shah was truly 'on a roll', as his American admirers would say at the time. The country was flush with billions of dollars in burgeoning oil revenues, the more so since the Shah, together with Libyan leader Muammar al-Qaddafi, had been a prime mover in nearly tripling world oil prices following the Arab–Israel crisis and war of 1973. He was determined to use his close alliance with the United States to his utmost advantage.

For decades, Thomas de la Rue in the United Kingdom had produced Iran's riyal currency. Senior advisers convinced the Shah that it would be much better if Iranian paper money were not produced in a country that generations of Iranians regarded as an adversary and rival for dominion in the Middle East, if not as an outright enemy, but rather by the Bank Markazi (the Central Bank) in Tehran. So some time during the final months of the Nixon administration in 1975, Iranian envoys approached US Secretary of State Henry Kissinger for an important favour.

The secretary of state under presidents Nixon and Ford, Kissinger was a firm supporter of the Shah. He had done his best to offer protection after the Shah's February 1979 abandonment of the Iranian throne and during his exile, right up until the Shah's death during his stay in Egypt as President Anwar Sadat's guest in 1980. Therefore there could be no objection to training Iran's central bank personnel in the proper production, including printing and incorporation of security devices, of riyal currency. The US was also willing to help catalyse the purchase from Switzerland of intaglio presses like those used to print the US dollar in Washington and the Bureau of Engraving and Printing's other facilities at Fort Worth, Texas.

Bank Markazi's director-general selected several senior Iranian engineers and technicians to train for several months with the Bureau in the US. There they observed and studied all of the processes needed to produce the world's favourite currency – privileges that the North Korean purchasers of the Giori equipment did not enjoy. Perhaps with the help of the huge CIA station in Tehran, which was often closer with the Shah than was the State Department, Iran purchased two intaglio colour-8 presses from De la Rue–Giori in 1973. These were to be shipped to the Bank Markazi. When the engraving, printing and engineering experts returned from their training in the US, they were already familiar with the presses and their operation.[8]

According to Klaus Bender, however, there were delays of 'over a decade' in the delivery of the presses. They had not even been unpacked from their crates in Tehran and the plant for them was still under construction when the Shah fell and Khomeini's partisans took power. Some aspects of the original purchase contract had not been fulfilled. The new adversary relationship between Washington, Giori's best customer, and revolutionary Iran gave Giori pause. The company turned to Thailand, another commercial friend of Gualtiero Giori. He transferred final outfitting of the Tehran plant and training of its personnel to Kassemchitta Asavachinda, technical director of the Thai government's printing establishment. Bender reports that the mullahs ordered two more Super-printing machine lines from Giori in 1987.

Bender also reports on North Korea's successful shopping trip to Lausanne in 1973. Giori lodged Kim Il Sung's buyers in a top hotel, where they enjoyed the scenery, the cuisine and the shopping. Their talks with Giori's people dragged on for months. When Lausanne's culinary delights had increased the Koreans' waistlines, says Bender, Giori obligingly bought them bigger suits. Payment in hard currency was a problem for the North Koreans. Western banks refused them letters of credit. Finally, the men from Pyongyang found a private bank in Zurich that granted a ten-year loan at a very high interest rate. The complete banknote printing unit was finally shipped to Pyongyang, where German and Italian mechanics set it up next to a barracks on the edge of the city. But the Zurich lender got badly burned: after just two instalments, the North Koreans defaulted on the loan.[9]

The Stasi Conundrum

East Germany's exact role in supplying Iran with the capacity to forge money remains surrounded by questions. That the communist regime in East Berlin was involved to a greater or lesser extent seems beyond doubt. Yet, as this book goes to print, the reliability of one of my key informants remains questionable. The true story, known to only a few, remains highly classified and well covered up. An official search of the Stasi archives in Berlin disclosed nothing at all about currency counterfeiting or the transfer of presses, other printing equipment or technicians from East Germany to Iran. But German friends and colleagues have speculated that archives spirited out of East Berlin in 1990 and sold to the CIA, or even those that remained in Germany, were 'sanitized' or purged of any references to the subject. It is known that a great deal of other material, including compromising reports on West Germans and other politicians, were indeed wiped from the records. The historical background, however, adds some plausibility to the unconfirmed story of the transaction.

In 1983, three years after Saddam Hussein's forces had invaded Iran, the Ayatollah's armies and the Pasdaran (Iran's Revolutionary Guards) had been holding their own for some months. They had repelled some Iraqi offensives on land as well as in the waters and airspace of the Persian Gulf, despite the help Saddam Hussein was getting from the British, French and Soviet governments.

Iraq received indirect help from the US government as well: loans, financial credits of various sorts, sales of 'dual-use' aircraft. The latter were supposed to serve Iraq's civilian air fleet, but Boeing 727 transport planes, Augusta-Bell helicopters and other aircraft were used by Saddam's military. Major US and multinational oil companies, with real or potential interest in Iraq's vast oil reserves, lobbied actively for more Western military aid – such as a dozen French 'Super Etendard' fighter-bombers 'leased' to Iraq for offensive operations against Iranian oil tankers and fixed oil installations in the Gulf.[10] In Washington, as in London and Paris, policymakers regarded Iraq as a bulwark against Iran's militant Shia revolution, which was already exporting violence to places such as Kuwait and Lebanon.

Although its military and civilians were hard pressed and suffering from the war, Iran was producing and selling plenty of its oil around the world for good, hard US dollars. It had ample hard currency and could use it to pursue programmes of destabilization in the West. The Tehran mullahs saw a promising trade partner in Erich Honecker's East German communist regime, with which the late Shah had initiated oil and other commerce. As 1983 began, the Soviet-backed bosses in East Berlin found themselves desperately short of hard currency. They also needed as much Middle Eastern oil as they could buy. Meanwhile, since operation of its Giori presses was presumably behind schedule because of previous delays, Iran may have yearned to reinforce its printing capabilities.

According to a single source – a former Stasi officer who never provided documentation to verify his story (although he promised to deliver such from Soviet 'friends', probably ex-KGB or GRU military intelligence officers, against substantial payment) – both sides agreed to a secret deal.

East Germany's big state machine-building firm of Polygraf AG in Leipzig manufactured superior-quality printing presses used for printing East German security documents and Stasi forgeries of passports, ID cards and the like, and probably of West German D-marks, dollars and other foreign currency. These presses were exportable. Some time in the winter or early spring of 1983, Mohsen Rezai, commander-in-chief of Iran's Revolutionary Guards, visited East Berlin. There he met with senior officers of Stasi and civilian trade officers.

The Revolutionary Guards were the de facto purchasing agent

and the Ministry for State Security the seller, on behalf of Polygraf AG, of two intaglio presses made in Polygraf's Leipzig factories. Each one cost about $15 million and came with high-grade security paper, plates to print US currency, as well as the loan of several skilled Polygraf or Stasi technicians. At least two former officers from the Stasi workshop for forged documents in East Berlin travelled to the Middle East and made a lot of money using their skills there. The Polygraf presses were shipped to Tehran in great secrecy and amid elaborate security precautions. They were placed under heavy guard at installations nominally under control of the Bank Markazi.[11]

The difficulties and ambiguities of this story soon became apparent. I did two follow-up telephone interviews with the East German spymaster Markus Wolf, the former head of intelligence for the German Democratic Republic. (Wolf was the star pupil of the KGB and is often said to be the model for 'Karla', the arch-chief of East Germany's espionage services in John Le Carré's memorable psychological thriller novels who ruthlessly fights Smiley, the fictional anti-hero of British intelligence.) While disclaiming his own knowledge or responsibility, Wolf identified the Stasi directorate that would have handled the deal. He suggested the name of Dr Alexander Schalk-Golodkowski, often called 'Alex' or 'Schalk' for short, as the hypothetical key intermediary in the deal, if it did indeed take place.[12]

Man without a Face, Wolf's highly readable memoir, is a mixture of reminiscence, self-justification and self-congratulations on his highly successful career. In it, without mentioning the supposed Polygraf transaction, he highlights his admiration for Schalk's talents. He describes Schalk as 'East Germany's financial wizard', 'Der Devisenschaffer' ('he who procures hard currency') and 'a massive man with copious chins, a barrel chest and a booming voice'. Schalk understood Western capitalism, its markets, its banks and financiers, and had excellent contacts throughout the world outside Europe, including in the Middle East. He had been introduced to Wolf in 1966 by Wolf's deputy, General Hans Fruck, former chief of the Stasi's large East Berlin bureau.

Schalk was made head of the Working Group for Commercial

Coordination, whose German initials (and somewhat derisive nickname) were 'KoKo'. He reported directly to Communist Party leader Erich Honecker and Günter Mittag, the politburo member in charge of the economy. KoKo exported a great deal of military material. In the Iran–Iraq war it first supplied Iraq. Then in 1982, through a shell firm called IMES GmbH, it began delivering military supplies to Iran.

In *Man without a Face*, Wolf gives away the fact that he did know about Stasi forgery operations after all. In describing the many shell companies Schalk created to bring hard money into the DDR's then-depleted treasury, he notes that 'Our ministry's central budget financed our technical work – falsifying passports, running specialized photo laboratories and the like . . .'[13] Published sources agree that the Stasi's forgery workshop was located near the centre of East Berlin in the former top-security Stasi compound next to Hohenschönhausen prison, a notorious place where Stasi political prisoners were interrogated, tortured and sometimes executed.[14]

The ex-Stasi officer who described the alleged Polygraf deal was scornful of Markus Wolf's pleas of innocence and the suggestion that Schalk had been involved. He insisted that Wolf was a liar and a master of deflecting from himself responsibility for delicate matters like the Supernotes operations.

Whichever printing system had been used to produce the notes, Giori's, Polygraf's or another company's, the Secret Service and the FBI in the United States had little doubt that the Supernotes circulating by the early 1990s in the US and Canada came from Iran as well as from North Korea. Law-enforcement officers in New York found evidence of Supernote distribution by Iranian diplomats such as Muhammad Razeh Shalhian. In the early 1990s he represented the Iranian Committee for the Oppressed, which was likely a front for Iran's Revolutionary Guards. Until the organization's office at 830 Park Avenue in New York City was closed down in 1993 and Shalhian, whose diplomatic immunity prevented him from being prosecuted, was sent home, a staff of about eighty Americans and foreign nationals worked there under the Pakistani flag and diplomatic cover. Pakistan represented Iranian diplomatic interests in the US after the Carter administration broke diplomatic relations during the 1979–81 imprisonment of American Embassy hostages in Tehran.[15]

Knut Royce, the *Newsday* reporter who broke the story of the Bureau of Engraving and Printing's missing thirty-two-bill $100 printing plate, spoke with the chief executive of a mid-sized Miami bank in the summer of 1996. Asking for himself and the bank to remain anonymous, this executive told Royce that fourteen Supernotes had recently slipped into his bank, and that they had been shipped to the Federal Reserve branch in Miami. A few days later, two Fed officials visited him with the fourteen notes, detected by German-made state-of-the-art equipment. 'They're absolutely perfect,' they told him. 'With the exception of this one little line. And you've got to use a magnifying glass to see it.' The Fed's man showed the banker the flaw on the left side of the note's back: a minuscule curl buried in the mass of white whorls superimposed on the green field. The official then stunned the banker by telling him: 'We're convinced that they [the counterfeiters] did that on purpose to distinguish their money from the real money.' The suggestion was that those behind the operation – 'an undisclosed government' – had vast amounts of both good and bad money.

The Miami Federal Reserve did not charge the Miami bank for the counterfeits. Royce reported that from 1991 through 1995, the Fed had written off about $10 million in Supernote issues. 'But no one knows how many Supernotes are in circulation,' Royce added. 'Nor does anyone know what percentage they represent of all counterfeits in circulation.' In 1990–2, when Supernotes were flooding much of the world, official US Treasury figures showed an average of $30 million in counterfeit American money seized abroad. By 1993 the total climbed to $120.7 million and to $137.7 million in 1994. Comparably high amounts were recorded in Canada.[16]

Washington's Countermeasures

At senior levels, the US Justice and Treasury Departments were unwilling to believe that evidence of the origin of the Supernotes in Iran (or in North Korea) was sufficient to go public with formal accusations. Although angry congressmen and some editorialists cited aerial or satellite images broadcast by ABC News and others of a site where the CIA believed the presses to be located, and even demanded that the US consider bombing them, such ideas remained hypothetical.[17]

President Clinton unquestionably sent friendly but serious warnings to Syria. He may have sent highly secret but more forceful ones to Iran. Only those given to Syria were publicized. On 16 January 1994 Clinton met President Hafez al-Assad of Syria in Geneva, and again in Damascus in October, and asked for help against traffic in both drugs and Supernotes. US Secretary of State Warren Christopher, who had much eventful experience dealing with both Damascus and Tehran in delicate matters such as the American diplomatic hostages held in Tehran in 1979–81, later renewed the request.[18]

On 27 October 1994, after presiding over the signing of the historic peace treaty between King Hussein of Jordan and Prime Minister Yitzhak Rabin of Israel, Clinton made a rapid stopover in Damascus. He pointedly asked for Assad's help in ending the counterfeiting drama as far as any Syrian role was concerned. He also requested more vigorous measures against the related matter of the druglords of the Bekaa Valley in Lebanon. According to a senior diplomat present at the meeting and its follow-up, Assad assured his guest he would do everything possible. Assad was as good as his word. Most of the serious counterfeiting activity and much of the drug traffic was suppressed (if only temporarily in the latter case) by the Syrian army.[19] Due to the poor image of Syria in the American media, the late President Assad has never been given significant recognition in public for this, as far as I know.

Iran's Bank Markazi periodically issued denials, none of which received much attention in the world media, that Tehran was engaged in the currency counterfeiting business. Some of these denials were issued by the permanent mission of Iran to the United Nations in New York. One came from the Iranian Embassy in Jakarta, Indonesia. After the 1 April 1995 edition of the Singapore *Straits Times* quoted a March *Reader's Digest* article accusing Iran, the embassy's letter published by the *Straits Times* said the accusations were 'baseless information provided by the agents of the CIA, Mossad and other western intelligence networks, as part of a series of concerted efforts or conspiracies to tarnish the image of Iran in the world'.[20]

How President Ali-Akhbar Hashemi Rafsanjani's government in Iran responded internally to the pressure, other than making public denials, is not known. Intelligence sources have privately speculated, without showing evidence, that either some or all of the printing activity was transferred out of Iran, probably to ex-Soviet republics of Central Asia. Russian, Kazakh, Ukrainian and other Asian and eastern European mafia-type organizations assumed a much greater role in the years after 1996, when the US Treasury, prodded by the counterfeiting threats, made the biggest changes since 1929 in the design and security features of the US currency, beginning with the $100 and $50 bills, and progressing at the turn of the century to $20, $10 and $5 notes.

During the years of the dollar's design changes, information or speculation about Iran as the source of Supernotes diminished almost to vanishing point. There were, however, sporadic reports that someone in Iran was still in the dollar-forging business. For instance, early in 2002, a newspaper in the former Soviet republic of Azerbaijan, since 1991 an independent state whose rulers were strongly tied in with the Western companies pumping their oil, complained that fake dollars from Iran threatened seriously to damage the Azerbaijani economy and reduce the local currency's exchange rate against the dollar.

According to the BBC Monitoring Service's summary of the article, Azerbaijan's state commission for organized crime warned that the Iranian-produced dollar banknotes, 'unlike those printed in Chechnya and Russia, are identical with real banknotes' and that available detection equipment was not successfully identifying them. Fake $100 notes were being smuggled from Iran 'through Lerik and Yardimli districts on the Azerbaijani–Iranian border'. The summary also quoted senior Russian law-enforcement officials and the director of the Central Bank of Russia.

Smugglers transport small consignments of money not only on

horseback, but also on foot. At the same time, Azerbaijan is not the final destination of fake banknotes. [They] even go to Russia, where its media often mentions Azerbaijan and Georgia as the main sources of fake US dollars . . . Experts think that the [Azeri] economy may really suffer because a substantial amount of mantas (the Azeri currency) will be withdrawn from circulation without being replaced due to the circulation of fake dollar banknotes in the market . . . In the future it might have a serious impact on the exchange rate of the manta against the dollar, or to be more precise, devalue the manta. Moreover, the fear of fake banknotes being circulated in the market might seriously undermine the local population's trust in the dollar. If we take into account that most of Azerbaijan's financial and trade operations are conducted in the American currency, then the 'loss of respect' for the dollar will lead to a confusion in the market and the temporary freezing of purchase and sale processes.[21]

North Korea, China and Iran and neighbours have been singled out as money forgers in our own time. But the practice is almost as old as history itself: forgery dates to the origins of money itself and parallels its development. Next we will move back through time to some of the same regions already discussed: ancient Persia (Iran), Mesopotamia (Iraq) and the Greek city-states.

Four

The Ancient Black Art of Money Forgery

Counterfeiting is a prehistoric art of gainful skulduggery.
Saint Clair McKelway, New Yorker, *1949*

In late September of 2006, a terse news bulletin from Bulgaria's Sofia News Agency recorded that a certain Georgi Ivanov and his son, Hristo, both from a village hard to find on any map called Yoakim Guevo, were being 'sued' by the state – an elliptical expression for being charged or indicted – for 'illegal possession of machinery, equipment and materials for the production of false euro coins'. Their confiscated equipment included '8,200 metal pulleys for the production of false two-euro coins [each worth about $2.60 at the time], matrixes and an all-purpose lathe'.[1]

A few weeks earlier in the prosperous monetary centre of Vienna, in the past a locus of hyperinflation and a favourite false-money market, a financial news magazine had reported that the 'forgery of coins is back in fashion' after generations of counterfeiters had concentrated on printing fake paper money, which yielded far bigger profits. Dietmar Spranz, the director of Austria's national mint, estimated that of 100 billion euro coins then in circulation the number of counterfeit coins totalled about 100 million. (For security reasons, he wouldn't disclose the amount circulating in Austria alone, though he acknowledged it was higher than the European average.) The false coins, as well as genuine gold and silver pieces from earlier times, were much sought-after by numismatists and amateur coin collectors.[2]

Delving into the history of money, one discovers many similarities between the position of coinage today and its situation in ancient times. Ingots or bars of bronze, silver and gold gave way in some places in the seventh century BC to coins cast or struck from the same precious metals. These were practically the only form of money until China introduced paper currency centuries later. Bartering has continued parallel to the use of money through the ages in societies around the world up to the twenty-first century.

Traces of money, along with religion, systematic farming and other essentials of human life, first appeared in ancient Mesopotamia and Egypt in the third millennium BC. Copies of the Law Code of Hammurabi, the king of Babylon (1810–1750 BC), refer to 'payments in weighted amounts'. Probably dating to the same general period, a passage of the Old Testament account of Joseph reads:

> Then there passed by Midianites, merchantmen, and they drew and lifted up Joseph out of the pit, and sold Joseph to the Ishmaelites for twenty pieces of silver, and they brought Joseph into Egypt. (Genesis 37:28, authorized version, 1611)

The seventeenth-century English translators wrongly thought this text referred to silver coins, which didn't exist then. Metals used for money in ancient Egypt and Mesopotamia in the second millennium BC were handled as bullion, not as coins, so their value was determined by weighing them. In Mesopotamia and Babylon, it was often the king himself who fixed the value of the bullion. Monetary values were also regulated in the temples.[3]

Historical records show that counterfeiters were quick to copy the products of the royal mints. Goods used for barter in the pre-metal or early precious metal days, such as animal skins and stores of foodstuffs, were represented by a kind of pre-coin: metal tokens engraved or struck in bullion and easily counterfeited. Once coins became current and more abundant around 250 BC, counterfeiters began clipping their edges and passing the originals on as payment. They would then melt down the silver, gold, bronze or copper they had clipped and use it to coat the lead cores of counterfeit coins. This practice is not unknown among the kind of money forgers operating with the euro and other coins today.

In the millennium before the start of the Christian era counterfeit tokens and coins proliferated on a scale comparable with the amount of phoney coinage circulating in the world today. The governments of ancient times, notably the Greek city-states, assumed the responsibility of checking for counterfeits, which was often the work of an enemy or rival city-state intended to weaken its adversary's currency. In Athens in 375 BC a law was passed decreeing that all coins, suspicious or not, had to be checked by public slaves.[4]

The use of electrum for the first known European coins was a boon to ancient counterfeiters. Electrum is an alloy of gold and silver, and has a pale yellow colour. It was used to strike coins in the Greek state of Lydia in the seventh century BC. Some of these proto-coins in the British Museum collection have an imprint of punches on one side and a figured design, such as the head of a lion, on the other. Such coins spread throughout the Aegean region until about the middle of the sixth century BC. The fact that a small amount of a base metal, usually lead, was added to the electrum coins provided a window of opportunity for forgers. By covering a lead core's surface with a very thin layer of a gold–silver mixture that would take the lion's head or other imprint used on legitimate coins, a counterfeiter who could pass enough of his fakes was able to turn a nice profit.

Croesus (595–546 BC) accumulated his legendary wealth by extracting electrum, which occurred naturally in a local river, from mines and by collecting huge sums in tributes and taxes from his subjects. Then the Persians conquered his kingdom. After the conquest, they continued minting both their own coins and the Grecian coins. The Lydian, Athenian and other Hellenes of the time may have worried about the intrusion of dubious foreign money from the Middle East, much as European bankers and law-enforcement officials today look on intrusions of counterfeit money from points east with a jaundiced eye.

One of the most blatant cases of political counterfeiting in the early Hellenistic world was that of Polycrates (538–522 BC), the tyrant of the island state of Samos, just off the coast of present-day Turkey. Around 530 BC, Polycrates was engaged in war with a complicated mix of other Greek city-states as well as rulers in Egypt and the Levant. A faction of his Samian opponents joined some of his enemies and enlisted the help of a tough military force from Sparta. When the enemy force made preparations to sail against him, Polycrates, who was something of an expert in monetary matters, had his mint strike a special issue of lead counterfeit coins covered with a wash of gold. The Spartans accepted these as genuine, and so were bought off from the hostile enterprise.

After a long series of costly wars with Carthage and Macedon, Rome had conquered both the Carthaginians and the Greek leagues and city-states by 146 BC. The Roman Senate ordered General Mummius to abolish the leagues, replace the regional Greek democracies with oligarchies, and place Greece under the authority of the Roman governor of Macedon, thus ending Greek and Macedonian independence. Until 31 BC Roman gold, silver and bronze coinage gradually became prevalent in the Roman Republic. It then spread through the domains of the empire until AD 527.

Greek and later Roman coinage surviving in museums and collections today bear the images of gods and goddesses, kings and emperors, and renowned persons such as Alexander the Great of Macedon, whose likness appears on ancient Greek coins still found as far east as Afghanistan and India where his armies conquered and founded colonies. The Roman imperial coins bear portraits of rulers, from Julius Caesar to Constantine the Great.

Counterfeiters who sheathed leaden or iron cores with coatings of monetary metals learned to duplicate the techniques of casting the designs using clay moulds for the molten metal. There was wholesale counterfeiting for profit and in some cases to debase and weaken a rival state or region's currency. It was the Emperor Nero (AD 54–68, born AD 37), however, who gave the black art of weakening money a quantum boost – by debasing and thus devaluing Rome's own currency. In effect, since Nero gradually counterfeited his own money, one could call him one of the first 'state counterfeiters'.

Nero's reign got off to a constructive start under the guidance of the philosopher Seneca and Nero's imperial guard, Burrus. But in spirit, Nero was what one today might call a ham actor. His ego expanded and corroded his relationships with those near and supposedly dear. He deserted his wife, Octavia, first for a commoner named Acte, then for Poppaea Sabina, the wife of his friend Otho. In AD 59 he murdered his mother, Agrippina. After the death of Burrus late in his reign in AD 62, Nero divorced, exiled and murdered Octavia, then married Poppaea.

His personal depredations were mirrored in his attitude towards the Roman economy. According to some accounts, he began by firing his freedman financial secretary Pallas, who may have dared to object to Nero's policy of progressively removing the silver content of Roman coins. The empire's economy was already experiencing inflation. As history shows, from Nero to Weimar Germany of the 1920s or North Korea in the early 2000s, counterfeiting often spikes during times of high inflation. Nero professed to be preserving Roman money. Calling it currency 'reform', he began adding copper alloy to Rome's silver denarius coins. But acid on the fingers of the handlers corroded the copper, wearing on the coin and causing the surface to slough off gradually, thus further reducing its silver content.

Nero's successors kept adding more and more alloy to silver and gold coins until the once solidly trusted silver denarius came to be minted with less than 1 per cent silver. In the later empire, older coins with a higher content of precious metal were sought out and hoarded; the intrinsic value of the metal was greater than that of more recent mintings of the same denomination. As the older coins ended up in people's strongboxes or hidden away in cupboards, the total amount in circulation dropped off sharply, requiring more coins – especially the lower-denomination bronze ones – to be minted in order to keep trade and everyday exchange flowing.

Severe punishments were sometimes officially prescribed for counterfeiting: Emperor Constantine the Great had some offenders burned alive. As the Roman Empire and its economy gradually slumped into its final decline and fall in the sixth century AD, however, there was less and less real prosecution of wildcat counterfeiting. After all, emperors themselves were involved. Privately forged coins that looked real circulated widely without being questioned, stimulating inflation but also boosting day-to-day commerce, especially in distant provinces such as Britain in the West, or Syria and Palestine in the East. Nevertheless, progressive debasement of Roman coinage through the government mint's Senate-approved adulteration and through counterfeiting unquestionably weakened Rome's military power.[5]

'To Counterfeit is Death'

Despite the tolerance shown during the decades after Nero began debasing Roman coinage, in general Rome could inflict ruthless punishment for counterfeiting its currency. During the early years of the Roman Empire, counterfeiters who clipped precious metal from coins were punished by having their ears clipped or cut off. They were also deprived of Roman citizenship, a precious commodity. Later, their noses were cut off too, and eventually they were castrated and thrown to be devoured by hungry lions. Despite the terrible penalties applied most frequently to poorer Romans, as the empire declined currency counterfeiting grew to be an increasingly popular pastime or trade among well-to-do and prominent people. In this atmosphere of financial liberalism, Nero had little trouble moving ahead with his state counterfeiting, which ultimately led to virtual collapse of the currency and economy during the last decades of the empire's decline.[6]

With the rise of Islam in the seventh century AD and the constant wars between Persians and Arabs, as well as others between Romans and Persians, the integrity of currency and resistance to counterfeiting grew in importance. At the end of the Persian Sassanian dynasty in AD 696, an Arab caliph, Abd al-Malik, decreed wide currency reforms. His powerful governor Al-Hajjaj bin Yusuf, who ruled what is now Iran and Iraq, and who is credited with establishing the first Arab mint in Wasit in AD 702–3, implemented the reforms. A caliphate official called the *muhtasib*, supposed to be of high moral character and possessing a thorough knowledge of sharia religious law, had the job of testing the weights and measures and checking for counterfeit coins. Al-Hajjaj bin Yusuf set up a branch mint to coin Persian dirhams where workers had their hands tattooed or branded. This practice extended also to public moneychangers, who were often closely supervised to ensure against freelance forging. Anyone caught counterfeiting could have his hands cut off.[7]

In the Far East the earliest record of money is attributed to a Chinese minister who died in 645 BC. A book he wrote that alludes to a hierarchy of currency, with pearls and jade at the top, gold in the middle and metal knives and spades at the bottom, did not emerge until 26 BC. Bronze coins with square holes were the next step. By AD 669, under the Tang rulers (AD 618–907), the Chinese Empire and its money extended southwards to Vietnam, north to Mongolia into Siberia, east to most of the Korean Peninsula and west as far as Afghanistan. The earliest Chinese coins were issued by private enterprise, and even after the state had assumed responsibility for the currency some private issues continued and were occasionally encouraged. Experts hired by contract to cast coins were required to use bronze, made of copper and tin. Anyone who dared to counterfeit by adulterating coins with iron or lead was to be punished by having his face tattooed.[8] By the seventh century AD, counterfeiters as well as their families and neighbours were subject to the death penalty.[9]

Under the legendary Mongol ruler Kublai Khan (AD 1214–94), whom the Italian explorer-trader Marco Polo visited and then served in sensitive tasks and missions from 1275 to 1292, the first paper money appeared in the Chinese Empire, followed by bills of exchange. The paper currency issued was limited to the face exchange value of 100,000 ounces of silver. Various Muslim financiers working for the court of the khans raised this to 10 million ounces at one juncture. However, confidence in the paper was shaky. As so often in history, the economy suffered due to inflation and counterfeiting, and by 1311 the imperial treasury was printing no more paper money.[10] Early Chinese banknotes often carried the warning of 'Death to counterfeiters' (echoed in colonial America as 'To counterfeit is death'). Banknotes would reappear in China only in the nineteenth century, during the period of conflicts and economic stress during and following the Opium Wars with Britain.

In early medieval times in Europe, Roman coinage gradually gave way in the north to bartering and crude copper and bronze coins, and in the south and east to Byzantine gold and silver coins. In Anglo-Saxon England under King Athelstan (924–40) coin forgers were tortured and executed if found guilty. Under King Canute (1014–35) coin forgers had both hands cut off. During the reign of King Edward II (1307–27), forgers of the royal coinage had an especially tough time. The Abbot of Messendem was condemned to be drawn (not quartered) and hanged, and other clerics were executed for counterfeiting.

Much later, under Henry VIII (1509–47), the royal mint returned to Nero's practice of debasing the king's own currency. He also granted licences, called 'letters patent', to some of his favourites to do so. Economic historians rarely treat the issue of debasing's impact on Britain's growing mercantile economy as a whole. It is safe to say that it brought inflation. Wildcat counterfeiters often ignored the terrible penalties for their activities, and money forgery thrived as it has from ancient times until today.

Thalers and Dollars: True and False

Today's age of mixed metallic and paper money economies began in the late fifteenth century. With Renaissance artists' images of the rich and powerful on their faces, coins began to resemble those of our time. Spanish and Portuguese colonial looting of the gold and silver mined and fashioned into religious and secular art by the natives of Africa and Latin America increased the amount of bullion available in Europe. As a result commodity prices climbed, systems for denominating the new gold, silver and copper coinage changed, and monetary use grew. The makings of a world economy based on trade and monetary exchange began to emerge.

European silver production peaked. Several main silver mines were responsible. The Schwaz mine in Tyrol produced so abundantly that its ruler, the Duke of Sigismund, earned the sobriquet of 'The Wealthy', whereas his father had been called 'The Penniless'. Mines of the Dukes of Saxony 'enabled their rulers to dine off silver tables', according to the British Museum's *Money, a History*. The best performer of all was the mining complex at Saint Joachimsthal (Jáchymov) in Bohemia. Coins struck at the mint located at this fabulously rich silver mine, called the 'Joachimsthaler Guldengroschen', gave rise to the generic term 'thaler' or 'taler', the direct linguistic ancestor of 'dollar'.[11]

New and often higher-denomination coins of gold, some of it mined in Europe but most of it looted from Africa and America by the Spanish and Portuguese *conquistadores* and freebooters, began to appear on the Continent by the sixteenth century. From 1501 on, gold and silver coins issued by a private guild, the Wendische Münzverein, became legal tender in the trading cities of the Hanseatic League. They were labelled as 'marks', probably the first appearance of what came to be known as the German mark (much later as the reichsmark and finally the deutschmark). During the sixteenth century, the mark coins spread from northern Germany around the Baltic to Sweden, Denmark, Holstein and the states constituting today's Estonia, Latvia and Lithuania. Finland adopted it later, and its official currency was the finnmark until it was replaced by the euro. In 1619 the Hamburg city council and local merchants got together and founded the first public bank of exchange, called the Hamburg Bank, in the so-called 'Holy Roman Empire of the German Nation', the grandiose title of the motley collection of counties, dukedoms and earldoms that together constituted most of Europe's German-speaking areas and territory outside it as well.

Towards the end of the sixteenth century, the silver mines in the Harz, Erzgebirge and Tyrolean regions were largely exhausted. The silver price rose until, in 1559, it was higher than the value of silver coins issued by the imperial mint. Clever traders then melted silver thaler and gulden coins and smuggled the silver abroad, where they got market prices for the bullion. The value of the older coins was so high that the various regional mints lost money in their coining operations. The result was a severe shortage of change, making things tough for both consumers and merchants as well as for the moneychangers and bankers. The private and public mints issuing the coins began to debase their product, just as Nero and many others after him had done.

Bad coins began to turn up in big numbers and were traded – in other words, laundered – for good ones. When it became necessary for the empire and its loyal subjects to fund the Thirty Years' War (1618–48), in which most of Europe's states were fighting either each other or the empire or both, the depredations of counterfeiters and money launderers had so weakened the empire's finances that there was a chronic shortage of money hard enough to buy the guns, cannon, ammunition, food and other needed war supplies. As far back as 1603, a session of the imperial parliament, the Reichstag in Regensburg, had tried to confront the problem and had foreseen the huge difficulties the counterfeiters would create in financing the brewing war. It called a Reichsmünztag or currency conference to try to deal with the situation. One of the measures that followed was an edict by Emperor Rudolf II (1576–1612), who was better at astronomy than he was at statecraft, that counterfeiters would be burned to death. Despite this, 'official' counterfeiting in the form of debasement seems to have continued. The silver content of coins declined until, in September 1621, anyone who wanted to change copper coins into one thaler had to give in return copper coins to the value of eight thalers. In Dresden and Annenberg (Saxony) alone, counterfeit coins with a face value totalling 12.5 million gulden were struck, greatly helping to feed hyperinflation.

In the rival Hapsburg Empire, a consortium of money traders paid Emperor Ferdinand II (1619–37) to let them issue all the coinage of Austria, Bohemia and Moravia for one year. Trader Albrecht von Wallenstein got together with friends, converted to Catholicism and, with all the debased money he had collected, bought up a good part of the Protestant assets confiscated in Bohemia during the wars of the Counter-Reformation: an authentic case of seventeenth-century money laundering.[12]

Colonial America: Pieces of Wampum and Pieces of Eight

In his book *Greenback*, a lively and erudite history of the American dollar, Jason Goodwin records that a European nobleman named the Count of Slik controlled the region of the lucrative Joachimsthal silver mines in Bohemia. He began striking silver thalers there in 1519. Only nine years later, the rising Catholic dynasty of the Hapsburgs took over the area. The imperial mint soon began issuing the 'imperial reichsthaler' (Englishmen called it the 'rix dollar'). It was valued at eight Spanish reals and was struck at the mint in Seville, Spain. Among Spanish and Portuguese explorers and freebooters colonizing and plundering the New World, this became known as the 'Spanish dollar'. In the popular lore of the time, its plural nickname became 'pieces of eight'. Like today's American dollar, it became a kind of reserve and trading currency for the whole world. Kings and queens collected Spanish dollars for their royal treasuries; pirates and bandits raided, robbed and killed for them. There were plenty of enterprising forgers, some more expert than others. Today treasure-hunters still dive for occasional hidden caches of the coins, both real and false, along the coasts of Central America and Florida.[13]

When British, Dutch, French and Swedish settlers first began to establish permanent settlements along the Atlantic coast, the currency of the Native Americans (or 'Indians', a name that has stuck since Columbus and contemporaries thought they had sailed to India) as far south as the Carolinas was called wampum. An Algonquin Indian word meaning 'white bead', wampum (or *wampumpeag*) actually came in both white and black. White wampum was made from the shells of periwinkles, or marine snails. They were worth half the value of dark beads made from clamshells (called *quahog*, from the Algonquin word for hard clam). Each bead was cylindrical, about half in inch in diameter and about a quarter of an inch in length, and highly polished and strung together on sinews. Both settlers and Native Americans recognized wampum as true money, and used it to trade. The main denomination was called the *fathom*, which had a different value in each colony. In Massachusetts in 1640, the standard bead count in a fathom was 240. One fathom was worth five English shillings, which like pounds and pence were legal tender in the English colonies. In Virginia, wampum was called *roenoke* (hence the early settlement and today's city of Roanoke). In Nieuw Amsterdam, which became New York when seized by the English in 1664, it was called *zeewand* or *zeewan*.

Because of the shortage of both real and forged coins in the early decades of colonial America, wampum predominated for a decade or so as the main medium of exchange.

The Pilgrims were a separatist sect of Protestants who sailed from England on the *Mayflower* and founded in 1620 the Plymouth Colony on Cape Cod, Massachusetts. Mostly folk of modest means, they did not bring much silver, gold or copper money from England. Some of them, however, were adept in the old art of clipping and shaving coins they did possess, such as Spanish milled dollars or English sovereigns. Under their first governors John Carver and John Winthrop, the Pilgrims did not know how to detect counterfeit wampum proffered by Indians in trading deals, and the Indians could not tell the difference between real and counterfeit coins. Each side took advantage of the other's ignorance. The settlers began making bogus wampum out of cheap porcelain fragments, bone, or glass beads made in undercover factories, first in England and later in America. The settlers traded the bogus wampum for corn and other commodities they desperately needed.

Both the Indians and the settlers began to cheat in their purchase and trading transactions by counterfeiting wampum. The Indians did this by making it from the far more abundant, and hence less valuable, blue clamshells. If a modern bank teller or his superior recognizes a counterfeit bill or coin, he rejects it with a warning if the customer is still in front of him, or notifies the police (and, in the United States, the Secret Service) if the customer has departed before the fake is detected. When the early settlers tried to pass counterfeit wampum back to an Indian, the latter would look at it, spit on it, drop it to the ground, fold his arms and shake his head. The early settlers learned to spit on the strings and rub the beads vigorously to make sure they were the hearts of genuine quaghog shells and not the common white seashells that Indian counterfeiters sometimes dyed blue with the juice of wild huckleberries.

Just as in ancient Rome, the anti-counterfeiting laws passed by early American colonial bodies were relatively mild at first, before harsher and sometimes capital punishments were applied later on. In Dutch-held Nieuw Amsterdam, Manahatta (Manhattan) Island was reputedly purchased from the Indians by Dutch adventurer Peter Stuyvesant for twenty-four 'dollars' (probably Spanish milled dollars). Forged wampum became so prevalent that the colonial council there passed a law in 1650 prohibiting the 'nefarious practice' of counterfeiting. Records are lacking for subsequent early penalties for counterfeiting in the colonies, but contemporary accounts show that wampum currency became thoroughly discredited by counterfeiting, and totally collapsed.[14]

Gold, silver and copper soon returned to their old supremacy. More momentous for the future, the era of paper money gradually dawned, both in Europe and in its American settlements and colonies. How the rise of paper money influenced history on both sides of the Atlantic is our next subject.

Five

Benjamin Franklin versus King George: America's Financial Birth Pangs

> But, matchless FRANKLIN! what a few
> Can hope to rival such as YOU,
> Who seized from kings their sceptred pride
> And turned the lightning's darts aside!
>
> *Philip Freneau*, c. *1790, from*
> *'On the Death of Dr Benjamin Franklin'*

It is altogether appropriate that Benjamin Franklin's is the face on the American $100 bill – both the pre-1996 note and, in a larger, more emphatic portrait, the newer one. After all, Franklin not only furthered the cause of paper money in the American colonies by printing it, he also devised a meaningful and artistic means of combating its forgery. Above all, Franklin (1706–90) was a close observer and a tireless player in the crucial financial aspects of one of the eighteenth century's biggest historical dramas: King George III of England's ill-fated attempts to crush both the American Revolution and in the prologue to the French Revolution. These events led to the world dominance of Great Britain's two greatest rivals and modern-day allies: the French and American republics.

Even before Franklin's Philadelphia print shop began turning out colonial currency for the governments of Pennsylvania, New Jersey and Delaware in 1729, the Massachusetts Bay Colony's rulers had become the first governing authority in the West to print paper money. Counterfeiting of coins had spread in the colonies like an epidemic, just as it would from the turn of the century onwards for the newer paper money. The counterfeiting and clipping of New England coins had become so prevalent that the Massachusetts authorities decreed in 1652 that all coins had to have a double ring on each side, along with other distinguishing marks. The double ring was supposed to guard against clipping. However, the minting of the 1652 New England coins was too amateurish to deter the counterfeiters. A report in the *Boston Transcript* newspaper a century later disclosed that numerous Pine Tree Shillings were forged in New York City and sold to antiquarian shops at huge prices.

As counterfeiters and their accomplices multiplied, their punishments grew in severity. In Massachusetts in 1679 Peter Lorphelin, a Frenchman whose offences included possessing counterfeiting paraphernalia, was sentenced to stand two hours in a pillory, to have both ears cut off and to pay a bond of £500, an immense sum in those days. He also had to pay prosecution costs and court fees.[1]

Paper Money Adventures in the West

In the seventeenth century, Spanish 'pieces of eight' were joined by trading coins of the republic of the Netherlands in Asia and the Middle East, and also in the form of ducats of gold and silver in Russia, India and China. The Austrian thaler, another highly valued silver coin, appeared in the mid-eighteenth century and by 1780 had begun to spread around the world as the Maria Theresa thaler. People in the Middle East, especially in the Arabian Peninsula, and in Ethiopia still use these old silver coins today. While living in Morocco, I discovered that the Maria Theresa thalers were still to be found there as well.

The ancestors of today's Western paper money appeared during the decline of European gold and silver coinage, which had spread around the world with the colonial adventurers and traders. By the end of the seventeenth century, paper notes and bills of credit were in use in Europe to pay off debts and cheques, make loans and interest-bearing deposits, and serve as promissory notes. In 1676 an anonymous pamphlet in England condemned goldsmiths for charging exorbitant interest rates on loans and bills of exchange. The pamphlet identified the basis for successful banking and use of paper currency: trust in the banker and the notes he issues, and sound financial backing (meaning gold or silver) for the notes.

The evolution of the West's gradual shift in preference to paper money over coins is fairly easy to trace. As the use of gold and silver declined, coins were replaced by fiduciary money: promises on paper to pay specified sums in gold and silver. Individuals or companies issued such a promise in the form of a banknote or as a transferable entry in a book called a deposit, which was a claim on gold or silver deposited with a bank or a merchant. As time went by, it became evident to the banker or merchant concerned that not all the holders of paper would claim the balance due to them at once. Thus the banker or merchant could profit by issuing more claims to the gold and silver than the actual amount stored in his vaults or strongboxes. He could then invest the difference or lend it at interest. The big weak spot was that if too many borrowers defaulted on their loans, or if the banker or merchant had committed a modified form of counterfeiting by issuing amounts of paper greatly in excess of the value of the precious metal he held, the bank could fail or the merchant go broke. Decades before Benjamin Franklin began printing money for the restless American colonies in 1729, some of the early experiments with paper money ended in damaged economies and ruined careers.

The first freely circulating banknotes in Europe were issued by a man named Johan Palmstruch. In 1656 he founded a private bank in Sweden called the Stockholm Banco. However, half of its profits were payable to the Swedish Crown, and the Crown's chancellor of the exchequer kept a controlling watch on the cash flow. Standard Swedish currency was then planted on clunky copper plates and was depreciating in value. So with royal permission Palmstruch began issuing paper 'credit notes' as a transitional alternate currency. But he lent too much money and issued too many notes he couldn't redeem. This landed him before a royal judge who issued a death sentence. He sentence was later commuted to prison.[2]

About fifty years after Palmstruch's fiasco came the much more grandiose efforts of John Law (1671–1729), a Scottish 'philanderer, gambler and duelist who invented modern finance', as he is described by his biographer Janet Gleeson in the subtitle of her book *Millionaire*.[3] The son of a wealthy Edinburgh goldsmith and banker, he wasted his large inheritance on drinking, gambling and womanizing. After killing a love-interest rival in a duel in 1694, he bribed his way out of death row in a Scottish prison and fled to France, which became his second home. There he picked up a wealthy Parisian married woman named Katherine Seigneur, and they roamed Europe's gaming casinos. Law's extraordinary mathematical skills helped him work out a system to break many a casino's bank and amass a fortune. In fact the word 'millionaire' was invented to describe Law as he was enriching himself with his financial schemes in France.

In 1705 Law published a pamphlet urging the establishment of banks to issue paper money backed by land or other collateral. The 1690 essay 'The Key to Wealth' by William Potter, an English bureaucrat working in a government land office, may have helped to inspire Law. Advocating the issue of abundant paper money to be backed by the value of government-owned land, rather than by gold and silver, Potter reasoned that the more money was in circulation, the more trade and production would increase. Although making no allowances for what counterfeiters might contribute to its growth, he predicted that the increased money supply would be absorbed by rising output and that prices would fall as a result. (This theory was echoed in the twentieth century by the gifted but eccentric American poet Ezra Pound, whose vague theory of 'social credit' proposed that usury, or abusive lending with interest, would disappear in favour of interest-free credit based on real estate or other concrete assets.) Economic historian Murray Rothbard credits the essay with establishing Potter as 'the first English inflationist'. Potter was not a conscious swindler, but future financiers would try with almost no success to put his theory into practice.

Both the Massachusetts Bay Colony in America and the Bank of England in London had been issuing paper money since 1690 and 1694 respectively. Yet Law's highly placed social and political contacts sat up and took notice of his scheme to print vast amounts of banknotes, which despite Potter's earlier essay seemed like a new idea on the Continent, especially in France.

The plight of France and England, and their colonies in the New World, during the seventeenth century is reminiscent of the ruinously expensive financing of contemporary wars of the twentieth and twenty-first. Named after the Wampanoag leader whom colonists had given an anglicized name, King Philip's War was a massive conflict between the dominant tribe in the Cape Cod region, who felt their power threatened, and New England colonists from Maine to Connecticut. In 1675–6, numerous colonial and Indian communities were devastated, and 500 white men and an undetermined number of Indians were killed. The war left Philip dead and the Indians defeated, but the colonies involved were close to bankruptcy. Repeated conflicts with the French and Indians also took their financial toll on the colonies. However, the main impetus for the Massachusetts Bay Colony issue of paper money in 1690 was a ruinously expensive military expedition organized by New England and New York against the French in Canada. The invading army was routed and the colonial soldiers returned home and demanded their pay long before the organizers had anticipated. Since the only way to raise the necessary cash was to levy taxation, already a *bête noire* for the colonists as His Majesty's authorities were already discovering, the Massachusetts authorities acted to print paper money in the amount of £7,000. Other military expeditions requiring quick paper-money fixes followed: the Carolinas' campaign against the Spanish in Saint Augustine, Florida, in 1702; new campaigns against the French in Canada forcing New York and Connecticut to print money in 1709. Pennsylvania printed money in 1723, Maryland in 1734 and Delaware in 1739. Virginia and Georgia followed in 1755 and 1760, respectively.[4]

But back to John Law's monetary adventures. These illustrate well the grey area between actual counterfeiting and the overprinting of officially sanctioned currency issued by a state. After he returned to Scotland in 1703, immune from further prosecution for murder, the Scottish parliament rejected Law's plan for a central bank that would issue paper money 'backed by the land of the nation'. Citing prosperous Holland, which had an export surplus and ample reserves of gold and silver to back its own paper banknotes, Law unsuccessfully tried to convince the dour and canny Scots that more money in circulation would boost employment and production as Potter had claimed. What he did not comprehend was that Dutch prosperity resulted from a positive trade balance and a solid currency basis, and that it was a state where counterfeiting was a grave offence and too infrequent to feed inflation.

Further legal troubles forced Law to flee to France a second time. In 1715, King Louis XIV's death finally gave Law the opportunity he sought to propagate his paper-money schemes. He convinced the Duke of Orléans, the French regent, to name him head of the Banque Royale, which issued all of the paper bills and notes. The notes were initially accepted for payment of taxes and were redeemable in silver. However, the hard currency backing was soon abolished. This gave the French Crown (and hence Law) the power to create unlimited debt.

By 1716 Law had full control of the monetary system in France and its empire. He was placed in charge of the Mississippi Company, an enterprise formed to exploit the huge French-held Louisiana Territory in America. Law issued huge quantities of notes supposed to be backed by the expanse of the Louisiana Territory, which reached from the Gulf of Mexico to Canada and was bigger than France itself. This massive increase in the issuance of government debts produced a hyperincrease of the money supply to feed the frenzy of hundreds of eager speculators. Promissory notes, bank credit, the nominal value of French paper money and prices skyrocketed from 1717 to 1720 in France, creating what financial writer Lewis J. Walker describes as the 'royal hyperinflationary mess that is known as the "Mississippi Bubble"'.[5]

Hard-money supporters in Europe and America were heartened when the bubble burst along with the French dream of paper wealth. Bankrupt and burdened by personal debt, Law fled France and roamed Europe until 1729, when he died in Naples while trying to persuade local politicians to make him their central banker. France experimented no more with paper money until the disastrous issue of the famous assignats by the revolutionaries, which induced hyperinflation in France. This was clandestinely fed by English King George III's covert and massive counterfeiting of the paper notes, intended to support the monarchy of Louis XVI and Marie Antoinette by bringing down the Revolution.

Richard Cantillon (1697–1734), an Irish entrepreneur, plunged into the Paris banking world in 1730 and was briefly Law's partner. However, he bet that Law's scheme would fail and is said to have accumulated a fortune following France's economic collapse. Cantillon wrote an 'Essay on the Nature of Trade in General', published posthumously in 1755, in which he became one of the first writers to recognize human greed and fear as catalysts in economics.[6]

Ben Franklin's Print Shops . . . and Their Customers

Nearly all mainstream American historians agree that Benjamin Franklin was one of the giants among the fathers of the American Republic. However, he deservedly earned a global reputation as a statesman, author and scientist (and, in France especially, as a ladies' man). He began his career in the American colonies of Great Britain as a journalist and printer. He ended it as the one man who probably did more than anyone else to secure a financial and military alliance with France. This was crucial in saving a revolution that nearly foundered under economic difficulties severely aggravated by the currency counterfeiting of Franklin's former sovereign, King George III, and in securing the former colonies' independence.

As a teenager in his birthplace of Boston Franklin picked up basic printing skills. In 1723, at the age of seventeen, he left for New York, hoping to find work with William Bradford, at the time believed to be the only printer in the colonies outside of New England. When the Bradford firm was not sufficiently responsive, young Ben took a job with a rival Philadelphia printer, Keimer. In his autobiography, Franklin commented that he found that Keimer

> tho' something of a Scholar, was a mere Compositor, knowing nothing of Presswork. He . . . was very ignorant of the World, and had, as I afterward found, a good deal of the Knave in his Composition.[7]

Ben needed a job badly, so he kept his opinions private and began to print pamphlets and other small jobs for Keimer. His impeccable work attracted the attention of Sir William Keith, the governor of Pennsylvania, who sent him to London in late 1724 to buy equipment and open accounts with stationers and booksellers. In eighteen busy months in London, Franklin learned the book trade. He then returned to Keimer's employ in Philadelphia, where he acquired new skills, including wood engraving and cutting type metal.

After a quarrel with Keimer Franklin set up his own printing house in Philadelphia, bought the *Pennsylvania Gazette* and soon earned a reputation as a journalist and pamphleteer. Spiced with wry humour, his shrewd comments on the colony's political and social scenes, along with some financial manoeuvring, won him an appointment as Philadelphia's postmaster in 1737. This eventually led to his elevation to deputy postmaster general for all of the American colonies in 1754 as well as subsequent diplomatic missions in England.

During his first twenty years as an independent printer and author of such famous publications as *Poor Richard's Almanack*, Franklin earned his bread and butter by specializing in job printing of books, pamphlets and whatever other assignments came his way. Ready money in the form of cash, whether in sterling, Spanish dollars or other forms of specie, was in short supply in the American economy of the early eighteenth century. As usual, Franklin did his homework in monetary affairs. Like Potter, John Law and other contemporaries, he became an enthusiastic proponent of increasing the money supply by printing paper money. He became a craftsman of paper money that would set a pattern for the American currency of the coming generations up to the present.

In 1729, six years after Pennsylvania began issuing paper money, Franklin printed his own manifesto: *A Modest Enquiry into the*

Nature and Necessity of a Paper-Currency. He won contracts to print banknotes for the governments of Pennsylvania, New Jersey and Delaware. Each individual note had to be numbered by hand and signed by one or more public officials. The Pennsylvania Assembly delegated authority for issuing the currency to the Loan Office, a sort of land bank issuing mortgages paid out in the new paper money. Farmers and tradesmen liked the increase this brought in the money supply. However, wealthy merchants and landowners (including the family of the colony's founder, William Penn) did not like it all, and tried to limit its circulation. 'The Rich Men dislik'd it; for it increas'd and strengthen'nd their Clamor for more Money,' as Franklin wrote in his autobiography. But the Pennsylvania Assembly, influenced by Franklin's *Modest Enquiry*, approved it.[8] Between 1729 and 1747, Franklin printed about 800,000 paper bills – a total of four currency emissions for Pennsylvania, Delware and New Jersey valued at 275,000 sterling, from which he earned about 1,000 sterling.

During this general period and beyond, the counterfeiting of paper money in the colonies peaked. A contemporary of Franklin, Mary Butterworth (1686–1775) became the mastermind of one of America's first successful counterfeiting rings. At the time, Rhode Island was issuing paper bills of credit denominated in sterling. In 1716, Mrs Butterworth, then thirty years old, began copying the bills using a unique method of her own. Her tools included a hot iron and starched muslin cloth. She would run the iron over a genuine bill and then impress the image on blank paper similar to that used by the Rhode Island bank of issue. With some confederates who were artistically inclined, she supervised filling in the images with a quill. They were then passed through a network of accomplices, including a local judge who had an impeccable reputation and was above suspicion.

Contemporary records omit the amounts of the laundered forgeries, but they indicate that Rhode Island's economy suffered considerable damage. The 'kitchen counterfeiters', as they came to be called, stayed in business for seven years without being detected. In 1723, the colonial constabulary arrested Butterworth along with a half-dozen co-conspirators. Although a quantity of the bogus notes was found in her kitchen along with the tools of the forger's trade, the conspirators managed to beat the rap when a court found the evidence insufficient to convict them. Butterworth and associates eventually went scot-free. The authorities in Providence did put her under close surveillance: this apparently prevented any new operations by the group.[9]

Franklin and a friend named Joseph Breintnall devised a unique artistic means to discourage counterfeiters of paper money. In the 1720s, Breintnall had been making nature prints of tree leaves. This inspired Breintnall and Franklin to ink leaves they had collected and place them between the halves of a folded sheet of paper, which they then passed through the printing press. Apparently using type metal cast from moulds made by pressing leaves into plaster of paris, Franklin made metalcuts of the leaves to print the leaf images on his banknotes. The first such cut was an impression of a plant called the Rattlesnake leaf, illustrating an article on the use of the plant in the 1737 *Poor Richard's Almanack*. The leaf cuts were so successful in the colonies that, until the fateful Continental issue of 1776, most money that Franklin and his successors printed incorporated them.[10] In 1776, however, King George's military commanders successfully counterfeited the notes in an effort to destroy the finances of the rebellious colonists and George Washington's revolutionary army.

The Bumpy Road of Revolution

Long before Paul Revere's legendary midnight ride warned the 'Minutemen', the armed farmers and townsmen of Boston and its suburbs, that King George's Redcoats were coming to crush the incipient rebellion, the entire British colonial enterprise in America had become a huge financial burden for the British Crown.

The acquisition of huge French territories in North America south of Canada in the 1763 Treaty of Paris forced the American colonies into the often dyspeptic view of Parliament in London, whose members were ready to legislate almost anything to finance the huge costs of maintaining the colonies without over-burdening the British taxpayer. Apart from one or two contemporary opponents of the Crown, like the rebel Englishman John Wilkes, the colonists had no representation in Parliament and little voice anywhere in Britain.

The Treaty of Paris led successive British ministries to focus on administering the thirteen colonies more efficiently and in particular to raise money there by a series of measures that were ultra-provocative to the colonists. Every American elementary school pupil learns about the Stamp Act (1765), Townshend's Duties, the experiment with the Board of Customs Commissioners (1767) and finally the Tea Act (1773) that led into the colonists' dumping of British tea cargoes at the 'Boston Tea Party'. All of these raised widespread economic and social unrest to the level of violence by the end of 1774.

The value of the money Franklin and others were printing was being steadily eroded by the widespread counterfeiting and other inflationary factors. After enactment of the Sugar Act, aimed at raising new revenues through direct taxation, Parliament passed the Colonial Currency Act in 1764. This prevented entities in the colonies from paying their debts in England with the depreciated colonial currency and forbade issues of money considered dodgy by the British authorities. The act caused a new shortage of money in the colonies at the same time the Sugar Act injured the colonies' West Indian trade in sugar, rum and molasses, which had brought in the hard currency needed for internal banking and commerce along the Atlantic seaboard.[11]

Supremacy of the 'King, Lords and Commons', stated in the English political bible, Sir William Blackstone's *Commentaries on the Laws of England* (1765), was contested by the growing patriot faction in an increasingly polarized colonial society. Many of the better-off tradesmen, bankers and professional groups tended to profess loyalty to the Crown once the onerous economic measures like the Stamp Act and stiff customs duties that hurt their livelihoods had been defeated or rescinded. The Loyalists shied away from attacking that 'firm Loyalty to the Crown and faithful Adherence to the Government which is the Safety as well as the Honour of the Colonies', as Ben Franklin, then still a loyal subject and a successful printer of the King's money, had put it in 1765.

After the Boston Tea Party on 16 December 1773, King George's favourite prime minister, Lord North, who kept his post from 1770 to 1782, became a main policymaker for the colonies. He was likely the authority who approved Lord Howe's counterfeiting operation against the American Continental currency after the British occupation of New York in 1776. In any case, in early 1774 North began to adopt and push through Parliament punitive measures that further wiped out civil liberties and eventually severely damaged colonial economies.

The so-called Coercive Acts that followed included the Boston Port Act, which closed and blockaded Boston's port after 1 June 1774, and the Massachusetts Government Act, which deprived the people of most of the rights they enjoyed under the colonial charter and gave the royal governor almost absolute power. Especially abusive was the Administration of Justice Act. This provided that anyone accused of a capital crime of rebellion be tried in England or a colony other than the one where the alleged crime was committed. The Quartering Act forced inhabitants of Boston and other towns to let British troops live in their homes. The Quebec Act was not envisioned in London as a punitive measure, but was so regarded by the colonists. It extended the boundary of the province of Quebec to the Ohio River, which cut across the claims of Massachusetts, New York, Connecticut and Virginia.[12]

On 5 September 1774, after calls from several of the colonies to hold an emergency meeting, the First Continental Congress convened in Philadelphia. A majority voted down Loyalist lawyer Joseph Galloway's proposal to avoid rebellion. Instead they drew up a Declaration of Rights and Grievances and decided on a boycott to prevent importation of British goods. In early 1775, two British plans for reconciliation were rejected and battles began at Lexington and Concord on 19 April 1775. In May, after the capture by the Americans of Ticonderoga and Crown Point, two British strong points in northern New York State, the crucial Second Continental Congress assembled in Philadelphia. They appointed George Washington (1732–99), a landed Virginia gentleman, as commander-in-chief of the hastily mobilized state militias called the Continental Army.

It was the 1775 Continental Congress that took the crucial financial measures to support the war. Its members began preparations to issue bills redeemable by the twelve confederated colonies (Georgia hadn't joined the confederation yet). As soon as the news of the new battle with the Redcoats at Bunker Hill (or Breed's Hill) near Boston reached the Congress on 22 June 1775, it ordered the issue of bills in the amount of 2 million Spanish milled dollars. The issue was divided among the twelve colonies in proportion to the estimated population of each colony, which was supposed to levy taxes for eventual redemption of the bills in hard currency. In November 1775 a new issue of 'Continentals', as the bills were called, of $3 million, was printed in fractional denominations – one-third, one-half and two-thirds of a dollar – and in larger denominations from $1 to $80. Virginia, the most populous state, received $496,278,000; Rhode Island, with the fewest people, was allotted just $37,219.50.

The design of the bills resembled that of the pre-Revolutionary colonial money. They measured two and a half by three and a half inches, framed in a square, decorative border of script and flourishes. The legend on a sample read:

> No. 19034 Eight Dollars
> This Bill entitles the
> Bearer to receive
> EIGHT Spanish milled
> DOLLARS, or the
> Value thereof in *Gold*
> Or *Silver*, according to
> The Resolutions of the
> CONGRESS, held at
> *Philadelphia*, the 10th of
> *May*, 1775. VIII DOLL.

Left of this was a patriotic slogan, *Majora minoribus consonant* ('The greater harmonize with the smaller'). Some accounts attribute the Latin inscriptions, different on each denomination, to Ben Franklin. Some of the objects portrayed on the Continentals appear on modern dollar banknotes of various denominations: the Great

Seal, thirteen stars (added after Georgia joined the confederation), the pyramid and the eagle. The Continentals were not printed from woodcuts like the previous colonial currency. They were engraved on copper plates and had only minimal anti-counterfeiting measures: many lacked Ben Franklin's leaf imprints. At first signatures of three of 195 authorized signers were affixed, but the practice was abandoned when the issues became too numerous.

George Washington's plans for an expedition to attack the British in Canada and another in Boston were hampered by a pitiful lack of cash, food, clothing, guns, ammunition and all manner of provisions for the Continental Army. Among other ways, low morale among the militia was manifested by a 10 September 1775 mutiny among the Pennsylvania riflemen, put down by General Nathaniel Green and a force of Rhode Island troops. Washington was dissuaded from his planned offensives by the counsel of wise men such as John Hancock, the president of the Continental Congress whose decorative signing of the Declaration of Independence in Philadelphia on 4 July 1776 would make his name a synonym for a forceful signature.

On 29 September 1776, the first $500,000 in Continental bills was delivered to Washington's headquarters at Cambridge, just outside the heavily fortified British positions in Boston, to give the troops there their first pay. Lieutenant Joseph Hodgkins wrote to his wife, Sarah, on 6 October, 'I send you eleven dollars' from his monthly pay of thirteen dollars.[13] Washington's troops besieged the British in Boston from July 1775 until 17 May 1776, when the British under General Sir William Howe finally evacuated the city.

Less successful was an American force commanded by Richard Montgomery that invaded Canada. They took Montreal, but troops under General Benedict Arnold, who later became the Revolution's most famous turncoat and joined the British, could not capture Quebec. By this time King George III and Lord North began hiring Hessians (German mercenaries from Hesse) to put down the rebellion, for which Britain's enemy France was already showing signs of sympathy and support.

As soon as the British left Boston, Washington moved to New

York where General Howe and his brother, Admiral Lord Richard Howe, were prepared to attack New York by land and sea. Admiral Howe had proposed peace terms, but the Americans had rejected them. On 27 August a British force landed in Long Island and defeated the Americans under General Israel Putnam, who retreated to New York. By 15 September Staten Island, Brooklyn and much of Manhattan had been captured by the British. Washington retreated to Harlem Heights. During this period, General Howe (and probably his brother as well) began to orchestrate a huge covert operation to undermine the Continental currency of the American rebels by massively counterfeiting it.

The counterfeiting of money in England for commercial use in the colonies was already an old story. It undoubtedly provided facilities as well as skilled printers and engravers whom Lord North's government could enlist in the new enterprise of economic warfare against the upstart Americans. The historical precedents went back to the early years of the eighteenth century. For example, on 30 July 1729, a sloop called the *Charming Sally* arrived from Dublin and docked at Philadelphia. During the voyage a passenger named Eaton had died. When his baggage was opened, it was found to contain 118 counterfeit pound sterling notes supposedly issued in New Jersey. Then in May 1739 Peter Long of Philadelphia arrived in his native city with 6,000 sterling in New England notes printed in England. The English printer who had forged the notes for Long also filled another order for Long's cousin and partner, Robert Jenkins of Salem, New Jersey. The printer then reported everything to the police in England. They informed the colonial authorities in Philadelphia and New York. When Jenkins arrived in New York and was placed under arrest, the colonial police found 971 counterfeit twenty-shilling Delaware notes. It emerged at his trial that before leaving England, Long had sent the English printer samples of genuine Jersey and Delaware notes, hidden in a saddle. He had ordered 1,000 forged twenty-shilling New Jersey notes and 12,000 Delaware ones. From 1740 until the outbreak of the Revolution in 1775, the newspapers in the colonies repeatedly cautioned the public about the proliferation of spurious banknotes and coins. Neither the warnings nor the severe punishments for counterfeiting did much good: the practice grew to be a cottage industry, making it much easier for the British operation to succeed.[14]

With or without counterfeiting, there was a general lack of faith in the paper Continentals almost as soon as they were printed. On 7 November 1775 the revolutionary Committee of Public Safety in Philadelphia learned that the Quakers of the region were refusing to accept the new bills. They argued that, since they were pacifists, they couldn't use money created to fight a war. The Quakers were reminded that they had used colonial paper money in the past to fight the French and their Indian allies. In January 1776, the Congress passed a resolution warning people 'lost to all virtue and regard for his country' who rejected the bills. (There is no record of any penalty for rejecting the bills, however.) The Congress also insisted that the Continentals would be redeemed in hard money when they became due. A proclamation told the public, 'A bankrupt faithless republic would be a novelty in the political world, and appear among respectable nations like a common prostitute among chaste and respectable matrons.'[15]

General William Howe, the British military governor of occupied New York, was backed in his counterfeiting enterprise by scores of British agents and Tory (Loyalist) sympathizers in New York and the other colonies. In the recent book *1776, America and Britain at War* by historian David McCullough, he is described as 'an easygoing, affable man who had never been averse to taking his pleasures when he could', wining, dining and gambling – all traits observed during his command in besieged Boston. He took with him to New York a 'stunning young woman . . . who became known as Billy Howe's Cleopatra'. She was the wife of Joshua Loring, Jr, of a prominent Loyalist family. A contemporary recorded that the general 'was fond of her. Joshua had no objections. He fingered the cash, the general enjoyed madam.'[16]

When not dallying with Mrs Loring, who after evacuating Boston with the British was comfortably installed near Howe's New York headquarters on Staten Island, Howe was pondering strategies to capitalize on tactical successes against Washington at the Battle of White Plains on 28 October 1776 and the November surrender of Fort Washington, located at the top of Manhattan Island and Fort Lee on the opposite bank of the Hudson River. At the same time, he and his staff, almost certainly coordinating with London authorities, were preparing and launching the counterfeiting campaign.

Much of the printing was done in England. At one point an American privateer intercepted and seized an English ship whose hold was packed with counterfeit bills. Much of the forgery was done in New York and Pennsylvania by Tory sympathizers. It also apparently happened aboard warships of the royal fleet anchored in and around New York Harbor and the Hudson River, under the command of Admiral Sir Richard Howe. In any case, private counterfeiters of the Continentals were given free rein by Lord Howe's occupation authorities to ply their trade – and to advertise their product.

Most historians who deal seriously with the issue reproduce one such 'advertisement', labelled as such in the *New York Gazette and the Weekly Mercury* on 14 April 1777. This was the newspaper that printed the official proclamations and edicts of the British occupying authorities. It invited 'Persons going into the other Colonies' to acquire 'for [only] the Price of the Paper per Ream', counterfeit notes 'in any number'. They were 'so neatly and exactly executed' that it was almost impossible to detect them. 'This has been proved by Bills to a very large Amount, which have already been successfully circulated,' the public notice assured potential customers. Interested persons were invited to 'Enquire at the Coffee-House [a prominent New York cafe] between the hours of 11 pm to 4 am.'

Contemporary accounts indicate that 'the pockets of English officers and men bulged with counterfeits' after the British captured Philadelphia in the winter of 1777–8. However, long before the occupation of Philadelphia, in 1776 British agents were sent from New York to the paper manufacturer who supplied the paper for the Continentals. The Council in Lancaster, Pennsylvania, reported in a letter to General Washington, dated 22 January 1778, that wagon drivers conveying clothing for English prisoners of war were jailed after a quantity of the forgeries were found on them. In a letter to Congress dated 7 December 1779, Washington confirmed that the British were obtaining paper from Philadelphia mills similar to that used for the most recent issue of Continentals and that their counterfeiting operation was continuing. A month earlier, President of the State Council Joseph Reed had told the Pennsylvania House of Representatives that the depreciation of the currency 'and its fatal consequences to the honour and interest of America' were so generally known that it was time to take firm action to counter it.

Continental issues of 12 May 1777 and 11 April 1778 were so extensively counterfeited that Congress had to recall all of both issues. By January 1780 $7,439,974 of the former and $12,407,294 of the latter issue had to be destroyed. The value of the bills became so minuscule that they lost nearly all their purchasing power. Thomas Jefferson reported that a total of about $200,000,000 (a Treasury report in 1843 gave the figure as $242,100,176), a gigantic sum in those days, had been printed in genuine Continental bills up to 1780, when the official value was reduced to forty paper dollars for one silver dollar. By September 1779, the notes were worth only 5 per cent of their original value and then became totally worthless. Jason Goodwin reports that Jefferson commented that the currency 'had expired without a groan'.

The phrase 'not worth a Continental' came into common use in the American language. A barber papered the wall of his shop with the notes. One old soldier with a serious leg wound reportedly used a bundle of notes from his pay envelope as a bandage. This gave rise to the American word 'shinplaster', later used to describe any piece of worthless paper money. During the war each state issued bills of its own, estimated to total $209,000,000 – also extensively counterfeited by the British, Tory sympathizers, just plain crooks, or a combination of the three.[17]

As McCullough records, the finances of the Revolution were in such desperate shape that often there were not enough Continentals to pay the troops. While Washington's men were struggling to hold off the British during the successful siege of New York by English and Hessian troops, the Americans were badly fed on sparse rations and many had received no pay for two months.

Their adversaries on the opposite side of the East River had plenty of food and other provisions from Long Island farms. The Hessians in particular proclaimed to contemporary journalists that they'd never had it so good. Later, when Washington had been driven south across the Delaware River and needed reliable intelligence about the enemy more desperately than ever, he is said to have assured his staff that 'Expense must not be spared in procuring such intelligence, and will readily be paid by me.' Since other funds were not available, he dug into his own savings in hard currency on this and numerous other occasions.[18]

During 1777, the British tried to sever New England from the other colonies and cut off the Continental Army in hopes of defeating it. British General John Burgoyne assembled a large force in Canada. Burgoyne was supposed to advance down the Hudson River and link up with the British troops sent up from New York City, but the plan collapsed when his army was routed at the Battle of Saratoga in October and forced to surrender. The defeat at Saratoga refreshed American morale, but the financial situation was rapidly collapsing, due in large part to the counterfeiting of the Continentals.

Up to that point, none of the states had made voluntary payments in their own currency to Congress to finance the war. The weakening Continentals had to compete with a wide assortment of other currencies for resources. States were still issuing their own individual currencies to help pay for their expenditures. Meanwhile, the massive British forging operations continued. Inflation was probably also enhanced by disruption of markets, the destruction of property and casualties among able-bodied troops and citizens. By the end of 1777, the Congress found that the Continental, at a fraction of its original value and still dropping, was supposed to provide 90 per cent of its revenue.

As things seemed to go from bad to worse for the rebellious colonies, Ben Franklin began to fold up his multiple peacetime pursuits and concentrate on winning a war he hadn't foreseen, but whose favourable course he was to influence mightily.

Franklin – and France – to the Rescue

After Philadelphia's subdued New Year's celebrations in January 1776, Franklin resigned from the Pennsylvania Assembly and the Committeee of Public Safety. He began to concentrate more and more on matters of defence. After long deliberations, on 29 November 1775 the Assembly had set up a Committee of Secret Correspondence to keep in touch with friends and sympathizers in Britain, Ireland and abroad. This was the first step towards answering the overt and covert warfare of George III and Lord North through the creation of an American diplomatic service. Its five members were Benjamin Harrison, Thomas Johnson, John Dickinson, John Jay and Benjamin Franklin. Ben Franklin was the only one who had already spent time on personal, scientific and quasi-diplomatic missions overseas. He soon became the leader.

Badly beaten in the Seven Years' War, France had lost many of its colonial possessions in the Treaty of 1763. Popular sentiment in the colonies was to let France keep Canada and take instead the sugar-rich islands of Martinique and Guadeloupe in the Caribbean. Arguments that Canada's wealth in furs, wood pulp, logs for construction and and minerals would be tremendous future assets won out. Britain let France keep the Caribbean islands and two tiny fishing isles off the Canadian coast: Saint-Pierre and Miquelon are still legally part of France today.

Franklin's and Revolutionary America's greatest European accomplice in rescuing the nascent new nation's fortunes was a young French diplomat, Charles Gravier, the Comte de Vergennes. He had proven his diplomatic prowess at the Ottoman Porte in Constantinople, where he defended French interests in the conflict between Turkey and Russia. When Louis XVI appointed him Foreign Minister, Vergennes turned his attention to vengeance against Britain. In 1775 he sent Achard de Bonvouloir to Philadelphia as a secret agent. Franklin already knew Bonvouloir through a Philadelphia bookseller where he had bought French works on science, especially electricity. Franklin had also sent his own articles to France.

The Bourbon monarchy in Paris was too weak in 1775 to

confront Britain openly. This would happen only in 1778, when it openly entered war with the British in Europe. Through the intermediary of the Philadelphia bookseller, Franklin met secretly with Bonvouloir, first alone, then with his four colleagues of the Committee. The Americans convinced Bonvouloir that they would openly declare independence by the end of 1776, which Bonvouloir in turn reported to Vergennes. Franklin then took up secret correspondence with Don Gabriel de Bourbon, the Prince of Spain, whom he regarded as another potential ally, and with French literary friends he had made on previous trips to Europe.

From Philadelphia, a French agent called Penet travelled to Paris to fish for contracts for munitions. Since the colonial currencies were unreliable and the Americans had no gold, they would be paid for by exports. Armed with Franklin's instructions and with letters to Franklin's Parisian friends, Silas Deane of Connecticut travelled to France in March 1776 disguised as a merchant looking for goods to trade with the American Indians. His mission was to meet Vergennes and repeat the assurances about independence Franklin had given to Bonvouloir, and to communicate with his American colleagues secretly.

At the same time, Franklin was dispatched to Canada on a hazardous mission that nearly cost him his life. Together with Congressmen Samuel Chase and John Carroll, both Catholics educated in France, he was supposed to win support for the American cause from unsympathetic French Catholics. Snow, ice and wintry winds delayed them on their journey up the Hudson River, Lake George and Lake Champlain. Franklin, now aged seventy, suffered through it all and finally reached General Benedict Arnold, who was unsuccessfully besieging Quebec. Arnold assured him that winning over the French Catholics was impossible. Arnold was broke and his troops were threatening mutiny: Franklin had to advance them over three hundred sterling in gold out of his own personal funds. An exhausted Franklin returned to Philadelphia just in time to help draw up the Declaration of Independence.

Franklin then began drafting proposals for friendship treaties with France and Spain, and even for a future treaty of peace with England. He parleyed with Lord Richard Howe, whom George III sent as a peace emissary, and rebuffed Howe's suggestions for an amicable settlement that did not include American independence. There followed a series of American reverses: Washington's loss of Manhattan, the battle at White Plains, the British capture and hanging of American spy Nathan Hale, and a disastrous fire destroying one-third of Manhattan.

In the dark months of 1776 unpaid soldiers were deserting almost as fast as they could be recruited. Then a light appeared for Franklin when he received a letter dated 10 June from his French friend, Dr Barbeu Dubourg. It reported on a meeting with Penet, the French agent Franklin had sent to seek aid. Dubourg thought Penet was most likely a British spy: Penet claimed to have left all his credentials and ID papers in Rotterdam for fear of border searches by customs officials. Despite his doubts Dubourg introduced Penet to French financial officials in Versailles. Using the cover 'M. de la Tuillerie' – the American cause was still not publicly respectable in France – Dubourg negotiated the 'loan' of 15,000 French 1763-model rifles, promising new ones to come. Driven by his sympathy for the Americans and his friendship with Franklin, Dubourg risked various other transactions, including contracts for a year's supply of the best Virginia tobacco. He also took Penet to see Foreign Minister Vergennes, who questioned him closely about the American situation. Later, Vergennes met secretly with Silas Deane. He assured Deane that everything possible would be done to help the Americans, but that it couldn't be done overtly before independence was an emerging reality or while France was not openly at war with Great Britain. Deane received help with his French contacts from Dr Edward Bancroft, whom Franklin also knew. Neither Deane nor Franklin realized until later that Bancroft was a British double agent who was doing his best to betray all of their projects to the Crown in London.

In a secret session on 26 September 1776 Congress formalized its quest for the aid of Louis XVI by appointing three commissioners to the court of France: Silas Deane, Thomas Jefferson and Benjamin Franklin. When Franklin arrived in Paris in late December, his fame as a scientist and his literary reputation had preceded him, partly because of his brief visits there in 1767 and 1769.[19] He found warm and occasionally intimate welcomes from Paris society, especially from well-read and fashionable French ladies. As recreation he concentrated on printing what American novelist John Updike calls 'flirtatious bagatelles for them, sometimes in French and sometimes in English, on a private press he had imported'.[20] During business hours, as it were, he concentrated on coaxing French loans of hard currency to shore up the already seriously weakened Continental dollars.

Franklin moved to the outlying Paris district of Passy, into a luxurious estate generously provided by Jacques-Donatien Leray de Chaumont, a contractor for the French government. Chaumont was appointed by Vergennes to handle secret aid to the Americans and to sell through a front company the prize cargoes captured from English ships by American privateers. After a delay of weeks, communications from the colonies brought plenty of bad war news. British troops had pursued Washington's ragtag troops through New Jersey and approached Philadelphia before Washington's surprise victory at Trenton. Congress had left for Baltimore. Unaware of the French loan Vergennes had approved and eschewing the British-forged Continentals, Congress floated an American loan of two million sterling, offering 6 per cent interest. To pay for the raising of nearly a hundred infantry and cavalry battalions, thirteen frigates, and three dozen guns, Congress not only pressed the trio of commissioners in France to get the required funds. To Franklin's chagrin, it also appointed new commissioners to other European courts where American envoys were already soliciting aid, including Spain.

On 15 November 1777 Congress adopted the Articles of Confederation and Perpetual Union, providing for a confederacy called the United States of America, and sent them to the states for ratification. The Americans' victory in the north over British General John Burgoyne's forces at Saratoga in New York State was offset in the middle states when Washington's forces had to surrender Philadelphia to General Howe in September. However, in France, the efforts of Franklin and his fellow American agents began to bear real fruit. After two years of covert financial and arms aid, Burgoyne's defeat and the surrender of his army to the Americans, along with Franklin's diplomacy and deals, led Vergennes to convince the reluctant twenty-two-year-old Louis XVI to sign France's Treaties of Commerce and Alliance with the United States on 6 February 1778. The Marquis Joseph de Lafayette and Baron Johann de Kalb had already arrived in America the previous summer to offer aid in men and materiel. The large covert aid operation run using a front company by the French playwright, tycoon and man-about-town Pierre de Beaumarchais could now go public.

From this point on, French aid and military and naval power began to bolster the American cause. Comte Jean-Baptiste d'Estaing commanded a French fleet sent to the Delaware Capes in July 1778, and Comte Jean-Baptiste de Rochambeau would land 6,000 French troops at Newport, Rhode Island in July 1780. Spain entered the war against Britain in June 1779, after French promises encouraged by Franklin and his fellow commissioners in Paris that the French would help Spain to recover Gibraltar (lost in 1719 to the British) and the Florida territories.[21]

Amid the ebb and flow of American and British military victories, and despite the injections of hard cash from France, the combination of British counterfeiting operations, hyperinflation due to overprinting of Continentals by an anxious Congress and the stifling of commerce by British blockades and other factors, the Americans' financial position was desperate in 1779. On 3 September Congress decided to stop its issues of currency. It set a ceiling of $200 million, beyond which all emissions would cease. By that date $160 million had already been legally issued, and perhaps twice that amount in counterfeits were circulating. The remaining limit of $40 million in legal money would last only a few weeks more. The states would have to assume the burden by again issuing their own paper money. A concerned Franklin wrote to Congressman Samuel Cooper an ironic letter about the virtues of paper currency – when it was trusted, which the Continentals were not. French and other European bankers and traders demanded American goods, hard to send through the British blockades. They would take only gold, practically non-existent in America, as payment.

Franklin had to admonish Ralph Izard, one of the American agents in Europe who had ample private means, that the Revolution's treasury could not go on subsidizing his expenses indefinitely. Franklin asked Izard to pay back previous subsidies in order to finance an exchange of hundreds of American and British prisoners he had been patiently working on for over a year and which had finally come to pass. Izard complained bitterly to Congress and vainly demanded Franklin's recall from Paris.

Congress passed the $200 million limit it had set itself. It asked the states to provide themselves the goods, food and services the armed forces required. This reduced the inflation caused by government purchasing agents who had offered high prices. The states got the power to make direct requisitions of needed commodities instead of making currency levies. The volume of now nearly worthless Continentals decreased. So did some of the fraud, waste and corruption that has plagued American military procurements from that time until the twenty-first century. In 1780 Congress further increased the states' power by asking them to meet the payrolls of soldiers recruited in their territories. This helped reduce the federal debt, but weakened federal government authority while strengthening advocates of states' rights (which would be a central issue until the Civil War of 1861–5).

On 18 March 1780 Congress enacted what amounted to a devaluation of the Continental currency still in circulation. Henceforth a newly issued dollar could be exchanged for no fewer than forty Continentals. This threatened all of the careful work Franklin had undertaken in Europe to establish American credit. The states would tax the new dollars virtually out of existence at the rate of $15 million a month. As the states delivered the old paper dollars, Congress would issue the new devalued dollars. These would be jointly guaranteed by state and federal governments. They would draw 5 per cent interest, payable in paper bills of exchange. This virtually repudiated all of the American paper money in existence. Anyone who had accumulated paper dollars or held promissory notes and loans faced a forty-to-one loss of their investment. This caused the Europeans to lose faith in all American currency and to demand payments in the form of goods only.

In Philadelphia, again the American capital, the French Minister the Chevalier de la Luzerne reported to Vergennes in April 1780 on corruption, mismanagement and conspiracies that were undermining the American war effort. Although George Washington and his French allies were slowly making gains against the British, there were acute new supply crises for their forces. Farmers and merchants didn't like to make sales for paper money.

Meanwhile, under heavy British pressure in the Carolinas and Georgia, American General Ben Lincoln was running critically short of supplies. After his failure to recapture occupied Savannah from the British, Lincoln had fallen back to Charleston, South Carolina. He had to hold it or risk losing the entire south to British invasion and occupation. Lincoln commanded about 1,200 regular troops and 2,000 militiamen, whereas British Commander-in-Chief Sir Henry Clinton, with Cornwallis second in command, was gathering a force of 8,500, of whom nearly 3,000 were Americans loyal to the British Crown. Clinton's fourteen warships were confronted by only three frigates and one sloop of war, the *Ranger*. After a month-long siege, the British captured Charleston on 12 May 1780 and found Americans ready to set up a Loyalist government there. By 21 June much of South Carolina and Georgia had been reconquered by a coalition of British troops under Cornwallis and Loyalist Americans.

Darkness Before Dawn

At this low point in the Americans' fortunes, John Adams nearly sabotaged Franklin's careful work in Europe by undiplomatic behaviour towards Vergennes and the court of Louis XVI. Despite a series of contretemps involving secret negotiations Spain was involved in with both the British and Americans, Vergennes notified Lafayette that in keeping with an old promise to Franklin and him Louis XVI was sending a naval and expeditionary force of 15,000 men under General Comte Jean-Baptiste de Rochambeau. The French squadron landed in Rhode Island on 9 July.

Rochambeau and Lafayette quarrelled, and the sad state of the Americans' finances dismayed their French allies. In August

Rochambeau reported that the paper Continental dollars had fallen to a new low ratio of sixty-to-one and that George Washington was unable to recruit a new soldier unless he paid him 100 'hard dollars'. One French staff officer wrote home:

> Instead of helping the Americans, we are a drawback to them . . . [O]ur victualizing makes provisions scarce for them . . . [B]y paying cash for our provisions we depreciate their paper money and consequently the purveyors refuse to sell provisions for their paper money.[22]

The American army now numbered only 3,000 men, and many Americans complained that the French should have sent 20,000 men and twenty warships to drive the British from their strongholds in New York instead of setting up camp in Rhode Island. Washington reported to Congress that any joint Franco-American offensive against the British in New York was impossible without more French help, especially arms and gunpowder.

As Cornwallis moved his forces into rebel territory in North Carolina, France was acutely feeling the expense of the war. Vergennes believed the Americans weren't doing enough on their own and were growing too dependent on France. Like other colleagues and predecessors, his powerful rival Jacques Necker, director-general of finances, had been opposed to helping the Americans from the start. The alliance seemed to be on the rocks by late 1780. Czarina Catherine the Great of Russia was urging the British to make peace with each American state separately and so to divide the Revolution. Prime Minister Lord North said Britain was willing to accept mediation and settle with France, but only if France would abandon its alliance with the United States.

The winter of 1780–1 saw George Washington's army and the civilian population of the rebellious states at the lowest ebb in their fortunes since 1776. Continental money was worthless, and despite obstruction at home in Philadelphia and from European adversaries and American rivals in Europe, Benjamin Franklin was hard put to it to wheedle Vergennes and Louis XVI into granting new injections of French hard currency. In January 1780 John Laurens, a new congressional envoy to France, brought an urgent written plea to Louis XVI for 25 million livres, in addition to the 25 million Franklin had obtained earlier. George Washingon advised Franklin by letter that foreign help was urgently needed, including cash, food and clothes for mutinous soldiers, along with much more French military support.

From America, Lafayette advised Vergennes of the great need of the Americans. Vergennes had to inform Franklin that the French Treasury couldn't bear another 25 million livre loan but that the King had generously offered a downright gift of 6 million livres, in addition to 3 million Vergennes had provided to Franklin. The funds were sent to a special account in the name of George Washington, and only Washington himself could sign for it. (Vergennes and Franklin both feared that Congress or others might divert funds away from the essential subsistence needs of the army.)

Laurens had arrived in Paris and, working almost separately from Franklin, raised 2.5 million livres in cash and another 2.2 million that, on returning to America, he left in France to pay for military stores. A dejected Franklin, ill with gout and other complaints and now in his seventy-fifth year, proffered his resignation in writing to Congress in Philadelphia. He was greatly buoyed by Congress's refusal to accept it and encouragements to continue his mission.

On 16 August 1780 American General Horatio Gates' forces lost the Battle of Camden, New Jersey, to General Cornwallis. Other defeats followed in the Carolinas. On 23 September a plot of General Benedict Arnold to surrender the American fortress at West Point, New York, to Sir Henry Clinton was discovered through the capture of British agent Major John André. Arnold escaped to lead new Loyalist and British attacks, but André was hanged as a spy on 2 October.

In January 1781, George Washington got some better news: General Daniel Morgan had defeated crack British cavalry units under Sir Banastre Tarleton. By the end of September, the British, harassed by American guerrilla militias, had pulled back from Carolina mountains and woodlands into Charleston. During this time, Washington used deception tactics to convince the British in New York that he had planned with his French allies a joint attack on New York, thus immobilizing a sizeable British force there. Meanwhile, Cornwallis was concentrating forces in Virginia, where they fortified themselves at Yorktown.

At this critical time, Louis XVI sent Comte François de Grasse with a major French fleet, twenty line-of-battle ships, to the Chesapeake Bay. Washington, Lafayette and Rochambeau closed in around Cornwallis at Williamsburg, Virginia. From 30 September until 19 October the allied Franco-American land and sea forces levied a relentless siege against Cornwallis, bottled up in Yorktown, and cut it off from supplies or reinforcements by land or sea.

On 19 October 1781 Cornwallis had no choice but to surrender with 7,000 men. The popular legend has it that his headquarters military band played 'The World Turned Upside Down' at the surrender ceremony. This did not end all hostilities, but it did convince George III and his ministers that a peace settlement with the Americans was imperative – and that it should avoid American independence, if at all possible. Britain should retain control of Canada, and French interests in the New World should not benefit by such a settlement.

Under fire in France for what many contemporaries saw as the prodigal generosity of his financial and military rescue of the Americans, Vergennes was also in a difficult position. He had to please both allies, Spain and the United States. This caused delays and the great impatience of Franklin, John Jay, Jefferson and the other American negotiators. Disregarding instructions from Congress in Philadelphia not to conclude a separate peace with George III that excluded France, they proceeded to do just that. Seeking American trade and friendship while hoping to frustrate French aspirations, the British agreed to such a peace.

The definitive Treaty of Peace between Britain and the United States, signed on 3 September 1783, did finally recognize American independence. Problems over the north-eastern and north-western boundaries of the new American nation would later lead to problems with Britain and helped bring on the War of 1812. The southern boundary provision led to trouble with Spain. The huge financial crisis arising from the valueless paper currency, defaulted debts and the general devastation wreaked by the war resulted in provisions that creditors of neither country should have legal difficulties collecting debts. The Congress would recommend restoration of the confiscated assets of the Loyalists. Neither provision was ever totally implemented. The Mississippi River, America's western boundary, was to be open to navigation by both British and US ships.[23]

During the drawn-out peace negotiations, Franklin managed to extract from the French Treasury another 600,000 livres and a promise to raise this eventually to 6 million once the funds were available – which they weren't. The monarchy in Paris and the Parisians celebrated the signature of the Treaty of Peace with a holiday, royal prayers for peace, free wine and sausages to the populace, and toasts to Benjamin Franklin, who would shortly return to his scientific and scholarly pursuits in Philadelphia. He died in 1790, a deeply fulfilled and universally respected founding father.

Despite draining their Treasury to rescue America and the rapid and infectious spread of ideas about democracy and freedom among their people, King Louis XVI and Queen Marie Antoinette did not realize that 'they were approaching the end of their regime'.[24] The American Revolution would shortly lead into the French Revolution, ushering in a new era of upheaval: economic dislocation again aggravated by currency counterfeiting by France's foreign enemies, a technique soon to be copied by other European regimes. This would be followed by the imperial conquests and the ultimate downfall of Napoleon Bonaparte.

Six

Soft versus Hard Money: Revolution and Consequences

> Of all the contrivances for cheating the labouring classes of mankind, none has been more effective than that which deludes them with paper money.
>
> *Daniel Webster,* c. *1850*

The wars with England in America, Europe and Asia (where they had fought over colonial conquests, especially in India) left Louis XVI's monarchy exhausted and nearly broke. The French Revolution (1789–99) was in part a consequence of this national exhaustion. The Revolution in turn brought more financial, commercial and social ruin to the French; its consequences in Napoleon's wars of conquest were serious for all of Europe. During all of these events, currency counterfeiting by hostile states was a factor.

Six years before the storming of the Bastille, France's finances were in deep trouble. An attempt by the King's Comité des finances at reform in 1783 failed. It began to dawn on the French people that Louis XVI and his ministers, even his highly capable finance minister who came from the ranks of Switzerland's redoubtable bankers, were unable to solve these problems alone. The benefits that hard-headed diplomats like Vergennes and visionaries like Lafayette alike had hoped to draw for France from their tremendously costly efforts in the American Revolution seemed to be fading fast. Peace in America allowed British competitors to make an energetic comeback and caused a severe drop in French–American commerce. The boom in British trade ensured the injection of capital into the British economy. Americans had already begun to compete in long-established French markets, such as the Turkish domains in North Africa, and they were moving into France's captive colonial markets in the Caribbean.

In 1789, when Paris mobs launched the armed revolution on 14 July, France was a fairly prosperous society with a bankrupt government. A rising middle class found that they could get good jobs in the royal bureaucracy. Government machinery was large and unwieldy, hardly suited to the requirements of a major trading and agricultural state. French commentators bitterly criticized its flaws. There were no truly representative assemblies, though local *parlements*, notably the *parlement* of Paris, often tried to assume the role of a real assembly. While landed peasants often supported the monarchy, they offered only passive opposition in the Revolution's early stages, and many joined it.

Like America, which it had just helped win its freedom, France's biggest and most urgent problem was a huge and ever-growing deficit. On 5 May 1789 at Versailles a meeting was called of the Estates-General, comprising well over a thousand delegates from the middle classes (called the 'third estate') and about 300 each of clergy, nobles and commoners. Squabbling over how the Estates-General could be converted into an effective legislative body, a constituent assembly, blocked any constructive action. The King grew impatient and concentrated royal troops near Paris.

Just three days before the storming of the Bastille, Louis XVI took the momentous step of firing his brilliant finance minister, Jacques Necker. Having seen the suffering caused by John Law's venture into hyperinflation and the accompanying counterfeiting of paper money, Necker was an eighteenth-century version of that familiar human symbol of rectitude, caution and secrecy, the Swiss banker.

Born in Geneva, Necker began his career as a bank clerk in Switzerland, moving to Paris in 1762 where he founded a bank and quickly got rich in speculative deals. In 1776–7 he was director of the Treasury and director-general of finances, and he attempted some needed reforms. Perhaps against his better judgement, he got involved in heavy borrowing to finance the American War of Independence by providing the loans and gifts that Ben

Franklin was busy gathering. For a time Necker managed to conceal the growing state deficit, but he was dismissed in 1781 after this was discovered. In 1788 he was recalled to be finance minister to cope with the growing bankruptcy situation of the monarchy. During the turbulent sessions of the Estates-General and constituent assembly he departed from his banking speciality and proposed some social and constitutional changes that sounded most unpleasant to Louis XVI and his advisers. Necker was popular, and his firing was one of the factors provoking the disorder that surrounded the storming of the Bastille.[1]

What followed in the economic sphere has been called the biggest attempt ever made in the history of the world by a government to create an inconvertible paper currency and to maintain its circulation at various levels of value. It was also one of the largest efforts made by a regime since the reign of Roman Emperor Diocletian to enact and enforce legal price ceilings on commodities. In late 1789, the revolutionary National Assembly touched off the operation by declaring Church estates public property. The revolutionaries then began ordering the printing of paper notes called 'assignats'. They were not secured by gold or silver and were not redeemable in either. They were supposed to be backed by confiscated ecclesiastical properties.

According to a key study written in 1912 by Cornell University economist Andrew D. White:

> The first notes were based on one-third of the entire landed property in France; choice property in city and country – the confiscated estates of the Church and of the fugitive aristocracy [who began leaving the country after the storming of the Bastille], and on the power to use the paper thus issued in purchasing this real property at very low prices.[2]

Initially the National Assembly planned to issue large-denomination notes in the value of 1,000, 300 and 200 livres. These were too large to be used by ordinary folk as currency but were of convenient size for purchasing the Church lands. They bore interest and so would tempt holders to hoard them. The Assembly reasoned that the total value of the confiscated lands (at least 2 billion livres) would constitute a solid backing, guaranteeing France a prosperous future. In debates it was argued that issuing 400 million livres in paper money (not as interest-bearing bonds, as first proposed, but in both large- and small-denomination notes) would stimulate commerce, enable the state to pay its debts and provide means for capitalists to buy up the confiscated estates. Necker, Honoré Mirabeau and Jean-Sylvain Bailly, the astronomer who was mayor of Paris and president of the National Assembly in 1789 but who would be guillotined during the Reign of Terror in 1791, were among those who expressed doubts during the Assembly's debates.

The Slippery Slope of War, Hyperinflation and Forgery

The second issue voted, with the King's endorsement, by the Assembly in September 1790 was to print 800 million livres in paper assignats. The law had a rider limiting the entire amount to be put into circulation in the future to 1.2 billion livres. As fast as the assignats were paid into the Treasury for land they were supposed to be burned in order to keep inflation down. Unlike the first issue they were not to bear interest. Just as was happening in the newly independent American states, there was loud public clamour for small-denomination bills. Paper was driving small silver and copper coins to disappear. Sixty-three different privately printed notes of hand, called 'confidence bills', circulated in Paris alone. Provinces and regions began to issue their own assignats.

From this time on, the revolutionaries' pledges to retire and not reissue old notes, and to keep to the 1.2 billion limit were gradually thrown to the wind. Rumours spread that the Bourbon ruling family and their allies, including British agents, were working to make hard money disappear and the rapidly depreciating assignats increase. The purchasing power of the livre, or franc, measured by the value of staple foods and other commodities, was a fraction of today's US dollar or euro.

Pressure on the Revolution's finances was soon ratcheted up by the outbreak of war with Prussian and Austrian rulers (1792–7). French reverses raised the level of revolutionary fervour, leading to the storming of the Tuileries Palace and the passage of power from the National Assembly to the Paris Commune and the Jacobin Club. It also resulted in the official abolition of the monarchy by a new National Convention that seized power in September 1792 and lasted until October 1795, which was dominated by radicals like Maximilian François de Robespierre (born in 1758, guillotined in 1794) and Georges Jacques Danton (1759–94; he met the same fate as Robespierre). After the trial and execution of Louis XVI on 21 January 1793, war was declared against Britain, Holland and Spain. The royalist émigrés, under the Prince of Condé, proclaimed the imprisoned young son of the dead king as Louis XVII. A royalist revolt began in the Vendée, with British and allied backing: at about this time the émigrés, with covert support from their host governments and especially the British Crown, began to print counterfeit assignats to undermine the already inflating finances of the Revolution.

By early 1793, the face value of the paper was about 3 billion francs. Previous issues were public, but under the new National Convention the radical Committees of Public Safety and Finance began to decree regular new issues in secret session. Growing poverty and agitation by the radical leaders led to a wave of riots in Paris on 28 February 1793: mobs looted hundreds of stores and shops of bread, cloth and luxuries, until a special issue of 7 million francs was handed out to buy off the mob.

Forced loans weighed heavily on the surviving middle class, and severe punishments like death and the burning of property were imposed on anyone hoarding farm produce or metallic currency. The Convention decreed that anyone selling gold or silver coins, or making any difference between the value of paper and specie, should be imprisoned in iron shackles for six years. Even tougher sentences were imposed on anyone refusing to accept assignats in payment. In May 1794, the Convention adopted the death penalty for anyone who questioned before a transaction what kind of money would be paid.

By the end of July 1795, circulation increased to 1.4 billion francs. The value of 100 paper francs dropped, first from 4 francs in gold, then to 3 and finally to 2.5. By February 1796, a gold louis d'or coin, originally worth 25 paper francs, rose to 7,200 francs. During the Reign of Terror in 1793–4, the dictatorship of Robespierre tried to stem the relentless rise of commodity prices by imposing ceilings on both prices and wages. Much of the scheme remained as texts in paper decrees, and the maximums were often violated. But the scheme did temporarily prevent the total collapse in value of the assignats and permitted provisioning of the armies, fighting wars on several fronts against Britain, Austria, Prussia and their allies. It was less a measure of socialistic control than a way to ration vital commodities during an emergency.[3]

During the mid-1790s, the allies fighting France joined forces with the royalist émigrés in a mighty effort to destroy the Revolution by counterfeiting its paper money. Enormous amounts of assignats, rising to 4 billion francs face value, had by this time been issued by the Revolution's despots. Criminals in various parts of France, royalist émigrés in the enemy countries and all manner of speculators began to print equal or even greater sums of counterfeit paper francs. The main source was London. Sterling notes, especially the 1 and 2 sterling bills, were easily copied by a competent copper-plate engraver, and counterfeiting became so prevalent that between 1797 and 1815 some 313 people were hanged in Britain for forgery-related offences. Some of the same engravers were apparently enlisted by émigré Comte Joseph de Puisaye to produce huge quantities of false assignats. De Puisaye dispatched cargoes of the carefully engraved and printed paper counterfeits through ports in Brittany and other centres of counter-revolution in France. General Louis Lazare Hoche, a loyal soldier of the Revolution, reported seizing one cargo with a nominal value of 10 billion francs.

The insurgent Royalists in the Vendée and other centres used local engravers and printers to produce notes bearing the emblems of the Bourbons: the fleur-de-lis, a portrait of the imprisoned dauphin as Louis XVII and the legend '*De Par le Roi*'. People in the insurgent areas were forced to accept and use these notes, which continued to appear as late as 1799, long after the Revolution had triumphed in every part of France that counted.[4]

A whole series of revolutionary decrees and what Andrew White calls 'financial juggles' were promulgated in desperate efforts to arrest the precipitous fall in value of the hyperinflated and counterfeited paper money.[5] All assignats above the value of 100 francs were supposed to stop circulating after June 1796. This was never honoured. Another decree edicted that 1 paper franc should be worth ten pounds of wheat. On 16 July 1796, they declared that all paper, whether assignats or Treasury bills called '*mandats*', should be taken at face value and that purchases and deals could be made in whatever currency people chose, including gold, silver or copper. The effect of this was to drive the real value of the *mandats* down to 2 per cent of their nominal value.

The climax came in February 1797, when the post-Terror Directory government that had been formed under the new republican constitution of 1795 threw in the towel and ordered destruction of all the engraving apparatus for the paper money. Neither assignats nor *mandats* could any longer be considered legal tender. Old debts to the state could be paid for a limited time with government paper at the rate of 1 per cent of their face value. In the spring of 1797, the Directory decreed that 21 billion francs still circulating in assignats should be annulled. On 30 September 1797 it edicted that national debts could be paid up to two-thirds in bonds. These could still be used to buy confiscated real estate. The remaining 'Consolidated Third' would be entered in the 'Great Book' of the national debt. This would be paid in the future as the government thought best.

Creditors of the state were forced to accept the bonds. These, like the assignats and *mandats* before them, sank rapidly in value, reaching 3 per cent. While the rising General Napoleon Bonaparte (1769–1821) was conducting his victorious military campaigns against the enemies of France in Italy and elsewhere, the debts of the Consolidated Third were mainly paid in new paper francs printed to replace the old. Under the new inflationary pressures, the newer paper money sank gradually to about 6 per cent of its face value.

Paper money in France, for two generations to come, was a dead issue. Assignats and *mandats* alike, to a combined face value of something like 70 billion francs, were consigned to the garbage dumps. Both France's impoverished masses and a tiny minority of the rich, including exceptionally astute merchants, profiteers and successful racketeers, experienced financial ruin. Some of the better-off people such as Jean Lambert Tallien (1767–1820), president of the Convention in 1794, were clever enough to become millionaires. Their dupes, who had cried out for more and more issues of paper money, had become paupers. Tallien survived the last throes of the Revolution. He was denounced by Robespierre, whom he conspired to bring down. He joined the ruling Council of Five Hundred under the Directory and went on to accompany Napoleon on his temporary conquest of Egypt in 1798.

At the end of the Revolution, republican society and its socialites like Madame Tallien underwent a transformation from previous simplicity to conspicuous consumption worthy of the fallen aristocrats. They were wildly extravagant, constantly seeking new luxuries when the return of hard currency made this possible. Of their husbands and lovers, they demanded huge sums to clothe themselves in the latest fashions and to satisfy their every whim. All this time, working people, salaried employees and anyone with a pension or other fixed income, especially city-dwellers, suffered great distress. Many had to subsist on handouts of government bread rations, often unfit to eat and distributed to long lines of men, women and children who frequently had to wait their turn from dawn to dusk.

When forced loans and other discredited measures faded along with the discarding of paper money, gold and silver coins from all over Europe began to filter back into society. At first their sums were small, enough to do small-scale business that had survived the collapse. Then, as business demand increased, so did the amount of hard currency flowing in to meet it. Recovery was gradual, and some historians insist that full stability didn't return until long after the end of the Napoleonic wars in 1815.[6]

During the last years of revolutionary government, Napoleon's steady run of military triumphs against both Austria and Piedmont in Italy established his military prowess and his credibility, both with the political world and with his own soldiers. By 1798, of the anti-French coalition only Britain remained at war with France.

Appointed commander of the Army of England, Napoleon realized that the greatly weakened French navy couldn't control the sea and prudently renounced a land invasion of England. Instead, he recommended attacking British commercial and economic interests wherever possible. One of the devices he conceived of using was the counterfeiting of enemy currency, the effect of which he'd acutely experienced during the Revolution.

Napoleon was elevated to First Consul of the Republic for life in 1799. After a series of French victories and defeats on Europe's battlefields, the Treaty of Amiens in 1802 ended the Revolutionary Wars. He set about completely revamping French law in his Napoleonic Code, which still governs much of French justice and society today. As he began reorganizing fiscal affairs, the financial collapse due to the hyperinflation and counterfeiting during the Revolution presented Napoleon with an appalling situation. There was a huge unpaid national debt. Government departments were largely bankrupt. Collection of taxes on any meaningful scale seemed impossible, due to chaos in the system of assessments. Even the armies had been largely unpaid for months. The biggest loan that could be floated was scarcely enough to pay the government's expenses for a single day.

At his first cabinet session as First Consul, Napoleon was asked what he intended to do about the financial disaster. He responded that he would pay hard cash or nothing. He carefully crafted the tax assessments, funded the national debt, and made payments in gold and silver coinage, much of which was apparently minted from jewellery and other objects collected and melted down by the Treasury.

The instrument for rescuing France from its indebtedness and the miseries accompanying it was Napoleon's creation of a national bank on 18 January 1800, three months after his accession to power. The Banque de France was the sole institution authorized to issue banknotes. It was under strict orders to limit new Treasury money issued to that covered by the level of its gold reserves. The bank was created as a private bank, and its shares were offered for sale on the Paris Bourse. Among principal shareholders was the family of his wife, Josephine Beauharnais. This was a kind of assurance to the nation that Napoleon firmly believed in what he was doing. Like many other promises he made during his reign over France and much of Europe, Bonaparte kept his promise that all interest on outstanding debts would be paid by September 1808. Martin-Michele-Charles Gaudin, Napoleon's finance minister until 1814 and the bank's first governor after 1820, had accepted from Napoleon the finance post he had refused to accept from the men of the Revolution.

Throughout Bonaparte's successive military campaigns of Marengo, Austerlitz, Jena, Eylau and Friedland, until the Treaties of Tilsit in 1807 with Russia and Prussia, there was only one short period when Napoleon had to suspend payment in specie. When the first wide array of European allies formed up a grand coalition against what had become the French Empire, Napoleon was under extremely heavy financial pressure. Ministers proposed resorting to paper money. He wrote to his finance minister that he would never pay with worthless money. His governments managed to command enough gold to meet France's main obligations. Even after defeat at the Battle of Waterloo on 18 June 1815, Louis XVIII's accession to power (he was effectively enthroned by the victorious Allies), and heavy war expenses and indemnities and reparations to pay, there was no financial distress in France comparable to that caused by the era of the paper assignats and their counterfeiting.[7]

When it came to turning the currency weapon against enemies, Napoleon and several other leaders of early nineteenth-century Europe had quite a different attitude: counterfeiting became an important arm in their covert arsenals. Orthodox historians have either avoided the subject, probably for lack of much documentation, or treated it only vaguely. However, collectors of paper money and dealers who sell it have been able to authenticate many of the cases.

Napoleon and his extremely clever and conspiratorial minister of police, Joseph Fouché (1763–1820), a kind of national security adviser and director of imperial intelligence combined, were certainly aware of European precedents to the counterfeiting of enemy currencies undertaken by Fouché and others under Napoleon's orders. During the Seven Years' War (1756–63) among France, Britain and their various European allies, Austrian and Russian troops marched through Poland and Frederick the Great of Prussia flooded the country with counterfeit money.

When Napoleon's forces occupied Vienna in 1806, his secret printers in Paris and Italy forged Austrian currency, known to collectors as Banco Script notes. After Napoleon divorced his childless aristocratic wife Josephine de Beauharnais and married the Austrian emperor's nineteen-year-old daughter, Marie-Louise, who in 1811 would give him a son, François Charles Joseph Napoleon, Bonaparte apparently decided that the bogus Austrian notes had done their work and he banned them. However, under the old axiom that bad money drives out good, the forgeries continued to circulate for some time afterwards. The only distinguishing characteristic of the fakes was that the paper tint was different from the original Austrian notes. From 1805 until his disastrous retreat from Moscow in 1812, Napoleon's minions in Paris and Moscow forged Russian 25 and 50 imperial ruble notes. Despite a lack of firm evidence, some collectors think it was possible that they also produced bogus British notes during this period.

Lessons for the Future

In 1991, the Federal Reserve Bank's branch in Minneapolis, Minnesota, took careful note of the modern relevance of the French Revolution's financial consequences. It published remarks by Thomas Sargent, a senior fellow at the conservative Hoover Institution at Stanford University, California, summing up the monetary and fiscal shocks of the period as the results of a struggle 'to unwind past commitments and elaborate new ones'.[8] He concluded that those who formulated the paper money policy of the Revolution abhorred the idea of defaulting on the French government's huge debts, both out of principle and because of the interests they represented. Their drastic experiments managed to postpone defaulting on the debt until 1797. By then, their experiments had failed, and their paper money and securities had lost nearly all value.

While they ignored the lessons that France should have learned through the hyperinflation and counterfeiting in the John Law era earlier in the eighteenth century, the monetary and fiscal expedients of the French revolutionary era in fact constituted a kind of forecast used by economically stressed governments during the twentieth. The plight of governments ruined by the First World War, their inflationary remedies and the criminal counterfeiting that accompanied them come to mind: especially Weimar Germany from 1919 to the late 1920s, but also Austria, Hungary, Portugal and the young Soviet Union. In the case of Germany and Portugal, the aftermath of the war was a weighty factor in bringing about fascist rule, as we will discuss later in this book.

The French theorists and the revolutionary dictators who implemented them show parallels with twentieth-century developments and monetary theories emerging since the Second World War. The revolutionaries provided the illusion of backing for the assignats, *mandats* and bonds they printed in such huge quantities: the confiscated lands of the Church and the feudal gentry. There were long debates about whether this would forestall depreciation, and whether the paper money was best administered by the government directly or through a privately owned central bank.

The roles assigned to the assignats evolved from an instrument of short-term credit into an instrument to reimburse the national debt. Finally, they emerged as a classic fiat currency, redeemable only theoretically, in which the public rapidly lost faith. When France's enemies in Europe waged war on the Revolution, the revolutionary leaders did their best to promote the demand for the paper money by severely limiting people's access to other assets, especially hard currency, and later by introducing the assignats into the French army's newly conquered territories. Adolf Hitler tried to do the same thing in the Second World War with the meticulously forged pound sterling notes printed by the Jewish slaves in the Sachsenhausen concentration camp – until Hitler's wiser financial advisers halted distribution of the counterfeits because of the damage they could do to the economic structures of the short-lived Nazi Empire in occupied Europe.

Few political and social revolutions have escaped phases of what a twenty-first-century commentator might be tempted to call 'terrorism'. The French Revolution's Reign of Terror was an outstanding example. Its leaders were intoxicated by their own sudden power. While they experimented with the national money and further impoverished society, they butchered each other on the guillotine.

One of history's most famous and notorious dictators, Napoleon Bonaparte, imposed conservative fiscal and monetary policies and enforced them in a rigorous police state. In his wars, he didn't shy away from using money forgery against France's enemies. His final military defeat and exile by the Allies ended this and temporarily restored the Bourbon monarchy. But neither France nor the rest of Europe would ever be the same again.

How these transatlantic cataclysms and the difficult emergence of democracy and its follow-ups in America further changed the world's dealings with its money is our next subject.

Seven

Drivin' Old Dixie Down: The American Civil War and the Birth of the Greenback

> Moneyed obligations of the Confederate Government are forged by citizens of the United States . . . [Union] complicity in the crime is further evinced by the fact that soldiers of the invading armies are found supplied with large quantities of these forged notes as a means of despoiling the country people, by fraud, out of such portions of their property as armed violence may fail to reach.
>
> *Jefferson Davis, President of the Confederacy to the Confederate Congress, 18 August 1862*

At sun-up on 23 February 1861 President-elect Abraham Lincoln arrived in Washington. He had sneaked through Baltimore after dark the night before to avoid rebel street mobs out to murder him and had taken a train to Washington's Union Station. From the Baltimore & Ohio station near the Capitol building, he took a carriage directly to Willard's Hotel. Its proprietors, two Yankees from the state of Vermont, Joseph and Henry Willard, gave him the house's best suite.[1]

Willard's was destined soon to become a de facto Capitol in its own right: headquarters of the Union's great and grand, but also a luxurious lair and dealing place for all kinds of legitimate and shady businessmen, war profiteers, agents of both the Union and Confederacy. It served as a rendezvous for clever and attractive women who were to play important roles, not only as spies extracting political and military secrets between the bedsheets, but also as secret couriers for a flood of bogus money and securities.

Confederate notes and paper were smuggled across the Potomac River and into the rebellious Southern states. Union counterfeit money and securities, notably bonds, were freely traded in the North and, like the Confederate paper, exported and sold in Europe, mainly on the London market. In the rebel South, the counterfeit paper would allow marauding soldiers to pay spies, procure specie or valuables, and above all to contribute heavily to the final ruin of the South's agrarian, cotton-and-slave-tied economy and consequently its war effort.

The Prelude: Currencies Galore

The years between the American Revolution and the Civil War of 1861–5 had been a boom epoch for the forgers of money. In the newly independent American Republic, people's faith in paper money was close to absolute zero. A bewildering variety of paper dollars and cents circulated: 3,000 to 5,000 different sorts, depending on the source of the estimate. Issuing them were state banks, municipal 'banks', trading firms, shopkeepers and private individuals. Denominations for the paper scraps ranged from 3 cents up to $1,000; later in the nineteenth century they went up to $10,000. As with the old Continentals or the French assignats, this plethora of paper blurred the distinction between what was 'real' (i.e., issued by chartered state or local banks) and what was freely printed.

In 1861, just before the outbreak of the Civil War, 1,600 state banks printed their own money. Counterfeiters had an easy ride. Criminals bribed or bought from amenable authorities permission to open their own banks and print money. Money forgers hired printers to put imprints of a bank on their products. The US Constitution of 1787 didn't authorize the federal government to issue banknotes. It could issue only paper notes and bills, some interest-bearing and some not, but that could not be circulated.[2]

The colossal struggle between paper money, both true and false, and gold and other specie has been a critical factor in financing

American wars up to the twentieth century. Along with bringing improvements in printing technology, it was also a key to fighting the counterfeiters, foreign and domestic. The run-up to the Civil War and the war itself were no exception.

The National Mint Act of 1792 had established the US dollar as the basic unit of American currency and placed the United States on a two-metal standard. It authorized the government to purchase gold at a rate of $1 for 24.75 grams of gold. Silver was to be bought at $1 for 371.25 grams. The Act provided for minting of gold and silver coins containing the proper amounts of the two precious metals in the alloys used. Few citizens offered their gold jewellery or other objects to be used for coinage in the following generations. Instead, gold was hoarded in America, just as it had been in most societies through the ages. The reason for this was that the official ratio between their prices was fifteen parts of silver to one part of gold. So Gresham's Law that bad money drives out good money kicked in with a vengeance. One could make a handsome profit by using gold to buy silver on the open market, then selling the silver to the US Mint.

Even during the generations before President Franklin D. Roosevelt took the US off the gold standard in 1933, few Americans used gold coins – they hoarded them. Counterfeiters seemed to shun the forging of gold coins because the US currency was based on silver, whose value wasn't as stable. When the expansionist war against Mexico erupted in 1846, President James Polk's government tried hard to bolster the Treasury's reserves of currency needed to fund it by both making and demanding payments in coin or in paper money, backed by or redeemable in bullion. Nevertheless, the hundreds of state and wildcat 'private' banks continued recklessly to issue their own paper money. In 1862, a year into the Civil War, half of the notes were deemed counterfeit or otherwise worthless.[3]

Public demand for small-denomination notes continued right up until the Civil War. 'Shinplasters', pieces of paper in denominations of 3 to 50 cents printed by anyone who took the trouble, were used as currency along with postage stamps. Both were extensively counterfeited. One of many booklets intended to guide people on how to tell good money from bad was Bicknall's *Counterfeit Detector* of 1839. It listed twenty issues of notes of imaginary banks, forty-three banks whose notes were worthless, fifty-four bankrupt banks and 254 banks whose notes were forged. It describes 1,727 different forged notes. The counterfeit threat led state legislatures to appropriate funds to finance anti-counterfeiting organizations.[4] The paper plague kept increasing until the Civil War, when counterfeiting the enemy's currency as well as one's own became a lucrative business and a potent weapon.

Financing the War, Part One: The Union

In November 1860, Abraham Lincoln was elected the sixteenth president of the United States, drawing no electoral votes from slave-holding states because of his Republican Party platform opposing further extension of slavery in western territories. On 20 December 1860 South Carolina became the first Southern state to secede from the Union in a declared protest against Lincoln's election. Despite futile efforts to save the Union through negotiations, including a 'peace convention' in Washington on 4 February 1861, between January and May of that year Mississippi, Florida, Alabama, Georgia, Louisiana, Texas, Virginia, Arkansas, Tennessee and North Carolina left the Union.

On 4 February, the very date of the Washington peace talks, the seceding states met in Montgomery, Alabama, and formed the provisional government of the Confederate States of America. On 8 February, Jefferson Davis was elected president and Alexander H. Stephens vice president of the Confederacy. The Confederates seized federal lands and property throughout the South. On 10 April they demanded the evacuation of Fort Sumter in Charleston harbour. Major Robert Anderson and his garrison resisted bombardment by the South Carolina militia's artillery on 12 and 13 April, but were finally forced to capitulate just as a federal naval relief force approached.

On 15 April Lincoln called for 75,000 volunteers to serve for three months in what was expected to be a short war due to the

North's overwhelming advantages: twenty-three states with almost 23 million people against eleven states with a white population of only 5 million and an indeterminate number of slaves (with a very few free blacks) with virtually no civil rights. The North's economic strength lay in its banking system, manufacturing infrastructure, better railway communications and a widespread telegraph network. The South depended mainly on cotton-growing, and its exports were soon badly hampered by the Union naval blockade of the Southern ports, proclaimed 19 April 1861. Davis' rebel government was encouraged on 13 May when Great Britain recognized the Confederate States as belligerents, a move that profited many a trader, banker, currency counterfeiter and blockade-runner on both sides of the Atlantic during the five years to come.[5]

Lincoln ordered the Union into the war with only $200,000 in real money in the Treasury. He and his cabinet, including his canny Treasury secretary, Salmon P. Chase, believed at first in a brief war that would not unduly task normal federal revenues including taxes, tariffs or stamp sales. The First Battle of Bull Run in Virginia upset all of Lincoln's modest planning. On 21 July 1861 General Winfield Scott's troops were routed by Confederate forces under the overall command of General Pierre Beauregard. They fled to Washington in disarray. Lincoln and Chase now realized that they had not a short police action but a possibly long and costly war on their hands. There was urgent need to raise cash to pay the volunteer Union soldiers. Chase began by borrowing money from Northern banks and selling war bonds.

In the spring of 1862, after more Union reverses and some victories, with Lincoln's accord Chase reluctantly decided to print paper money. In April, he got through Congress the momentous law creating the 'greenback' dollar: paper dollars printed on their face in black and on their reverse in green ink. The first greenback issue was for $150 million. The notes were to be legal tender for all debts, public and private, except for customs tariffs on goods entering the country and interest owed the government on its own debt. In the fall came a second issue of $150 million, including millions of $1 bills. Government bondholders were to be paid in gold, the hoarding of which was accelerated by the flood of new paper money. The same original act of Congress also authorized a $500 million government bond issue. The government was to sell to 'the people', as Carl Sandburg relates in his classic four-volume book on the war and Lincoln's career, but actually to investors and banks, $500 million worth of its promises to pay. Lincoln told Chase he did not pretend to understand because he 'had no money sense'. Chase did understand. He had plenty of contacts in the business world to make the money-raising scheme work. He knew that it had to work, because without it '[m]oney cannot be supplied much longer to a demoralized and homesick army'.[6]

Throughout all of these operations, Chase was ideologically hindered by the philosophy he shared with other Northern policy-makers. He instinctively distrusted any form of payment other than specie. He preferred to pay debts by physically moving gold out of the Treasury instead of transferring money from demand deposits using cheques. Chase and his colleagues were also reluctant at first to use established private banks in New York, Boston and Philadelphia as repositories for federal funds. However, mounting debts, a shortage of specie and the menace of inflation led Lincoln and Chase to seek new ways of raising taxes and borrowing money. Chase turned to Jay Cooke, a business tycoon and major operator on the Philadelphia banking scene, to administer the sale of war bonds. Cooke launched a sophisticated marketing campaign of newspaper ads appealing to citizens' patriotism, and a field force of 2,500 legmen persuaded nearly a million Northerners (about 25 per cent of normal families) to buy bonds. Sales topped a whopping $3 billion, a truly gigantic sum in those days. This set a precedent for the successful war bond campaigns during America's twentieth-century wars. Purchasers of the Civil War bonds paid with the new greenback dollars, but were allowed to collect the interest in gold valued at pre-war levels.[7]

Opinion in the Northern states was strongly polarized between those who favoured the new paper greenbacks and those who didn't. Chase realized that there was a widespread lack of trust in their value. 'There are some persons,' he acknowledged to Lincoln and others, 'and some institutions which refuse to receive and pay them.'[8]

Lincoln feared that the issuance of the new dollar notes would heighten the already formidable threat of counterfeiting. He told Chase:

> [T]here seems to be no protection against a duplicate issue of every bill struck, and I can see no way of detecting duplicity until we come to redeem the currency, and even then the duplicate cannot be told from the original.

A joint committee of Congress was formed to consider safeguards to be incorporated into the engraving process.[9] But real improvements in security of the banknotes were slow in coming and spread over several decades that followed the Civil War.

The value of the greenbacks in silver or gold fell with Union victories and rose with Union defeats. In August 1863, after the Northern victories of Gettysburg and Vicksburg, the greenback was worth 82 cents in specie, but dropped to 35 cents in June 1864 after some Southern successes. Hoarding of specie reached the point that during one week in June and July 1862, in Boston and New York, all silver quarters, dimes and three-cent pieces disappeared. Most went to Canada, which in 1858 had adopted its own dollar and decimal system. Chase suggested use of postage stamps to fill the demand for small denomination currency. This was at first resisted by Postmaster-General Montgomery Blair, who had nightmares about his post offices being overrun by street vendors, crooks and speculators, all of whom abounded in the Northern cities. But by spring of 1863, the Treasury hadn't paid the Post Office for issue of more than $20 million in stamp currency, which soldiers stuffed into their boots and pockets to pay for drink, gambling and professional ladies.

In March of 1862, when greenbacks were still somewhat of a novelty, Lincoln told a delegation of wealthy New Yorkers who, fearing Confederate subversion or even a direct naval attack, were asking that federal funds finance a gunboat committed to the protection of their city:

> Gentlemen, I can't do it . . . The credit of the government is at a very low ebb. Greenbacks are not worth more than 40 or 50

> cents on the dollar, and in the condition of things, if I was worth half as much as you gentlemen are represented to be, I would build a gunboat and give it to the government.

At the end of 1862, three gold dollars would buy four greenback dollars.[10]

In May 1863, after more than a year of greenback circulation, the *Bureau County Patriot* in Lincoln's home state of Illinois and hundreds of other newspapers ran a cartoon under the heading of 'Abe Lincoln's Valentine'. It showed the president receiving a valentine in the shape of the American Eagle. The regal bird was busy picking up and swallowing gold coins. As Sandburg delicately puts it, 'at that portion of the bird most remote from head was a pile of "Greenbacks", into which the yellow coin seemed to have been mysteriously transmuted'. Lincoln showed it to Chase, who was not amused. He said he'd give a million-dollar reward to find the anonymous cartoonist. Abe replied that the idea 'sounds liberal', but that he could judge better if Chase would tell him which pile to use for payment. Chase's anger didn't abate. Abe dismissed him with

> Oh, never mind, never mind. After the war is over, we'll remedy it by turning the bird end for end, and get him to eating greenbacks. All will come out all right![11]

By the first months of 1862 it was clear to Lincoln's government and his top military men that something had to be done to end intelligence failures and fill the huge void of reliable military, political and economic information about the Confederacy. They also had to curb the growing counterfeiting of the greenbacks.

Scottish immigrant Allan Pinkerton had opened the first financially successful private detective agency in antebellum America. After his arrival in the US, Pinkerton worked in an Illinois town west of Chicago named Dundee at the trade handed down to him by his father in Scotland: making wooden hoops to wrap around barrels. On an expedition to gather wood for his barrel hoops, Pinkerton ran across the campsite and base of a gang of roving counterfeiters. After watching them for several days, Pinkerton led a sheriff's posse to catch the gang red-handed burying storage quantities of their bogus banknotes. The local town council then asked Pinkerton to set up a sting operation against a shady landowner named Crane, suspected of counterfeiting. He contacted Crane's agent, John Craig, offering to buy $4,000 of Crane's product. As he was handing over $125 in real money and getting a mass of bogus bills in return at a hotel bar, two plainclothesmen nabbed Craig. The Cook County sheriff then offered Pinkerton a permanent job as investigator. Pinkerton accepted, and he settled into his lifelong career as a detective. Eventually he would become the Union's first chief spy in the Civil War.

Spies and Counter-Spies

While on detective business in the Baltimore area shortly before Lincoln's inauguration on 4 March, Pinkerton got a tip about an assassination attempt against the new president. He warned Lincoln, who altered some travel plans. After the war's outbreak, Lincoln summoned Pinkerton to reward him for his loyalty, bravery and prescience by asking him to organize a secret service in Washington, DC, where Willard's Hotel and a few other sites were hotbeds of Confederate sentiment, subversion and espionage. When he presented Pinkerton to the Cabinet for approval, it turned out that the ageing General Winfield Scott, commander-in-chief of the army, preferred to appoint Lafayette C. Baker, an adventurous ex-lawyer from Ohio who had earned a reputation as a crimebuster by using rough tactics to smash waterfront gangs in San Francisco.

While awaiting Lincoln's final decision between the two men, Pinkerton found himself recruited for intelligence work by General George McClellan, commander of the Army of the Potomac charged with the defence of Washington. When Winfield Scott retired in 1861, Lincoln named McClellan commander-in-chief in Scott's place. Before he was later fired by Lincoln for his sluggish conduct of the war, McClellan used Pinkerton and several of his operatives from the detective agency as spies. They operated out of an office in I Street in Washington.

One female operative was the young and attractive Kate Warne. She collected a lot of information on military movements. At one point, she spotted the actor John Wilkes Booth, Lincoln's future assassin, as a dangerous Southern sympathizer. Another successful female spy for the Union was Elizabeth Baker. She managed to penetrate the Tredegar Iron Works in her home city of Richmond, Virginia, and brought back to Pinkerton and Navy Secretary Gideon Welles descriptions and sketches of the Confederate navy's experimental submarine, one of the first such designs ever. Pinkerton's man Timothy Webster specialized in snooping on the Southern secret society called the Knights of the Golden Circle, which spied for the South in Northern cities. Pinkerton also began to use his sixteen-year-old son, William, for spy missions around Washington. William was present at an early effort at aerial reconnaissance: the launching of a hot-air balloon used to watch Confederate movements south of the Potomac in Virginia.

But the greatest counter-espionage coup the Pinkertons accomplished against the South was the arrest of the glamorous Rose O'Neal Greenhow, widow of a pro-slavery editor. Through her own social graces and her sister's marriage to the nephew of Dolly Madison, widow of the late President James Madison, Greenhow met and threw parties for the great and famous at her fashionable home on 16th Street, near the White House. Among her dinner guests were Lincoln's predecessor, President James Buchanan, Secretary of State William H. Seward and Senator Henry Wilson. Using the cipher of the Confederate Army's Signal Corps, she relayed a number of important Union military secrets to Confederate espionage chief Thomas Jordan in Richmond. While walking with her daughter Mrs Greenhow was arrested on 23 August 1861 by Pinkerton's men and was placed in house arrest. In her home detectives found coded letters, diagrams, contact addresses in the South and a journal that recorded her dealings with other Confederate agents. In line with the chivalry of the times, and perhaps for convenience in interrogations, Greenhow and her daughter were never hanged. Remarkably, the War Department released her earlier than agreed upon, perhaps due to officials with an undue affection for Rose O'Neal. She was escorted back to Richmond where it was thought she couldn't do any more damage to the Union. They couldn't have been more wrong.

Timothy Webster had been supplying invaluable intelligence, serving the Knights of the Golden Circle in Baltimore with disinformation while reporting to Pinkerton on vital Southern subjects. At one point he was so esteemed in Richmond that Judah P. Benjamin, the Confederate secretary of war, hired Webster as an adviser to his intelligence network. When Pinkerton learned to his horror that Mrs Greenhow, who almost certainly had knowledge of Webster's operations, was free in the rebel capital, he dispatched a scout to Richmond. By the time the scout arrived, it was too late: Mrs Greenhow had spotted Webster and two of his associates. They had been arrested in their hotel, and after a vote of the Confederate Congress, they were hanged as spies.

This disaster to Northern intelligence ended Pinkerton's espionage career and helped to hasten the appointment of Lafayette Baker. As Lincoln's new spy chief, Baker became deeply embroiled in cracking counterfeiting operations in the North and arranging trips to the South by his couriers and spies, especially women. During frequent trips into Dixie, many of them helped to pump counterfeit Confederate currency into the Southern economy.

Pinkerton returned to detective duties in the North, especially tracking crooked suppliers who overcharged the Union for supplies. He also continued to use his expertise against the forgers of money and bonds. But he always regretted that he was not in charge of the president's security on 14 April 1865 – the day Lincoln signed the US Secret Service into its long mission to protect both US currency and presidents, and the evening on which John Wilkes Booth would murder Lincoln during a theatrical performance.[12]

Financing the War, Part Two: The Confederacy

The South began the war with a financial strategy quite different from the North's. A devil-may-care philosophy of personal gain fostered domestic counterfeiting in the Southern states, along with the bewildering proliferation of thousands of kinds of banknotes. This already plagued the antebellum South when South Carolina's artillery opened the war by bombarding Fort Sumter in Charleston harbour. First based in Mobile, Alabama, then moved to Richmond in May 1861, the hastily assembled Confederate government did not have the bureaucratic machinery needed to levy or collect domestic taxes. Citizens lacked the degree of compliance with tax laws prevalent in the North. Neither hard money nor paper money was abundant, and the majority of Southern capital was tied up in land and slaves in a mainly agrarian economy that was highly vulnerable to inflation.

A variety of methods of raising revenue to finance the war through taxation had proved unsatisfactory. The Confederate Congress in 1861 enacted a tariff that contributed only $3.5 million over the four-year war period. The Congress also legislated a small direct tax of 0.5 per cent on real estate and personal property, but the government in Richmond had to rely on individual states to collect it. As during the American Revolution, most of the states did not collect the tax at all. They tried to meet their quotas by borrowing money from their citizens – or printing more state banknotes.

President Jefferson Davis' Treasury secretary, Christopher Menninger, was an immigrant born in Nayhingen, Württemburg, Germany in 1803. He eventually used his training in the law in Charleston to get elected to the South Carolina state legislature and was one of the principal drafters of the constitution of the Confederate States. Although the rebels seized the federal mints at New Orleans, Louisiana; Chattanooga, Tennessee; and Charlotte, North Carolina, there was precious little gold bullion in their safes and vaults, so no coins were minted for general circulation. The very few coins minted are now in museums or sought by collectors, who pay very high prices for them.

The hoarding of coins, including old Spanish silver and other forms of eighteenth-century specie, and widespread failures of Southern banks began immediately after secession. The Confederate regime immediately began to contract with established banknote printers such as the Southern Banknote Company in New Orleans (the hastily renamed former subsidiary of the American Bank Note

Company in New York) and Hoyer & Ludwig in Richmond to issue paper money.

Desperately experimenting to ward off inflation, the government tried to fix official ceiling prices. This was a miserable flop, as it would prove to be in Weimar Germany. The 'fixed' price of a bushel of beans, a staple of the Southern diet, jumped from $1 a pound in May 1863 to $4 and eventually to $30 before the war's end. The familiar inflationary trap ensued: the more paper money the Confederate regime issued, the more prices rose. The more prices rose, the more pressure increased to print banknotes. Estimates of the amount of paper currency issued in the South range from $1 billion to $2 billion, not including bonds and currency issued by individual states, counties, cities and private businesses. Even the Native American Cherokee Nation in the South was issuing its own money, redeemable in Confederate currency.

Davis and his cabinet hoped to cover the cost of the war and their banknote issues through European loans (especially from Britain, where there was sympathy with the Confederacy) and the sale of its coveted long-fibre cotton abroad. During the early war years, the stringent Union naval blockade worked against cotton exports. But in barter trade, Spain's Cuban colony was a good market for the South's cotton in exchange for durable goods and foodstuffs like sugar. Then the Union navy moved into Cuban waters, raising diplomatic tensions with Spain, and seizing dozens of blockade runners. By autumn 1863, far fewer Confederate craft were visible in Havana harbour.

Inflation was fed by many other causes apart from the counterfeit notes smuggled into the South by Union soldiers, spies and female courier-spies, including domestic counterfeiting and the bewildering variety of locally printed notes. The Confederate Congress tried to fight inflation by forced funding. On 23 March 1863 they ordered gradual sinking of the interest rate of bonds that people could purchase with notes. But the same law authorized Treasury Secretary Menninger to issue $50 million of notes every month. In any case, rocketing inflation made bonds a progressively poorer investment.[13]

Some of the first genuine Confederate currency was printed by the high-pressure intaglio process, used today by the majority of reputable banknote printers, including the US Treasury. Requiring much time and care for production, the intaglio process utilized incised metal plates. The process produced 'fine-line detail quality often unobtainable by stone lithography', the process used subsequently for most of the genuine Confederate notes. These genuine notes often varied in quality and bore cruder images than those produced by intaglio, but they were faster to print. Speed and quantity, rather than quality and the more deliberate production pace of intaglio, were in great demand in the South.

Different printing establishments contributed designs for the same denominations. The vignettes used to print the designs were used by most printers in both North and South. Added to this were shortages and inconsistencies in ink and paper used. All this added up to one thing: the work of counterfeiters on both sides of the Mason–Dixon line dividing North and South was greatly eased. The result was inevitable: Menninger began to receive reports of many counterfeit Confederate notes in circulation. Some were 'crude copies printed from electrotype plates produced from woodcuts'. But the majority were lithographs, some superior in quality to the original lithographically printed notes.[14]

The Reign of the Counterfeiters

Before the war, currency counterfeiting in the United States was centred mainly in New York, Philadelphia and Saint Louis, Missouri, and the trade was practised purely for personal gain. When war broke out, the aim of each side to destroy the other's economy became mingled with the greed factor. By 1862, the *New York Times* estimated that Lincoln's fears about the greenbacks were being realized – fully 80 per cent of all banknotes in circulation had counterfeit counterparts. By the time the newer, easy-to-forge Hoyer & Ludwig Confederate notes began to circulate, Menninger suggested that the Confederate Congress legislate a compulsory death penalty for forging Confederate currency, a measure that did not pass until over a year later.

On 20 August 1862 Assistant Confederate Treasurer B. C.

Pressley in Charleston telegraphed Menninger that bogus $50 notes circulating there were causing bank tellers to 'reject all 50s of that plate because the difference [between the counterfeits and] the genuine is too minute'. Reports streamed in from Treasury agents and bankers in Charleston; Columbia, South Carolina; Atlanta, Savannah and Augusta, Georgia; and Montgomery, Alabama, of high-quality $20, $50 and $100 counterfeits in circulation. Menninger immediately recalled all three denominations of the Hoyer & Ludwig issue. As a result of the uncertainty and rejection in some quarters, Confederate currency expert George B. Tremmel reports that '[A] monetary panic erupted among the public, merchants and bankers. People stopped accepting these particular notes and in some cases any Confederate treasury notes at all.'[15]

Menninger planned to replace the recalled notes with 6 per cent interest-bearing Treasury certificates. These in turn were to be exchanged for interest-bearing Treasury notes when the notes became available. The acute shortage of money during the war's first year also led Menninger to recommend stamping counterfeit notes as 'Valid' and recirculating them. Neither of these proposed solutions worked. Deeply concerned about the impact of counterfeits now turning up in the pockets of captured Union soldiers and returned Confederate prisoners, the Confederate Congress passed new legislation: imprisonment for three to ten years; fines up to $5,000 'or death by hanging for producers and passers of counterfeit and forged notes'.[16]

The records of the First Confederate Congress, second session, on debates prior to the passing of this legislation show the heated rhetoric that surrounded Yankee counterfeiting. One legislator testified:

> An immense number of these counterfeit notes have found their way into our banks . . . Wherever their armies have invaded our country . . . these notes have been scattered . . . [This is] one of the most destructive blows made against our government. Its aim and tendency is to destroy all faith in the currency of the country . . . No method could be too speedy and summary for

> the trial and punishment of the unscrupulous Yankee scoundrels . . . [The] offences . . . are done with the complicity of their government.[17]

Virginia newspapers reported that in Culpepper County, Yankee soldiers had bought up almost the entire stock in trade of a country merchant with

> counterfeit Confederate notes printed in the United States . . . They come among us as felons in the garb of soldiers. They come not only with arms in their hands but with counterfeits in their pockets.[18]

Menninger told Speaker of the House Thomas S. Bocock on 18 August 1862:

> Organized plans seem to be in operation for introducing counterfeits among us by means of prisoners and traitors; and printed advertisements have been found stating that counterfeit notes, in any quantity, will be forwarded by mail from Chestnut Street in Philadelphia, to the order of any purchaser.[19]

The mention of Philadelphia's Chestnut Street refers to one of the most ambitious of the Northern counterfeiters. His products found their way in huge quantities into the South, through both official and unofficial channels. Samuel Curtis Upham was born in Montpelier, Vermont, on 2 February 1819. He grew up and worked in New York, Richmond and other cities of the South. After a long career in the US Navy including sea duty abroad, he re-entered civilian life in Pensacola, Florida, in 1845. After many adventures in California during the 1849 Gold Rush and a period spent working on and publishing newspapers in Philadelphia, he settled finally in Philadelphia in about 1857 and opened a newspaper and stationery shop. He moved the shop to 310 Chestnut Street in 1862, then sold it and moved again to 25 South 8th Street. For the rest of his working life, Sam Upham used the 8th Street shop to peddle everything from patent medicines and perfumes to 'patriotic' wartime stationery.

Upham began his eighteen-month career as a currency forger

after noticing that the 24 February 1862 issue of the venerable *Philadelphia Inquirer* sold out due to an image of a Confederate banknote on the first page. People were buying the newspaper to have a souvenir of Rebel currency. Upham got electrotype plates from the *Inquirer* and *Leslie's Weekly Magazine* in New York. He began printing souvenir copies of Southern money 'wholesale or retail'. He offered to pay a premium 'over face value in gold for new samples of Southern currency' that he could copy and sell. He then branched out into offering notes on high-quality banknote paper with his imprints omitted and with blank signatures and serial numbers. Richmond newspapers began to denounce Upham's 'Yankee scoundrelism' and published means of detecting his false notes. In a post-war letter, Upham recalled hearing that Confederate Congressman Henry S. Foote of Tennessee told the Confederate Congress that Upham had done more to damage the Confederacy 'than the whole Union Army'. Upham wrote in the same letter that he had learned that Jefferson Davis has offered a $10,000 reward for his 'corpus, dead or alive'.

The other main Yankee culprit in Southern eyes was Winthrop E. Hilton of New York City, who operated a printing shop at 11 Spruce Street in Manhattan. However, Confederate Secret Service operatives based in Richmond succeeded in bringing him down through an elaborate sting operation, perhaps one of the most subtle and successful during the entire Civil War. After learning of Upham's success in Philadelphia, Hilton began turning out his own Confederate counterfeit banknotes in the autumn of 1862. He called them 'facsimiles', which he probably considered a good euphemism for Upham's 'souvenirs'. In ads placed in *Harper's Weekly* magazine from October 1862 until April 1963, Hilton boasted that his products were 'so exactly like the genuine that where one will pass current the other will go equally well'. The high quality of the Hilton forgeries was such that Sam Upham had to reduce the price of his products to keep up with the competition.

Hilton's presses rolled almost continuously until 16 December 1863, when US Marshal Robert Murray and a team of federal officers descended on the Spruce Street shop, arresting Hilton.

They seized $1 million in Confederate Treasury notes, $6 million in Confederate bonds, as well as dyes, presses, lathes and all the other requisites for engraving and printing, as the *New York Times* reported on 31 December 1863. Hilton was incarcerated in the prison at Fort Lafayette, New York.

But how come? Were the Feds really interested in stopping an operation which was a de facto part of the Union war effort by adding to Southern inflation, acquiring Southern property and undermining confidence of the Southerners in their money? According to Tremmel's thorough and convincing research based on an exposé published by the Richmond *Daily Disptach* of 10 May 1864, the answer is that the Rebel government had Hilton in its sights almost from the beginning of his operation. Its agents perpetrated a clever sting operation to eliminate the Manhattan printer as a threat to the Confederate cause by having the Yankee government seize and neutralize him.

According to Tremmel, it worked as follows. Early in Hilton's career of counterfeiting Confederate paper, New York was teeming with Southern spies and sympathizers (called 'Copperheads'). Rebel agents noticed that the bogus $100 Confederate notes being hawked by newsboys at 5 cents apiece came from Hilton's Spruce Street premises. Many of these notes bore the signatures, forged or real, of the Confederate registrar and treasurer. They were being sold to people approaching or intending to cross into the Rebel states, where they concluded private deals with Southerners to launder, use or pass them. The Southern spies discovered that Hilton had a secret arrangement with George H. Briggs, formerly of Atlanta, who had come North to pick up bonds to be sold and circulated in the South. Tremmel reports that this operation had become so successful that

> the South was flooded with spurious bills . . . until [it] fairly broke down the currency of the Southern States, so that they were obliged to destroy their old plates, call in their old issues and print entirely new money.[20]

Hilton was thus able to damage materially the Southern cause. As had been the case with Upham, a rebel agent was sent to New York to stop his operation.

In fact, Hilton had signed contracts with Confederate agents to print *genuine* Confederate money and securities. These could be exchanged for good specie, gold, silver and whatever had purchasing power abroad, especially in the United Kingdom's markets. There is a good possibility, Tremmel believes, that Hilton was also counterfeiting Union paper money. Only a smoking gun was needed to nail him. This was provided by three Union cryptanalysts, code-breakers who solved a ciphered message the federal authorities intercepted between a Confederate agent based in Canada to another in New York, mentioning Hilton's activities. If the Feds had been deliberately ignoring Hilton's Confederate productions, believing they would be used to weaken the South, they moved in on him when he began to threaten Union finances.[21]

The Northern counterfeiting offensive was especially wounding to Southern pride. Confederate currency was artistically decorated with elaborate pastoral and sentimental themes, portraying the plantation society of the rural Old South and its heroes and leaders. There was an especially strong tradition among the bankers, merchants and ordinary people of Louisiana, where French language and subculture lived on long after Thomas Jefferson purchased it from Napoleon for $15 million. In 1833 New Orleans saw the foundation of the Citizens Bank of Louisiana, which issued ornately decorated banknotes of up to $1,000. These came to be accepted as far north as Pittsburgh, and were in constant use by gamblers and other patrons on the Mississippi riverboats.

The $10 note was the most popular. Like most Louisiana imprints, the currency was bilingual, so both 'Ten' and the French '*Dix*' were printed on each note. Americans in the vast southern and western regions where these were current began calling a $10 bill a 'dix', and there was more confidence in them than in much other paper money of the time. Steamboat travellers in the North used to say they were going south 'after dixies'. Like most other currency, 'dixies' were extensively counterfeited.

A Northerner who had enjoyed a summer in New Orleans was inspired to write a song inspired by a bucolic vision of the South.

'Dixie' was first played at a performance in Mechanics Hall, New York City. When war broke out between the states, General Albert Pike of the Confederacy wrote patriotic words for the tune.

I wish I was in the land of cotton,
Old times there are not forgotten,
Look away, look away, look away, Dixie Land.

It became a mildly worded battle hymn and marching song for the South.[22] Dixie became the favourite sentimental name for the Confederacy as a whole, and has survived until now. More than a century after the Union victory in 1865, Robbie Robertson of the Band wrote another song about the night in Richmond when the exhausted Rebel Commander-in-Chief Robert E. Lee surrendered: 'The Night They Drove Old Dixie Down'.

Colonel Baker, the Lady from Havana and High Jinks in the US Treasury

Much of the gossip whispered in the plush recesses of Willard's Hotel in Washington concerned Colonel Lafayette C. Baker, Alan Pinkerton's successor as chief of the Detective Bureau and effective chief of the North's intelligence and counter-spy operations from then on. Carl Sandburg's four-volume account of Lincoln at war calls Baker 'a czar of various underworlds' because of his connections in the North's criminal milieu and his use of spies and counter-spies, especially women. By late 1863 Baker commanded a core of 1,000 agents and a total of 2,000 men and women who intermittently operated under his orders. He kept a kind of mental card file on evildoers as well as loyal people of all descriptions. William O. Stoddard, a White House staffer who handled Lincoln's mail but who may also have played a strategy-adviser role with the president, commented once that any man even appearing suspicious who had spent some time in Washington was known to Baker.

Baker's grandfather, Remember Baker, was a member of the Green Mountain Boys, the Vermont state militia commanded by Ethan Allen during the American Revolution. Lafayette Baker went east, then west, where he joined the Vigilante Committee, which used big sticks rather than limp carrots to restore order to an openly lawless San Francisco, especially among unruly Irish immigrants in 1856. Lincoln's secretary of war, Edwin M. Stanton, admired Lafayette Baker's early espionage exploits in the South and raised Baker to the rank of brigadier general, though for most people and historians he has remained the more familiar 'Colonel' Baker.

Baker was described by contemporaries as 'red-bearded and ferret-eyed'. Like many another chief of spies, he developed a reputation for disregarding the civil rights of those he tracked, captured and interrogated. From his official headquarters at 217 Pennsylvania Avenue he gradually began to run his service like a vigilante organization. He often wore a badge in public, melodramatically inscribed with the motto, 'Death to Traitors'. Among his lasting accomplishments was creation of the first comprehensive US criminal dossier and criminal photo file.[23]

Baker was well prepared for a major role in helping to distribute the bogus Confederate money throughout the South. Shortly after his appointment by General Winfield Scott to run Union intelligence, Baker was captured, by his own account, about fifty miles behind Rebel lines. Suspecting his identity and top role in the Union war effort, his Confederate captors delivered him directly to President Jefferson Davis in Richmond. At the time Baker was using one of his many aliases, that of Samuel Munson of Knoxville, Tennessee, a real person whom Baker had met during his California days.

While Baker waited in Davis' office, the Confederate chief sent aides to find some citizen of Knoxville who could verify 'Munson's' identity. Within a short time a gentleman named Brock sent his calling card, and Davis had Brock shown in. Baker contrived to show recognition of Brock, who looked surprised. But then Brock acknowledged his old crony Munson, whom he'd known in their youthful years in California. Baker listened carefully to Brock's chatter about the good old days in California and managed to give answers that satisfied both Brock and Davis. Davis ordered 'Munson's' immediate release. On his way out, however, a voice cried,

'Why! Baker!' To his consternation, the father of a child Baker had saved from drowning on a ferryboat twelve years earlier had recognized him. Baker told him curtly that he had the wrong man, and walked away.

He probably headed for Fredericksburg, Virginia, for which he had been given a Confederate safe-conduct (Jefferson Davis had given him a written pass allowing him to travel to Frericksburg). After twice dodging arrest, he dared not show his face in a public eating place or tavern. He found two Dutchmen living in a tent on the bank of a creek, which eventually fed into the Potomac. They kept a boat in the creek. Baker stayed overnight in their tent. At dawn he made a break for it and stole their boat. The Dutchmen summoned him back, and then one pointed a shotgun at him. Baker had managed to keep or purloin a revolver. With one shot he downed the Dutchman, whose companion called for help. Escaping into the Potomac, four miles wide at that point, under a hail of bullets from a posse of Confederate soldiers, he sculled for two and a half hours to arrive safely at last on the Union shore.[24]

Soon after, Baker would cross paths with one of the most extraordinary women ever to sprint across the stage of American history and live to write about it. Published in 1876 with a title that tries to do justice to her tumultuous career, *The Woman in Battle: A Narrative of the Exploits, Adventures and Travels of Madame Loreta Janeta Velazquez, Otherwise Known as Lieutenant Harry T. Buford, Confederate States Army* portrays its author and some of the characters who crossed her path during a tumultuous career of fighting, spying, amorous affairs and trading in bogus currency and securities of both the Union and the Confederacy.[25]

Born in Cuba of French and Spanish parents, Velazquez consistently claims to be a true patriot of the Southern cause. She probably had as much or more to do with massive financial fraud of the Confederate cause. Professional historians who have studied her narrative, notably Professor Richard Hall, believe that despite some exaggeration in her narrative, there's enough truth in it to make it an important document of Civil War history. Velazquez claims her fervent devotion to Dixie made her don a Confederate uniform, provide herself with false credentials as Lieutenant Harry Buford, complete with a man's wig and a false moustache. She learned how to walk like a man, to smoke cigars and pad her uniform to make her look bigger and tougher. As Buford, before beginning her spying career, she fought at the First Battle of Bull Run, Fort Donelson and Shiloh. She was wounded at Shiloh, and Confederate army doctors treating her wound discovered her gender. Denied permission to return to combat duty, she went to Richmond and persuaded Confederate spy chief General John H. Winder to enrol her as a spy and courier for the South. During the final year and a half of the war (1864–5), after convincing Lafayette Baker into hiring her, she became a Confederate double agent.[26]

Her career as a double began with winning the confidence of Baker by completing several courier missions for him. Apparently having carried considerable quantities of counterfeit Southern money behind Confederate lines, she observed that Baker and his agents were using the fake bills to finance espionage in the South. She also noted that Baker considered that distribution of the bogus currency was a good opportunity to undermine the Southern economy.

In Washington gambling and vice were rampant. One of Baker's self-appointed tasks was to fight these evils. Sometimes led by Baker himself, he would frequently raid the bordellos and shady hostelries, such as the Canterbury Hotel. One of Baker's concerns was the elite class of gambling casinos where, according to Sandburg's book on Lincoln, 'Faro and poker were the principal games' and one 'needed an introduction: there were governors, members of Congress, department officials, clerks, contractors, paymasters'. At the bottom of the ladder were dives 'where smooth-spoken women plied the young [Union] infantrymen with drink and played them out of their last payday greenbacks'. Baker reported to Stanton in the summer of 1863 that '163 gaming-houses in full blast required attention'.[27]

What troubled Stanton and others in the Lincoln administration, however, was that Baker was using Treasury Department women employees as spies. As sometimes reported in the

Washington newspapers, nocturnal goings-on involved young Treasury ladies and such officials as Spencer Morton Clark, the acting engineer in charge of printing Union currency and producing the finished greenbacks that were then delivered to private banknote companies for distribution. By spring of 1864, the *New York World* and other newspapers hostile to the Lincoln administration were publishing stories about women in the Treasury's printing bureau dressing in men's clothes and attending 'lewd performances' at the Canterbury Hotel, to which only men were supposed to be admitted. The *New York Tribune*, no friend of Colonel Baker, editorialized that this was a conspiracy on the part of the 'conniving' Union spy chief and that he used a disreputable actress (perhaps Loreta Velazquez, who did do some acting on the side) and 'women of the streets' as informers and operatives 'to discredit women employees of the printing bureau and thereby cast a shadow over the Treasury Department'.[28]

Chase, whose own portrait was printed on the $10,000 bill, worried about everything: Baker's spy ladies and the possibility (which turned out to be a fact) that counterfeit securities of both the North and South were either being printed or that plates to print them 'privately' were being smuggled out of the Treasury. Chase petulantly offered his resignation fourteen times, but was cajoled by the president to remain until Lincoln reluctantly accepted it in June 1864.

By then, Lincoln was being informed by other advisers and by the press that the gold price had reached new highs in London. Greenbacks were down, and there was plenty of counterfeit money around in the North despite Baker's best efforts. Even worse, at one point Registrar of the Treasury Lucius E. Chittenden reported that he had caught Baker in the act of forgery – Sandburg doesn't say what Baker was forging – and 'Perfectly unabashed, without a blush, the fellow smiled as he looked me in the face and said, "That game didn't work, did it?"'[29]

Meanwhile Loreta Velazquez, remaining a loyal servant of the Confederacy, wormed her way into Baker's confidence. In 1864 Baker began to send her on secret investigative and espionage missions. After he was transferred to the Treasury Department in

Washington and put under Salmon P. Chase's authority, Baker asked her to look into the well of corruption he correctly perceived there. She recorded that within the Treasury building and its printing bureau, there was the 'headquarters of a gang of thieves and counterfeiters'. It had been operating for many months and with the knowledge of prominent people. Velazquez added that not only were Confederate bonds and notes freely manufactured in the North, without any interference on the part of the government, but that federal officials actually made use of this bogus Confederate paper whenever they found it convenient to do so.

Baker, she found, often used promissory notes to pay his spies in the South. These were 'supposedly issued in Richmond, but in reality manufactured and given to the world in New York and Philadelphia', a reference to the operations of Upham and Hilton. Since Baker appeared to believe in using the counterfeit paper as a proper weapon against the rebels, 'we rebs had the right to do the same to the Union'.

Velazquez solicited the help of Treasury clerks. One whom she doesn't name believed that bogus Union bonds could be printed 'in Washington'. She explained that the bonds should be floated, as much as was possible, in Europe. This could be done by selling them in Europe at rates that undercut the official rates offered by Union agents who were selling the more expensive genuine article. Velazquez began to travel between New York, Philadelphia and Washington, carrying the bonds, Treasury notes and bogus plates, and calling herself a 'confidential manager'. Brokers were doing the financing. The British were 'fair game' to receive the bogus currencies and paper of either side, 'for we regarded their conduct as treacherous to both parties in the great contest'. Therefore they should be made to pay 'some of the expenses of conducting it . . . it was determined, therefore, to go for Johnny Bull's pocket'. Velazquez made at least one 'sales' trip to London for this purpose.[30]

In Chapter 41 of her lengthy tome, Velazquez explains how she worked, sometimes at night, in the Treasury with Spencer C. Clark, head of the National Currency Bureau, and other officials. For their counterfeiting operations these officials used 'abandoned women' who 'had the habit of carousing in their offices at midnight'. Exposure in the newspapers caused the public scandal that led Chase, before Lincoln finally accepted his resignation and replaced him, to have Baker investigate the nocturnal goings-on in the Treasury.[31]

Another woman, Velazquez relates, smuggled electrotype duplicates of genuine plates to outside co-conspirators. This, she gleefully claims, defrauded the Union of 'vast quantities of money', as the counterfeit Confederate and Union bonds were sold on the London market. She describes another episode in which she bargained over the price of an electrotype plate, which she had delivered to her Washington residence, Kirkwood House, and kept locked up in a trunk. The plate was for printing bogus $100 compound-interest notes, which might be called the 'Supernotes' of the time!

During the same period in 1864 Velazquez received $55,000 dollars' worth of Union securities, left for her in a package under a cedar tree in the gardens of the Smithsonian Institute. On a trip to Philadelphia, she contacted brokers and other intermediaries and acquired from them a large amount of bogus Confederate bonds. She took her haul to a room she had rented in a private house in Greenwich Street, New York City. She and her brokers exchanged the bonds for sterling and gold at market rates, which were then converted into greenbacks. Despite the considerable profits she earned from this trafficking, she adds that 'the amounts that passed through our hands only represented a very small proportion of what was issued during the war'. The main centres of the trade, Velazquez claims, were in Wall Street and Fulton Street in New York's financial district, although a number of these swindlers were located on Broadway, 'many with unimpeachable reputations'.

Summing up her operations, Loreta Velazquez records that she and other Confederates used these transactions 'not only to replenish our treasury', but that they 'worked in many ways to turn the criminal selfishness and unpatriotic greed of people, with whom were were brought in contact, to account, for the benefit of our cause'.[32]

There is no sure record of Velazquez' life and adventurous career after the war, or confirmed data about the date and place of her death. Historians will doubtless argue for years about the truth of the exploits in her book. What seems clear is that she'll always be associated with the role of counterfeiting and big-time financial fraud in the service of selfish interests as well as the Southern cause throughout the Civil War period.

Gone with the Wind

The big question for Civil War historians and their readers is just how much counterfeiting the South's currency led to its economic collapse and its ultimate defeat. No one would argue that it contributed more than did the Union's crushing military campaigns. General William Tecumseh Sherman's devastating, scorched-earth march through Georgia, the North's victories in the western states, or the repulse in Pennsylvania of Confederate General Robert E. Lee's invasion of the North, among many other factors, were of course decisive. And yet, as North Carolina author George B. Tremmel has recently shown, the attack on the South's currency did much to undermine both Southern morale and the largely agrarian bases of its slavery-based economy.

Tremmel's analysis of the combined impact of counterfeiting and inflation on the Southern economy – each of the two factors aggravating the other – begins with inflation measured by the standard American Lerner Domestic Price Index. Prices of basic commodities in the Confederate states rose from 101 in January of 1861 to 5,824 in January 1865 (a fifty-eight-fold increase).

Inflation spurted upwards at a rate of between fifty-eight to ninety-five times during the war. From early 1861 until early 1865, the Confederate money supply grew eighteen-fold, putting a total of $1.54 billion in circulation. This was backed not by specie but by a promise to redeem the paper money 'six months to two years' after a hypothetical Southern victory.

In Margaret Mitchell's masterpiece Civil War novel *Gone with the Wind*, further engraved in the American memory by the 1939 film starring Vivien Leigh and Clark Gable, Scarlett O'Hara experiences this bitter state of affairs. After the guns fall silent in 1865, she finds her hopes of paying Reconstruction taxes to the victorious federal government in Washington shattered. Her father had converted all of his money into Confederate war bonds, rendered worthless by the South's defeat.

During the same period, competing Southern currency issued by states, banks, local governments and 'private' issues from Southern railroads and insurance companies added, Tremmel calculates, perhaps $10 million more. His most conservative guess at total counterfeit Confederate currency in circulation is $45 million (which would be in the neighbourhood of $1 billion or more in 2007 dollars).[33] In comparison, the value of the gold dollar on the New York money market in Union greenback currency was $1.03 in January 1862 and $1.79 in March 1865, as the war drew to a close.

Long before that time, Dixie's Treasury was broke. The Confederate state of Texas realized by mid-1864 that Southern currency was virtually worthless and discontinued its use as legal tender. Trade from then on in Texas was based on barter, very dubious locally issued money or Union greenbacks. When the South surrendered in 1865, its total Treasury assets were only $85,000 in gold, $36,000 in silver coin and $700,000 in Confederate paper currency.

One of the supreme ironies of Civil War history is that although millions of dollars' worth of Confederate notes, genuine and counterfeit, were used as fuel or dumped and destroyed by the defeated Southerners, thousands of surviving notes in later decades drew huge sums from collectors, especially at the time of Civil War centennial celebrations in 1965, and prices continued to rise afterwards. One historian records that by 1992, an uncirculated $1,000 Confederate bill produced in Mongomery, Alabama, was worth over $18,000 in real money.[34]

Tremmel concludes that the fact that inflation increased so much more than the increase in the supply of currency appears to be due to the South's gradual realization, beginning in 1863, that the war was not going well and that 'time was running out for the Confederacy'. Among the less measurable but doubtless real effects of counterfeiting was that it drained the already limited resources of the Confederate Treasury, local banks, businesses and ordinary consumers. There was the added drain due to expenses, time and effort of pursuing and trying to capture the counterfeiters in both the South and the North. Confederate Treasury headaches, Tremmel finds, were worsened by management of counterfeiting scares and the need to recall many banknote issues. In sum, 'counterfeiting not only abetted the increase in the money supply but also compounded the loss of confidence in the monetary exchange system'.[35]

The US Secret Service: A Civil War Heritage

During and after his involvement with the likes of Loreta Velazquez, Lafayette Baker used (and sometimes abused) his vast powers to pursue Confederate agents, counterfeiters and all manner of real or suspected malefactors. The birth of the greenback dollars in 1862 soon gave rise to what the *New York Times* of 30 July 1862 called 'a startling increase of counterfeiting'. Baker and his men spent much time and energy tracking down a master counterfeiter named Peter McCartney, operating like many other currency forgers in Indianapolis, in the Union state of Indiana.

McCartney worked with a prominent criminal dynasty, the Johnson clan of Lawrence, Indiana. McCartney used a technique still current today: he'd scrape the $1 denominations off real bills he earned as a sales agent for a farmer and affix higher numbers to the same bills. Later he studied with a German immigrant forger named Ackerman, an engraver, and married his mentor's daughter Martha Ackerman in 1852. He developed his engraving and printing skills to a fine point. By the summer of 1864, McCartney and the Johnson clan together had successfully circulated over $100,000 in phoney greenbacks, a huge sum at the time.

Baker's Treasury detectives captured McCartney and the Johnsons in raids in Indiana in summer of 1864, but McCartney managed to gain his freedom by jumping off the rear platform of a train on the Penn Central Railroad carrying him and his colleagues towards captivity in the notorious Old Capitol Prison in

Washington, DC. He was free and operating when the war ended on 9 April 1865.

On the afternoon of 14 April 1865, Lincoln met with Chase's successor, Secretary of the Treasury William P. McCullough. The secretary outlined the critical seriousness of the counterfeiting situation and suggested creating a 'regular permanent force whose job it will be to put these counterfeiters out of business'. In one of his final acts before actor and Confederate supporter John Wilkes Booth assassinated him that night at Ford's Theatre in Washington, Lincoln agreed. Political turmoil and intrigue delayed creation of the official Secret Service, as it is still known today, until 5 July 1865.

Lincoln's successor, President Andrew Johnson (1808–75), became Baker's foe when he discovered that Baker had created his own network of spies inside Johnson's White House. Johnson fired Baker and closed down the new Secret Service. When Johnson was impeached and tried before a Congress that hated him for his conciliatory policies towards the defeated South (but nevertheless acquitted him of the charge of 'high crimes and misdemeanours'), Baker testified against Johnson. Baker in turn was accused of returning to one of his favourite black arts, forgery, and producing false letters to incriminate Johnson.

The Secret Service was soon revived and placed under the Treasury Department, where it remained until President George W. Bush transferred it to his new Department of Homeland Security in 2002, just before the start of the Iraq war. William P. Wood, another avid foe of counterfeiters who had done favours for Lincoln, was appointed to head it. A veteran of guerrilla warfare during the Mexican War of the 1840s, where he had become known as 'the Daredevil Leader of Company C', Wood and the small band of agents he recruited pursued counterfeiters like McCartney and the Johnsons ruthlessly.

One of their quarries during a rugged campaign to protect the nation's greenbacks was William E. Brockway, an early associate of McCartney who came to be called 'The King of the Counterfeiters'. Brockway once turned out $1,000 US Treasury bonds so perfect that they fooled the Treasury into redeeming $75,000 worth of them for hard cash. But after Wood succeeded in tracking down and seizing Brockway, the Treasury secretary reneged on his initial offer of a $20,000 reward and told Wood he could only afford to give him $5,000. Disgusted, Wood handed in his resignation as first Secret Service chief on 5 May 1869. His replacement, second in a long line of directors, was a former lieutenant-colonel in the Union Army named Hiram C. Whitley.

Through the decades that followed, the Secret Service's duties expanded to detecting other kinds of fraud against the federal government and running down the Ku Klux Klan's racialist crimes in the South. Finally, during the administrations of President Grover Cleveland (1885–9 and 1893–7), it received its second main mission: personal protection of the United States president, and eventually the vice president, visiting statesmen and sometimes celebrities. It has both succeeded and failed in this mission, from James Garfield, killed in 1881 by a disappointed office-seeker, and William McKinley, murdered in 1901 by an anarchist, to Ronald Reagan, whose life the Secret Service preserved from a would-be assassin in 1981. During the Spanish–American War in 1898, the service became involved in both espionage and counter-espionage work against the nation's Spanish adversaries.[36] Through all of its ups and downs the Secret Service has pursued the anti-counterfeiting task given it during the Civil War.

The ramifications of that task and of currency forging on a grand scale are among our next subjects.

Eight

Britain's Goal: Undermine the Kaiser's Economy

> There was nothing very new to learn about this war or the end it was fought for; England had destroyed, as in each preceding century, a trade rival.
>
> *John Maynard Keynes,* The Economic Consequences of the Peace, *1920*

On the evening of 25 January 1916, Royal Marine Lieutenant-Colonel Maurice Hankey sat in his London home at 52 Oxford Terrace writing in his leather-bound diary. He was, perhaps unwittingly, recording for posterity one of the best-kept secrets of the First World War: the deployment against Germany and the other Central Powers of a weapon whose manipulators, other than Hankey, would not write down its name. It is most likely still protected by Britain's Official Secrets Act. It was expert forgery of German money intended to undermine Germany's economy and weaken its war effort, which together with that of Austria-Hungary and Turkey was proving formidable.

At thirty-nine, Hankey was much more than just a successful artillery and naval intelligence officer, accomplished in seven languages, and with a record of sea and combat duty in the Mediterranean and Near Eastern theatres. As secretary in a high-level War Committee, he had become a confidant of King George V and Prime Minister Earl Herbert Henry Asquith. He would remain an adviser to the next prime minister, David Lloyd George, and he was already privy to a number of top secrets of the war, most recently those connected with the disastrous campaign in the Dardanelles to capture Turkey's Gallipoli Peninsula and push on to conquer Constantinople. Long before Hankey's death in 1963, three prime ministers – Lloyd George, Winston Churchill and Clement Attlee – would all bar him from publishing personal memoirs that might contain top secrets.

Hankey's diary entry from that January night was preserved in a book, written by his naval intelligence colleague, friend and admiring biographer, Captain Stephen Roskill, that slipped by the keepers of Britain's secrets. The entry recounts how Sir Edwin Montagu, a Treasury secretary and Munitions Minister, had come to Hankey's office that day. The purpose of the visit 'was to explain a scheme of his for placing forged German banknotes in circulation, in which I promised to try and help'. Hankey noted that the governor of the venerable Bank of England, Walter Cunliffe (1855–1919), 'with the knowledge of the Chancellor of the Exchequer and Prime Minister, has produced some marvellous forgeries. It seems rather a dirty business, but the Germans deserve it and Napoleon used to do it.' He could have added that before Napoleon, George III's regime had also done it to the fledgling rebel American and French Republics. 'There is reason to suspect that the Huns have already played this game on us . . .'[1]

The basis for Hankey's diary remark about 'the Huns' is unclear. German commentators on the First World War mention in passing that Dr Hjalmar Schacht, the brilliant banker who had helped to rescue the Weimar Republic from the oblivion of post-First World War hyperinflation and who would later serve Hitler as central banker, had directed counterfeiting of currency in German-occupied Belgium. This was primarily to serve the purchasing and consumption needs of the German occupiers. They do not allege, however, that Schacht or other Germans serving Kaiser Wilhelm II were forging British or other Allied currency at the time.

In any case, Hankey rapidly followed up his consent to the Montagu scheme by calling on Captain (later Admiral) Reginald 'Blinker' Hall, the formidable chief of Britain's wartime Naval Intelligence Division (NIS). Hankey's diary entry for 27 January records that he had 'asked him [Hall] to help in the banknote scheme'.[2] In Hall's black operations in the Admiralty's legendary 'Room 40', a team of military and civilian experts including linguists and other academic experts seconded from Britain's universities were engaged in breaking both enemy and Allied codes and ciphers. (In 1917 it was they who deciphered Germany's Zimmerman telegram instructing the German ambassador in Mexico to offer up large swathes of territory in the south-western United States after a hypothetical German victory if Mexico would agree to join the Central Powers and open hostilities against the US.) The codes cracked there included the personal cipher used by American Colonel Edward M. House.

At the time of Hankey's diary notes about the forgery campaign, the US was still neutral. Colonel House was in London as US President Woodrow Wilson's personal envoy on an exploratory peace mission. He was seeking a way to ease the British naval blockade and the growing German submarine warfare, if not to stop the entire war. The Germans, however, not only refused Wilson's terms for settling the sinking of the Cunard liner *Lusitania* on 7 May 1915, which had resulted in a huge loss of American lives, they were also preparing to wage a wider war in the Atlantic with larger U-boats, as intelligence in the deciphered telegrams showed. On several occasions Hall's code-breakers in Room 40 jubilantly showed to insiders like Hankey the plain texts of House's telegrams with Wilson.[3] There does not seem to be any indication that Colonel House, President Wilson or any other American leader at the time was aware of the top-secret British counterfeiting scheme; indeed, only a handful of Britons knew about it.

The reason Hankey and the other planners turned to Captain Hall of NID and not the five-year-old Secret Intelligence Service (SIS) can only be inferred. For one thing, Hall's NID network commanded stations and active agents, especially in accessible neutral seaports such as those in Holland, Norway and Sweden. There was also the possibility of diplomatic mail to Switzerland. The Royal Flying Corps had already dropped bombs on Germany; its pilots were also capable of dropping the forged money and stamps produced by the secret counterfeiting cabal. Using the Royal Navy and merchant shipping mobilized for the war, Hall was better situated than the acutely understaffed and under-resourced SIS to handle the clandestine distribution of the forged banknotes, stamps and other documents of the Central Powers.

The SIS (later MI6) had been effectively started up in 1909. At the war's outset in 1914 its foreign section was commanded by a young lieutenant named Mansfield George Smith-Cumming, who had a background in naval intelligence and was also a trained military pilot. However, his junior rank and status worked against him. Smith-Cumming was not granted the rank of acting captain until January 1915. Unlike 'Blinker' Hall at NID, Smith-Cumming did not yet command overseas stations or agents. After war broke out in Europe, SIS was moved. In the words of British intelligence historian Nigel West, it was juxtaposed with the NID under the aegis of the Admiralty.[4]

The secret government 'counterfeiting committee', if the insiders could be called that, found ready and discreet allies and recruits in the Bank of England. The man directing them was the current head of the bank's huge printing department, Herbert G. de Fraine (1870–1958). In effect, he let slip the capital secret in his own memoirs, *Servant of This House*, published posthumously in 1960 by his daughter, Joan de Fraine. However, de Fraine was more cautious than Hankey: he used only the phrase 'forged German documents' to describe the mass of banknotes, stamps and other forged paper that the bank's busy presses, often working in twenty-four-hour shifts, turned out under conditions of the tightest secrecy.

De Fraine's vague time reference, 'after the war broke out', raises the possibility that the counterfeiting scheme was first conceived and begun, at least in the design and printing stage, as long as two years before Hankey and Hall were told about it and asked to cooperate in the distribution of the 'documents'. De Fraine relates that 'one day', Bank Governor Walter Cunliffe, a martinet who already bore the nickname 'tyrant of the City', visited him in his printing office.

> [He] told me that he had promised Captain (afterwards Admiral) Hall, Director of Naval Intelligence, to provide him with imitations – in plain English, forgeries – of certain German

> documents. He said that I and my Deputy, S. B. Chamberlain, were to place all the resources of the Printing Department at Captain Hall's disposal, also that this was highly confidential and that the three of us – three, no more – were to share this top secret between us.

De Fraine wrote that the bank's printers were able to take on the huge extra workload and guarantee secrecy of the forging operation

> by re-distributing some of the ordinary work [of printing sterling, Imperial currency like that of India and miscellaneous British security documents] to free accommodation and seal it off with double iron gates. Incidentally, we sealed it off so effectively that the Governor himself was refused permission to enter, and had to come down and ask me to go up and vouch for him. This pleased him mightily, as indication of the thoroughness of our [security] arrangements.[5]

Since long before the First World War, premises of the Bank of England's printing works in the main buildings off Threadneedle Street had been too small and cramped for the bank's huge printing tasks. Expanded quarters were found by incorporating Saint Luke's mental hospital, once called 'Saint Luke's Hospital for Lunaticks', in Old Street. Built in the early eighteenth century, this was a huge building close to the bank with a frontage of 500 feet. In October 1915, the bank found out that the governors of Saint Luke's were prepared to sell their City of London buildings and move to the country. In April 1917, after long haggling, the bank obtained possession and began reinforcing the wooden floors with steel and otherwise adapting the former hospital to accommodate heavy presses and other apparatus to handle the bank's main printing works.

Already in 1916, before the move to Saint Luke's, de Fraine had supervised installation of the machinery needed for the forgery and other expanded printing operations, including some 'specialities' that had to be ordered on the outside. There was a sixteen-man team consisting of old employees: 'Servants of the Bank', as they were more grandly called. Night watchmen, firemen, window cleaners, carpenters and normal maintenance and ordinary security personnel were all barred from the premises.

Initially, the designing, printing and engraving team worked two twelve-hour shifts, from Monday morning to Friday afternoon. On Friday there was a rigorous cleaning and search for 'any scrap of paper that might be recognizable'. Some of the printing presses had to be half-stripped for this search. All of the week's waste paper was then burned in a dustbin inside the restricted area and 'the ashes scrupulously examined'.[6]

A Cooperative Venture

Hall, on the intelligence side, and Sir Walter Cunliffe and de Fraine, in the bank, enlisted helpers in British industry and academic life. Hall's recruits included Claude Sercold, a London stockbroker; Thomas Inskip, later Lord Chancellor; a fellow of All Souls College named Sir Philip Baker Wilbraham; the short-story writer A. J. Alan; and a City wine merchant, James Randall.[7] It is uncertain how many of these gentlemen became involved in the counterfeit scheme. Their talents were needed for other black operations, including Room 40's code-breaking functions and the necessary analysis of the solved texts. This required a great deal of expertise, especially in languages such as German, Turkish and Russian. However, it is likely that wine merchant Randall, at least, could have been privy to the counterfeiting scheme. De Fraine records that

> completed documents [i.e., the forged banknotes, stamps, etc.] were nailed down in ordinary wine cases. We packed the cases in brown paper, labelled them with stick-on railway labels we had printed ourselves, and added a few hieroglyphics in blue pencil.[8]

The 'goods' were delivered by taxi on Sunday mornings, consigned personally to Captain Hall at the Admiralty. There, two naval guards 'wheeled our goods down to his room, more like a drawing-room than an office', provided with a Chesterfield with cretonne loose covers, comfy armchairs, 'and a charming light flowered carpet'. A white Pomeranian dog that 'trotted up to make our acquaintance' added to the homey atmosphere, de Fraine noted.

De Fraine admiringly described the 'dynamic little Captain', as he called Hall:

> on the short side, clean-shaven, with chin thrust out; and with one glance of his remarkable eyes he took our measure completely. He was bald on top, but had the sides and back of his head whitish hair, fluffed out as though he solved many difficulties by torturing it.[9]

De Fraine marvelled at the extraordinary variety of the helpers working for Hall, running far-flung agents and solving puzzling enigmas concerning the enemy and the Allies. It was all happening in the surrounding suite of rooms constituting what was collectively called 'Room 40': Royal Navy officers in and out of uniform, some over military age; fellows of colleges at Oxford and Cambridge; a director of the Bank of England; a famous music critic; an ex-president of the Oxford Union; an art expert; and a world-famous dress designer.[10] Truly, an impressive array of experts required to run global black operations in a global war!

Some of the outside expertise was evidently supplied by the long-established banknote printing firm of Waterlow & Company, most probably at Waterlow's plant in the London suburb of Watford, although other Waterlow offices were located in the City, not far from the Bank of England. (Bogus German and Austrian stamps that turned up much later in auctions and private collections bore in tiny letters the notation 'Printed in Watford'.)

During the post-war period of the 1920s, the firm would rise to a peak of activity, printing legitimate banknotes for foreign and imperial customers. Ironically, Waterlow's slow decline in the 1930s and eventual disappearance was speeded by involvement of Sir William Waterlow, a senior partner in the firm, in the twentieth century's biggest and most ambitious counterfeiting scheme: the Portuguese banknote scandal, which we will look at later in detail.

As the company's responsible representative, in 1930 Sir William (elevated to the post of Lord Mayor of London in 1929–30) had to submit to a fraud trial, appeal and final conviction and fining in the UK's highest judicial instance, the House of Lords. A strong hint of the super-sensitive nature of the German banknote operation and its probable coverage by the Official Secrets Act briefly emerged during this drama. At the first trial, a judge asked Sir William if his unwitting complicity in printing the millions of dollars' worth of spurious high-denomination Portuguese escudo notes in the 1920s was 'the most confidential thing he had ever done'.

'I said yes,' Sir William replied.

Later, at the appeals trial before the august House of Lords judges, he admitted

> it was not so, my Lord [Justice Wright] . . . The most confidential business I have ever undertaken was Secret Service during the War. I never told a single colleague of mine what was done . . . If you want to have it I will write it down.[11]

In his memorable book about the Portuguese scandal, Murray Teigh Bloom comments, 'Justice Wright, sensibly enough, did not want him to [write it down]. It seemed to some spectators Sir William was visibly disappointed.'[12] Bloom and other commentators who followed him (the first publication of his book was in 1952) have all agreed that Sir William's cryptic reference was to the forgeries during the First World War.

Evidence of the forgeries leaked in London in 1980. In November Harmer's, a long-established dealer and agent for the sale of collections catering principally to philatelists, published a catalogue for the auction of a collection of postal forgeries. It advertised

> Outstanding Austria, France with Allied intelligence forgeries, Germany with Allied intelligence and propaganda forgeries. One of the world's most complete collections of wartime espionage and propaganda stamps.

Inside the catalogue, buried among multiple listings of the bogus and satirical stamps issued by the contending powers in wartime, appeared 'Lot no. 1391', listed as a 'Circa 1916 forgery of 20-

mark bank note, uncirculated and fine'. The catalogue estimated its value at £7. A collector bought it for £15. (Harmer's has not responded to an email request for more information about this or subsequently discovered forgeries.)

Herbert A. Friedman is a retired master sergeant of the US Army, living at the time of this writing in upstate New York. He has had much experience with wartime forgeries in the US Army's psychological warfare (PSYOPS) division, which has printed forgeries of enemy money, stamps and propaganda leaflets since the Second World War. Friedman spotted the transaction and published a copy of the forged 20 imperial reichsmarks note (serial no. F3530024, dated 21 April 1910) in a long Web site report. It provides many details and some reproductions of the British First World War forgeries, especially the stamps but also the banknotes. Other examples of the bogus reichsmarks were later to emerge in private collections.[13]

Black Ops and Economic Warfare

It is easy to imagine a mixture of urgency and resignation in Maurice Hankey's spirit as he made his diary notes about the forgeries that night in 1916. His pre-war and wartime active service in the Royal Marines before his elevation to the inner councils of the war with the king, the prime minister, Sir Winston Churchill and others enabled Hankey fully to grasp how badly the war against Germany, Austria-Hungary and Turkey had been going. The Royal Navy's blockade of German ports and its successes against the German fleet on the high seas had been the main achievements so far.

At the beginning of 1916, Allied plans in the Balkans, a favourite of Hankey's senior contemporary (and occasional detractor) Winston Churchill, had virtually dissolved. Bulgaria had joined the Central Powers, despite British efforts to bribe it (recorded in Hankey's diary notes). Tiny but pugnacious Serbia, where the war had begun with the murder of the Austrian Archduke Ferdinand in 1914, had succumbed to Austria-Hungary. The Greek government of Prime Minister Eleftherios Venizelos, still one of Greece's most revered national heroes, was an enthusiastic advocate of Allied action against Greece's enemy and occupier, Ottoman Turkey. However, Greece's King Constantine hoped that Greece could ride out the war as a neutral. Venizelos' government fell. When Allied troops (mainly French) later occupied Salonica (Thessaloniki) to tie down Turkish forces in the region, Greece for a time was politically divided between neutral and pro-Allied advocates.

The British, ANZAC and French efforts to break through the Dardanelles to capture Constantinople and cripple Turkey had collapsed after the landings on the Gallipoli Peninsula. British and Allied troops there were slaughtered in vain, the Australians suffering the most casualties. The Allies had to 'cut and run', as President George W. Bush and his supporters of the disastrous US operation in Iraq nearly a century later would probably have described the Allied withdrawal.

In the mud and mire of the dismal trench warfare on the Western Front, a British offensive at Loos, carried out contrary to the advice of Field Marshal Sir Douglas Haig, commander of the First Army whose men had to carry it out, left 60,000 British corpses after a gain of about 8,000 yards. Another 50,000 British and French soldiers perished in futile autumn offensives in Champagne and the Artois region.

In the East, German Lieutenant General Erich von Falkenhayn's drive at Gorlice cost the Czar's allied Russian armies *two million* dead, imprisoned and incapacitated troops. The Italian allies fighting the Austrians at Iszorno were routed in December 1915 after horrendous Italian losses. In Mesopotamia (modern Iraq), British Major-General Sir Charles Townshend's advance from Basra towards Baghdad had bogged down in Kut al-Amara. The combined Turkish–Arab forces had surrounded them. Between 7 December 1915 and 29 April 1916, the British and Anglo-Indian forces made three vain attempts to relieve the garrison. Floods and mud proved to be as great enemies as did sandstorms and enemy activity in all of the desert wars of the twentieth century in North Africa and the Middle East. An effort was made to buy off the Turks just before start of the disastrous Gallipoli campaign. The only result was fiercer Turkish resistance at Gallipoli. On 29 April

1916 the ten thousand British-led troops trapped in Kut al-Amara surrendered to the Turks and their Arab allies.

Although undocumented, it is a reasonable assumption that the Gallipoli and Mesopotamian reverses helped motivate the secret counterfeiting committee in London to try to undermine further the decrepit Ottoman economy by forging the Turkish lira. As in the German case, the evidence appears in the collections of philatelic auctioneers and private collectors. As Scott E. Cordry commented in the journal *Coin World* of 13 July 1988, the British had plenty of reasons to 'disrupt and discredit' the money supply in Turkey and Turkish-ruled Palestine and other Arab territory. '[W]ith the discovery of excellently made counterfeit Turkish 10-livre [sic] notes dated 1918, we have some physical evidence of just such a scheme.'[14]

Such forgeries began to turn up in collections around 1969 and in greater numbers in 1987. Like the German reichsmark forgeries, they were of high quality and bore different serial numbers. However, Friedman notes that there was one 'remarkable' error on all of the bogus lira that have turned up: the Roman and Islamic 10-digits along the left border on the backside face towards the outside of the banknote instead of towards the inside as on the genuine article.

Devalued and counterfeit money occupies an especially ignominious niche of Turkish history. It has haunted Turks since early Ottoman times. Orhan Pamuk, the 2006 Nobel Prize–winning Turkish novelist, eloquently expresses this in a narration in his novel *My Name is Red* by his fictitious seventeenth-century Ottoman protagonist:

> [T]he problem of devalued money was the same everywhere. It was rumoured that Flemish and Venetian merchant ships were once filled with chests of counterfeit coin at the royal mint where 500 coins were once minted from 500 drachmas of silver, owing to the endless warring with the Persians, 800 coins were minted from the same amount. When Janissaries discovered that the coins they'd been paid actually floated in the Golden Horn like the dried beans that fell from the vegetable-sellers pier, they

> rioted, besieging Our Sultan's palace as if it were an enemy fortress . . . [A] pickle seller . . . said that the counterfeit coins – the new ducats, the fake florins stamped with lions and the Ottoman coins with their ever-decreasing silver content . . . were dragging us toward an absolute degradation from which it would be difficult to escape.[15]

Seizing Germany's Colonies

British colonial military reverses in German East Africa evidently led to a similar attack by the counterfeiting cabal in London on the currency issued by the German colonial authorities.

Prussia's prime minister and the Chancellor of a unified and imperial Germany after he deliberately provoked the Franco-Prussian War of 1870–1 and defeated Napoleon III, Otto Eduard Leopold von Bismarck (1815–98) was not especially eager to found an overseas German colonial empire. However, during the late nineteenth century European nations were competing for whatever territory, raw materials and markets for their new manufacturing industries they could lay their hands on. Bismarck gave in to Germany's powerful pro-colonial lobbies, the Colonial Association and the Society for German Colonization. After 1880 Germany seized and began to settle parts of East Africa, South West Africa, the Cameroons, Togoland and several South Pacific islands.

After Bismarck's resignation in 1890, Kaiser Wilhelm II embarked on a new course: Germany, he proclaimed, must become a *Weltmacht*, a world power. He began building up the German navy to a point where it could challenge the Royal Navy. Between 1897 and 1899 Tsingtao in China, the Caroline, Marianna and Palau islands and parts of Samoa were added to the empire. Wilhelm and Chancellor Bethmann Hollweg had their eyes on North Africa as well. A premature outbreak of war was narrowly avoided when Germany sent a warship to Agadir in Morocco in 1911 – finally making a deal with France, which also coveted Morocco. France was already moving troops into its territory, had seized what became the big port city of Casablanca and in 1912 formally established a French Protectorate in all but Morocco's northern strip, which was already under Spanish control.[16]

When the First World War began, British, French, Australian and New Zealand forces captured most of the under-garrisoned German colonies during the first months of the conflict. In the Allied camp, Japan seized most of the German possessions in China and the South Pacific early in the war with the help of small British detachments.

German East Africa proved a much tougher nut to crack. In the eyes of the Asquith government and their secret helpers, it necessitated the undermining of the German colonial economy there. In August 1914 the British promptly began hostilities against the Germans in Tanganyika. The Royal Navy bombarded the coastal towns of Bagamoyo and Dar es Salaam, capital of today's independent Tanzania. British-commanded Indian forces were then moved to East Africa for the campaign. However, the German commander General Paul Emil von Lettow-Vorbeck proved to be a formidable adversary. He defeated a hugely superior Allied landing force in November 1914. The Allies made little progress until November 1915. Royal Navy units won control of Lake Tanganyika. In the summer of 1916 landing forces occupied Tanga in July and Bagamoyo. Portugal had entered the war on the Allied side. South African General Jan Smuts and a Portuguese force pushed Lettow-Vorbeck's forces back into the south-east corner of the colony by the end of 1916.

In 1917 Lettow-Vorbeck went over to the offensive. He captured Mahiwa in Tanganyika, then invaded Portuguese East Africa (modern Mozambique). By then commanding only a band of 3,000 Europeans and 11,000 Askaris (African suppletives), Lettow-Vorbeck waged daring raids and guerrilla warfare against a combined Allied force of 375,000. On 2 November 1918, as the exhausted Allies and defeated Germans were winding down the war in Europe to the armistice signed 11 November, Lettow-Vorbeck invaded the British colony of Rhodesia. He was still fighting when the armistice was supposed to take effect in Africa on 14 November. He didn't surrender his forces in Mozambique until 25 November. It had taken the British two weeks to find him and tell him the war was over. The East African campaign cost the British about 60,000 casualties. Lettow-Vorbeck's Askari colonial troops enjoyed such prestige in Germany that the Weimar Republic later gave them pensions. Germany's defeat in 1918 ended the German Empire for good. The Versailles Treaty split German East Africa among the Allies, giving the eastern part to Belgium as Ruanda-Urundi, a small patch south of the Rovuma River to Portugal for Mozambique and the rest to Britain, which named it Tanganyika.

During his four-year campaign, Lettow-Vorbeck had tied up almost a million Allied troops from the Gold Coast, The Gambia, Nigeria, South Africa, British East Africa, Uganda, Zanzibar, the Belgian Congo, Mozambique, India, the West Indies and Britain. Clearly, German East Africa was an important target for black British economic warfare.

News of the British counterfeiting campaign against German East Africa, like those against Germany and Turkey, trickled slowly out of philatelists' circles. The British forgers produced bogus stamps, some of them obvious parodies and propaganda stamps, a phenomenon repeated in the Second World War and since by warring governments, including the United States. In the First World War the British printed five labels imitating regular German East Africa stamps and depicting Kaiser Wilhelm's yacht, which became known as the 'Hohenzollern Yacht Series'. Optimistically, the British printers overprinted 'G.E.A. BRITISH OCCUPATION'.

The British Royal Navy's blockade of much of Europe was well under way when Maurice Hankey agreed to join the banknote counterfeiting scheme, which also included African seaports. The British blockade halted the import of raw materials and supplies for Lettow-Vorbeck's forces in East Africa. The local banks ran out of imperial reichsmarks imported from Germany. So in March 1915 the German authorities approved production of 'interim banknotes' in the colony. They believed that the war would soon be over with a German victory and that the notes would not be needed for long.

Two important sources for these British forgeries are Bernard Schaaf's article in *The Currency Collector* for the year 1972 and his article 'The Paper Money of German East Africa' in *The Bank Note Reporter* for November 1976. Schaaf reports that genuine 'interim 20 Rupien notes' were printed in Tabora dated '15 März 1915'. He continues:

> In the neighbouring colony of British East Africa, the British forged the notes in an attempt to destroy the economy of the German colony. The British forgeries are rare, but easy to identify. The paper is not three-layer [as in the genuine notes], the colour is a deeper shade of pink, and the handwritten serial number of the front of the note does not match the printed serial number on the back of the note.[17]

A dealer who had sold one for $400 in June 1983 told Friedman that the forged note was possibly identical with one sold in another collection in 1979. 'It is apparent,' Friedman comments, 'that this is a very rare forgery and few have surfaced in the eighty-plus years since the end of the First World War.'[18]

What were the Real Allied War Aims?

Dismantling, seizing and partitioning Germany's short-lived colonial empire and taking over its markets and labour forces had become one of the successful accomplishments of the victorious First World War Allies, Britain and France. In Europe their primary goals, neither of which they achieved, had been the total destruction and rollback into Germany's own territory of the imperial German armed forces as well as their total defeat at sea.

The ultimate Allied victory depended to a large extent on the near-destruction of imperial Germany's economy. The war and the ensuing peace settlements achieved this. Financial historian J. Orlin Grabbe goes so far as to declare flatly:

> The war of 1914 . . . was fought by England, not on France's behalf nor on Belgium's, but . . . to dispose of Germany, if possible, for good, as an economic rival. In 1916 there set in, side by side with the military war, a systematic economic war, to be carried on when the other inevitably came to an end.[19]

Grabbe and other writers see the onerous financial burdens the Allies imposed on Germany in the Versailles Treaty reparation requirements as a kind of extension of the 1916–19 economic warfare.

Especially after Prussia's defeat of France in the 1870–1 war, Bismarck's Germany had not immediately experienced an economic boom. The German economy did not really recover until 1895. After that, with the exception of two minor recessions in 1901 and 1908, it enjoyed relative prosperity not only for the big industrialists and the private bankers, but also for the middle and even working class. In the later 1890s, an early form of globalization swept the world. This helped Germany to catch up with its European neighbours, as well as the British and French colonial empires. Its components included electrification, the coming of the automobile and resulting motorization, and above all, wireless communication.

In 1914, Allied economic warfare, running parallel with the successful British sea blockade, included the counterfeiting operations and the discreet but powerful currency wars conducted by the Allied governments and their central bankers.

Germany, like Britain, France and other principal European players, possessed a stable currency, the imperial reichsmark (afterwards referred to as the mark). It was valued at 4.2 to the US dollar. Under the pressure of the British blockade and other measures as the war progressed, the mark began slowly to inflate and lose value: it stood at 8.9 marks to the dollar at the end of the war in 1918. This soon escalated into hundreds, thousands and millions of marks to the dollar. By 1923, the runaway hyperinflation, accompanied and certainly augmented by the disclosure of huge amounts of counterfeit money in the system, had dropped the mark's value to about *one trillion* to the dollar, a phenomenon examined in some detail in the next chapter.

When the war began, all the belligerents, including Germany and Austro-Hungary but excepting Great Britain, went off the gold standard and suspended convertibility of their paper monies into gold and silver. Governments and central banks in the belligerent states officially controlled markets and regulated financial transactions. However, neutrals such as Switzerland and Sweden operated free money markets, a pattern largely repeated in the Second World War. The private bankers and moneychangers in these countries reaped windfall profits. It was almost certainly to these markets, especially those in Holland, where British intelligence had many officers and agents, that Captain Hall directed the contents of his sealed wine crates stuffed with counterfeit banknotes and stamps. Some of the forgeries could easily have been dropped from the air over Germany or smuggled in across land frontiers.

In the neutral free markets, the value of the French franc fell by 8 per cent soon after the start of the war. Italy's lira dropped by 17 per cent, and Czarist Russia's ruble plummeted by 28 per cent. Sterling was initially stronger, given a lift by a flight of capital from the Continent. Already challenging sterling for the title of world reserve currency, the US dollar remained stable. The French franc eventually stabilized. The Belgian franc buckled and nearly collapsed under the German occupation of Belgium. As already mentioned, the Germans were rumoured to be counterfeiting Belgian money during the war. Britain remained the principal banker to the Allies, until German submarine warfare and President Woodrow Wilson brought the US into the conflict in 1917.

However, in 1915, the year in which the British were preparing their covert forgery of German marks, large flows of gold into the US threatened to weaken sterling. The Bank of England then pegged the dollar–pound rate at $4.764 to £1. To support sterling, Britain intervened in the New York market in an operation managed by the J. P. Morgan Bank. It was financed by loans floated in New York and by obligatory surrender by British investors of their US dollar assets. According to bankers, the $4.764 rate was a gross overvaluing of sterling. It gave Britain access to the huge quantities of dollars it needed for massive purchases in North America of munitions, foodstuffs and all manner of goods needed for the war effort.

Post-War Financial Vulnerability

The values of currencies during the conflict came to be seen as a way of measuring how successful each nation was in its war effort.

The German mark, floating at the time, and the Russian ruble were the most sensitive and vulnerable of the belligerents' monies. All the other European states supported their currencies, but the Kaiser's financial strategists were the most aggressive currency warriors.

As Cornell University professor Jonathan Kirshner points out, a German war aim was to achieve a separate peace with Russia. Even without any known counterfeiting of rubles by the Central Powers, the Czar's money steadily sank in value with the military reverses that eventually drove Russia to abandon the war, which helped bring about the Bolshevik Revolution in 1917. The German strategists who facilitated Lenin's return from exile to lead the revolution in Russia knew very well that the weaker Russia's money became, the more Russia had to gain from leaving the Allied coalition and concluding a separate peace.

Before the war, the ruble was almost totally covered by gold and was convertible into gold and silver. By the time of the Russian Revolution, gold coverage had dropped to 8 per cent. Speculators bet against the likelihood of Russia winning the war, and the ruble continued to fall; a fall probably assisted by domestic counterfeiting.

In 1916 when Moscow began making its first overtures for a separate peace with Berlin, the Kaiser's financial warriors collected all the rubles they could buy and dumped them at bargain rates in the Stockholm free money market. The further devaluation this brought about raised the pressure in Russia for a separate peace. The Germans gained valuable hard currencies such as Swedish kroner and Swiss francs that enabled the Kaiser's men to buy needed war supplies. They also used the hard currency to buy up marks and so slow their decline in value, which in all probability had been accelerated by the British counterfeiting operation.

To protect the German and Austrian currencies, both nations banned the publication of foreign exchange data. Profiteering speculators had to operate in the dark. In Geneva, Zurich, Stockholm and other neutral markets the Germans and traders in their service began buying up marks in great quantities and selling French francs and other currencies. This did little to stop deterioration of the mark against the US dollar, but it did temporarily lift the value of the mark from 60 to 90 French francs. Germany's dumping of rubles in Sweden didn't win the war with Russia or bring about the Peace of Brest-Litovsk on 3 March 1918, in which Russia abandoned its conquests or jurisdictions in Poland, the Ukraine, Lithuania, the Baltic provinces, Finland and Transcaucasia. But, as Kirshner points out, Germany's ruble dumping was the first modern case of 'direct currency manipulation for political ends'.[20] It was a precedent for the massive Nazi counterfeiting and other currency manipulations during the Second World War.

Both the Allies and the Central Powers juggled exchange rates and counterfeited enemy money. All did their best to shore up the value of their own currencies and undermine that of their enemies. The after-effects of the Allied operations speeded the inflation, hyperinflation and ruin of Weimar Germany's economy and middle class. These in turn paved the way first for the rise of communism, then for the rise of Adolf Hitler and his fascist Nazi Party.

Conflicting and ineffectual efforts of the First World War Allies in the 1920s to prevent all of this; the economic ruin and partial recovery of the Weimar Republic; and the post-war counterattacks against the Allies by Fascists and clandestine money forgers in defeated Germany, Austria, Hungary and the rest of Europe are our next subjects.

Nine

Forgers, Fraudsters and Fascists: The Weimar Years

> Germany had lost a war and almost sleepwalked into a republic for which it wasn't prepared . . . It was a time of great misery, with legless war veterans riding the sidewalks on rolling planks in a nation that seemed to consist of nothing but beggars, whores, invalids and fat-necked speculators.
>
> *Hans Sahl,* Memoirs of a Moralist, *1934*

German Jews and others who managed to survive the economic, political and moral miseries of both the Weimar era in the 1920s and the Hitler era in the 1930s and 1940s can never forget either. These two twentieth-century disasters are joined in history like Siamese twins. The collapse of German finances from 1918 onwards drove them both.

At New York's Council on Foreign Relations in 1965, Walter Levy, a German-born international oil consultant, talked about having been a boy in the impoverished post-First World War Weimar Republic. He related how in the prosperous, pre-war Germany of 1903, his father had signed up for an insurance policy. Faithfully he had paid his premiums every month on the twenty-year policy. When it came due at the height of the German hyper-inflation of 1923, the elder Herr Levy cashed the policy. With the proceeds – a load of banknotes with face denominations in billions of marks – he was able to buy a single loaf of bread.[1]

Yesterday's journalists and today's historians agree that the misery and starvation of both Germany's working blue-collar and its clerical white-collar classes helped to boost Adolf Hitler and his National Socialist German Workers (NSDAP or Nazi) Party to power in 1933. They have traced many of the causes of the relentless fall in value of the paper reichsmark to the point of total worthlessness. Plenty of counterfeit notes of unknown or forgotten origins circulated in that downward spiral along with the Weimar government's mass-produced official paper money and other notes printed by the banks or authorities of the *Länder* (states) or even of cities and towns. What no one has been able or perhaps willing to probe and measure is how much of the wartime and post-war currency forgery by Britain or other Allies fed the 'fevered' (to use Walter Levy's term) German hyperinflation.

Currency counterfeiting by a master criminal forger was directly instrumental in producing the form of fascism, sometimes called 'corporatism', adopted by the stern and austere thirty-six-year Salazar regime in Portugal. (This case is considered in the next chapter.) Currency counterfeiting is also a historical culprit in failed attempts by Stalin in the 1920s and the much more concerted operation by Hitler in the 1939–45 World War to destroy Western economies and societies. Because Benito Mussolini and his fascist advisers in Italy were shrewd enough to head off both severe inflation and to fight counterfeiting with drastic methods, neither ever seriously threatened his dictatorship.

It is worthwhile to look at a few clues to counterfeiting's role in the rise of history's supremo of fascism, Adolf Hitler. The rise and the accompanying collapse of Germany's middle classes during the Weimar years were tragedies that could have been, and at times almost were, avoided by the main actors. These actors included vindictive Allied statesmen, especially the French and Belgians, who had suffered so much at the hands of Germany during the war that they imposed the oppressive and unrealizable conditions of the Versailles and other peace agreements. Other culprits included many of the post-war German politicians, from focused extremists and negligent democrats to bankers, honest and otherwise, to fascist and communist ideologues, and all manner of adventurers and criminals, some of whom we will presently discuss.

Revolutionary Times

America's entry into the First World War in April 1917 had thrown into the scales huge quantities of money, manpower and weapons that decisively tipped the balance in favour of the Allies. Linked with efficient economic espionage, Allied economic warfare, especially the British blockade, overwhelmingly worked. Submarine warfare, the Kaiser's main response to the blockade, had failed, thanks largely to the men and women of Room 40 in British naval intelligence. When they were not forging the enemy's currencies (evidently more a side activity than a principal one), they were breaking their codes and ciphers, and so predicting and ultimately intercepting the movements of their submarines and surface ships.

Although some hard money and strategic materials were sneaked into Germany, Austria-Hungary and Turkey from neutrals, the shortages of food and fuel in the parts of Europe the Central Powers controlled were soon acute. In Germany clothing as well as food became scarce. People in Germany, Austria-Hungary, as well as in countries and areas they occupied, such as Belgium and Serbia, began to suffer unbearable living conditions. As staple grains like wheat and rye were vanishing, people often had to make do with bread made from potatoes and turnips. Vast numbers of cattle, sheep, goats and horses were being slaughtered for food, leading to livestock shortages across most of Europe.

By the late summer and autumn of 1918, the last great German offensive in France had failed. The German commanders-in-chief, Generals Paul Ludwig von Hindenburg and Erich Ludendorff, warned Kaiser Wilhelm II that October 1918 would offer the last chance to make any kind of honourable peace with the Allies. Prince Max of Baden, Wilhelm's cousin, was appointed chancellor. As such he asked President Woodrow Wilson for peace terms. The Allies were willing to dictate, rather than negotiate. They imposed the harshest terms deemed possible in the armistice signed at Compiègne, France, where Hitler would later impose his own harsh terms on a France defeated in the German *Blitzkrieg* of 1940. The signers were supreme commanders French Marshal Frederic

Foch and German General Wilhelm Groener. Some historians believe the Allies should not have agreed to an armistice before they could militarily occupy any territory inside Germany. This school of thought also holds that President Wilson erred by refusing to deal directly with the German Supreme Council, the real leadership at the helm.

The result was that the German people as a whole had no idea how truly total and disastrous their defeat was. In this view, there arose the enduring German myth, fondled, amplified and propagated by Hitler and his chief ideologues such as Josef Goebbels, of 'the stab in the back'. Germany had not really lost the war, ran the tale; instead it was betrayed by 'subversives' at home – 'pacifists, liberals, Socialists, Communists and especially Jews [specifically certain bankers] had so weakened the domestic front that the military arm could no longer function'.[2]

The distinguished historian and media commentator Niall Ferguson has powerfully summarized the causes of Weimar's eventual collapse in *The War of the World*, published in 2006. Ferguson argues that by creating a socialist welfare state while seeking to pay (but also to evade, Ferguson could have added) the huge reparations imposed by the Versailles Treaty, the Weimar regime tried to do the impossible. This produced the hyperinflation of 1923, the year of Hitler's failed Beer Hall Putsch in Munich. During his resulting imprisonment Hitler wrote *Mein Kampf*, still a bestseller in neo-fascist and anti-Semitic circles today. After a few years of recovery, a world depression began in 1929 and the steep German deflation followed. The inflation, Ferguson reminds us, signalled to Germans the collapse of their formerly solid middle-class society. There was no more of the *Ruhe und Ordnung*, 'the peace and order that had been so dear' to earlier German society. These qualities were wiped out by the rapid series of communist and rightist coups and upheavals, many bringing with them bloodshed, from 1918 until the hyperinflation eased in the mid-1920s. Germany's political disintegration, which opened the door to Hitler's victory in free elections in 1933, 'had begun seven years prior to the election breakthrough of 1930, with the wheelbarrows of worthless cash that symbolized Weimar's bankruptcy'.[3]

The upheavals had begun before the war's end, with a brief German naval mutiny at Kiel in mid-October 1918. There followed a far-leftist revolt in Munich inspired by socialist journalist Kurt Eisner (1868–1919). He put the full blame for the war on Germany, not exactly a popular idea at the time. The Bavarians were broke. They profoundly distrusted their inflating paper reichsmarks. Bavaria was being innundated with counterfeits as well. Many believed that even more counterfeits would follow if victorious Allied troops occupied southern Germany (the First World War Allies never did). King Ludwig of Bavaria fled, and workers, peasants and soldiers formed Soviet-style ruling councils. They proclaimed a short-lived republic on 7 November. The agitation spread to Berlin. There, a former saddle-maker named Friedrich Ebert was being sworn in as chancellor of a new all-German republic, which was soon to move its capital to Weimar, following the Kaiser's abdication.

A marriage of convenience temporarily joined the moderate Majority Socialist Party and the Bolshevik-inclined Independent Socialists. Challenging this shaky union were 'Spartacists' led by people like pro-Soviet Karl Liebknecht and Rosa Luxemburg. Both communist leaders were killed amid considerable bloodshed in Berlin. Against the Reds, President Ebert successfully used the reborn 'republican' German army, the Reichswehr, comprised of some war veterans and hungry young recruits who needed employment and bread. The armistice terms and the later Versailles Treaty would deprive them of their heavy weapons, armour, and their warships and aircraft. These had to be junked or turned over to the Allies.

Armed with strict instructions not to yield to exorbitant Allied demands, Ebert government delegates went to Versailles in April 1919. When the Allied dictating of terms was over, the Germans had to accept things they had never dreamed could be so draconian: Germany gave up one-eighth of its territory, 6.5 million of its people, all its colonies everywhere in the world and all foreign investments. The investment clauses meant of course that Germany had already lost hundreds of millions in hard currency in foreign hands before it even began trying to pay reparations. Territorial losses in Europe included Alsace-Lorraine, which returned to

France; Eupen, Malmedy and Moresmot went to Belgium; parts of Upper Silesia went to Poland and the new state of Czechoslovakia; West Prussia and Posen went to Poland; Danzig was lost to a League of Nations mandate; Memel went to Allied rule; Kiachow in China went to Japan; and all the remaining Pacific and African powers were given to the Allied nations under nominal League of Nations mandates. The Allies were temporarily to occupy the Rhineland. The Reichswehr was limited to 100,000 men and conscription abolished. The navy was limited to just a few surface ships and no submarines. The German General Staff was abolished. The crowning humiliation was the Treaty's Article 231, holding the Central Powers responsible for all losses and damage of the war. This clause was the basis for the huge reparation obligations.[4] All this, of course, was grist for the nationalist and soon, the Nazi propaganda mills.

Counterfeits . . . and Countermeasures

From 1914–18, while the government kept printing money to finance the war, the imperial reichsmark lost its value only slowly. In August 1914 it had stood at 4.20 marks to the US dollar. The tightening and continuing Allied economic warfare, mainly the British blockade, made it necessary to keep printing money also to supply outlying outposts of the German Empire with funds – mainly, as seen in the last chapter, in the case of the British-printed German East Africa marks.

German bankers at first saw little danger in the inflation, reasoning that some inflation happens during any long war. Big creditors and industrialists even welcomed it, figuring that some day they would be able to make windfalls by calling in debts that had to be paid in much more valuable hard currency. But during the rioting and unrest through the period of the armistice and the first weeks of 1919, even before Versailles was signed, the mark had dropped to 8.90 per dollar. The costs of demobilization and of handing over huge amounts of war material and fuel to the victorious Allies accelerated inflation. Mindful that Germany ended the war with a national debt of 144 billion marks, of which 89 billion were in long-term bonds and 55 billion in other paper, the government and the Reichsbank spurred the new republic's presses to keep printing more and more paper money.[5]

At the same time, more counterfeit paper cash of varying quality, printed either inside or outside the country (most likely both), began to pour into the economy. The rumour spread that the Reichsbank and private banks, including the big Deutsche Bank, were perhaps unwittingly accepting false notes and reissuing them. (There was a somewhat similar but brief problem in America in the early 1990s. Testing at the US Federal Reserve Bank in Miami, Florida, failed to detect some of the Supernotes coming from the Middle East. Their value was covered by issuing new genuine notes to replace them.)

In June 1919 the Reichsbank issued an official statement denying the allegations of its acceptance of forgeries published by two leading Dutch periodicals, the *Nederlandische Financier Bourskourant* and the *Algemeen Handelsblad*. Germany's *Deutsche Allgemeine Zeitung* also cited the *Handelsblad* as charging that Russians were handing out forged Bavarian provincial banknotes at Berlin's posh Adlon Hotel. Bavaria's bank of issue, its central bank and its government were all notified of the allegations, but they seem not to have followed up on them.[6]

In mid-1920, French troops marched into the Ruhr without consulting the other Allies to try to force reparations payments and seize German assets, including railway rolling stock, coal and even telephone poles. By this time, the quantities of forged paper money surfacing in the German economy had reached enormous proportions. The French operations gave rise to rumours that the occupation troops brought forged German money with them, to spend for their own needs and wants. The Berlin police president, together with the Reichsbank, found it necessary to create a new special anti-counterfeiting unit. The old anti-Semitic bias of many Germans, which Hitler and his Nazi ideologues were already busy developing into a virtual national religion, appeared in German press stories about alleged illicit currency traffic by Russian Jews.[7] Ironically, even as circulation of counterfeits began to get out of hand, official inflation temporarily dropped.

The respite was brief. By the first weeks of 1922, the exchange rate had crept up to 20 paper marks to one US dollar. 'In other words,' as one of Germany's most perceptive journalists and historians, Sebastian Haffner, observed, 'Germany's monetary assets had disappeared.'[8]

What were the main causes of the hyperinflation? And what average proportion of the masses of paper marks were counterfeits, imported or domestic? The first question is much more easily answered than the second. Other world currencies have inflated, hyperinflated and collapsed. It happened in Shanghai awaiting takeover by the Maoists at the end of the Chinese Civil War in 1949. In Argentina during July 1989, prices rose by nearly 200 per cent. But Germany's paper money plague was the worst ever to batter into ruins an advanced (although war-weary) economy. It followed political events rather closely, including the stages of Hitler's rise. By the time of his Beer Hall Putsch on 9 November 1923 the mark quotation for one US dollar had galloped from 17,972 in January to 40,000 in July. It then rocketed to 4.2 *trillion* in November. Most historians identify the main cause of this acceleration as impoverishment by the punitive French (and later Belgian) occupation of the Ruhr during the previous winter and spring, after French President Raymond Poincaré had declared Germany in default of its Versailles Treaty reparation obligations.[9]

Deeper origins of the crisis, of course, lay in the 1914–18 war. Less than 10 per cent of budgets came from taxation by the wartime parliaments. Sir Edward Montagu, Prime Minister David Lloyd George and the other architects of British and Allied economic warfare, including the British currency counterfeiting enterprise, must have known that wartime German parliaments continued to suspend the citizens' rights to convert paper banknotes into gold. The Reichsbank was authorized to use government and commercial paper securities as reserves. Law required such reserves to be held against newly issued banknotes. So, to finance the war, the German and Austro-Hungarian governments simply ran the printing presses at ever-greater capacity.

From 1919 to 1923, there was a huge German deficit, measured in billions of gold marks. Taxes never climbed above 35 per cent of expenditures. Money printing, some of it by private and provincial banks, reached what the British newspaper *The Economist* called 'heroic' proportions.[10] As John Maynard Keynes and other economists had vainly warned the French and other Allied governments, the reparation demands formalized and hardened by the start of the crisis year of 1923 were far beyond the value of all of Germany's assets. Demands comprised not only compensation for physical war damage and casualties. They also included paying the pensions of Allied soldiers, dead and alive. Even ignoring some paper that today's financial wizards would probably call 'junk bonds', the total came to the value of $17.5 billion. This was an astronomical figure in those days, about half of Britain's gross domestic product (GDP). The Allies, especially the French, did not want to see Germany boosting its exports. Nor were they eager, as *The Economist* noted, to supply any of their labour to help rebuild Europe.

So as printing presses spewed out all manner of official and bogus notes, the total money supply in Germany in face values rose from 29.2 billion marks in November 1903 to 497 *quintillion* (that is, 497 followed by eighteen zeros) in November 1923, the duration of Walter Levy's father's ill-fated insurance policy.

The Weimar government promoted a wide campaign of positive resistance to the French and Belgian occupation troops. (One of its activities was secret counterfeiting of French currency, as we will see below.) To pay the workers involved in the general strikes that erupted in the occupied towns and industries, the Weimar government printed still more paper marks.[11] As in other hyperinflationary epidemics, during the American and French Revolutions for example, the boundary between 'official' and 'counterfeit' money grew thin and dissolved in people's perceptions. Germans rushing to buy bread, beans or books before prices went up had neither time nor inclination to scrutinize the individual banknotes in the packet needed for the purchase. Prices sometimes rose ten-fold in a single day. City governments began to print their own money on silk, linen or leather, which had far higher intrinsic values than paper. It was called *Notgeld*, emergency money. Other print shops, private and piratical, printed notes too. At the height of this pandemic of forgery, over 300 paper mills and 2,000 print shops worked twenty-four hours to meet the demand for anything that looked like real money.

In November 1923, when the Levy family cashed in their twenty-year insurance policy for a piece of bread, there was truly what Walter Levy, historian Louis Snyder and others call a 'fever dance'. In Berlin, a woman hopefully entered a butcher's shop, bearing a basketful of million- and billion-mark notes. She left it on the ground at the entrance to queue up for whatever meat might be available. She turned to find the load of marks dumped into the gutter and the empty basket stolen. Streetcar conductors would accept fares only at the end of a passenger's ride because the value of the mark would sink during the few minutes of the trip. On the other hand, 'fat cats' with foreign currency were in seventh heaven: a few $1 bills would buy the royal box at the opera. Householders had to shop several times a day for food; a pound of butter or a slab of cheese might rise in price by 500 per cent in twenty-four hours. A woman had to pay six weeks' wages for a pair of shoes.

A British couple about to celebrate their golden wedding anniversary in Berlin in 1923 received an official letter. It advised them that the *Bürgermeister* (mayor), in accordance with Prussian custom, would call and present them with a gift of money. Next morning, the mayor and several aldermen in robes arrived at the aged couple's home. They handed over, in the name of the Prussian state, 1,000,000,000,000 (one trillion) in paper marks. It was worth one halfpenny of the English couple's money.[12]

Consequences in German society of the paper money plague jump out of the printed pages and records and recordings of theatrical, musical and picture images of the period, such as the Expressionist paintings of Max Beckmann, George Grosz and others. Audiences can read works such as Christopher Isherwood's *The Berlin Stories*, published in 1946, or watch either the later stage version, *I am a Camera*, or the musical *Cabaret*. One contemporary writer described a Berlin street where

> a portrait of the Kaiser was flanked by nude women; the Crown Prince of Meiningen stood cheek by jowl with 'documents of

> feminine beauty' . . . Further down you were invited to behold the 'Anatomical Wonder Cabaret' . . . Prostitutes, pimps, peddlers. From raincoats to cocaine, from jewels to love – everything on hand, immediate delivery . . . Since one part of the population had sold everything it possessed and another exchanged its dollars only for 'tangible goods', a clearance sale in human beings began. As in normal times people sell their labours, strength or intelligence, today they they sold themselves, body and soul . . . Everything had its price, and with the dollar at millions of marks, the price was very low.[13]

People bartered what possessions of any value they had, especially those of precious metal, for food, clothing or medicine. Germany's fat-cat capitalists with access to dollars, sterling or other real money acquired huge fortunes, especially by holding on to the debts others owed them. However, people with fixed incomes and bank accounts, insurance policies and pensions all in marks were ruined. The middle classes, who like the impoverished blue-collar wage earners would later embrace Hitler and his policies of state-subsidized full employment, lost whatever savings and property they had. Some of the biggest firms, like ThyssenKrupp and I. G. Farben holding foreign currency reinforced by American and other lenders, continued to prosper through the worst months, despite the bleeding of German assets for reparations. Big creditors, like some private banks, reaped bonanza profits by holding old debts of foreigners denominated in depreciating marks, which had to be paid off in gold, silver, dollars or sterling from abroad.

Americans to the Rescue . . . Sort of

A glimmer of salvation appeared amid the shadows, just before Hitler's first failed bid for power in Munich in November 1923.

Gustav Stresemann (1878–1929), the most statesman-like of all the Weimar politicians, had become prime minister in August 1923. He soon set to work to lift Germany out of the abyss. Stresemann's government set up a new Rentenbank to issue new currency to replace the flood of worthless and counterfeit paper which was soon officially recalled or otherwise junked. Dr Hjalmar Horace Greeley Schacht (1877–1970), the same reported earlier to have been counterfeiting Belgian francs during the 1914–18 German occupation of Belgium, was appointed as special currency commissioner. He put an almost instant halt to the official printing of paper money. Schacht's Rentenbank began issuing the new Rentenmark, meant to be backed up by land and property values (shades of John Law and the French assignats of the eighteenth century). Schacht gave the Rentenmark the same value as the pre-war gold reichsmark: 24 US cents.

Enter the Americans. Charles Gates Dawes (1865–1951), an American banker who was to share the Nobel Prize in 1925 for rescuing Germany and would serve as Republican vice president of the US under President Calvin Coolidge from 1925 to 1929, now stepped in. Dawes was named head of a committee also including European allies tasked to manage German reparations. After a long and careful study of Germany's real ability to pay reparations, Dawes and his staff produced the so-called Dawes Plan of April 1924. It established effective foreign control of Germany's finances. It indexed actual reparations payments levied to Germany's revenues, such as a new transport tax, railway bonds, industrial debentures and revenue from sales of commodities like beer, tobacco and sugar. However, it set no final deadline for winding up payments. Germany would have to keep paying indefinitely, without knowing how long it had to keep paying. The deal was sweetened by a series of liberal US loans.

So American funds now began pouring into Germany. Germany used the dollars, or some of them, to pay reparations: this recycled funds to the US as well as partially satisfying the Versailles Treaty demands of the other Allies. Britain and France, receiving most of the reparations money, were supposed to pay their multi-million-dollar war debts to the United States. America in turn would send more money to Europe, especially Germany, as funds and investments.

German politicians and industrialists soon fell into the habit of expecting an indefinite flow of US dollars, which by 1927 (as explored in the next chapter) Stalin was already trying to undermine by counterfeiting despite his own urgent need for real dollars. The Great Depression, triggered by the US stock market collapse of 1929, would soon disabuse Germans of the illusion of a perpetual dollar intake: the investments and loans dried up.[14] There were disastrous bank failures, like that of Vienna's Creditanstalt in 1930, and resulting depression and strengthening of fascism in continental Europe.

During the first months of the Stresemann administration in 1923–4, along with the new Rentenmark came government 'gold loan' notes, maturing and payable in 1935. Much more quickly than it rose, inflation dramatically declined. Prices soon stabilized. Consumer goods, from meat and butter to bread made from real wheat and rye, replaced the ersatz bread of the worst months. However, the hyperinflation had left indelible scars on German society. Millions of Germans lost their life savings. Later, fanned by the Nazi propaganda of men such as Josef Goebbels and editor Julius Streicher, to say nothing of Hitler himself in *Mein Kampf*, they came to believe in the old conspiracy theory: Germany since 1914 had been stabbed in the back by a cabal of Jews, international financiers and local appeasers of the reparation-thirsty Allies.

Elias Canetti, a German author who won the Nobel Prize for literature in 1981, used principles of group psychology to weave the plots of his novels. He compared the Nazi treatment of the Jews to the Weimar hyperinflation: depreciation and degradation to the point where the Jews, like Germany's former reichsmark, could be 'destroyed with impunity by the millions'. *The Economist* in 1999 editorialized that Canetti strained the analogy, but added that 'he was right that a debauched currency was one reason why a whole country could lose its virtue'.[15]

Some Counterattacking Counterfeiters

Budapest in the early 1920s was the capital of a defeated, impoverished and bankrupt Hungary, beset by inflation and currency counterfeiting and fearing increases in both. The 1920 Treaty of Trianon deprived the old Hungarian portion of Austria-Hungary of nearly three-quarters of its territory and two-thirds of its inhabitants. The new smaller Hungary agreed to pay the Allies reparations, to keep an army of only 35,000 men, and to assume part of the old Austro-Hungarian debt. Its eight million remaining inhabitants had suffered a revolution in late 1918. They afterwards failed to establish a republican government, run by a partnership of a liberal-minded aristocrat, Count Michael Karolyi, and Bela Kun, a Hungarian Bolshevik henchman of Lenin who had been imprisoned in Budapest after his return from Moscow. Bela Kun soon turned Hungary into a brief communist dictatorship. He was driven from power and had to flee when Romanian troops invading Hungary reached Budapest, which they thoroughly looted as they withdrew in February 1920. Before signing the Trianon Treaty, Nicholas Horthy (an admiral without a navy) took over as head of state. He proclaimed Hungary a monarchy with a vacant throne – Austro-Hungarian Emperor Karl had fled to Swiss exile.

The situation in post-war Hungary was highly conducive to criminal counterfeiting. The peace agreements decreed that the old Austro-Hungarian banknotes had to be overstamped by the succession states including Hungary and later replaced by a new currency. The stamps used on the old imperial notes were very easy to forge, resulting in the circulation in Hungary of a great flood of the old notes. This helped produce inflation and finally hyperinflation. After the fall of Bela Kun's Soviet republic, the former imperial central bank in Vienna declared all the korona (crown) banknotes, the first post-war Hungarian currency issued by the Bela Kun dictatorship, to be counterfeit. In 1925 the korona gave way to the new pengö, at a rate of 12,500 korona to one pengö, in a currency reform that in some ways resembled the one in Germany.

The conspiracy against the French franc, hatched in Berlin and carried out in Budapest, actually began earlier, in late 1923 and early 1924. German author Georg Kretschmann reports on one of the triggers for the attack on the franc:

> The French, during the occupation of the Ruhr in 1923, brought with them vast quantities of counterfeit Reichsmark notes, in order further to shatter the already weak finances of Germany.[16]

Kretschmann doesn't specify where the bogus marks were printed. If his information is authentic, it would be fair to speculate that they were either printed in France or Belgium, or were perhaps leftovers from undelivered contents of the wartime wine cases of British naval intelligence chief 'Blinker' Hall.

Karlheinz Walz is another German who enjoys the advantage of a professional career with the post-Second World War German Bundesbank and other financial institutions, and who has made a special study of German money forgery. In one of his books Walz reports that the intelligence service of Weimar's army, headed by General von Seeckt and sometimes dubbed the 'Black Reichswehr' because of its covert violations of the Versailles disarmament provisions in secret cooperation with the Soviet Union,

> commanded the printing of French francs and Soviet Russian banknotes. Colonel Max Hoffman recruited for this purpose former officers and criminal Russian emigrants, who did their forging with the knowledge of German government circles.[17]

The enterprise was conceived and carried out by fraudsters and fascist-minded political adventurers in Hungary in 1924. It eventually attracted so much international attention that it was one of the factors leading to creation of Interpol, the International Police Organization now headquartered in Lyon, France. The main players, all sources agree, were informal 'subcontractors' of the Weimar secret service, led by Colonels Max Hoffman and Max Bauer. They facilitated the conspirators in Hungary with their printing presses, plates and other equipment.

Main financier and effective boss of the enterprise was the scion of an old Austro-Hungarian aristocratic family, Prince Ludwig zu Windischgraetz. His family were feudal landowners, holdovers from the so-called Holy Roman Empire (which, as is often pointed out, was neither holy nor Roman: an anachronistic title of a non-existent entity that in its latter generations was roughly equivalent to the Hapsburg domains). Both the name and the Hapsburg reality expired with the post-First World War Treaty of Trianon. This deprived the Hungarian part of Austria-Hungary – transformed, like Austria itself, into a small and impoverished state beset by political and economic chaos – of two-thirds of its former territory and 58 per cent of its Magyar-speaking people. In 1924, Windischgraetz was thirty-eight years old with an adventurous past: involvement in the Russo-Japanese War of 1904; mishaps that landed him in a New York City jail during a sojourn in the United States; lion hunts in Africa; undercover work for Austro-Hungary in Serbia; losing much of the family fortune in Europe's gambling casinos and in betting on horses.

When Windischgraetz returned to Hungary after the war, he was cash-poor and laden with debts but loath to sell or barter away the family estates, whose vineyard produced Hungary's popular Tokay wines. He had badly bungled the sale of the Hapsburg family jewels and paintings for the deposed Emperor Karl. And like most of his compatriots the Prince was bitterly resentful of what the Allies had done to his impoverished country. Added to his personal grievances, the political situation in Hungary convinced him that salvation for him and Hungary might lie in the massive anti-Allied counterfeiting operation proposed by General von Seeckt and his senior intelligence officers in Germany.

Seen from Budapest or the princely Windischgraetz estates, Hungary was in desperate straits. Hungary was nominally ruled by Admiral Nicholas Horthy as regent, later described as a dictator. The dominant Union Party, led by Prime Minister Stephen Bethlen and holding 169 of 245 parliamentary seats, favoured the totally chimerical objective of restoring the Hapsburg dynasty. One of the other strongest political forces was a federation of ultra-nationalist and fascist clubs and armed militias called by its Magyar initials, the TECZ, which resembled the rightist clubs and militias simultaneously plaguing the Weimar Republic.

In late 1923 or early 1924, Windischgraetz met both General Ludendorff, who had tried to be Hitler's partner in the Beer Hall Putsch, and intelligence expert Colonel Max Bauer. Both of these German officers were desperately seeking solutions to the awful problem of paying war reparations. The Weimar army bosses had gone so far as to recruit a team of scientists, led by a Nobel Prize-winning German chemical genius Dr Fritz Haber, to extract the needed gold from seawater! That had floundered because of the astronomical costs of the theoretically possible process. When a self-styled alchemist, thirty-nine-year-old Franz Tausend, tried and failed to make gold out of iron oxide and quartz in a high-profile public experiment in Munich, hopes for that golden solution died.

Weimar's intelligence chiefs concluded that the best alternative was to forge masses of hard, gold-backed paper currency and use this to pay reparations and purchase whatever goods possible. France's gold-backed 1,000-franc notes looked like the best bet. To make the plates, the German spooks tried to recruit an expert Berlin engraver named Arthur Schulze. General Paul Hindenburg, a defender of old-fashioned Prussian virtue, objected on moral grounds to using money forgery as a weapon and vetoed using Schulze.

Windischgraetz returned to Budapest from his meetings in Germany to recruit others. He was sold on the forgery scheme. He sold it in turn to a motley crew of Hungarians eager both for personal gain and revenge against France. His fellow conspirators included Hungarian State Police Chief Emmerich von Nadossy and Army Major Ladislaus Goeroe, technical expert of the Hungarian Cartographic Institute, where the phoney francs were to be printed. Windischgraetz was able to get Arthur Schulze in Berlin secretly to supply paper for the 1,000-franc notes and a convicted professional counterfeiter named Julius Meszaros to help.

Author Murray Bloom lists three main aims that Windischgraetz outlined to his fellow plotters:

1. To produce $100 million worth of the 1,000-franc notes (then worth about $32 each), which they believed could wreck the French economy if properly disseminated.
2. To plan and finance a fascist-monarchist putsch in Hungary on Christmas Day 1925.
3. To restore to the vacant Hungarian throne Hapsburg Archduke Albert (Emperor Karl had died in 1922).

Windischgraetz agreed to find and put up funds for the venture. He secretly planned to take 40 per cent of its profits from laundering the bogus francs, a fact he didn't reveal to his fellow conspirators. He soon realized that he needed a lot of real money to make fake money. He could contribute only about $1,300. Gabriel Baross, director of the Postal Savings Bank and head of the fascist TECZ organization, made an unsecured loan of $6,000 taken from Postal Bank funds. Materials including a special printing press from Leipzig were brought from Germany, some of them on Hungarian tugboats navigating the Danube. To avoid detection by officers of the Allied Military Commission still in Budapest, dynamite was planted in parts of the Cartographic Commission in case of an inspection or raid.

By the summer of 1925, lack of funds and resulting substandard technology limited production to less than a thousand 1,000-franc notes per day. Even though they had already scaled down their goal to a mere million banknotes, worth about $32 million in American money, Prince Ludwig cut the objective to only one hundred thousand banknotes, worth $3.2 million. The plotters abandoned hopes of collapsing the French economy by breaking the Banque de France, and aspired simply to finance the planned *coup d'état* of December 1925.

Further complications developed when Baross showed their productions to Hungarian banker friends. They told him that the imitations were hopelessly poor, and wouldn't pass even a superficial inspection. Baross panicked. If a Budapest banker spotted the fakes so easily, how could he easily launder them in Western capitals familiar with the 1,000-franc notes? Baross decided to confide in Prime Minister Bethlen, who urged him not to try to circulate the notes in Hungary.

In early December 1925 the conspirators went ahead with their distribution scheme anyway. Head distributor was to be Colonel Aristide Janckowicz, who had a good military record but few if any financial skills. However, his brother-in-law, Count Caroly Czaky, the defence minister, recommended him and joined him in the 'patriotic' enterprise. Another distributor was to be Georg Marsovsky, an artillery captain, former aide to Admiral Horthy and secretary to Julius Goemboes, founder and leader of the Hungarian Fascist Party. Marsovsky was also a good friend of Archduke Albrecht, whom the monarchist-fascist plotters hoped to restore to Hungary's throne. Once the counterfeit francs had been circulated, but no later than Christmas Eve, Goemboes' fascist storm troops were to occupy Budapest. Archduke Albrecht would then be crowned King in Saint Stephan's Cathedral by Bishop Zadravetz, another of the plotters. Admiral Horthy would become royal commander-in-chief; other plotters including Goemboes would get the top cabinet posts, with Prince Ludwig Windischgraetz as prime minister.

The printed notes were stashed in the Windischgraetz family castle at Sarostpak, near Tokay and the Czech border, and at Bishop Zadravetz's home. Prince Ludwig's butler, Kasper Kovacs, sent six of the 1,000-franc notes by registered mail to a Dutch bank cashier friend named Severing, asking him to convert the 6,000 francs, worth about $192, to Dutch florins at the current exchange rate. This was done. That the fakes had initially passed muster in the Netherlands encouraged Windischgraetz to dispatch the money couriers on 12 December to the target European capitals. Each carried about $250,000 worth of the bogus French notes. A nervous Colonel Janckowicz detrained on Sunday 13 December in Amsterdam after trouble at the Dutch frontier because the masterminds in Budapest had forgotten to get a Dutch visa stamped into his diplomatic passport. He was warned to get his passport in order at The Hague by Monday. In his hotel room he opened one parcel addressed to the Hungarian minister at The Hague; took out twenty-five 1,000-franc notes, worth $8,000, and carried them to the Amsterdam Bourse in his overcoat pockets. There, by pre-arrangement, he met Marsovsky and another courier, Georg Mankowicz, who travelled under false names with forged Romanian passports. Janckowicz turned the notes over to them. By mistake, two notes fell out of their wrappings. Janckowicz lodged them in his wallet along with two genuine 1,000-franc notes and some Dutch florins.

On Tuesday Janckowicz travelled to The Hague and had his passport fixed. His mistake – which turned out to be fatal for the destiny of the entire conspiracy – was to mistakenly extract a phoney 1,000-franc note, which he believed to be one of the genuine notes, to change it for Dutch money at an exchange office.

The clerk took one look at it and angrily asked him how he dared present such a clumsy counterfeit. He phoned for the police. Janckowicz grabbed the note, stuffed it into his sock and ran. Police caught up with him. At the police station, he first tried to claim he'd obtained the note from a bank; then he claimed diplomatic immunity against arrest. At the Hungarian Legation, the Hungarian minister, who wasn't in on the plot, wouldn't vouch for him. A note the police found on Janckowicz implicated and gave the hotel addresses of the two other couriers he had met on Sunday. Police soon secured all the notes the four were carrying. At first they refused to talk. But their luck had run out: a commissioner from the French Sûreté in Paris, summoned when the six 1,000-franc notes sent by Kasper Kovacs were detected as counterfeit, remembered advance reports that Prince Windischgraetz was hatching an anti-French counterfeiting plot. K. H. Broekhoff, the Dutch State Police chief, took their confessions and wired Budapest and Paris. In Budapest, police Lieutenant Raba, one of the conspirators, wired the thinly coded message, 'AUNT ILL. COME HOME', to all the couriers. One of them, in Copenhagen, had already been caught with $200,000 worth of the fakes.

Back in Budapest, Prime Minister Bethlen and his cabinet, now under international investigation, were about to induct Hungary into the new League of Nations, with Bethlen scheduled to head the delegation to Geneva. The League was offering financial help to replace the hyperinflated korona – 67,000 to one US dollar at the time – by the new gold-backed currency, the pengö. Well aware that if he tried to block the investigation, Hungary's international standing and financial support would crumble, Bethlen knew he would have to sacrifice some close cronies and political supporters for the good name of their country.

In destroying the printing equipment and other evidence, the plotters forgot about stocks of the banknote paper Schulze had brought from Germany. Police found them, and arrests began on 2 January 1926 with Lieutenant Raba and Windischgraetz's butler Kovacs. Despite tough press censorship in Budapest, Bethlen's name repeatedly cropped up. He told the *New York Times* that he was sure that two such trusted employees must have been duped by Hungarian fascists. Then, on 4 January, Windischgraetz was arrested and Police Chief Nadossy suspended. The two were soon ensconced in cells in Budapest's grim central prison.

One of forty French detectives arriving from Paris to join the investigation, Henri Collard arrived without Hungarian money and asked his cab driver to change a genuine 1,000-franc note. The socialist cabbie took Collard to the nearest police station, claiming a reward for turning in another member of the forgers' ring!

Little by little, the conspirators in Hungary and in Germany, including Arthur Schulze, were rounded up. The General Staff of the Reichswehr, denying accurate press reports of Colonel Max Bauer's involvement, issued an admission that Murray Bloom calls 'the frankest public statement ever issued by any General Staff':

> It is admitted that the General Staff received many communications for overcoming the country's financial plight by counterfeiting foreign monies – English and American. Though these proposals were discussed, they were never adopted and preparations for making counterfeit money were never begun.[18]

Most of the conspirators were caught. Arthur Schulze and George Hir, a leader of Hungary's Fascist Awakening Party, died under suspicious circumstances: Schulze, in a padded cell in a Berlin insane asylum where he had been sent for violent behaviour in prison, and Hir, in a Budapest hospital soon after telling parliamentary investigators that he had seen a 'safe conduct guarantee' for the plotters signed by Prime Minister Bethlen. There were rumours that the two deaths had been arranged by a fascist secret society founded by Admiral Horthy and supporters, 'The League of Blood of the Double Cross', an ideological precedessor of the Hungarian Fascist Arrow Cross Society that became prominent in the nation's affairs during the Hitler era.

At the trial, which opened on 7 May 1926, of twenty-four conspirators including Windischgraetz, twenty-three parliamentary deputies testified for the defence. Franz Ulain, a fascist deputy and an attorney for Windischgraetz, called the prince an adventurous dreamer. He compared him to Poland's Marshal Josef Pilsudski and first post-First World War president, and Edvard Benes, then the Czech foreign minister and later the anti-Nazi and anti-Soviet president of Czechoslovakia. Ulain reminded the court that Napoleon had counterfeited British sterling, and that British statesman William Pitt had permitted the counterfeiting of fake French assignat currency.

The court's vedict on 26 May gave ex-Police Chief Nadossy four years' hard labour and a fine of about $2,000. Windischgraetz got four years without a fine. Goeroe, who had made the sloppy plates, got two years. Others got lesser sentences. Eventually the highest appeal court relieved Windischgraetz of hard labour. He was later transferred to the prison hospital where his wife regularly brought him gourmet food from the best Budapest bistros. A national petition for his amnesty got one hundred thousand signatures. He was given a 'leave of absence' for medical reasons and never returned to confinement.

In October 1931, when Julius Goemboes became the fascist Prime Minister, he allowed a military Court of Honour to rule that Windischgraetz accepted the legal responsibility for the forgery of the French francs to protect the Hungarian State and Nation from harm. Late in 1932, the Prince dropped his Hungarian nationality and was naturalized a German, just before Hitler's election to power in 1933. His son Aladar became a Nazi *Sturmbannführer*. Windischgraetz helped to reinforce Nazi propaganda with the ridiculous claim that the counterfeiting plot hadn't been masterminded by General Ludendorff and Colonel Bauer of Weimar's Reichswehr, but was actually the work of the Weimar democrat Gustav Stresemann, Chancellor in 1923 and Foreign Minister until his death in 1930. Stresemann shared the Nobel Peace Prize in 1926 with Aristide Briand, the French statesman who would help to conclude the Kellogg–Briand Pact of 1928 outlawing war. Accusing Stresemann suited the Nazis. They wanted to smear the Weimar Republic and also sought an excuse to end Frau Stresemann's widow's pension.

In 1940 Wilhelm Hoettl, a Nazi intelligence operative, interviewed the Prince to get tips on how to forge money in preparation for the Nazis' 'Operation Bernhard' against the Allies, the biggest counterfeiting operation of all time. Windischgraetz, embittered over his treatment for his 'patriotism', outlived many of his fascist and monarchist colleagues. He died in relative obscurity in Vienna some time in the late 1950s.[19]

Stephan Bethlen resigned as Prime Minister in 1931, mainly because he couldn't cope with renewed inflation and other financial problems. After a brief effort by Bethlen's friend, Count Julius Karolyi, to cope with the problems, Julius Goemboes took the helm as Prime Minister in October 1932. He immediately began to cosy up to Benito Mussolini's Fascist Italy in order to realize Hungary's territorial claims against Romania and Czechoslovakia. He soon visited Berlin to do the same with Hitler, as Nazi agitation and demonstrations grew in Hungary.[20]

Following the Dawes Plan, pre-Nazi Germany's post-hyperinflation stability was temporarily boosted by another American, lawyer Owen D. Young. In January 1929, shortly before the collapse of the stock market on Wall Street heralded world depression, Young became head of an Allied committee to re-examine and finally finesse the war reparations issue. After some German counterproposals, the Young Plan, as it came to be called, was announced in June.

Germany was to undertake responsibility for transferring payment in German marks into foreign currency. A new Bank for International Settlements in Basel, Switzerland, was created to handle this. All of the West's main central banks were represented on the board. Germany was supposed to pay annuities ending in 1988, increasing gradually for the first thirty-six years. The annuities were secured by a mortgage on German state railways. The total annuity of 1.7 billion marks was less than Germany had been successfully paying under the Dawes Plan, and so its creators believed this would be a permanent settlement.[21] After Hitler became German chancellor and dictator in 1933–4, he repudiated all of the 'Versailles *diktat*', including disarmament and reparations and began preparing for new German conquests in Europe.

By the mid-1920s, Europe's pandemic of currency forging had already begun spreading. It was also helping to spread fascism to other countries, notably Portugal. And with the help of a crooked

Berlin Bank, Soviet dictator Josef Stalin had decided to counterfeit and distribute vast quantities of American dollars, with the objectives of paying Soviet spies abroad; buying whatever vital commodities could be bought with expertly forged dollars; and undermining the American capitalist economy, which had saved the infant Soviet Union both before and after Lenin's death in 1924 from the mass starvation that followed the Bolshevik Revolution and civil war that followed. These are the subjects of the next chapters.

Ten

Portugal: Clever Crook Empowers Durable Dictator

> This small country, with its variety of climates and mixture of racial strains, is an assiduous copyist, mimic and borrower . . . The rich in Portugal are said to be the richest in Europe.
>
> *Mary McCarthy, 1955*

The most ambitious 'private' criminal counterfeiting scheme of the twentieth century led to the longest-lasting fascist regime anywhere: the 1932–68 dictatorship of Portugal's António de Oliveira Salazar. His quasi-fascist, 'corporatist' *Estado Novo* (New State), modelled in some respects after Mussolini's Fascist Italy, eventually succumbed to democracy in the mid-1970s. It had witnessed the gradual crumbling, then final loss of Portugal's large colonial empire.

The jewel of that empire was considered to be Angola, rich in petroleum, diamonds, phosphates and copper, and since 2006 a member of the international oil cartel, OPEC. The financial panic and chaos wrought unintentionally by Artur Virgílio Alves dos Reis, a master forger who dreamed of riches and devised an almost perfect currency counterfeiting scheme, arguably contributed heavily to the loss of Angola.

After a bloody struggle, Angola won independence in 1975, the same year that Portugal emerged from dictatorship. Alves Reis, a chastened dreamer and ex-jailbird, had seen his dreams of wealth and power in a future, prosperous Portugal and Angola dissolve. There is much irony here: the huge, sprawling and run-down African colony of Angola was rich in resources but notoriously misruled. It was also the country where Alves Reis began his career of skilful white-collar crime.

Alves Reis hoped that his impeccably printed Portuguese escudo banknotes, wisely invested, would help Angola to blossom into a colonial paradise and enrich himself and his small band of fellow schemers. Instead, his fantastic and daring but eventually failed enterprise was followed by many years of economic, social and political upheavals in the Portugal that Alves Reis had once dreamed of dominating himself.

Though largely forgotten now, the Salazar regime and Portugal's empire survived a premier among terrorist challenges: the first successful hijacking of a cruise liner on the high seas, not unlike a classic act of piracy. On 24 January 1961, former Portuguese Navy Captain Henrique Galvão and a posse of Latin American revolutionaries, together with a band of mercenary guerrillas they'd recruited, seized control of the Portuguese luxury cruise liner *Santa Maria*. They shot dead a ship's mate who resisted, and wounded two crewmembers. They then proclaimed the start of a 'liberation struggle' against Salazar, acting in the name of General Delgado, former military attaché in Washington, where he had picked up liberal and democratic ideas. Delgado had been defeated in an apparently rigged presidential election in 1958 by Salazar's official candidate, Admiral Amerigo Tomas. The *Santa Maria*'s seizure panicked the Salazarist authorities in Lisbon into calling for help from their British and American allies. Galvão's plan was to steer the ship and hostages to Fernando Po, a Portuguese African colony, then to Angola to raise army mutinies in the two colonies. He hoped the rebellious contagion would spread to mainland Portugal and overthrow Salazar.

US and British planes and ships shadowed the errant liner, which changed course for Brazil after Portuguese warships were readied off the African coast. On 2 February Galvão surrendered. He released and disembarked the 607 captive passengers and crew at Recife, Brazil. The Brazilian government gave Galvão and his cohorts asylum and returned the liner to Portugal.[1]

'Galvão messed up badly,' Delgado told me over coffee at my home in Casablanca's suburbs. 'He – and we – should have planned better in advance with all of the Portuguese military.' By this time, the austere, deflationary and impoverishing policies of Salazar, initiated to clean up after the 1920s counterfeiting scandal, and an army and navy demoralized by revolts in the African colonies made the country ripe for revolution, Delgado believed.[2]

Unfortunately for Delgado, he never factored into his thinking economic and social factors like the strength of the Portuguese currency (which under Salazar had become solid) and the possible mobilization of a repressed labour movement. He thought, in old-fashioned, Bonapartist terms, that he and fellow military dissidents could excel what the military rebels of Portugal's myriad coups had done in the First Portuguese Republic in the teens and the 1920s, by provoking a general mutiny of the armed forces that would sweep Salazar and the fascist bureaucracy from power, essentially without civilian help. Diamantino Machado, a historian who takes Delgado seriously, called him 'the hope and the spokesman (indirectly) of the petite and middle bourgeoisie', which had been in steady decline since.[3]

On 31 December 1961 came Delgado's last hurrah, which he invited me to cover, but which I missed because I didn't take his advance tip seriously enough. With a couple of like-minded brigadier generals and colonels, Delgado raised a force of about a hundred men and tried to spark a general military uprising by attacking loyalist army barracks at Beja. In the bloody nocturnal fiasco the Portuguese army secretary was killed. Many of Delgado's men were slain or captured. Delgado escaped in disguise and travelled by ship to Casablanca, where I again met him and his Brazilian lady-friend and 'secretary', Mme Arajaryr Moreira de Campos. Both were crestfallen, but neither seemed to be questioning the fundamental wrongness of Delgado's tactics. This, to my lasting regret, was my last meeting with Delgado and his confidante. Salazar's secret police, the PIDE, murdered both of them in 1965 after luring them into a trap in Spain, near the Portuguese border.

No one tried violent military insurrections after Beja: the 'velvet revolution' of the officers who in 1974 overthrew Salazar's successor, Marcelo Caetano, was nearly bloodless. They eventually refashioned Portugal as a parliamentary democracy and European Community and European Union member. The legacy of Salazar was conservative, deflationary banking and fiscal policy he had instituted to cleanse the system after the catastrophe of Alves Reis' massive forgery scheme.

Arturo Alves Reis: Gentleman, Master Penman and Crook

The man who shook the all-powerful Central Bank of Portugal and who aspired to supreme power by taking control of it was born on 8 September 1896. Artur Virgílio Alves dos Reis was the scion of a self-taught Lisbon bookkeeper, who also did some occasional moneylending and tried his hand at managing a funeral parlour.

Schooled during the final years of the old monarchy, which was overthrown in 1910, Alves Reis couldn't enter university after his graduation from high school in 1914 because the family was nearly broke. As the First World War erupted and a nominally neutral Portugal gradually embraced the Allies and became embroiled in African fighting in and around Germany's colonies, the Reis family, like so many others, lost their savings. These disappeared in a black hole for investments that opened in Angola, where the Portuguese Petroleum Company was then vainly drilling for the oil that American and European companies triumphantly began to pump later, during Salazar's 1932–68 rule.

Alves Reis studied engineering at a technical school for a year. At age twenty, he married a short and plump but presentable girl named Maria Luiza Jacobetti d'Avezdo, whom he had met at a beach picnic. After much nudging by its old ally Britain, its best customer for its fine port wine and other products, Portugal declared war on Germany on 9 March 1916.[4] Alves Reis avoided joining the 40,000-man Portuguese force shipped off to the Western Front's muddy and deadly trenches.

He cheated the military draft using his first big forgery: he carefully penned and had printed a forged 'diploma' from a non-existent 'Polytechnic School of Engineering' at Oxford University, held in great awe by the Anglophile Portuguese. The only genuine parts of the document, attesting to his supposed proficiency in a bewildering variety of academic disciplines from geology to civil, mechanical and electrical engineering – he would henceforth often be identified as 'Senhor Engineer' – were a friendly notary's stamp and seal.

With wife and two young sons, Alves Reis was welcomed in Angola in November 1916. Skilled graduates, especially white professionals, were scarce in the colony. He discovered a land twice as big as Texas and fourteen times the size of mother Portugal. Its population then was about 20,000 whites, 10,000 coffee-coloured mulattoes and about 3,000,000 black Africans – the latter called by the white settlers '*japas*', a Portuguese equivalent of 'niggers'. It was an agricultural colony, exporting coffee, corn, sugar, tobacco and rice. It lacked coal and sufficient iron for heavy industries.

At first Alves Reis held a dull Public Works job. Then, moonlighting as a supposedly qualified 'Oxford graduate' mechanical engineer, he used his undoubted mechanical knack to repair Angola's ageing and decrepit locomotives. Using the labour of fifty natives he branched out into saving the threatened tobacco crop of a settler friend through an irrigation scheme. He began travelling with Maria around the country to buy up crops for resale in Luanda, the capital, leaving their baby sons in the care of servants. By 1919 he had entered the lucrative trade in war-surplus items and became prosperous enough in 1922 to return to Lisbon. There, with two partners, Alves Reis set up his own trading company, A. V. Alves Reis Ltd, renting a luxurious twelve-room apartment. Temporarily he held the local distributorship for American Nash automobiles.[5]

But times were hard. In 1917 during the war, General Sidonio Pães had led a pro-German uprising. He arrested and deported the pro-Allied President Bernardino Machado, and made himself president and dictator. On 14 December 1918 a radical opponent assassinated Pães. A nominally parliamentary democratic regime was restored, amid general economic and social chaos. This was very bad for business, especially for small businesses like A. V. Alves Reis Ltd. The economy of a country then 65 per cent illiterate couldn't function well. One government succeeded another. The average duration of each was about four months. Amid repeated coups and upheavals, the financial conditions went from bad to worse. As American historian William Langer observes, '[M]ultiplication of offices, widespread political corruption, appalling inefficiency characterized the decade from 1918 to 1928.'[6] All this provided Alves Reis and his associates with the ideal stage for their theatrical swindles.

Unable to make a go of his trading firm, in 1923 Alves Reis found out that he could buy a controlling interest in the Royal Trans-African Railway Company of Angola (Ambaca) for only $40,000. This was because the company's shares had plummeted in value and bondholders were demanding cash for unpaid dividends and interest. So Alves Reis wrote a 'kited' (uncovered) cheque on an account he had opened in the National City Bank of New York. There wasn't any transatlantic air service in those days. It took at least eight days for seaborne mail to reach New York from Lisbon. By the time his cheque reached National City Bank, it was no longer phoney. Alves Reis had used it during the week to buy control of Ambaca. He cabled $40,000 from Ambaca's cash reserves to New York in time for the cheque to be covered before arriving at the New York bank. With another $60,000 of Ambaca's cash, he bought control of the South Angola Mining Company. Even though it was not commercially productive, Alves Reis and friends lauded its supposed assets among the punters in the small and conservative Lisbon market, lifting the value of the shares. During this operation, he met one of his key associates in their subsequent giant counterfeit currency operation. José Bandeira, a Portuguese diplomat serving in the Netherlands, claimed to represent a Dutch company then drilling for oil in Angola.

Some of the suspicious stockholders of Ambaca discovered how Alves Reis was using the company's cash to speculate in gambling on a big strike in oil or gold in Angola. They accused him of embezzling $100,000 of Ambaca funds and had him arrested on 5 July 1924. Jailed in Oporto, his two partners, Bandeira and a shady German businessman named Karl Hennies, visited him in jail and tried to persuade him to return to the straight and narrow by selling the Ambaca shares he held and putting the cash back in the company treasury. He argued against this idea, and they gave up trying to convince him. He was brought to trial and found guilty. After spending fifty-four days behind bars, Alves Reis raised $10,000 bail by selling his wife's jewellery and their home. Upon his release, friends gave him a cordial surprise party at a posh bistro. He learned that a conviction for forgery in the Portugal of that day did not necessarily make you an outcast.

It was during his Oporto confinement that Alves Reis hatched his master scheme for gaining control of the Bank of Portugal and eventually, he hoped, of the country itself. He had brought with him the detailed statutes of the bank and studied them carefully. He learned that the bank was *not* actually government-controlled; it was semi-private. The government held only a minority of the shares. Crucially, it held the exclusive right to issue all Portuguese banknotes: unlike the situation in Germany and other European countries at the time, there weren't any private or provincial enterprises printing Portuguese money. Alves Reis' careful reading of the bank's statutes and some later snooping after he left jail showed, oddly enough, that no one on the bank's staff was responsible for monitoring banknotes for duplicate serial numbers, a sure way to discover counterfeits.

The power and value of money, he reflected, was largely in the eye of its holder. Portugal had long ago abandoned the gold standard. Money presses, working overtime, were already bringing a measure of prosperity back to Germany with the new, post-hyperinflation, *de*-flated marks. The presses were doing the same in Hungary and in Mussolini's Fascist Italy. So, why not find a way to generate money himself, indistinguishable from the official Portuguese currency then being printed, under contract from the Bank of Portugal, by the eminent firm of Waterlow & Company in England?[7] The work was given to Waterlow because after the war, Portugal was too broke to afford the necessary machinery to do it itself.

(Of course, neither Alves Reis nor anyone else knew at the time that Waterlow had been helping produce the counterfeit German reichsmarks and stamps during the First World War, probably by making plates and doing some of the printing for the Bank of England; not that it would have made any difference if they had known.)

Alves Reis also discovered that the Bank of Portugal's profits were proportionately divided between private stockholders and whatever government was in power at the time. By law, the bank was not supposed to circulate notes worth more than three times its paid-up capital. However, he discovered that by 1924 the bank had followed the examples of its counterparts elsewhere in Europe by issuing notes with a face value of more than 100 times its capital. (Fortunately, the resulting inflation was far below the level of that in Weimar Germany of 1919–23). Since Portuguese paper money had not been convertible to gold or silver since 1891, the only expenses involved in generating more 'genuine' money was the cost of the paper, ink and printing.

Alves Reis' next big step up the ladder of ambitious forgery was also a crucial step towards achieving his aim of grabbing control of the economies of both Portugal and its colony of Angola. He carefully forged a contract specifying that he was an agent representing the Bank of Portugal. On it he traced the signatures of the high commissioner of Angola, the minister of finance and a technical representative of the Angolan colonial government. The contract, said his carefully crafted text, authorized him to request the printing of the equivalent of $5 million in large-denomination escudo notes of Angolan currency. This was to be paid to an 'international group of investors'. These, in turn, would loan the Angolan colonial authorities the same amount, but in British sterling. A notary's assistant authenticated Alves Reis' signature, and so (although only symbolically) the document itself. Then Alves Reis got French, German and British consular offices to affix their seals, further dignifying his bogus text and forged signatures.[8]

Obviously, the place to present the phoney contract and commission the printing was Waterlow & Company, which had been printing the official 500- and 1,000-escudo notes for the Bank of Portugal. Alves Reis' next problem was to find the right partners for his enterprise. They would have to be men who would not shy away from taking big legal risks and who were not intimidated by the size of the sums being manipulated. At least one of them should have diplomatic immunity, so that he could act as a courier, easily crossing frontiers with his sensitive baggage, ultimately including millions in the escudo notes ordered by Alves Reis, letters bearing his carefully forged signature of the Bank of Portugal's governor and other sensitive documents. He already knew this third man: José Bandeira's brother, António, was an accredited minister at the Portuguese Embassy in The Hague, and part of the group of Dutch and German financiers probing the possibility of exploiting Angolan oil resources.

His other partner, Gustav Adolf Hennies, was a German who had emigrated to the United States as a boy of eleven and had followed a progressively clever fraudulent career in helping to fabricate or distribute counterfeit money in Brazil and the Netherlands (where he worked for German intelligence during the 1914–18 war). Later in Albania he and other operatives tried to set up a bank to pay off the small monarchy's debts before Mussolini's men, already muscling their way into Albania, chased them out.

The final member of the team was Karl Marang, a skilful Dutch trader who had built up a thriving import–export business. Among his lucrative sidelines was purchasing titles of nobility and honorary offices (such as consulships) for wealthy war profiteers and other would-be tycoons. For himself, he had bought the title of Venezuelan Consul in The Hague. Since the purely honorary consulship didn't entitle him to a real one, to go with it he had bought for a hefty sum a forged Venezuelan diplomatic passport. This gave him diplomatic immunity at frontier customs posts. António Bandeira's younger brother, José, a corrupt and reckless gambler and chaser of women, also soon became an important accessory in the venture.

Alves Reis paid personal visits to all three and talked them into joining his scheme. He withheld one crucial detail: that on the commissioning letters to be presented to Waterlow for printing the banknotes the signatures from the top officers of the Bank of Portugal, including that of Governor Comacho Rodrigues, had been forged by himself. Reis told them that he had 'highly placed friends' in the bank who would facilitate matters, and who had produced and signed the supposedly genuine documents for him. Reis did confide to Marang that he'd get the $5 million, the first instalment of Waterlow-printed escudos to give to the Angolan colonial government in exchange for sterling, by using the escudo notes to buy gold, his backing for the needed credit. Marang swallowed this thin fable only after Reis, through his connections, had managed to introduce Marang to Portugal's current president, Teixeira Gomes (to be succeeded in December of 1925 by Bernardino Machado, who was elected to a second term after one of Portugal's many failed military coups).[9]

Although Marang and Bandeira at first preferred the venerable Dutch banknote-printing firm of Enschede of Haarlem to print the new escudos, they soon learned that Enschede didn't want to take the business away from their competitor Waterlow. Enschede may have also sniffed something wrong with the whole deal. In any case, the Bandeira brothers got a letter of introduction from Enschede. It gave Marang in effect a legal power-of-attorney to act for Alves Reis of Lisbon. After forging the Bank of Portugal's letterhead on some impressively heavy paper and studying the Waterlow situation in London, the Reis group decided to target Chairman Sir William Waterlow. He had a reputation for pomposity, and was impressed by honours and titles in people he dealt with. Sir William was often scornful of the advice of his associates and underlings (some of whom would later vainly caution him to think twice about the business with the Reis group). Reis decided that Marang was the ideal emissary to Sir William; their personalities matched.

Marang embarked for London and put up at the Ritz Hotel, from where it was easy to phone and get an appointment with Sir William Waterlow. On the morning of 4 December 1924, they met in Waterlow's first-floor office on Great Winchester Street in London's financial district, the City. The visiting card Bandeira presented identified him as 'Consul General of Persia' (a fiction). The confidential letter he gave Sir William from 'His Excellency António Bandeira, Portuguese Minister at The Hague', certified that the bearer was carrying official dispatches of the Portuguese government. It bore the signature of Bank of Portugal Governor Senhor Comacho Rodriguez, which Reis had traced from the signature on a legitimate 500-escudo note. A final factor impressing Sir William with the Reis group's importance was a lapel rosette Marang wore:

the Order of Christ, a high distinction in overwhelmingly Roman Catholic Portugal that Sir William recognized and admired.

Marang outlined to Waterlow the Angolan loan scheme. The $5 million worth of 500-escudo notes the Reis group was ordering, he said, would be overprinted by them with the stamp 'Angola'. This would distinguish them from escudo notes circulating in Portugal, which weren't legal tender in the colony. On 6 January 1925 Waterlow agreed in writing to supply the Alves Reis group with 200,000 notes of 500 escudos each, total value about $5 million. The total price translated into dollars was $7,200, giving the counterfeiters a profit of $700 for every dollar they paid Waterlow for the print job. Reis and his men worried that Sir William might try to verify his trust in the two personal emissaries (Bandeira replaced Marang on some future trips) by opening direct communication with Bank of Portugal Governor Rodriguez by sending him a letter by ordinary mail, confirming the 'confidential' printing transaction. In fact, Sir William did write such a letter, apparently mailed by an underling. The Reis group's extraordinary good luck held firm: the letter never arrived at the Bank in Lisbon. Its receipt would have doomed the whole enterprise; Portugal's future might have been quite different.

Before 10 February 1925, the date set for the first delivery of the Waterlow notes, Reis urgently consulted Hennies. Hennies agreed that despite what Marang and Bandeira had been telling Sir William Waterlow (as they continued to visit him to make sure all was going smoothly with the printing), about using the notes in Angola, this would be impossible. Instead of stamping 'Angola' on them, as they'd assured Waterlow they would do, they had to swiftly launder the Reis escudos in Portugal by exchanging them for British, American, French and other hard currencies. They would spread the exchange transactions around through respectable banks and moneychangers. There was to be minimal use of the notes for purchases in shops or kiosks. The total amount they could safely launder in Portugal, they reasoned, shouldn't exceed $15 million worth of 500-escudo notes, anticipating future orders and deliveries of about $10 million more. More, Reis and Hennies agreed, would be dangerous: the law of averages meant that sooner or later, there'd be duplication of serial numbers between the official notes and the Reis issue. Reis did not have, and in fact never fully figured out, the numbering and lettering codes used by the Bank of Portugal, which they would have needed to beat the system. (In the end, this would prove their undoing.)

Reis then confided to Hennies the final, triumphant step in his projected scheme: to buy up a majority of the Bank of Portugal's shares and so win control of it! Since the central bank was the final decider of what was genuine money and what was not, as the new senior officers of the bank, they would eventually totally control Portugal's money supply – and would be immune from prosecution. Alves Reis chortled with glee. Hennies also broke into uproarious laughter. Author Bloom describes this as 'almost the laughter of two small [he might have added, very naughty] boys who had found a riddle that had hopelessly perplexed their parents'. Hennies kept repeating, 'How can they arrest us when they're us and we're them?'[10]

Bandeira and Marang picked up the first delivery of notes from Waterlow & Sons on schedule and shipped $500,000 worth in a trunk accompanying them on a boat train to the Netherlands. Bandeira's diplomatic card got them through Dutch customs without a search. At Marang's office in The Hague, two of Reis' Lisbon employees were put to work shuffling the new bills around, so that the packages of fresh money would not have consecutive serial numbers when handed into the enterprises chosen for their exchange into sterling or dollars, or Swiss or French francs. For these laundering transactions, they paid black-market rates slightly above the legal ones. Such transactions left no paper trail, for the simple reason that they were illegal, although very widespread. New deliveries of notes from Waterlow followed on 25 February and 12 March. By the end of March, Alves Reis' group was busy laundering $5 million worth of banknotes. These were passing the inspection at the Bank of Portugal and being pronounced legal tender.

Reis and his associates decided that they needed next to create their own bank. This could not only launder their new notes more efficiently and safely; it would also serve as a licensed, legitimate institution to make investments in Africa which would, in effect, buy up the economy in Angola and facilitate acquiring majority and controlling shares in the central Bank of Portugal itself. This, Reis believed, would be his ticket to total power in Portugal. The new bank was to be called the Bank of Angola and Metropolis. After delays caused by the authorities' hesitation because of Bandeira's past shady record, his name was dropped from the list of directors. More of the new notes changed hands and in July, the new Banco Angola e Metropóle opened for business with branches in Lisbon and Oporto.

The Reis gang had not been following their own advice about caution in public buying sprees. Reis' wife, Maria, loaded up on fancy jewellery and *haute couture* from Paris shops. Reis and colleagues bought mansions, stocks and shares in all kinds of enterprises, and even settled some of their big debts with the new notes. As soon as this new bank's charter had been approved, Alves Reis and wife Maria voyaged to his favourite colony, Angola. He and the money he announced he was bringing were royally received. During his triumphal tour of the colony, Reis conceived a grandiose plan for the prosperity of Angola and its white masters: he would renew its infrastructure with new and improved streets, railways and harbours. He managed to buy up about a million acres of land and was lauded in the popular press as Angola's Cecil Rhodes, the British colonial statesman for whom the former British colony of Rhodesia was named.

At home in Portugal, the new Reis bank was very forthcoming about loans of all types, including property mortgages, at very attractive rates. If you could pledge solid securities, the bank gave you *very* advantageous interest rates. With the millions of dollars' worth of currency now circulating, due to the laundered Alves Reis notes, there was an illusory upswing in Portugal's financial fortunes. The gang decided they needed more 500-escudo notes, so Marang visited Sir William Waterlow again on 29 July 1925 with another forged letter from the Governor of the Bank of Portugal. This time he collected 380,000 of the 500-escudo notes bearing the Portuguese explorer Vasco da Gama's likeness, the same images as Reis had ordered earlier and identical with the older official

Bank of Portugal issues. Marang paid Waterlow 2,850 sterling, or about $14,000.

Rumours began circulating, some of them printed in the Lisbon newspapers, of a great quantity of forged 500-escudo notes turning up in daily commerce. This caused the Reis gang temporarily to suspend their laundering operation for short periods. However, each time the Bank of Portugal tested the notes originating with the Reis Bank of Angola and the Metropolis, it pronounced them absolutely authentic. Reis and Hennies channelled $100,000 or so worth of the notes into Angola by investing in public utilities, whereas Marang and Bandeira quickly and prudently moved their shares of the take to Brussels, Amsterdam and German banks.

José Bandeira, however, drew attention to himself by spending $150,000 worth of the Reis notes on three big estates from three noblemen: the Count of Garda, the Marquis of Sagares and the Marquis de Funchal. He bought a fleet of taxicabs in Lisbon, a majority interest in the shirtmaker that supplied him with his fine linen and a popular Lisbon barbershop. He also drove around Lisbon and the countryside in a chauffered Hispano-Suiza car. This prosperity greatly impresssed his long-time girlfriend and companion on vacation trips, the popular Dutch actress and singer Fie Carelsen.[11]

Reis assigned to José Bandeira management of his dreamt-of enterprise: gaining control of the central Bank of Portugal by acquiring a majority of its shares. José and others working for him gradually acquired something less than 40 per cent of the shares, but as news about the transactions spread through the banking community, the price of the shares grew alarmingly high. Alves Reis had taken a huge cut from the top. He claimed he owed this to his imaginary patrons at the Bank of Portugal. The other members of the gang seemed to accept this demand. Bloom and Sam Burton, an American financial analyst, believe their acquiescence 'would seem to indicate that they were doing the bidding of legitimate, if corrupt Portuguese officials'.[12]

The only American who became (marginally and unwittingly) involved in the enterprise made a brief appearance on the scene in later summer of 1925. He was George U. Rose, Jr, then sixty,

Waterlow's only American staffer and manager of the Waterlow banknote printing and engraving plant in Scrutton Street, London. Rose had worked for the US Bureau of Engraving and Printing on US currency. He had then moved to the private sector to help manage the American Banknote Company's banknote printing plant in the Bronx, New York. Sir William Waterlow heard of Rose's great technical competence and hired him away from American Banknote with a fat seven-year contract. When the Bank of Portugal's supposed super-expert in counterfeit detection, Senhor Pedroso, visited Waterlow in London to look over their numbering equipment to see if the Bank of Portugal could somehow copy or duplicate it and return to printing Portuguese money on home soil, Rose followed through on the print job by helping Marang and another Waterlow employee escort the latest print run of banknotes to the initial part of their usual route to the Continent, the Liverpool Street railway station. There is nothing on the record to show that Rose wasn't as completely duped by the Reis enterprise as Sir William himself and the rest of his staff.

The undoing of Reis, his associates, and the destabilization of Portugal's financial system, resulting in the Salazar dictatorship, began to unfold during the final months of 1925. By that time there had already been suspicions, some of them published, about the plethora of new 500-escudo notes moving through the system. Although the gang often took pains to artificially age and wrinkle the notes, they didn't always do so: many were crisp and new-looking. What had saved them up to then was, of course, that the three main elements – the printed images, the paper and the ink – were all totally authentic and without flaws. What finally brought the operation down was the serial numbering system. This was Reis' only real – but totally decisive – failure.

In Oporto, a teller in a rival bank who purchased foreign exchange for the Bank of Angola and the Metropolis was struck by the fact that the 500-escudo bills his jeweller boss bought from that bank were not in numerical order. At the bank, he also noticed that pages in the account book on which foreign exchange deals on the Reis notes were entered were afterwards torn out of the book and were missing. On 4 December 1925 he talked with his banker boss about his suspicions. The boss quickly alerted the Bank of Portugal, where alarm bells sounded. On the very next day, 5 December, police closed the Bank of Angola branch in Oporto and arrested the branch manager, who had been aware of the scam since June. Bank of Portugal officials hurried to Oporto to inspect the suspicious 4,000 500-escudo notes in the bank's vaults. Once again, they pronounced them genuine. However, a check of the serial numbers disclosed duplicates. More arrest warrants were issued.

On the following Monday morning, 6 December 1925, the authorities instructed all Portuguese banks to call in the 500-escudo Vasco da Gama notes and replace them with other 500-escudo notes of a different design. Anyone showing up to change more than two hundred of the da Gama notes would have to present his ID and sign for the bills (the same precaution taken by many banks in Europe for *each* $100 bill presented in the early 1990s, the era of the 'Supernotes' believed to have been printed in Iran and North Korea).[13]

Meanwhile, on 4 December Reis and his wife and friends had ended their African junket and were returning to Lisbon aboard the German steamer *Adolf Woermann*. While still at sea, but nearing Lisbon at the mouth of the Tagus River, the ship's German purser warned his fellow countryman, Hennies, that the steamship line's Lisbon office had cabled him not to accept any more Vasco da Gama 500-escudo notes, now considered fishy and under investigation. Hennies called Reis to his stateroom and broke the bad news. He urged Reis and his wife not to disembark at Lisbon, where they faced certain arrest. He, Hennies, would stay aboard. He already had a record as a forger and fraudster. He was also being fingered by public rumour and the Portuguese press as a possible German spy, conspiring to turn over Portuguese possessions in Africa to the Weimar Republic. So he would seek safer havens in Paris, Amsterdam or Berlin.

Alves Reis Falls: Fascism Rises

Reis bitterly responded to Hennies that if only they had had another month, they could have won control of the Bank of

Portugal. 'We don't have that month,' Hennies said. Reis told him he would 'fight this rap' by claiming that it was all a plot originated by the corrupt officials in the Bank of Portugal itself. When the pilot boat arrived at 7 a.m., Hennies rode ashore on it and had coffee at a quayside cafe. Afterwards, he would reboard the steamer, whose complicit captain awaited his return before sailing, and eventually disappear into the woodwork of post-war Europe, secure with his alternate identities and fat bank accounts. At 9 a.m. the police boarded and arrested Alves Reis. From his cafe table, Hennies watched his former boss and colleague being whisked away in a police car.

After brief interviews with the civil governor of Lisbon and the head of the Criminal Investigation Department, Reis was escorted to a cell. He would later describe this as 'a horrible hole' that 'poisoned every decent instinct in my heart . . . Scandal would be my revenge and I, coolly, calmly planned to attack innocent people – the Governor and Vice Governor of the Bank of Portugal, the High Commissioner of Angola, politicians.'[14]

Since the notes with duplicate numbers could not be distinguished from the real thing, the Bank of Portugal officials and the forensic police concluded at first that the plates and other materials must have been stolen. Before his arrest, Reis had been furiously forging documents indicating that the governor of the Bank of Portugal and some of his directors had been the original plotters. The phoney documents looked so genuine that the police hastily arrested Governor Comacho Rodriguez and Vice Governor Dr Mota Gomes. They were held for only twenty-four hours, but their arrest and the allegations, which continued to make headlines in the populist press for months afterwards, shook the bank's board of directors into offering their resignations. A shaken Sir William Waterlow arrived in Lisbon. He was roughly questioned during a whole week, then allowed to leave. Police would not guarantee his safety from the public anger already sweeping Portugal unless he left incognito, as 'Mr Smith'. Some newspapers headlined that the plot originated in Soviet Russia (only a bit later, Stalin was indeed cooking up the massive counterfeiting of US dollars), others that it was brewed in Weimar Germany, notorious for counterfeiting and its worthless paper money. With the help of friends (his wife was temporarily incarcerated and later charged as an accomplice), Reis was making wild accusations from his cell against Portugal's top bankers and financiers. However, both Bandeira and Marang, caught and questioned, were spilling the beans. Reis' fantasies found less and less credibility among the panicky and outraged citizens. They began to form long lines to withdraw their deposits before the banks' expected failure, which in many cases soon followed.[15]

Thousands of people who had lost their life savings or their pensions behaved, in general, much more violently than had their counterparts in Weimar Germany during the hyperinflation there. Riots erupted in Lisbon, Oporto and some other towns. Portugal's downtrodden workers began to organize into anarcho-syndicalist groups and organized illegal strikes. Armed militias of the republican and monarchist parties and clubs began to fight each other in the streets and sometimes in the countryside. Martial law was declared and the army replaced the police in many of the centres of disorder. The economy spiralled downwards, with the remaining legal escudo banknotes in circulation rapidly sinking in value and the cost of living rising to fourteen times what it had been in 1914.

Gradually groups who craved a return to the pre-1911 monarchy began to get the upper hand over the republican and liberal politicians. On 25 May 1926 an army movement inspired by a monarchist-minded politician named Mendes Cabecedas and led by General Gomes da Costa declared in the royalist town of Braga that they would lead a march on Lisbon to overthrow the government of President Machado and the cabinet of Prime Minister António Mara da Silva. Both of these had been acquaintances, if not close friends, of Alves Reis during his high-flying days as a rich tycoon.

A full-fledged military revolt, supported by most of the army, erupted in northern Portugal. General Gomes da Costa, a vain and audacious officer with little political sense or know-how, was momentarily praised as a national hero. After considerable bloodshed, the Machado–da Silva government was overthrown. The victorious putschists dissolved parliament and broke up the legal political parties. However, Gomes da Costa and the cronies he installed in his regime proved to be disastrously incompetent. On 9 July 1926 another general, Antonio de Fragoso Carmona, led some of the troops in deposing Gomes da Costa, who was 'honourably' exiled to Portugal's Azores Islands in the Atlantic.[16]

During these tumultuous events, the Portuguese Embassy in London pressed for an investigation of Waterlow & Company. Colonel José Auguste dos Santos Lucas of the Embassy found deposits from Reis' defunct Bank of Angola and the Metropolis in branches of the Midland Bank and the Westminster Bank. There was nearly half a million dollars' worth of the suspect sterling deposits in both, although much of the balance in the Westminster Bank had been withdrawn. With Scotland Yard Inspector F. J. Eveleigh, Colonel Lucas called on Sir William Waterlow. They trod carefully: Sir William was an alderman (with every expectation of becoming lord mayor) of the City of London, which had its own police force. Scotland Yard had to ask permission to enter the City. Sir William admitted that Waterlow had printed over $15 million worth of 500-escudo notes for the Reis group on the basis of instructions from the Bank of Portugal. Colonel Lucas told him these had been forged. But formal charges against Waterlow followed much later.

Amid confusion accompanying and following the temporary arrests in Lisbon of Bank of Portugal officials, the Lisbon police sent extradition orders to London and other European capitals for Henry Romer, Waterlow's former representative in Portugal, and for members of the Reis gang in their various hideaways. In Lisbon police had violated the diplomatic immunity of the Legation of Venezuela – the apartment of the Venezuelan minister, Count Planas-Suarez, where they found 85,000 of the counterfeit notes. Though arrested, the Count was later allowed to leave the country: he pleaded successfully that he had stored the notes as a favour to the Reis group without knowing they were forged.[17]

Alves Reis enjoyed privileges and amenities in jail. Sympathetic magistrates seemed to consider him as much a benefactor of Portugal as a crook who had compromised Portugal's international financial reputation. While Reis and associates, the Bandeira brothers and Francisco Ferreira, Reis' complicit secretary, awaited trial in prison, the country was spiralling rapidly downwards towards the dictatorial rule that followed the economic decline and that would be its destiny for the next half-century.

The financial chaos and confusion resulting from the economic and psychological damage done by the Reis group continued. The military dictatorship under President Carmona couldn't seem to remedy it. Between 3 and 13 February 1927, new uprisings erupted, first in Oporto, then in Lisbon. They were described by the military regime as 'communist', probably because they had support from industrial and other workers influenced by the anarcho-syndicalist movements. Actually much of the inspiration came from a group of reform-minded academics and intellectuals called the Seara Novo. After bloodshed and some tough fighting between loyalist and rebel troops and militiamen, with army artillery fire nearly levelling much of Oporto, the government crushed the movement. One hundred and twenty-two rebels were killed, and the others were exiled to the Azores and Cape Verde.[18]

President Carmona and his advisers had believed for over a year that the one man who might be able to pull Portugal out of its morass of corruption and public penury, or at least its fiscal aspects, was Professor António de Oliveira Salazar, chair of economics at Coimbra University. Born in 1889, the studious Salazar had been educated to become a priest. He had switched to law studies and finally economics, where he embraced many of the classic theories of the most conservative economists. Carmona's men consulted Salazar. They made him a kind of unofficial finance minister in 1926, but without powers, especially the power he sought most: to veto all government expenditures and to watch over dubious banking practices. From the first public breakout of the Reis scandal, Salazar had been deeply interested in the history of the forged banknotes. After all, his admirers reasoned, hadn't he written his doctoral thesis on the evolution of Portuguese currency?

Following a period of relative political calm but continued financial turbulence, General Carmona was elected for a new presidential term on 28 March 1928. Carmona remained president until his death in 1951, although from 1928 on Salazar was the only supreme authority in the land. Power and the spoils of state remained in the hands of the military, not the parliament. On 27 April 1928, when he was about to turn thirty-nine, Professor Salazar became minister of finance in fact as well as in name. He took his oath dressed in sombre black, the standard garb of Portugal's top professionals. Bloom writes that he was 'so thin and pallid that some unkind critics thought he looked like "an underpaid funeral parlour assistant who would bury Portugal's finances for good"'.[19]

Nothing could have been further from the truth. Within a few months, most of the old high-denomination escudo notes had been recalled and replaced with new ones whose printing was closely supervised by Salazar's Finance Ministry. Meanwhile, Salazar's supporters worked towards securing their primacy, under his leadership, in a new fascist, one-party state. Its economy was henceforth to be based on strict accounting and accountability of all government departments, a deflationary fiscal policy and a careful control of currency values, along with extreme vigilance against currency counterfeiting.

The first big political step towards Salazar's intended *Estado Novo* was the formal foundation, on 30 July 1930, of the ruling *parti unique*, the National Union. All others were prohibited. Its architects methodically laid the foundations for the *Estado Novo*. Just as Hitler's rise to power in Germany, built on the ruins of the Weimar Republic, was slow and methodical until Germany's crucial electoral period of 1932–3, so was Salazar's accession. On 5 July 1932 President Carmona named him prime minister. National Union Party stalwarts hammered out a new constitution, promulgated on 22 February 1933, just as Hitler and Mussolini were consolidating their dictatorships, and as General Francisco Franco and fellow conspirators against the Spanish Republic were beginning their preparations for their revolt, which would lead to civil war and Franco's 1939–75 supremacy.

The Salazar constitution preserved a façade of democracy, with Mussolini-type corporatist underpinnings. The elected president was to serve successive seven-year terms. The president appointed a cabinet responsible to him alone. The National Assembly was a kind of parliament, chosen by the best-educated heads of families. There was a corporative chamber built on Mussolini's Italian model representing occupations and trades, but with only advisory power.[20] Salazar created a tough secret police, the Policea Internacionale e por la Defesa del Estado, known as the PIDE. This evolved into a kind of Gestapo and became the dread of Salazar's opponents, whom it imprisoned, tortured and sometimes killed.

Despite sporadic assassination plots and continued opposition from the illegal Portuguese Communist Party and from more liberal movements and individuals such as General Delgado, the system solidified following suppression of a leftist revolutionary movement in 1934 and elections in 1935. These gave Carmona his first constitutional seven-year presidential term. When the civil war erupted in Spain in 1936, Portugal immediately sided with Franco and became a main channel for German aid to Franco's insurgents.

The Second World War allies, especially Britain, had to strain hard to keep to their traditional alliances with a neutral Portugal. They did so partly because of their urgent need for the bases that Salazar granted the US in the Azores for the anti-submarine war in the Atlantic. The Lajes Field base in the Azores was useful in the Cold War. It still serves the US under the current democratic Portuguese regime.[21]

Legal and Commercial Consequences

Through wheeling and dealing with his high-level contacts and use of his still existent bank accounts, after his arrest and initial incarceration in 1926 Alves Reis and his lawyers managed to delay his trial for over four years. It finally opened on 6 May 1930, in the military court at Santa Clara, Portugal. The presiding judge, Dr Simão José, was close to the ruling military junta. A six-man jury consisted of six other judges. Reis pleaded guilty to all counts. He argued that his associates be released because they were acting in good faith and believed he was acting for the benefit of Portugal's interests in Angola. His defence counsel contended that Reis wasn't really a forger but an 'inflationist' who was carrying out official Bank of Portugal policies without cost to the bank. Reis had paid Waterlow for printing the notes, which Reis was *duplicating*, something different from counterfeiting. The verdict handed down on 20 June 1930, after 12,000 pages of testimony in sixty-six volumes, was that Reis was guilty – not only of introducing 330,000 false 500-escudo notes into Portugal but, grotesquely, of falsely using the title of engineer. His sentence was twenty-five years of exile in the Azores, or a combination of twelve years' exile and eight years' imprisonment. In 1931 his sentence was revised to a straight twenty years of jail. Bandeira and Hennies also received twenty years, Hennies *in absentia*. José Bandeira got six years. The bank clerk who had mixed Reis' notes in The Hague drew three years. Senhora Maria Reis got ten months and eight days, but since she had already served more jail time than the sentence she was released. Marang, tried in the Netherlands, was found guilty and appealed. He then jumped bail and fled to Belgium.

In London, the Bank of Portugal had brought suit against Waterlow & Sons for $3 million, the amount of damage it claimed for the firm's improper use of its escudo plates. The amount would have been much higher if the Bank of Portugal hadn't recovered about $2.5 million from the Bank of Angola's assets, and the personal assets of Reis and the Bandeira brothers. Reis had deliberately kept about $8.5 million of his illegal notes out of circulation, some of which he withheld out of fear that irregularities in the coded serial numbers would attract suspicion. The remainder of the notes he just hadn't had time to get laundered and into the system.

The London court case had been postponed to begin only after Sir William Waterlow's one-year term as lord mayor of London had expired. It opened on 24 November 1930, and after dragging on through months it ended in Britain's highest court of appeal – five members of the House of Lords. The decision against Waterlow came on 28 April 1932. Trials and appeals cost almost a million dollars. Bankers, the banknote printing community and government finance ministers followed it with what Bloom calls 'morbid fascination'. Waterlow's counsel, Sir John Simon, argued in defence that all that had really happened was an exchange of one set of paper banknotes for another and the only real cost to Portugal had been the printing fees, paid in real money. As noted in the last chapter, during the first trial the judges avoided airing publicly Waterlow's connection with printing the counterfeit imperial reichsmarks during the First World War. They concentrated on the real damage to Portugal's finances – also avoiding mention of the political consequence, the rise of the Salazar dictatorship.

In the end, the Bank of Portugal won by a split 3–2 vote in the House of Lords. Waterlow had to pay the Bank of Portugal $3 million in damages. Surprisingly, after a gap of six years the Bank of Portugal again gave its banknote printing business to Waterlow & Sons, with elaborate safeguards this time to avoid a repetition of the great scandal. Sir William Waterlow died shortly after the court award, which floored the company financially for some time, and psychologically as well as financially undoubtedly led to its ultimate demise. Up to his death, Sir William refused to believe that such a scheme had been the work of an obscure Portuguese forger and swindler. He kept private detectives on the case, trying to trace the imaginary real brains of the scandal, which had cost him the chairmanship of the firm and his professional standing.

Marang avoided arrest and trial, sending Christmas cards to Waterlow from Belgium and Germany, and a box of cigars to a Waterlow company friend. Always insisting he was the innocent victim of a villainous gang and probably keeping most of the $2.5 million the gang had sent out of Portugal, Hennies was tracked by the new Interpol organization but never found. He was rumoured to have survived in Germany into the Nazi era under his German name, Adolf Doring. José Bandeira and brother António served prison and exile sentences respectively.

Alves Reis began his twenty-year sentence in the Lisbon Penitentiary in October 1930, but was released in May 1945 because of the pre-trial time he'd served. While in jail he wrote memoirs entitled *The Secret of My Confession* and converted to Protestantism. After his release he went to Oporto. In a church ceremony he repented his sins and informally became what would now be called a 'born-again Christian', a faith he and his wife and two grown sons then tried to spread in Brazil. Returning home from Brazil in 1950, Reis pursued petty and unsuccessful business deals until he died on 6 July 1955, two years after his wife's death. The biggest twentieth-century swindler in Iberian history was buried in an unmarked grave.[22]

One of the consequences of the Portuguese and other European counterfeiting epidemics of the 1920s was the creation and gradual evolution of Interpol, the International Police Organization, into the useful, if not omnipotent, tool of law-enforcement it has become in the world today. After Interpol's creation in 1923, law-enforcement in Europe, the Americas and the Far East faced a new state-sponsored threat: Soviet dictator Josef Stalin's multifaceted effort to produce and distribute enough forged US dollars to finance Soviet and communist espionage abroad and, if possible, to make massive purchases of food, fuel and military supplies urgently required by the struggling Soviet economy. Stalin's early covert economic warfare is our next subject.

Eleven

Stalin's Dollars: Biting the Hand That Feeds You

> In order to destroy bourgeois society you must debauch its money.
>
> *Vladimir Ilyich Lenin,* c. *1918*

On 23 January 1930, Walter Krivitsky, a senior Soviet GRU (Glavnoye Razvedyvatelnoye Upravlenic, the Red Army's military intelligence service) officer in Europe, was flipping through the *Berliner Tageblatt* on a Vienna–Rome train when he noticed a banner headline across the top of an entire page: 'WHO COUNTERFEITS THE DOLLARS?' The story had a Berlin dateline and the lead read:

> The news of the circulation of counterfeit $100 banknotes formed the topic of conversation today in banking circles and on the [Berlin] Stock Exchange. So far neither the counterfeiters nor their plant has been discoverered. But recent investigations have established that Franz Fischer of Neue Winterfeldstrasse 3 who undertook to pass the counterfeit notes in Berlin returned from Russia in March 1929.[1]

A cold chill must have run down Krivitsky's spine. As recorded in his memoirs (published four years after his defection to the West in 1937 and eight years before his assassination by the KGB in Washington, DC, in February 1941), he said to himself: 'What the devil! This must be *our* affair.'

Unlike many of his colleagues in the growing Soviet secret services, Krivitsky had both an instinctive and learned grasp of international politics, economics and strategy. He was hostile to the counterfeiting project. He believed, first of all, that it was impossible for Soviet presses to print enough phoney $100 bills or for communist networks to distribute them to make any real dent in the US economy. Worse, he reflected, the Soviet Union would be blamed sooner or later. Counterfeiting as an extreme criminal enterprise and weapon of economic warfare had a terrible international reputation. Moscow yearned for US diplomatic recognition. It had been refused by President Herbert Hoover and his predecessors, Coolidge, Harding and Wilson. If news of the Soviet origin of the dollar forgeries became public, that yearning would not be fulfilled.

From the media and from colleagues, Krivitsky learned that a group of American promoters of Canadian mining shares had acquired a private Berlin bank, Sass & Martini, founded in 1846. The buyers soon turned the bank over to the ownership of Berliners, including a certain Paul Roth. This Roth was a former communist member of the Berlin Municipal Council. Krivitsky knew him as a staffer at the embassy in Berlin.

Krivitsky had also known Franz Fischer, a principal customer of Sass & Martini, since 1920. He had worked with him in 1923, when Weimar Germany was wracked by hyperinflation, political unrest and secret deals with Moscow. In that year Krivitsky had helped Fischer to organize what Krivitsky called a 'military staff' for the German Communist Party. Fischer had served the GRU for years under the supervision of Alfred Tilden (a.k.a. 'Tilten' or Pacquet), long known in secret service circles only as 'Alfred', a top military intelligence officer who since 1927 had been operating mainly in the United States as the GRU *rezident* or illegal spy (the term was used for men and women operating from Soviet embassies or consulates, or otherwise with diplomatic cover or immunity).

Krivitsky recognized the Soviet acquisition of the Sass & Martini bank as a classic cover operation by Soviet intelligence. While he knew Franz Fischer to be a 'thorough-going idealist' who would never pursue the laundering of bogus money for his own personal gain, Krivitsky correctly concluded that he must have been acting under political orders from Moscow. Josef Stalin's evolving dictatorship had obviously bought the respected bank in order to inspire confidence in the expertly forged counterfeit American dollars it would be called upon to handle.[2]

Fighting the 'Red Peril' . . . and Helping Its Domestic Victims

The Soviet counterfeiting operation of the late 1920s and early 1930s brings to mind impoverished Communist North Korea's counterfeiting of US dollars. Since the Korean War of the early 1950s, US administrations often encouraged China, South Korea, NGOs and others to send North Korea desperately needed food and medicines. The US tried to use promised fuel oil deliveries as an incentive to halt Pyongyang's nuclear weapons programme in 2007, even while the US Treasury and North Korea were engaged in a bitter spat over the North Korean dollar forgeries. Similarly, despite their policy of not recognizing the Soviet government and wishing for regime change there, Herbert Hoover and other conservative American citizens and presidents in the 1920s staved off starvation in post-revolution Russia with food and medical aid. The American Relief Administration (ARA) alone sent Russia $50 million in food, clothing and medicine during the famine of 1921 under the direction of Herbert Hoover, then secretary of commerce. Hoover believed that this relief would succeed where Allied military intervention had failed in causing a popular counter-revolution and bringing down Soviet rule. Instead, even though they saved millions of Russians from starvation, the ARA's relief efforts actually helped to consolidate the Bolshevik government and to prevent a counter-revolution.

From 1921 on, with his so-called New Economic Policy (NEP) Lenin seemed to be abandoning extreme Bolshevism, with its xenophobia and confiscation of private industry and property. The NEP was intended temporarily to encourage private enterprise and attract foreign investment in order to rescue the country from the abyss of misery and starvation that the revolution had opened up. Lenin's argument was that socialism could be built at home once economic health had been restored. He believed that he could attract desperately needed capital by offering American industry concessions that would guarantee them profits. At first, the Americans were slow to respond. In 1925, a year after Lenin's death, only eight of ninety active foreign concessions were American. The eight included W. Averell Harriman, later President Roosevelt's ambassador in Moscow, and Armand and Julius Hammer, who got concessions for asbestos mining and manufacturing pencils.

During 1928–32, Soviet and communist agents in New York worked to purchase or steal US economic and military know-how. At the same time Soviet dictator Josef Stalin wished to undermine the capitalist US economy. All this was to be accomplished by systematic espionage, and by the covert or 'black' operation of expert forging of fake US dollars made in the USSR. Four years after Lenin's death in 1924, Stalin had his expert printers and engravers turn out millions of bogus dollars. In addition to acquiring capitalist goods and undermining the capitalist economy that was helping him, with the counterfeit US cash Stalin and his underlings sought to finance Soviet espionage and communist revolutionary activity around the world, especially in China, then in revolutionary flux.

It could be reasonably speculated that the dollar operation may also have been partly motivated by the Soviet leadership's desire for vengeance against America. President Woodrow Wilson considered himself a peacemaker with lofty ideals. He had tried to keep the US out of the First World War, until actions by Germany made this impossible by early 1917. Nevertheless, as the war ended in 1918, Wilson tried to help bring about regime change in the fledgling Soviet Union by military means, by supporting the counter-revolution there. The US joined the other First World War Allies in sending troops to Russia to back up the White armies in their ultimately unsuccessful civil war against the victorious Reds in 1918–21. American military intervention began on 11 June 1918, exactly five months before the general armistice on the Western Front in the First World War. Advance US troop units that arrived in June in Murmansk and Archangel were followed by an American expeditionary force of about 5,000 men. They landed on 19 August 1918 in Vladivostok (occupied by the Japanese since 1917) to assist the White forces against the Reds in Siberia and the Far East.

One of Lenin's reactions was to send an admonitory and at the same time encouraging letter to the American Workers Party (AWP), responding to a workers' rally in Seattle, Washington, against the US military intervention. In 1920 the AWP would merge with the fledgling American Communist Party. A number of the party's early adherents soon began assisting Soviet intelligence operations in the United States. Documents of the old American Communist Party donated to New York University were publicly exhibited by NYU in March 2007. The 1920 AWP merger document lists 'Dix' as the secret party name of Earl R. Browder, later the Communist Party's general secretary, and 'L. C. Wheat' as that of Jay Lovestone, who was privy to the counterfeiting operation but who later recanted his communism to work with the anti-Soviet US labour syndicates, the AF of L and CIO, and the CIA.

After unsuccessfully fighting against the Bolsheviks, Allied troops, including the Americans, withdrew from Archangel and Murmansk in September and October 1919, and from Siberia in 1920. By 1922 all Allied forces had been forced out of Soviet Russia.[3]

Lenin's attempts to woo American economic and technical help had begun even before American intervention against the Reds ended. Lenin enjoyed limited successes, marred by sporadic early episodes of Soviet espionage in America. Early in 1919 L. K. Martens was named by Moscow as official representative of the Russian Socialist Federated Soviet Republic in the United States. Though lacking diplomatic status, Martens opened an office in New York. From 9 to 16 March 1919, with the consent of both President Wilson and British Prime Minister David Lloyd George, diplomat William Bullitt went to Russia, tasked with exploring and possibly halting 'military conflict' (read Allied intervention in the civil war) by May of that year. Lenin had succeeded in establishing the Society for Technical Assistance to Russia. Its main mission: to assist American workers and technicians desiring to work in Russia. On 5 October the Chicago *Daily News* published an interview with Lenin, who insisted: 'We are definitely for economic accord with America and all other countries, but especially with America.' In December there followed the creation of the

American Commercial Association to Promote Trade with Russia, a non-governmental organization for the US business community.

By July of 1920, the US State Department had authorized the export of American goods to Russia. There was a condition: trade had to be carried out by private businessmen at their own risk, without guarantees or support by the US government. However, by that time federal investigators had discovered that Soviet intelligence had begun espionage operations under the cover of the L. K. Martens trading operation. In December Martens was expelled from the United States. Despite its desperate need for economic aid in almost any form from the US, the Soviet Foreign Ministry retaliated by cancelling all American private business contracts.

This left the Society for Technical Assistance to Russia still functioning. It managed to send representatives to Russia, where the Soviet Communist Party and government leased the Moscow Auto Works to them. This prompted the Soviets to appeal to President Warren G. Harding to normalize business relations between the two nations. On 25 March Secretary of State Charles Evans Hughes gave a cautiously positive response, citing Soviet Russia's guarantees to protect private property rights as a condition of American–Soviet trade. One big barrier to this trade – and to the activities of Soviet intelligence in the US – disappeared in May 1921, when postal service, interrupted after the 1917 Russian Revolution, was restored between the US and the USSR.[4]

Long before his election to the US presidency in 1929, Herbert Clark Hoover was a champion of humanitarian aid to struggling and starving people overseas. Born in 1874 in the little town of West Branch, Iowa, Hoover lost both his father and mother at the ages of six and nine respectively. He went through a Quaker school, the Pacific Friends Academy in Newberg, Oregon, then worked his way through newly established Stanford University in Palo Alto, California, majoring in geology. After jobs involving evaluating and inspecting mines, Hoover moved to China and worked as a mining engineer until 1902, then went on to the same work in Australia and eventually other parts of the world, opening his own mining consulting business in 1908. By 1914 he was a skilled engineer and the wealthy owner of profitable Burmese silver mines, assisted by his wife, also a geologist, in all of his mostly profitable ventures abroad. He was a successful capitalist with charitable instincts, somewhat like Bill Gates or George Soros today. After running the US Food Administration for President Wilson during the First World War, Hoover was named to head the relief effort that channelled 34 million tons of American food, clothing and other supplies to Europe. Besides the $50 million in humanitarian aid later sent to Bolshevik Russia, this programme helped people in nineteen other nations.[5]

In 1928, after defeating Leon Trotsky and his followers in a fierce policy and succession struggle (the Trotskyites had advocated giving top priority to promoting global Bolshevik revolution) Stalin went ahead with his project of building socialism in Russia by promulgating his First Five-Year Plan. Stalin dropped the policy of granting foreign concessions. He shifted to getting foreign technical assistance on a contract basis. This was more attractive to most American entrepreneurs. Many began flocking to the Soviet Union for the first time since the 1917 revolution. Bilateral US–Soviet trade, mostly in US exports to the USSR, increased twenty-fold between 1923 and 1930, reaching $114,399,000. By 1930 the US was the USSR's main supplier, furnishing 25 per cent of all Soviet imports. The Soviet Union was America's eighth-largest customer by 1930 and the single largest foreign buyer of American agricultural and industrial machinery.[6]

However, Moscow was still unable to get long-term credits from American banks. This was discouraged by the US government. Moscow was refusing to pay war and other debts owed from the Czarist era, and there were no formal diplomatic relations between the two countries. Heavy Soviet purchases of foreign machinery and all the materials Stalin needed to industrialize Russia were exhausting the meagre foreign exchange reserves held by the Soviet Treasury.

One of Stalin's remedies was to put into circulation throughout the world what Walter Krivitsky estimated at about $10 million in bogus US currency. Krivitsky wrote that from 1928 to 1932, the duration of the first Five-Year Plan,

> the globe was circled by a trail of spurious $100 Federal Reserve banknotes of the United States. The bogus bills first trickled and later flooded into the United States from Shanghai and San Francisco, from Houston and New York, from Montreal and Havana, from Warsaw, Geneva, Bucharest, Berlin, Sofia, Belgrade.[7]

The excellent-quality fakes were almost certainly printed by Section Six (the Printing Bureau) of the Fourth Department of the Razvedupr (GRU), the Red Army's intelligence service. US military historian Raymond W. Leonard, in his book *Secret Soldiers of the Revolution*, describes this task of Section Six as an offshoot of the old Bolshevik revolutionary use of underground presses to further communist revolutionary activities. The Section's printing plants turned out everything from posters and leaflets to forged identity documents – and counterfeit money.[8]

Soviet Espionage, the Counterfeiting Game and the Players

Serious Soviet espionage and the accompanying GRU 'black' operation to distribute counterfeit US dollars developed in the late 1920s. This was later than their use in western Europe, China and elsewhere. As David Dallin observes in his comprehensive account of early spying by Moscow's men and women, *Soviet Espionage*, there were only occasional and isolated early spying efforts in the US. They occurred during visits of agents of the Comintern, the semi-covert Third Communist International formed in March 1919, American zealots aided by Soviet 'commercial' emissaries, such as the exposed, discredited and deported L. K. Martens. Once US troops had been withdrawn from Russia, the America of Presidents Wilson, Harding and Coolidge avoided active involvement in adventures outside the Americas. Moscow was satisfied that American operatives and operations were rarely involved in the multitudinous western European or Far Eastern anti-Soviet projects. This helped keep Russian covert operations and 'dirty tricks' in the US to a minimum in those early years. Also, the US communist movement never reached the size or strength of sister parties overseas. Early communists in America in the 1920s and early 1930s were mainly immigrants, legal or illegal, from pre-revolutionary Russia and its subject or satellite peoples – Poles, Balts, Ukrainians and Jews of various nationalities.[9]

The military GRU was the first of the two Soviet spy agencies, the other being Obiedinenoye Gosudarstvennoye Upravlenie (OGPU), to come to the United States. In 1924 it played an important part in forming the American Trading Organization (AMTORG), whose official Russian name was Amerikanskaia torgovaia. Its offices were at 269 5th Avenue in Manhattan. Overtly AMTORG was a merger of two above-board Soviet corporations. Covertly, it evolved into a cover for military and economic espionage, as well as being a legitimate trading operation intended by Stalin to purchase as many American goods as possible. However, Stalin did not trust many of AMTORG's mostly American members and agents, many of whom were not communists. He assigned the Soviet civilian secret police organization, the OGPU, to keep tabs on it. (At that time, the civilian OGPU and the military GRU had been and would continue to be fierce rivals. They competed for Soviet funds, often spied on each other, and were not disinclined to play 'dirty tricks' to discredit one another.)

The first GRU *rezident* in the US was a certain Comrade Chatski, first name unknown. He was in America as an employee of AMTORG. Working with him was the Latvian-born communist Alfred Tilden mentioned earlier and Lydia Stahl, both of whom eventually helped to recruit, organize and operate the American branch of the counterfeiting operation. Both had previously served the GRU in espionage tasks in France. Tilden at first operated from the office of a shipping company near Manhattan's Battery waterfront. There, with the help of communist seamen and their trade unions, he organized a GRU courier service. This was to prove useful in distributing the bogus $100 bills, many of which were shipped to New York from Hamburg, Germany, on liners of the North German Lloyd Line.[10]

Among all the colourful characters involved in the counterfeiting operation, many of whom could have been figures in a Graham Greene or Alfred Hitchcock story or film, Lydia Stahl was outstanding. She was born Lydia Chkalov in Rostov, southern Russia, in 1885. Her husband, Stahl, was a wealthy Russian nobleman. During the revolution the Stahls, like so many others of their class, lost their estates and wealth, and emigrated to the United States. Lydia had a command of French and perhaps German as well as English and a good basic knowledge of international finance. She went to work at the New York Stock Exchange and took courses at Columbia University. Husband and wife both became naturalized Americans. Their only son died, probably in the global influenza pandemic in 1918. Grief-stricken, Lydia returned alone to Europe. She settled in Paris as a university student and began associating with communists. Dallin describes her in Paris after the First World War as living in a 'small and mean' apartment; a naturally attractive, elegant woman, 'she dressed poorly; with her tousled hair and worn-down heels she gave the impression of untidiness'. An expert photographer, she set up a studio in Paris where communist agents had secret documents they'd obtained photocopied. This was an important preparation for her later operation of the photocopying studio and lab Tilden managed to acquire for the GRU on upper Broadway in New York's Harlem. There, purloined espionage documents as well as the bogus dollars shipped over from Germany would be copied.

Stahl's role as a student in Paris was more than just a cover for espionage: she was deeply interested and far from ignorant in the sciences. At Columbia University she had studied medicine without graduating, and she dabbled in law studies in Paris before shifting to Oriental languages, probably in preparation for hypothetical future GRU assignments in the Far East. Her principal boyfriend and partner from 1923, during her first stay in France, was Professor Louis Pierre Martin, a former attaché at the French Naval Ministry and an officer of the Légion d'honneur.[11]

About the time Moscow was launching the counterfeiting operation, Stahl had returned to the US to work with Tilden and with Felix Wolf (a.k.a. 'Nikolai Krebs'), who ran the AMTORG cover operation for the GRU in New York from 1924 to 1929. Although it is unclear whether he was operating with or in a separate 'cell' from Stahl and Tilden, another GRU associate was Dr Philip

Rosenbliett, a New York dentist who was later the GRU contact (or case officer) of the American agent for the Soviets Whittaker Chambers, who defected in 1938, some time after his ideological break with communism, and exposed many secrets of Soviet espionage in his 1952 book, *Witness*.

In 1928, the GRU station in New York began to rack up some successes. Notable was the purchase for the USSR through AMTORG of two examples of a revolutionary new battle tank, originally designated the M-1928 and later the M-1930, designed by US armaments expert J. Walter Christie. After protracted attempts and vain efforts to sell the tank design to the US defence bureaucracy in Washington, the Soviets came up with the cash before the Americans. The two advanced models were shipped in crates labelled 'Tractors' to the USSR from New York on 24 December 1930. These Christmas presents to Stalin became the prototypes for a whole generation of Soviet armoured vehicles: the T-34 series of tanks, assault guns and tank destroyer used in the 1930s and 1940s. The Soviet Union produced and fought the Germans with them in the Second World War. By 1945, variants of the Christie suspension system were being incorporated in tanks designed in Poland, Nazi Germany, Britain and the United States.

Nicholas Dozenberg, code-named 'Arthur', was another Latvian-born GRU agent who eventually joined the Soviet counterfeiting ring in New York – for which he would later serve a year term in US federal prison. He had lived in the US with his family since 1904. After serving in leftist organizations including the old American Socialist Party in Boston, he joined the communist precursor to the American Workers Party in 1921. Later the Communist Party's politburo put Dozenberg in touch with Lydia Stahl. He took the cover name of 'Nicholas L. Dallant' and joined Soviet military intelligence. After Lydia Stahl's arrival in New York, Dozenberg rented facilities in the back rooms of a photography shop owned by a Joseph Tourin at 1180 Broadway in Harlem. Later, Dozenberg purchased the shop outright from Tourin. There, Stahl used her Paris experience to set up a photo shop and lab.

The lab's original purpose, for which it was extensively used before the dollar operation began, was photocopying stolen espionage documents in coordination with the AMTORG operatives. As well as these operations, done mainly at night, Stahl ran her own subnetwork of agents. She managed to acquire for Moscow from an unidentified 'cooperative and venal American officer' the blueprints for the British battleship HMS *Royal Oak* while they were being sent from Canada to Britain. After their theft and copying in Stahl's lab, the plans were returned. British and US authorities discovered the theft only years later.[12]

The GRU's Harlem photo shop at 1180 Broadway began the reproduction and distribution of the bogus $100 Federal Reserve notes printed in Russia and shipped from Germany some time in 1928. But even before this, the notes began to appear in Europe, the Caribbean and the Far East. After his defection to the West in 1937, Krivitsky began claiming credit for stopping the global operation. He believed this had spared the Roosevelt White House, which followed Hoover's Depression-shadowed presidency in January 1932, from having publicly to blame the Soviet Union. Official public blame would have turned public and congressional opinion against Roosevelt's planned normalization of diplomatic relations with Moscow, as Krivitsky well knew.

Krivitsky versus Stalin

Walter Krivitsky was born Samuel Ginsburg (a name appearing in some of his many passports) to poor Jewish parents in Podwoloczyska, Poland, on 28 June 1899. He was eighteen when the Bolshevik Revolution erupted in 1917. He joined the Communist Party and enthusiastically embraced Lenin's version of Marxism. He saw it 'as a weapon with which to assault the wrongs against which I instinctively rebelled'.[13] Despite the enmity and warfare between Russia and his native Poland, he was soon serving the Soviet GRU faithfully throughout Europe, especially in Germany. There he used his considerable diplomatic talents to build a close relationship between Soviet intelligence and the secret service of Weimar's semi-covert army, the 'Black Reichswehr'.

According to Krivitsky and other contemporaries, Stalin was naturally inclined to the criminal counterfeiting scheme because he had a criminal mind. Once an informer for the Okhrana, the Czar's secret police who spied on his early Bolshevik colleagues, Stalin is identified by Krivitsky and other contemporarics as a natural despot who in a crisis would use criminal methods as a first rather than a last resort against enemies. 'Even in his early twenties,' writes British Kremlinology scholar Donald Rayfield, 'Stalin attached himself to two sorts of men. One sort, like [Mikhail] Kalinin and [Dr Viktor] Kurnakovsky – doctrinaire, self-educated Marxists – would constitute his inner circle. The other sort were killers.'[14]

Krivitsky believed that Stalin's counterfeiting of US dollars revealed

> the primitiveness of this Georgian's mind – his ignorance of modern world conditions, and the readiness with which in a crisis he turns to the expedients of common crime. Stalin first rose to prominence in the Bolshevik Party as an organizer of 'expropriations' – that is, bank robberies designed to replenish the party treasury.[15]

Stalin and his immediate henchmen viewed the forging of dollars and their laundering as ideal expedients to secure genuine gold or genuine hard currency, desperately needed by the Soviet Treasury for the industries to be built during the First Five-Year Plan. Also, both the GRU and the OGPU were pitifully short of cash, just at the time when they were called on to expand operations. The quest for valuta, gold or hard foreign currency, was entrusted to a special 'Valuta Bureau' of the OGPU. Its task was to extract foreign currency and any kind of valuables it could from Soviet nationals anywhere in the world. One of its operations was the so-called Dollar Inquisition: remittances sent to Soviet citizens in the USSR from relatives in America were systematically extorted by imprisoning and torturing the recipients, where necessary, until the ransom money arrived.

Such practices were public knowledge. However, like other counterfeiting operations by regimes in history – George III and William Pitt against American and French revolutionaries, Napoleon and Prussia against their enemies, Britain against the

Kaiser's Germany, Hitler's Germany in the Nazi counterfeiting operation against Britain and the Second World War Allies or present-day North Korean or Iranian forging operations against America – Stalin's cunning global operation against the American dollar between 1928 and 1932 was intended to be a deep secret. Actually, it was for long a better-kept secret than most of those just mentioned. Until Krivitsky's revelations in 1939, the source of the counterfeit $100 notes of the late 1920s and early 1930s, though suspected by many law-enforcement and justice officials, remained a 'riddle inside an enigma', to use a Churchillian expression.

General Jan Berzin was the GRU chief and the highest authority charged with implementing the project. Berzin's underlings worked as much as possible with organized criminals – American racketeers operating in eastern Europe or in America with known Chicago gangland figures. Other helpers were non-criminal, purely ideological communists and fellow travellers who took little or no profit, acting mainly from political motives.

In January of 1930 Krivitsky, and shortly thereafter German law-enforcement officials, learned that Krivitsky's communist acquaintance Franz Fischer had exchanged at the Sass & Martini Bank in Berlin $19,000 in $100 bills. Sass & Martini in turn had deposited them with the solid and prestigious Deutsche Bank, which sent many of them to the Bank of New York. When they finally reached the Federal Reserve Bank in New York, they drew suspicion because they were of an old, large-sized series of Federal Reserve notes, the dimensions of which had recently been reduced in a new issue by the Treasury. Under microscopes, the bigger notes turned out to be counterfeits of a pattern already known to the Treasury. On 23 December the Federal Reserve cabled Berlin that the notes were bogus. It also warned German banks and law-enforcement agencies that these were the best forgeries ever discovered.

Berlin police commissioner von Liebermann ordered raids on Sass & Martini. He discovered the bank's doubtful antecedents (although not their Soviet government connection), and it was soon closed down. German investigators traced all the bogus bills to Franz Fischer, who had meanwhile disappeared. The Berlin police theorized, incorrectly, that the ring originating the counterfeits operated either from Poland or the Balkans.

Krivitsky worried that eventually Moscow's central role would be unmasked and that this would compromise ongoing Soviet espionage operations that he was running. In Rome, he voiced his strong objections to Vladimir Tairov (a.k.a. 'the Gregorian'), a personal envoy of Stalin then on an inspection tour of Soviet covert activities abroad. 'Don't worry about it,' Tairov told him. 'The Boss is in on it.' Krivitsky realized that 'the Boss' was Stalin and that General Berzin would not have launched it without Stalin's authorization. Tairov defended the scheme, while acknowledging that the GRU had purchased Sass & Martini for the sole purpose of laundering and distributing the Soviet forgeries. After further argument, Tairov admitted that the operation was perhaps causing harm to Russian interests in Europe. 'But you must understand,' he added, 'this business was organized primarily with an eye on China. Over there we're floating millions of these dollars, and we need them there.'[16]

By 1928, the counterfeit dollars were indeed badly needed to finance Stalin's agents in China. Leon Trotsky and his followers, eager to foment global ideologically 'pure' Bolshevik revolutions around the globe, argued that the Chinese Communist Party, then dependent on Moscow, should stay independent and not hobnob with the rightist Kuomintang (KMT). The KMT had triumphed in the battles between rival warlords that followed the overthrow of the last Manchu emperor in 1911. Stalin, however, maintained that since a real 'socialist' revolution in China was unlikely in the near future, Moscow should back Sun Yat-sen's KMT as the only effective 'revolutionary' force in China. Sun's deputy, General Chiang Kai-shek, began studying at Moscow's Frunze Military Academy. GRU operatives poured into China. But Sun died in 1925. In an ensuing power struggle within the KMT, Chiang began winning. His security forces arrested, interrogated and tortured Chinese Communist Party (CCP) militants. The communists nevertheless resisted and seized control of the KMT in Canton. They expanded recruiting among workers there and in Shanghai. In

1926, after complicated internal struggles in which Stalin's agents lacked enough real money effectively to bribe officials and pay spies, Chiang set up in Nanking a KMT government that excluded communists. By late 1927, political strife and military battle between KMT and communists had brought about in Wuhang, China, a communist rival regime to the KMT supported by Stalin.

The GRU's Moscow Centre sent into China such senior operatives as Ho Chi Minh, later the founder, leader and hero of the successful Indo-Chinese wars against the French and the Americans in Vietnam. They joined other GRU and Comintern agents, including American communist leader Earl Browder, in fomenting a communist uprising in Canton in December 1927, which Chiang's KMT ruthlessly crushed. The GRU and Comintern were defeated in Canton by the KMT's lack of ready cash, armaments, and training, all of which cost the kind of valuta that Moscow couldn't provide in sufficient quantities.

Political consequences of the Canton failure included Stalin's final crackdown and exile of Trotsky and his supporters – Trotsky was murdered in Mexico City in 1940 by Stalin's agent Ramon Mercador – and the perception by the GRU chiefs that they could not succeed in revolutionary ventures without enough cash for payoffs; hence their resorting to Stalin's false dollars. The Canton episode was the last time before the Second World War that Red Army intelligence tried to sponsor armed rebellion. In subsequent ventures, the GRU used the Comintern and the Comintern's often ill-paid or unpaid agents rather than its own officers.[17]

Following a Berlin police warning that millions of dollars' worth of the false $100 notes were circulating undetected in Europe, reports and warnings flowed between the US Treasury and many corners of the world in 1930. One US warning on 23 January tipped off the Swiss Federal Police Department in Bern that the counterfeits were circulating in Switzerland. The Berlin police the next day reported discovery of the forgeries with about $40,000 face value. They announced a reward for the capture of Franz Fischer. From Havana, Cuba, came news that many of the $100 forgeries were lodged in Cuban banks and the Havana branch of the National City Bank of New York. Many of the notes were being laundered into good money at the Casino National, a top-drawer Havana gambling joint.

On 29 January the German attorney Dr Alphonse Sack (who during the Nazi era would appear for the defence in the notorious Reichstag Fire Trial) told a Berlin court that he could prove the bogus $100 notes had been produced in the Soviet State Printing Establishment in Moscow. The *New York Times* reported on 30 January that the Soviets had circulated $2.5 million in forged sterling and dollar notes. In February discoveries of the same forged cash were made in Warsaw and Lwow, Poland, and in Antwerp, Belgium, where forged $10 and $500 notes (the Federal Reserve was issuing the $500 denomination at the time) led to the arrest of a Romanian, a Hungarian and a Czech national.

In the United States the US Secret Service and the FBI had been summoned to deal with the counterfeits being spewed out of the GRU copy shop in Manhattan. The Federal Reserve Bank of New York issued a circular on 22 February 1930, identifying minute errors by which to identify the fakes. In March they began to turn up in Mexico and Czechoslovakia. Alerted by the alarm bells ringing in Europe and the Americas, GRU boss Tairov informed Moscow of the potential danger of wholesale exposés of the campaign in Europe and the Americas. Krivitsky claims in his memoirs that Tairov was ordered to entrust him, Krivitsky, with 'liquidating' the affair.

In Vienna, Krivitsky met current GRU station chief 'Alexandrovsky', who was angry at the GRU's Alfred Tilden for sending Fischer to Vienna and for obliging Alexandrovsky, with reference to orders from Stalin, to protect Fischer and supply him with false passports for flight to Moscow.[18] Krivitsky knew and Fischer probably realized, Moscow would be the end station for him: Stalin wouldn't allow him to survive.

Tilden, whom Tairov blamed for the operation that he had now come to recognize as potentially dangerous to the USSR's reputation in Europe, was also in Vienna. Krivitsky met Tilden at the Café Künstler. In response to Krivitsky's scolding about the whole operation, Tilden replied in its defence:

> But you don't understand. This is real money. It isn't like ordinary counterfeit currency. It's the real stuff. I got the same paper they use in the United States. The only difference is that it's printed on our presses instead of in Washington.[19]

If such a conversation had been known at the time to US law-enforcement or the US Treasury, it would have been a bombshell. Paper for genuine US currency was supplied by the Crane Corporation, an old family paper manufacturing business located among the Berkshire Hills in Massachusetts. Crane had existed since 1801 and had begun supplying the paper for President Lincoln's new greenbacks during the Civil War. In 1879 it became the Bureau of Printing and Engraving's main supplier (it still is today in 2007), with minor exceptions when contracts were given to competitors such as the American Banknote Company. The exceptions ended in 1978. Crane has remained the monopoly supplier of genuine dollar currency paper ever since, despite challenges for the business by major British manufacturers De la Rue and Portals (which operates a paper plant in the US state of Georgia).

In their rare interviews with the media, Crane executives have consistently claimed that their security system was 100 per cent secure and that no stocks of their paper have ever been lost or stolen. This could be true provided all of the 'genuine' paper detected among the Russian forgeries was that of genuine $1 bills, bleached and overprinted as $100 Federal Reserve notes. Around the time that Krivitsky noted that the Soviet gang had obtained real US paper, Crane in 1928 added to its security measures by inserting silk threads in its paper. (Later, these were followed and replaced by metallic threads and fluorescent threads, common devices among most world currencies today.)

Nicholas Dozenberg and his friend and assistant, Russian-born Dr Valentin Burtan, a prosperous New York physician, had carefully cultivated contacts at the US Bureau of Printing and Engraving (USBPE) where the Crane paper was regularly delivered by train. A GRU officer named J. Polyakov was sent to the US under AMTORG cover. His mission was to further cultivate the USBPE contacts made by Dozenberg and Burtan. Several US federal employees, never publicly identified, may have been induced by the Soviets to provide technical data. Two of them reportedly approached Polyakov to ask him to arrange for their transport to Russia. One of these, possibly one whom Krivitsky vaguely refers to as Latvian-born 'Nick' who might have been Nicholas Dozenberg, reportedly helped the Soviets obtain a large stock of genuine US banknote paper. Printed as $1 bills or blank, this was apparently forwarded to the Soviet Union in the 1928–30 time-frame.[20] In the light of Crane's denials and perennial US Treasury secrecy about counterfeiting details, uncertainty remains as to whether any pristine, blank Crane paper really ever got into Soviet hands.

Krivitsky says that he believed he had 'liquidated' the counterfeiting campaign during the early months of 1930. Alfred Tilden returned to Moscow in May 1930. So did Fischer. In June, Krivitsky arrived in the Soviet capital to meet with General Ian Berzin and Tairov. Berzin expressed gratitude to Krivitsky for cleaning up the mess in Europe caused by the police raids and subsequent collapse of the Sass & Martini Bank. He repeated that the whole scheme had been planned in order to deal with Soviet espionage needs in China, admitting that it was apparently not suitable for the West.

Tilden was transferred to Minsk, near the borders of Poland that had fought a war against the new Soviet Union during the domestic civil war between Reds and Whites. Franz Fischer, in disgrace, was assigned to OGPU's construction division and sent off to remote Kolyma, in north-east Siberia. He was rarely heard of afterwards and probably perished in a Gulag. General Berzin sent Krivitsky on a troubleshooting mission to Vienna in late autumn, 1931. There Krivitsky first encountered Nicholas Dozenberg and Dozenberg's pretty young wife.

Tall and well dressed, Dozenberg acted the part of a successful young American businessman. He was working for the GRU in Romania, under cover of operating the American–Romanian Export Film Company. In Vienna, with Krivitsky's help, he solicited GRU funds to travel back to New York to buy some expensive film equipment, which could also serve for espionage. The Dozenberg couple travelled to the United States in early 1932.

During Dozenberg's new American sojourn he worked with some of the old GRU gang and their communist fellow travellers. This coincided with a fresh epidemic of counterfeit dollars on both sides of the Atlantic. Early in April, Swiss banking authorities suddenly warned all European banks to watch out for the same old bogus $100 bills. On 29 April Berlin's *Börsen-Zeitung* reported the appearance of the notes once again in Vienna and Budapest. The affair exploded publicly in the United States months later.

On 3 January 1933 US Secret Service agents at Newark Airport arrested on his arrival from Moscow a man carrying documents in the name of 'Count von Buelow'. By contemporary accounts, he ranked among the most colourful characters involved in Stalin's currency war against the US dollar. He is said to have affected a monocle and to have resembled a Hollywood German villain of the ilk of Erich von Stroheim. Investigators soon established that his real name was Hans Dechow. He was an experienced con man who had a police record in Chicago. He was charged with being part of a counterfeiting ring operating in Canada and Mexico. Although the Soviet Union was not mentioned in the court papers charging him, Dechow, who spoke Spanish and Portuguese, had actually been tasked with trying to distribute the bogus dollars in Latin America, especially in Guatemala, and possibly in Canada by bribing finance ministers and central bankers to accept them. He was also to take a cut on laundering operations and put the fakes into circulation. As it turned out, the GRU's valuta stocks were too low to give him enough genuine hard currency to corrupt the lofty officials he tried to target.

On 4 January 1933, during the final days of the outgoing Hoover administration, Secret Service agents intercepted Dr Burtan as he arrived in New York by train from Montreal. The *New York Times* reported that he was arrested on a charge of counterfeiting 'within twenty-four hours after that of "Count von Buelow". The arrest followed disclosure from Chicago that agents of the ring had passed $25,500 in a Loop bank of that city.'

W. H. Moran had capably headed the US Treasury's Secret Service ever since his appointment by President Wilson in 1918. In March 1929, when Moran saw the first seized Russian counterfeit, he realized that this was truly professional work. Secret Service laboratories confirmed that the paper was original paper; apparently new-condition $1 bills, bleached and overprinted as $100 bills. This was a device commonly used by more skilful counterfeiters since the Civil War period. It was more prevalent before the laser colour printers and other reprographic copying processes of the late twentieth century.

A US Treasury circular warned that 'This is an extremely dangerous counterfeit . . . unusually deceptive, and great care should be exercised in handling notes of this variety and denomination.' By February 1930 three additional types of the Soviet $100 forgeries, larger-size Federal Reserve notes bearing Ben Franklin's portrait, turned up in circulation. Ever-stronger warnings were issued by the Treasury. However, most accounts agree that the Soviet-printed bogus notes, identified as such and seized, probably never exceeded a face value of $1 million. Stalin's forgers might have had more success if they had shifted to reproducing the new, smaller Federal Reserve notes first issued in July 1929. Appearance of the new genuine smaller notes led foreign banks and other overseas holders of US currency to ask the US Treasury Department to clarify rules about redemption of the large, older currency notes.

Under questioning, Dechow decided to turn state's evidence. In return, his case was suspended from the federal courts' docket. His confession gave federal authorities a fairly complete account of his dealings with Burtan and the Chicago underworld. Crucially, however, Dechow observed GRU security discipline and omitted any mention of the operation's Soviet origins. Dechow said he was involved in the munitions business, especially in procuring chemical warfare equipment, and had met Burtan in New York in summer of 1932. Since Dechow had connections with the Chicago underworld, in November 1932 Burtan told him he had $100,000 in $100 bills given him by a patient who happened to be a member of the legendary Arnold Rothstein's gang. The money was implied to be 'hot' – proceeds from illicit gambling, of which Rothstein at the time was an undisputed monarch (he was later murdered in an unsolved gangland killing), or of prostitution, alcohol bootlegging or other rackets. As such, the hot money could not safely be exchanged or otherwise laundered in New York, Burtan had explained in his fable to Dechow.

Shortly before Christmas of 1932, Dechow took some of the phoney Soviet-printed $100 bills from the cache in the Harlem photo studio with him to Chicago. There he offered the laundering deal to some of his underworld contacts. A private detective named Smiley helped make the contacts. Eight of the Chicago racketeers, named later in court papers, were involved. 'Smiley's people' agreed to help. They had the bills checked by several bank tellers who passed them as authentic. Burtan arrived and worked out an agreement: 30 per cent of the take in good money would go to the racketeers laundering it. They were given $100,000 in the bogus bills for exchange. But they were still ignorant of their bogus nature.

According to Krivitsky, banks accepting the notes included the Continental Illinois National Bank and Trust Company, the Northern Trust Company and the Harris Trust and Savings Bank. They exchanged the bills. These were of the old oversized variety of Federal Reserve notes. On 23 December 1932 the banks forwarded the bills in parcels to the Federal Reserve Bank of Chicago. Suspicious Fed officials called the Secret Service, which sent a very senior and experienced agent, its Chicago office chief Thomas J. Callaghan. After careful examination Callaghan pronounced the notes counterfeit. He identified them as similar or identical to those that had turned up in Berlin in 1930 and many other places in the world since 1928. All Chicago banks were alerted. This resulted in the arrest of a man at the First National Bank of Chicago. He had tried to change 100 $100 bills for ten $1,000 bills, which while not too common were legal tender at the time. Following this, the FBI and Chicago police were able to bust the underworld syndicate. Its members were furious to discover their planned swindle had failed because they had been swindled with counterfeits. They surrendered the $40,000 in forgeries they still held and offered to cooperate with the federal authorities.

Dechow came under pressure and threats from the Chicago gang to give them good money in exchange for the bogus bills. An OGPU agent appeared in New York and warned him to take the next boat for Europe. Instead Dechow fled to Canada for an inconclusive crisis meeting with Burtan at the Mount Royal Hotel in Montreal in early January 1933. The OGPU man who had warned Dechow in New York then reappeared in Montreal and again urged him to flee to Europe. But Dechow took a plane to Newark Airport. There he was promptly arrested, as already mentioned. He led federal agents to Dr Burtan's office on 58th Street in Manhattan. The *New York Times* of 24 February 1933 reported that investigations of Burtan and Dechow had traced the origins of the fake $100,000 passed in Chicago to the Soviet Union. It added that the bills resembled others passed in China and deemed by the US Treasury to be 'the most genuine-appearing counterfeits ever uncovered' and printed six years earlier.[21]

The same *Times* story said Burtan was under investigation for reportedly working for the Soviet government. But during his questioning and subsequent trial, he never admitted this. Nor did he betray names of his American and other communist accomplices. Eventually, on 4 May 1934 a federal jury in Chicago convicted Burtan simply of possessing and passing counterfeit money. In the long trial Dechow, who had been given immunity in return for his evidence, was the main prosecution witness. Burtan was sentenced to fifteen years in the federal penitentiary at Lewisburg, Pennsylvania. He served ten years and paid a fine of $10,000. His physician's licence was revoked.

Soon after Burtan's arrest in February 1933, Dozenberg returned to Moscow. Alfred Tilden also reappeared there and had probably denounced Dozenberg. Like Franz Fischer before him, Dozenberg got a chilly reception from Stalin: no posh hotel accommodation and no privileged ration card of the sort agents of the GRU and OGPU operating abroad were accustomed to in Moscow.

Valentin Markin (a.k.a. 'Walter', 'Herman' and 'Oscar'), a senior OGPU operative in the United States described by David Dallin as 'an able and devoted Communist . . . summoned the courage to go to Moscow personally to report on the mischief' caused by the rival GRU's counterfeiting and other schemes. Markin made his case against the GRU, criticizing General Berzin's leadership and management directly to Prime Minister and

Foreign Commissar Vyacheslav Molotov. Markin won: Stalin approved his recommendations and ordered a virtual freeze of GRU operations in the US. The Soviets hoped that as a result the incoming Roosevelt administration would soon grant the long-sought American diplomatic recognition of the Soviet government. This came to pass in November 1933, when Secretary of State Cordell Hull and Soviet Foreign Minister Maxim Litvinov exchanged letters of agreement.

Soviet intelligence operations in the US were transferred to the OGPU under the authority of its notorious chief Genrikh Yagoda. Appointed to clean up the aftermath of the counterfeiting operation and other 'messes' left by the GRU, Markin was found apparently murdered in a bar-room brawl in a 52nd Street hallway in Manhattan. Later, an OGPU chief, Abram Slutsky, told Krivitsky that Markin had been a Trotskyist and a traitor. For Krivitsky, this implied that Markin had been murdered under Stalin's orders by Yagoda's OGPU, which was renamed the NKVD (Naroddnyi komissariat vnutrennykh del, or People's Commissariat of Internal Affairs) in July 1934.[22]

Burtan died some time after his release from Lewisburg prison in the United States, without ever publicly admitting his Soviet connection. Dozenberg, never indicted, was undertaking new GRU assignments in Germany and Romania by 1932. He was later transferred to Tientsin, China, for military intelligence missions related to the Sino-Japanese war and to the growing tensions between the Kuomintang and Mao Tse-tung's rising communists. Disillusioned with Stalinism, he returned from Moscow to the United States, as Dallin writes, 'a disappointed and disillusioned Communist'. He was tried for having made false statements in a US passport application and served a year in prison. After his release he stayed on in the US, changed his name, and disappeared from public view.[23]

Lydia Stahl also escaped prosecution in the United States. The GRU transferred her back to her original operational zone in Paris. There she joined the GRU residency headed by a Markovich (first name unknown, probably a Yugoslav national). By the end of 1933, the French Sûreté closed in on the network. Just before

Christmas, they arrested Stahl and eleven other GRU agents including a husband-and-wife team of American communists, ex-US Army Corporal Robert Gordon Switz and his wife Marjorie (a.k.a. 'Marjorie Tilly'), who had also worked in New York for the GRU. Switz turned evidence against the others, and as a result Stahl served two years in prison before later dying in France, her operational zone and former place of asylum from Russia.[24]

Aftermaths: Who Gained, Who Lost?

After the end of the counterfeiting operation, Walter Krivitsky loyally served Stalin's Kremlin in western Europe until Stalin's wholesale purges of 1937–8. Threats and attempts to recall him to Moscow following the execution of Soviet Marshal Mikhail Tukhachevsky and scores of other top military and political figures who had built and then fought for the Soviet regime since the days of Lenin, pushed Krivitsky to become, as British intelligence historian Nigel West observes in his introduction to Gary Kern's account of Krivitsky's life and career, *A Death in Washington*, 'one of the first and most significant examples of that most remarkable phenomenon, the Soviet intelligence defector'.[25]

Anticipating that Hitler would conquer and occupy France in the new war threatening Europe, Krivitsky fled to the United States. Under the name Samuel Ginsberg, he took passage on the French liner *Normandie*, arriving in New York on 10 November 1938. After days of detention as an illegal immigrant on Ellis Island, powerful figures such as Ambassador William Bullit and columnist Dorothy Thompson finally got him admitted to the United States on a temporary non-immigrant visa. Emigré writers David Shub and Isaac Don Levine helped him establish himself as a freelance contributor. With Levine as ghostwriter, he signed up for eight articles for the *Saturday Evening Post* for the fee (astronomical at the time) of $5,000 each. The State Department's hardline Soviet specialist, Loy Henderson, welcomed him in Washington and steered him to important US intelligence circles. Krivitsky's published articles about the counterfeiting and other Soviet operations displeased the FBI's jealous supremo, J. Edgar Hoover, who found himself reading about matters that he would have wanted locked in FBI files. Despite the coolness and sometimes downright hostility based on indifference and ignorance of many American officials concerning the value of Krivitsky's encyclopaedic knowledge of secret Soviet operations, he managed in the end to make vast contributions to Western knowledge of those operations, including Stalin's counterfeiting programme.

Even before 1939 when he published his history of the counterfeiting operation and other Soviet operations in Germany, the Spanish Civil War, China and elsewhere, Krivitsky feared that Moscow would target him for his revelations. Time and again he told friends that Stalin's spies had deeply penetrated many branches of the US government.[26]

Known as Ginsberg to most of those he met, Krivitsky hobnobbed with other ex-spies, including Whittaker Chambers. He was able to overcome charges that his Soviet past as 'General Walter Krivitsky' was fictitious. One time, he staved off INS efforts to deport him when his temporary visitor's visa wasn't extended. His help to the State Department's passport division's head, Ruth Shipley, helped to identify numerous cases of passport fraud by American communists and Soviet agents. Uninformed FBI interrogators tended to concentrate on unimportant individuals who interested them. They apparently did not permit Krivitsky to unveil much about important Soviet operations, such as the counterfeiting campaign: those revelations would appear in print in his later articles and his 1939 book.

Krivitsky had long been closely following secret Nazi–Soviet relations. Therefore he was one of the few experts not surprised by the Soviet–German non-aggression pact signed by Molotov and Nazi Foreign Minister Joachim von Ribbentrop on 23 August 1939. This was the immediate prelude to Hitler's 1 September assault on Poland, the partition of Krivitsky's native Poland between Germany and Russia, and the outbreak of the Second World War. He impressed Martin Dies' House Committee on Un-American Activities (HUAC) with testimony about Soviet and communist activities in October of 1939. He also lectured in public, adding to his high profile and increasing his personal vulnerability to Soviet assassination.

Kept ignorant by the other agencies of his huge value as an intelligence source, the INS cancelled Krivitsky's visitor's visa late in the year. He and his family travelled by train to Canada with the help of an escorting officer of British intelligence, MI6. Far more conscious of his value than the American officials he'd encountered, that service facilitated his passage to Britain, where he arrived in Liverpool on 19 January 1940. After intensive debriefing by British intelligence in the Langham Hotel in London during the coming three weeks, he returned to Canada. Grateful British authorities arranged substantial cash payments. These he banked to support himself, his wife Tonia and their two children for at least another year. At the end of October 1940, with the help of British, Canadian and American friends he managed to re-enter the United States, this time on the Russian immigration quota under the name of Walter Poref. He settled with his family in the Bronx, New York. During this second and fatal stay in the US, he refrained from publishing articles or briefing US agencies. He was in frequent contact with fellow émigrés and specialist friends such as Paul Wohl and David Dallin and tried to purchase a farm in Virginia.

Krivitsky was conscious that a Soviet murder net was closing in on him. He told friends that if they read in a newspaper that he had committed suicide, 'you must know that I was suicided'. He apparently bought a gun for self-protection and turned up on the farm he wanted near Charlotteville, Virginia. His fatal shooting followed some time in the early hours of 9 February in Washington's Bellevue Hotel, near Union Station. A 38-calibre revolver was found by his body. Sergeant Dewey Guest of the District of Columbia homicide squad diagnosed his death as a suicide, and so did the coroner. However, the consensus of the media and of Krivitsky's highly placed friends, family and associates was that former General Walter Krivitsky, the most important defector from the Soviet secret services in history, was indeed murdered by Stalin's agents, hundreds if not thousands of whom he had exposed or destroyed. Still, no investigations ever turned up conclusive proof of murder.[27]

By the time of Krivitsky's death, the Soviet counterfeiting

operation he had exposed in his articles and his memoirs was already being forgotten by the media, if not by the US Treasury and the Chicago and federal law-enforcement agencies. The operation had given invaluable help to Soviet espionage and other 'black' operations in China, several European countries and perhaps elsewhere, but it hadn't appreciably hurt the US economy, already badly limping from the 1929 Stock Market crash and the Great Depression which followed. President Roosevelt's preference for a rapprochement with 'Uncle Joe', as he began to be called affectionately in the American media after Hitler attacked Russia in June 1941, certainly helped to prevent political fallout.

The official Soviet forgery of American currency had other important effects as well. Non-political and non-governmental swindlers and crooks exponentially increased in the 1930s and beyond, often successfully counterfeiting money in the United States and Europe. This resulted in the strengthening and new successes of the US Secret Service. It also led to the rise of Interpol, which fell under Nazi control just prior to their own counterfeiting operation – the biggest of all time.

Twelve

Hitler's Counterfeit Campaign: The Lessons of the Second World War

> Mr Churchill ought perhaps, for once, to believe me when I prophesy that a great Empire will be destroyed . . .
>
> *Adolf Hitler, Reichstag speech, 19 July 1940*

The twentieth century's currency wars in Europe and America were preludes to the climactic main event in those conflicts: the Nazi scheme to counterfeit sterling and dollars to pay agents and spies, and to attempt destruction of the West's banking and financial systems. 'Operation Bernhard' gave rise to great anxiety among top Allied financial policymakers about the stability of their currencies – anxiety veiled for the most part from the public by the Bank of England's excessive secrecy and government censorship.

Despite wartime secrecy and post-war indifference, coverage of Operation Bernhard in print and visual media has accumulated over the years. One of the best recent treatments is a full-length German film called *Die Fälscher* (*The Counterfeiters*), first shown at the March 2007 Berlin International Film Festival. While making the film, first-rank Austrian director-screenwriter Stefan Ruzowitzky received the close personal advice of two of Operation Bernhard's living survivors, both of them in their nineties. They were among 144 artists, printers, engravers and other skilled Jewish workers, inmates of Nazi death camps such as Auschwitz and Mauthausen who were collected in Sachsenhausen concentration camp near Berlin. Though they were given far better living conditions than the other slave labourers, they were still forced under pain of death to produce millions of top-quality counterfeit sterling notes and other forgeries, eventually including US $100 bills. A chief virtue of Ruzowitzky's film, lacking in earlier documentaries and in the fictionalized feature film *5 Fingers* (released in 1952 and starring James Mason as the spy 'Cicero'), lies in its portrayal of the moral dilemma faced by the 144 captive counterfeiters. Most hostages and prisoners of armies, gangsters and terrorists (the Nazi SS operatives running the camps were of course all of these) still face this dilemma: cooperate with your captors to preserve your life and in so doing perhaps help them to win their war or further their cause, or oppose them by passive resistance or active sabotage and face almost certain doom.

Adolf Burger, a Slovak Jew who was impressed into Operation Bernhard, is ninety-two years old at this writing. He simply but eloquently portrays this dilemma in his well-illustrated and -documented book of memoirs, *Des Teufels Werkstatt* (*The Devil's Workshop*).[1] The makers of *Die Fälscher* identify Burger's book as the chief inspiration and source for the film. Burger worked closely with Ruzowitzky and reportedly thanked him after the film's release for doing such a splendid job.

Prelude to Operation Bernhard: Interpol and Its Nazi Takeover

Earlier counterfeiting stimulated the rise of two of the world's most important law-enforcement agencies: the Secret Service and Interpol. Around 1900, most law-enforcement officers viewed crime as a localized affair. Whether it was murder, politically motivated terrorism, counterfeiting of money or assorted swindles and rackets, crime was usually dealt with as specific acts inside specific borders. However, one academic expert in the Kaiser's Germany saw that crime and detection were destined to become more and more transnational. Professor Franz von Liszt of Berlin University wrote in 1893:

> We live in an era when the professional thief or swindler feels equally at home in Paris, Vienna or London; when counterfeit rubles are produced in France or England and passed in

> Germany; when gangs of criminals operate continuously over several countries.[2]

The trouble was and still is, although to a lesser extent today, that a French or English policeman could not easily bring about, for example, detention of either a fugitive suspect or confirmed crook in Germany. Interpol and Europol (the European Union's police organization) are still working on this by improving their international databases and computer networks.

It was largely due to Prince Albert of Monaco, the great-grandfather of the late Prince Rainier, that the world's senior police officials took action. They decided that it was time to put a stop to international crime and fraud by exchanging information about perpetrators across borders. In 1914 Prince Albert, then sixty-six years old, was the ex-husband of an American socialite, Alice Heine. She had shared her millions with him, and he was anxious to use them for worthy purposes. In April 1914 he invited senior world jurists, police officers and lawyers to attend an 'International Police Congress' in Monaco. Some 188 delegates, including three women, showed up. The only US delegate was a judge from Dayton, Ohio. The UK sent a magistrate from Hove on England's Sussex coast as well as a barrister and two solicitors from London. The congress was a success. Resolutions passed called for creating centralized criminal records (as now exist at Interpol's central bureau at Lyon, France) and standardized extradition procedures (which, though still non-existent, are the subject of urgent lobbying in many countries).

It took a canny policeman to take the next step towards fighting crime on an international scale. He was Dr Johann Schober, police chief of Vienna. He also headed the police for all of post-war Austria, where inflation and counterfeit currency had become twin plagues by 1923. Both as a top cop and as Austria's chancellor from June 1921 until June 1922, Schober became keenly conscious of the bogus money menace. He followed up Prince Albert's 1914 initiative by inviting over 300 police chiefs around the world to a 'Second International Criminal Police Congress' in Vienna in September 1923. In the end, of the 138 delegates who came, seventy-one were Austrian and only sixty-seven from abroad. The meeting ended on 7 September 1923 with creation of the International Criminal Police Commission (ICPC). Its permanent International Bureau was established in Vienna. Annual general assemblies were to be held in other European countries. Its official name wasn't changed to Interpol until 1946, after the 1938–45 Nazi control over it had ended with Hitler's defeat.

One of the early and enthusiastic delegates was New York police chief Richard F. Enright, who had to swim against a powerful and negative federal current to attend the 1923 meeting. The American FBI's top boss, J. Edgar Hoover, was then a revered figure in American folklore and schoolbooks. Hoover kept the US out of Interpol for most of his forty-eight-year rule over the FBI. Ironically, he finally permitted the US to join in 1938 – the year of Hitler's takeover of Austria, and thus of Interpol. In that same year, most other countries stopped participating. Nazi security supremo Reinhard Heydrich deposed the Austrian secretary-general Michael Skubl. ICPC then effectively ceased to exist as an international organization.[3]

One of ICPC's temporary German officials was also among the architects of the Nazi plot to take down Britain's banking system and overseas empire through falsifying sterling. He was Arthur Nebe, a senior civil servant in the Weimar days who had become an early Nazi Party member. His dedication and his knowledge of the criminal underworld in Germany made him Hitler's natural choice as chief of the criminal police of the Nazi SS (Schutzstaffel), originally an elite security and protective force for the Nazi Party.

Hitler liked Nebe, who had helped the Führer to consolidate control of the German armed forces in 1938 by outing the new wife of War Minister Werner von Blomberg as a former prostitute. As Lawrence Malkin reports in *Krueger's Men*, his comprehensive study of the Nazi counterfeiting scheme, this forced the old Prussian general to resign in disgrace. Even before Hitler's empowerment, Nebe was the German representative on the ICPC. When the Nazis seized Austria in 1938, they transferred the ICPC's head offices from Vienna to Berlin. This gave them access to fifteen years of case files. Nebe suggested culling from them the names of professional counterfeiters.

However, Heydrich did not want to discredit German control of ICPC by such use of the files. As the titular head of Supreme Security Chief Heinrich Himmler's Reichssicherheithauptamt (RSHA, the Reich Central Security Office), Heydrich preferred to use the net in Europe to track down Jewish and other anti-Nazi fugitives in the Reich. Once J. Edgar Hoover had brought the FBI into the ICPC, Heydrich also hoped to get US passport forms for the forgery of American passports. However, the FBI broke contact with the ICPC until just before Japan's 7 December 1941 attack on Pearl Harbor.

Just two weeks after the outbreak of the Second World War, on 18 September 1939 Nebe, Heydrich, Propaganda Minister Josef Goebbels, Economics Minister Walther Funk and other inner-circle Nazis met in the Finance Ministry at 61 Wilhelmstrasse, Berlin. The agenda was a discussion of how to bring about the collapse of the British economy and the Allied war effort by printing vast quantities of forged British sterling banknotes. Nebe outlined his ideas of how this might be done. Now Heydrich, who was already planning from his offices in Berlin's Gestapo building the systematic extermination of Europe's Jews, agreed. Only Funk disagreed, arguing that counterfeiting violated international law, that it would blacken Germany's name and that, anyhow, it would not work.

As the titular head of the Reichsbank Funk maintained liaisons with German industry. He did not want any bogus money distributed in German-occupied territories because it would cause the subject peoples to reject German occupation scrip for what they thought was real sterling. 'The last thing he needed while bleeding their resources for the Reich,' relates Malkin, 'would be an infusion of forged pounds soaking up his overvalued and suspect occupation currency.' Funk refused use of the Reichsbank's print shop in its central Berlin laboratories.[4] Despite this, the inner circle decided to follow through on Nebe's plan anyway.

Adolf Burger and other German-language sources relate that an 'idea man' for the counterfeiting enterprise was one of Heydrich's closest confidants: SS-Sturmbannführer Alfred Naujocks, an early, rowdy Nazi Party member and an amateur boxer who loved getting into fistfights with communists during the Weimar era. Having joined the SS in 1931, by 1934 he was a trusted member of Sicherheitsdienst (SD). At the outbreak of the war in 1939 he was the head of Department VI of the RSHA. Among his specialities was forgery of passports, ID papers and foreign banknotes for SD agents sent on foreign missions. He had come to the attention of Himmler and of Hitler himself by orchestrating the Nazi disinformation operation that launched the Second World War: a simulated attack on a German radio station at Gleiwitz, on the Polish border. Naujocks dressed up Polish prisoners in Polish army uniforms, and then had them shot by guards at the radio station. Goebbels' propaganda machine represented this as the intended opening shot of a general Polish assault on the Reich, and used it as a pretext for the massive air, land and seaborne attack on Poland at dawn on 1 September 1939.

Shortly after the secret Wilhelmstrasse conference had decided on the counterfeiting operation, Walter Schellenberg entrusted Naujocks with a new mission. (Schellenberg would later become chief of Department VI of the RSHA, and still later he would be one of the intelligence officers who envisioned kidnapping or sequestering the Duke of Windsor in neutral Portugal to install as a puppet king of England after a Nazi victory.) In November 1939 two British intelligence officers were lured into a rendezvous, supposedly under a flag of truce, at Venlo on the Dutch–German border. A Nazi squad under Naujocks' command then kidnapped them to Germany in their own car, where they were blamed by German propaganda media as instigators of an unsuccessful bomb plot against Hitler on 8 November 1939 in Munich's Bürgerbrau beer cellar. (The real attacker, a German carpenter named Georg Elser, was arrested by the SS as he tried to escape into Switzerland. Elser was questioned by Gestapo and criminal police in Munich, then sent to Sachsenhausen and later to Dachau, where he was murdered in April 1945 during the war's final days.) Naujocks got a medal – Iron Cross, First Class – for capturing the two British officers, and he was allowed to keep their automobile for his own personal use.

While still basking in the glory of his success, he took the opportunity to outline to Heydrich his scheme. By laundering the forged paper pounds into genuine hard currency or gold, silver and precious stones, the SD would have the wherewithal to buy the strategic materials the Reich needed to win the war.

While researching past counterfeiting operations, Naujocks' staff in September 1940 consulted Wilhelm Hoettl, a young historian with a PhD from the University of Vienna and since 1938 an SD expert on Balkan affairs. Hoettl showed Naujocks a report he had written about the counterfeiting operation against French francs led by Prince von Windischgraetz in Hungary in the 1920s. Naujocks dismissed it scornfully. 'Don't you understand?' he asked Hoettl. 'I am not interested in forging banknotes to finance some miserable secret society, as in Hungary. I want to break the Bank of England.'[5]

If the Nazis could print about a billion sterling in false notes, Naujocks believed, the Luftwaffe could scatter them over the British Isles from the air. (Naujocks apparently got this idea from British RAF flights in late 1939 that dropped counterfeit ration coupons over Germany.) Although some English patriots might turn them in to the authorities, many others would bank the cash or go on shopping sprees, adding to the growing wartime scarcity of staples of food and fuel. After a few such flights, Naujocks believed, the British banking system would collapse and a demoralized England would be an easy target for invading German forces.[6]

After the basic decision to undertake the operation, Naujocks was made technical boss of the Nazi counterfeiting factory at Delbrückstrasse in the up-market Berlin district of Charlottenburg. It was initially called 'Operation Andreas', apparently after the Saint Andrew's cross on the Union Jack. According to Burger, Heydrich gave Naujocks the following 'top secret' order:

> The operation is not to be forgery or copying [of banknotes] in the usual sense. It must be a thorough, unauthorized production. The notes must resemble the originals to such an extent that the most experienced British specialists for pound notes can find no difference.[7]

Naujocks wasn't qualified to manage the technical aspects of such an operation. Relying on Nazi archives and other original sources, Malkin points out that 'what he really did was to cut red tape with great speed since his operations were known to have Hitler's backing'.[8]

Since Nebe had left the operation after Heydrich would not let him use the international police files he had so meticulously assembled to identify the forgers needed for Operation Andreas, Dr Albert Langer was given operational control under Naujocks' direction. Langer was a physicist and mathematician who had served as a cryptanalyst first for Austria's military between the wars and then in the political police. After Hitler's annexation of Austria, Langer joined the Nazi Party. He was a bespectacled and physically fragile intellectual who fed the Hitlerian love for mysticism with projects such as articles on symbolism of the Freemasons and King Arthur's Round Table.

Although at first the Charlottenburg premises lacked even the most basic materials, Langer soon found that through the power of the SS Naujocks could provide everything needed, from printing machinery and paper to ink and the plates needed for the engraving process, all on a fairly tight budget of 2 million reichsmarks (about $10 million today).[9] Naujocks and Langer faced four fundamental and difficult requirements in launching Operation Andreas in 1941. First, they had to reproduce the paper used by the Bank of England. It had to be absolutely perfect chemically and have the exact same security devices embedded in it or added to its surface. Second, the plates had to be carefully prepared so that even the tiniest details matched the Bank of England's own notes. Third, mathematicians under Langer's expert direction had to work out the coded system of applying serial numbers on the genuine notes. Fourth, a distribution network had to be created in all of the world's important financial centres.[10]

The Reichsbank could not spare the meagre supplies of £5 and £10 notes in their vaults needed for purchase of strategic war materials like Swedish steel and Turkish chromite. So the Andreas team got some sample genuine pound notes from the police. Microscopic study and chemical analysis of the paper (made since 1725 exclusively by a family firm called Portals at Laverstoke, Hampshire) revealed that the ingredients were a combination of linen and ramie, a fibre spun from a nettle plant common in many parts of Asia. Germany's linen supplies, made from flax, were adequate, and its ally Hungary grew ramie plants.

Richard Schell, director of the Hahnemühle paper factory in Bütten, Germany, was summoned to RSHA headquarters in Berlin's Dahlem district. After he was sworn to secrecy, Operation Andreas was explained to him. He was told the firm must perfectly duplicate the English paper. Hahnemühle's operations chief, Robert Bartsch, realized after some tests that he could not duplicate the Bank of England's watermark in the duplicate paper. The RSHA then entrusted this task to another firm in Düren, Germany. After bringing together all of the needed ingredients, including the chemically correct paper, and following many tiresome test runs, the final product was pronounced satisfactory. Hahnemühle's paper production would begin in 1942 and continue until German defeat loomed in April 1945. In early 1942 printing began in the photo studio, etching, engraving and galvanizing rooms at the Delbrückstrasse installation in Berlin. The shop foreman was August Petrich, a loyal Nazi Party member who owned a printing business.

From the beginning, Naujocks wanted the Luftwaffe to drop the forged notes over Britain, before the invasion which Hitler had wanted to launch and after the fall of France in June 1940. Reichsmarshal Hermann Göring and his subordinate Luftwaffe brass apparently knew little of the drop plans. The RAF's victories in the air war during the Battle of Britain soon made this virtually impossible. German bombers were needed to drop bombs, not paper; and the RAF's Spitfires had so preoccupied Germany's best fighter pilots that none was available to protect air drops, whether of propaganda leaflets, the counterfeit British stamps that were being printed in Germany or the vast quantities of banknotes that Naujocks had envisioned would be required to sabotage Britain's economy.

Before the notes produced in the Delbrückstrasse plant could be circulated, they had to pass the acid test of examination by professional foreign bankers. The best way to do this was to send them to Switzerland and try to exchange them there. The SD emissary who travelled to Zurich posing as a German industrialist (the exact date is in doubt: Burger says 1 March 1941, but it may have been later) carried with him some of the fake sterling notes and a letter written by the SD but with the false signature of an imaginary business firm. The letter warned the Swiss bank that some of the notes the 'industrialist' had obtained might be counterfeit. Adequate technical means to check them out were not available in Berlin. Would the Zurich bank please check them out, with the usual Swiss *Gründlichkeit*?

After three days of rigorous tests, the Swiss bank executives assured the German emissary that the notes were absolutely genuine. To be certain the SD agent requested one final test. He asked the Swiss to cable the Bank of England to make sure that the serial numbers, dates of issue and other details were correct. The Swiss bank's telegraphed reply:

> ALL IS WELL STOP BANKNOTES WITH THE GIVEN DATES ARE IN CIRCULATION STOP

Naujocks was thrilled, and Heydrich gave the order to go ahead with Operation Andreas. But Naujocks' standing with Heydrich soon fell to zero. One of Naujocks' more routine tasks was bugging the bedrooms in Kitty's, a famous Berlin bordello, and recording all of the pillow talk to glean intelligence for the SD and provide material to recruit or blackmail agents. Unfortunately for Naujocks, Heydrich patronized Kitty's. A family man, Heydrich learned that his own exploits with one of the girls had been taped by Naujocks. The consequence for the former ace of dirty tricks was a transfer to the status of an ordinary SS trooper in the Leibstandarte Adolf Hitler, a unit on the Russian front.[11] An angry face-to-face scene between Naujocks and Heydrich had apparently preceded this in the spring of 1940. In the presence of Heinz Jost, head of SS foreign intelligence, Heydrich asked Naujocks how long it would take to produce some counterfeit Norwegian notes to be used in what was soon to be German-occupied Norway. When Naujocks replied that it would take four months, Heydrich lost his temper and called the currency forging operations of Naujocks 'alchemist's humbug'.

Hitler elevated Heydrich to Reich Protector of occupied Bohemia and Moravia, the two Czech provinces, in September 1941. There Heydrich became known as 'The Butcher of Prague'. The Czech exiled government and MI6 in London parachuted two agents into Czechoslovakia who assassinated Heydrich in May 1942. The brutal Nazi reprisal was the destruction of the town of Lidice and the massacre of its population.[12]

Operation Andreas limped along throughout 1941, but ultimately failed. A number of quality sterling notes were produced, but it is uncertain from existing sources how many were actually distributed and how many remained stored in the Delbrückstrasse installation. After the war, an unnamed print worker explained to a Frankfurt newspaper the reasons for failure.[13] The main one was that the SD-hired technicians were often overruled in methods or pace of their work by their SS bosses and guardians. Since his technocratic entourage could not get along with the Nazi political leadership, Langer was dismissed.[14] The project remained in suspended animation until its revival as the massive 'Operation Bernhard'.

Rescue from the Holocaust

Operation Bernhard's namesake and effective chief was Bernhard Krüger (often spelled 'Krueger' in English). He was born to German Lutheran parents on 26 November 1904 in Riesa, a town east of Leipzig. Recognizing his son's aptitude for using tools, Krüger's father, a civil servant in the government telegraph offices, sent him to Chemnitz Technical University. There he learned to use machine tools and textile machinery. He then worked in various factories in Poland and France. During the 1929 economic depression in Weimar he was laid off work and soon joined the Nazi Party. He became an SS man in 1931 and rose rapidly through the ranks. His rapid promotions during the 1930s were due largely to his effective work for the SD, including monitoring foreign radio traffic and assembling personnel to control Czechoslovakia's ethnic German Sudetenland when Hitler seized control there in 1938. He was posted to the SD's Department VI in occupied France in 1940, in charge of stealing or seizing US, British and Canadian passports; American merchant seamens' papers and ID cards for Canadian airmen. These were used to produce nearly perfect forgeries for SD agents and spies.

While Operation Andreas was turning out some of the Nazi counterfeit sterling notes, Krüger was tasked with surveying the black market in France as a vehicle for distributing the bogus pounds, dealing with former prime minister and Nazi collaborator, Pierre Laval. After a mission in Russia, following the Nazi invasion of the USSR in June 1941, he returned to Germany, married and worked at solving some of Operation Andreas' technical problems, including the duplication of the Portals British banknote paper.

Once the paper problem had been solved, a Berlin firm called the Gebrüder Schmidt produced the necessary inks. Stenz, manufacturers of printing machinery, sold the needed presses to the SD. By August 1942, all was ready to transfer the operation from the Debrückstrasse facility in Berlin to Sachsenhausen concentration camp near Oranienburg, 25 miles north west of Berlin (and today the site of a special museum commemorating some aspects of the Holocaust). Barracks No. 19 (and later No. 18) was cleared of starving and skeletal inmates on death row, and surrounded with a ten-foot barbed-wire barrier to segregate the block completely from the rest of the camp. Regular camp guards around the block were replaced with a special detachment of 'Deathshead' SS to watch over its inmates.

Heinrich Himmler and Walter Schellenberg decide that the man most likely to succeed in the Sachsenhausen venture was Bernhard Krüger. In his personal memoirs, still unpublished at the time of writing, Krüger described how he got the order to proceed – and his latent misgivings about the whole enterprise. Krüger was summoned to the office of Schellenberg, then chief of the SD, the secret intelligence service of the SS and of Krüger's Section VI, on the morning of 8 May 1942. Such a personal summons was highly unusual. Krüger knew that he faced some task far out of the ordinary. On the way to Schellenberg's headquarters in Berlin's Berkaerstrasse, he recalled that after waking at sun-up that morning he had seen a spider spinning her web. He remembered that his mother, 'in a brief fit of superstition', had once warned him that 'nothing good' would happen on a day when he had seen that.[15]

Once seated in Schellenberg's office, the SD chief told him that SS-Reichsführer Heinrich Himmler had given the order to begin producing the counterfeit English pounds immediately. He went on:

> The SS-Reichsführer has ordered that a secret printing plant be set up in the Sachsenhausen concentration camp. The work force must be taken from the pool of prisoners of Jewish origin. I proposed [to Himmler] that you be assigned to carry out this venture. It will be designated 'Operation Bernhard' . . . The SS-Reichsführer agreed unconditionally to my proposal. Judging by your previous achievements, I'm convinced that I recommended the right man. Krüger, take hold of this assignment with your full strength. I place my full trust in you. Tomorrow you travel to Sachsenhausen. Report to the camp commander there. He has been informed of your arrival and has received the appropriate orders.[16]

Krüger replied that although this was a tough assignment it was an order he could not refuse. He recalled that Operation Andreas had 'quietly died' and was not sure that the new attempt would not also fail. Success depended on 'the skill of the prisoners as well as on the capabilities of the people directing them'. Krüger added in his memoirs, 'my thoughts went back to the spider. There was trouble and strife ahead.'[17]

Krüger asked Schellenberg whether he was free to decide all technical and organizational matters himself. Schellenberg brusquely told him that he was. Krüger then agreed. Later he met with his section chief, an SS officer named Faustin. He argued with Faustin about who would be the right people to act as Krüger's deputies. Over strong objections from Krüger, Faustin insisted on appointing two SS men named Herbert Marock and Heinz Weber. Krüger maintained that they were unreliable and incompetent. But rather than risk a major fracas within the SS and the SD at this early stage, he gave way, perhaps reflecting at the time that

Schellenberg's assurance of his freedom of decision was not worth a *pfennig*. Later, both SS men performed miserably, bullying the workers, playing the black market, gossiping outside camp about the programme, and bedding the wives of absent officials. This would provide Krüger and his Jewish charges at Sachsenhausen with plenty of trouble and strife. August Petrich was enlisted to teach the workers how to use the high-tech machinery.

At first about thirty, and later 144 Jewish inmates of Nazi death camps were gathered up and put to work in Blocks 18 and 19 at Sachsenhausen. The Hitler leadership hoped the massive forging of British and other Allied money could turn the tide of war. Since the invasion of Russia in June of 1941 and above all America's entry in the following December, this was beginning to turn against them. The story of the physical and moral ordeals of Krüger's slave team of skilled workers was best told by Adolf Burger.

'We were like dead men with a stay of execution,' Burger recalled to a German interviewer just before the release of the film *Die Fälscher*. Before Krüger selected him and the other starters, Burger had almost starved to death in Auschwitz, been infected with a near-fatal case of typhus in Birkenau, had a frostbitten toe amputated by a fellow captive, had his front teeth knocked out by an SS guard – and, like his companions, narrowly escaped being shot by the Nazis at the war's end.

Burger was born in 1917 to poor Jewish parents in the town of Velká Lominca, in the High Tatra mountains of Slovakia. As a teenager, learning the printing trade and later opening his own print shop, he joined the leftist-Zionist Hashomer Hatzair organization. After Josef Tiso, a fascist and anti-Semitic priest, took power, Burger joined the illegal Slovak Communist Party. He was arrested in Bratislava in 1942, sent first to Auschwitz, then Birkenau and finally to Sachsenhausen. There his quick wits and fluent German helped to save him.

Burger's capture by the Nazis interrupted marital life with his new bride Gisela, whom he described as 'in love with life and full of hope'. Weeks after their marriage, and one day before his twenty-fifth birthday, 11 August 1942, Gestapo agents appeared at his print shop. They seized the couple and prodded them on to one of the cattle cars bound for Auschwitz. 'No one can imagine such a night,' Burger told a CBS news interviewer. 'Sixty people and sixty suitcases in a livestock car. Then the train finally stopped . . . The doors were opened and they shouted "Everyone out, everyone out."' The SS guards separated the couple on the platform at Auschwitz. 'She told me, "Think about me every night at eight o'clock, and I will think about you,"' Burger recalled. '"In this way, our thoughts will come together."' They never met again. Gisela was murdered with thousands of others in the 'showers', as the Nazi guards called them, with Zyklon-B gas. Her husband spent much of his time during his subsequent Sachsenhausen counterfeiting tasks dreaming of finding her alive, only to get confirmation of her end when the war was over and he was free again.[18]

Burger's amply illustrated, factual account of sufferings at Auschwitz, Birkenau and elsewhere of himself, the millions of Jews, Gypsies and assorted real or imaginary adversaries of the Hitler regime, is of course only one among many of the true accounts of the Holocaust told by survivors. Like others, it should be obligatory reading for history students and especially of Holocaust deniers. What concerns us here, however, is how the Sachsenhausen team remained alive because the Nazis needed their skills for their gigantic counterfeiting scheme – and, some of the survivors would argue, because of a combination of the iron will to survive and Divine Providence.

Krüger summoned the ninety or so prisoners sent to Sachsenhausen from the other death and work camps on the basis of their declared printing, engraving, mechanical and other skills. As they stood meekly in ranks not knowing what new horrors might await them, Krüger surprised them by speaking briefly and politely with each one, selecting thirty-nine in the end. He chose an engraver, a paper salesman, a banker, two carpenters, an electrician, a mason, several graphic arts specialists and four printers.

He added a Polish doctor to watch over the health of the team. Later the doctor would try to conceal serious illnesses among them from the SS guards. They became cases treatable only in the camp infirmary, where they might violate security by talking to doctors, hospital staff or other patients about their top-secret work. (At least four were shot during the operation. Krüger falsely denied responsibility for this.) One Norwegian, Moritz Nachstern, an anarchist stereotyper on an Oslo newspaper, was told at Auschwitz-Birkenau that they had been picked on the basis of the occupations listed in their prisoners' card files. According to Malkin's book, the card files were part of a system the Nazis acquired from the US firm International Business Machines (IBM).[19]

In the privileged enclave of the working group, food, clothing, bedding and general living conditions were far better than those of the miserable slaves confined outside. They even had a Ping-Pong table where they played during time off, sometimes with the guards, and they could listen to piped-in music and have a day of rest on Sundays. This made the rest of the camp seem like a distant planet. According to Adolf Burger's carefully compiled figures, the number of miserable inmates grew along with the expanding camp's perimeters from 10,577 prisoners in sixty-eight barracks to 47,409 in May 1944. Of over 200,000 victims sent to Sachsenhausen, according to Burger's statistics, over 100,000 were murdered. During three autumn months in 1941, as Hitler's Russian campaign reached full force, 18,000 of the 20,000 Soviet war prisoners were shot. Prisoners who weren't executed by the SS often committed suicide by running into the nine-foot perimeter wall containing nine watchtowers and barbed-wire carrying 1,000 volts of electricity.[20]

The team members soon fell under Petrich's direction designing and engraving new plates for fake sterling notes of £5, £10, £20 and £50. (The RSHA and SS had decided that counterfeiting £100 notes would be tempting discovery: their rarity in circulation would subject them to much more exacting scrutiny than those of lesser face value.) Oskar Stein, a former Czech businessman, secretly kept a ledger listing the notes produced. Various sources give different values for the total number and face value of the output. Malkin says Stein's record is the most reliable one: nearly 9 million banknotes with a total face value of £132 million.

Per Krüger's instructions Stein divided the notes in categories. The most perfect counterfeits were destined for German spies abroad to use and to pay contacts and sources. The second category had only minor errors, and Allied investigators often had trouble identifying them. The third type had more serious flaws, but these were sometimes also found in real pound notes. They were sent abroad to purchase raw materials in neutral countries like Sweden and Switzerland, and were sometimes detected. The fourth category was stored for planned airdrops by the Luftwaffe over England. After the RAF's victories in the Battle of Britain as well as the shortage of Luftwaffe planes and pilots precluded such missions, the SS passed the rejects for whatever use could be made of them.[21]

Early Allied Reactions

The British government and the Bank of England soon received word of the enterprise. As early as 21 November 1939, only two months after the secret planning session of the currency war in Berlin, a Russian émigré in Athens named Paul Chourapine somehow learned of Operation Andreas. He passed a detailed memorandum on the scheme to Sir Michael Palairet, the minister at the British legation in Athens, who relayed the stark warning to London. Palairet, acquainted with Nazi methods after serving as Minister in Vienna in 1937–8 and assigned to the capital of neutral Greece, had tried to keep aloof from covert operations. MI6 then relied on a group of British businessmen in Athens known as the 'Apostles' for whatever information it could garner in Greece on German and Italian intentions in the Mediterranean and Balkans.[22] However, the Chourapine report was so detailed and serious that it commanded immediate attention as soon as Palairet had forwarded its substance to London, which in February 1940 shared it with Washington.

The stability of sterling and the need to preserve it, as well as the possible use of counterfeiting against Germany for the second time since the First World War, had been on the mind of Winston Churchill since the European financial and counterfeiting episodes of the 1920s. On 24 September 1939, then first lord of the Admiralty in the government of Prime Minister Neville Chamberlain, Churchill proposed in a note to Chancellor of the Exchequer Sir

John Simon that the RAF drop 'forged notes of marks in bundles or tempting little packets', over Germany, instead of just propaganda leaflets and forged ration books, as was being done. Simon passed the note to David Waley, principal assistant secretary in the British Treasury. Apparently Waley advised against it. On 4 October 1939 Simon replied to Churchill that after the Treasury had looked at the idea, 'I am bound to say that, on balance I think the Noes have it.'[23]

Two months later, the warning from Palairet arrived from Athens. At the Treasury, David Waley rebuffed Basil Catterns, deputy governor of the Bank of England, who scoffed at the idea that a German counterfeiting operation might succeed. After some deliberation the bank's governor, Sir Montagu Norman, approved a security measure for the bank's most used and perhaps most vulnerable low-value notes: metallic thread enclosed in a cellulose strip, a common security feature of many of today's world currencies, including the euro.[24] In 1940, when the new notes were issued, the bank and the government continued to preserve secrecy about the real reason for the new security strip, discouraging the mass-circulation tabloid *News of the World* from publishing a story about the Nazi scheme.

Eventually, the bank withdrew from circulation all notes worth £10 or more, with a public claim that this was to cramp the style of black marketeers operating mainly with cash. The old printing plant of the bank in what had been before 1920 Saint Luke's mental hospital, used in the First World War reichsmark scheme, was evacuated from east London, anticipating the Luftwaffe's battering of the city in 1940–1. In 1943 the bank stopped printing large-format bills as part of the defence scheme. On 20 August 1940 it prohibited repatriation of its own banknotes, somewhere between 10 and 20 million sterling held abroad. The purpose was to prevent high-denomination Nazi fakes from infiltrating the domestic economy in Britain. Later, the £5 notes were also withdrawn and replaced. Despite these precautions and official silence about the operation, it emerged in later years that by the war's end in 1945, approximately 40 per cent of sterling notes in circulation in the United Kingdom were eventually identified as the Sachsenhausen counterfeits.

The Distribution Network

The main man involved in spreading the counterfeits around the world was an independently wealthy German freebooter with connections in far places, including the United States, Fritz Paul Schwend (a.k.a. 'Dr Fritz Wendig' and a number of other false names). Schwend was born in 1906. While working as a lowly petrol station mechanic, he married the aristocratic and wealthy Baroness von Gemmingen-Gutenberg, a niece of the assassinated liberal Weimar politician and foreign minister Baron Konstantin von Neurath. Schwend joined the Nazi Party in 1932, just in time to add power to the wealth he already enjoyed. He moved to Los Angeles, California, where he managed the personal finances of his wife's aunt, of the Bunge family. The added wealth he acquired through an international agribusiness conglomerate was useful in encountering the German consul-general, Georg Gyssling, who had good introductions to Hollywood stars. Later he lived briefly in Woodside, Queens, amid a German colony. In 1938 he moved to Italy. Still working for his wife's aunt, he bought on contract, often in the black market, foodstuffs and industrial goods for Hitler's Germany from a base at Abbazia, an Adriatic Sea resort (now part of Croatia). However, the war cut him off from the Bunge fortune in America, and his baroness wife divorced him. His next spouse was Hedda Neuhold, daughter of a rich Austrian engineer who became Schwend's business partner.

After Mussolini joined Hitler in the war in 1940, Hitler helped his new Axis partner defeat Greece and then occupy it. Following the Nazi invasion of Yugoslavia, Schwend manoeuvred himself into trouble with the Gestapo because he was trying to con British agents into buying fake plans for a new submarine. The suspicious Gestapo jailed him in Austria in the spring of 1942, but he was sprung when an SS money launderer in Italy named Willi Groebl enlisted him as an SS major with the task of managing the flow of Bernhard counterfeits. Schwend's chief became Ernst Kaltenbrunner, the SS chief who replaced the assassinated Heydrich and who was eventually condemned to death at the 1946 Nuremberg trials.[25]

A centre for distributing the 'B-notes', as top Nazis called the Sachsenhausen forgeries, became Labers Castle near Merano (known to Germanophones as South Tyrol's Meran), in Italy's Alpine north. On the basis of his former business travels in all of Europe, the Far East and the American continents, from Alaska down to Tierra del Fuego at South America's southern tip, Schwend fashioned a worldwide network. By agreement with his RSHA superiors, he got a hefty 33 per cent commission in good money on the earnings from laundering the counterfeits worldwide. However, he had to pay his principal deputy 25 per cent of his own share. Schwend's people laundered the fakes in several African countries, the United States, Argentina, Brazil, Chile, Honduras and Uruguay, as well as in India, China and Japan.

In Europe he operated with businessmen, senior officials and diplomats, including a staffer of the German Embassy to the Vatican. Commercial attachés of German embassies and legations in Ankara, Bern, Geneva, Madrid and Rome received consignments of B-notes. They used them to pay spies, make purchases for the German war effort or simply launder for their own profit. The SD, through these channels, used the counterfeits to buy up gold, precious stones, jewellery and hard currency. Burger's memoirs list the European locations most useful in the laundering operations: Andorra, Belgium, occupied Denmark, France, Greece, Ireland, Italy, Yugoslavia, Lichtenstein, Monaco, the Netherlands, occupied Norway, Portugal, Sweden, Switzerland, puppet Slovakia, Spain, Turkey and Hungary.[26]

Operation Bernhard was extended to eastern Europe and the Balkans. Along with counterfeit postage stamps, passports, ID papers, American merchant seamen's papers and other documents, the enslaved Jewish artists, photo-engravers, engravers, printers, sorters and product inspectors at Sachsenhausen were also forced to forge Balkan and eastern European currency. When Adolf Burger arrived at the camp in the spring of 1944 his first assignment, he says, was the 'relatively light task' of counterfeiting Yugoslav money and securities. From 1942 well into 1944 partisans operated in all of the German-occupied nations, from France through the Czech and Slovak regions into Yugoslavia, Greece and (after Mussolini's fall and the Italian surrender) Italy.

In Yugoslavia partisans commanded by Josip Broz Tito and Drazha Mihailovitch (who later opposed Tito and effectively helped the Germans) liberated parts of Yugoslavia. The areas held by the guerrillas were larger than the territories of Austria, Hungary and Switzerland combined. Villages in the 'free' portions of Yugoslavia in November 1942 formed a 'People's Council of Liberated Yugoslavia'. This body organized the economic base and the infrastructure for the use of the partisans fighting the German and Italian occupiers.

The partisans badly needed cash to buy weapons, food and everything else required to survive and fight. They used any currencies accepted by their suppliers in the population: Hungarian pengö, pre-invasion Yugoslav dinars, German occupation scrip, Italian lira, and also dollars and sterling when they could get them. Finally, on 13 January 1944, the partisan People's Council floated the first Yugoslavia-wide loan of 500 million dinars, also called 'kuna'. Similar provincial partisan loans for lesser sums were floated in Croatia, Slovenia, Montenegro and Bosnia-Herzogovina.

What the citizens of the liberated zones got from the People's Council in return for their cash were promissory notes. These became the first 'partisan currency'. This was used as legal tender in all of the liberated areas. In Ljubljana, capital of 'free' Slovenia, a bank of issue called Denarni zavod Slovenije had soon printed millions in the new currency. It was the first free bank in German-occupied Europe. Gestapo agents reported to Berlin that the proceeds of the loans had lifted partisan morale and aided their war effort. Countermeasures were needed.

So Adolf Burger was put in charge of printing false Yugoslav 'Tito notes', which had also begun to appear in the liberated zones, and counterfeits of the promissory notes issued by the People's Council. Burger says the copies closely resembled the originals. German agents circulated his products throughout the liberated areas in an attempt to undermine their reawakening economies and their war efforts.[27]

Solly, Jacobsen and the Dollar Syndrome

One day in September 1944, Bernhard Krüger appeared in the Sachsenhausen counterfeiting workshop to proclaim: '*Meine Herren*, from today we'll produce dollars.' He instructed SS officer Kurt Werner to choose eight team members who were to produce only dollars. Salomon Smolianoff was among those chosen.

Under the name Salomon Sorowitsch, Smolianoff is played by the prominent German actor Karl Markovics in *Die Fälscher*. True to the real Smolianoff, he is the only truly professional criminal counterfeiter the Nazis manage to recruit for their operation. Perhaps less believable (but more entertaining for cinema audiences), 'Solly Sorowitsch' becomes a gambler, womanizer and sometime gigolo in the film. Whatever the truth or the degree of the real 'Solly's' addictions, he was good at his chief source of income before his incarceration by the Nazis: designing and working through all the stages of producing fake currency.

Bernhard Krüger was delighted to discover Solly's talents. These had saved Solly's life earlier in Auschwitz, where he had drawn flattering portraits of the SS guards. These talents were also enlisted in the late-1944 enterprise ordered by Himmler to print bogus $100 bills.

Berlin sent new machinery and new banknote paper, copied from the US banknote paper produced by Crane & Company. Krüger turned over some genuine $50 and $100 notes to copy. A new difficulty: it would take too long to produce good intaglio-engraved plates. Impatiently, Krüger overrode the team's reservations and insisted that photo-offset be employed. By using a glass plate covered with a film of gelatin and a layer of ammonium bichromate dried at a temperature of 50 degrees centigrade, one could get very sharp images of Benjamin Franklin on the $100 bill.

The team was separated from their co-workers in three isolated rooms of the block. They practised at producing playing cards and postcards by photo-offset. Then they began experimental printing of the $50 and $100 notes.

(Ironically for Burger, just at that time his brother and sister, both kibbutz residents in Palestine, succeeded in getting the Jewish 'Palestine Office' in Switzerland to send Burger a printed authorization to immigrate to Palestine. Sent at first to Birkenau, then forwarded to Sachsenhausen, Krüger presented it to Burger with an ironic smile. They both knew, of course, that Burger hadn't a chance in heaven or hell to use the certificate and flee to Palestine.)

In late 1944 the team reached a consensus. Since the tide of war was turning so strongly against Hitler, with the advance of the Russians in the east and the Allies in the west, it seemed wise to delay as much as possible producing the false dollars so that the Nazis could not use them in their failing war effort. Despite the influence of Solly, who was producing excellent dollar negatives in line with his pride in his own professional craftmanship, Abraham Jacobsen evaded the hawk-eyed surveillance of the SS guards. He was determinedly sabotaging and thus slowing the production of usable dollar fakes by spoiling the gelatin film on the glass plates.

Under pressure from Schellenberg and Himmler, Krüger now demanded results. Peter Edel, Burger's fellow printer, took it on himself to tell Krüger that in order to fashion the tiny fine lines so important in the printing process, he needed to have sent from his home his 'Chinese' brushes with needle-thin points. Krüger, for fear of failure and therefore of his own possible fate, swallowed his scepticism and sent an SS courier with a written request to Edel's mother. Delighted to have this sign of her son's life, his mother quickly handed over Edel's entire art kit including the brushes. The courier speeded back to Sachsenhausen with the kit.[28]

'Produce Dollars – or Die'

The SD leadership had originally demanded that the team produce 200 perfect \$100 specimens. Jacobsen's subtle sabotage had prevented that. Impatience overcame Himmler. He issued an order, relayed by Krüger to his anxious charges, that if preparations to print the false dollar notes were not completed within four weeks, the prisoners involved were to be shot.

The team continued their experiments. Within four days of the deadline, they had no satisfactory product to show for their labours. On the two hundred and fiftieth attempt, Solly's retouched negative looked perfect as always. Jacobsen placed it on the illuminated glass plate covered with gelatin. He poured glycerin on to it, drawing the dollar image from the paper on to the plate. Burger then placed the plate and turned on the press. The result was twenty-four perfect $100 counterfeits. The photo process had worked after all. During the same night the team printed the required 200 bills, face value $20,000.

When Krüger arrived the next morning, he placed thirty genuine Ben Franklin notes among a selection of the new but artificially aged counterfeits on a green-covered tabletop. Krüger and some SS men with him tested the tactile qualitites of the notes between their fingers. They pronounced more than half of the forgeries to be real. That evening, Krüger telephoned Himmler that everything was ready for the presses to roll.

Several days later on 2 February 1945 the team boss, Werner, transmitted a new order from Schellenberg and Himmler: they had, in two daily ten-hour shifts, to counterfeit a total value of $1 million. But before production could begin, Berlin and its environs were rocked by Allied bombing, clearly visible in Sachsenhausen. A secret joy that they dared not show in front of their captors swept over all the prisoners. Hitler had clearly lost the war. The radio broadcasts they were allowed to hear (not including BBC or other enemy broadcasts) now told them that the Soviet armies had smashed through Poland and East Prussia, and were nearing Berlin. The Americans, Free French Forces and other Allies approached from the west.

On 20 February 1945 a new order from Berlin reached Sachsenhausen: 'Stop work!' Burger recalls that most of his teammates feared this meant they would soon be sent to the gas chambers. Their SS guardians stopped talking with them, clearly anxious about their own fate, until one of Krüger's deputies appeared and gave the order to pack up the machinery and prepare to move out. Everything had to be disassembled and packed within thirty-six hours. By working together around the clock, the 140 Jewish workers (four had been killed from the original 144) managed to have all of the paraphernalia of forgery, as well as its products – fake currencies, postage stamps, ID documents and assorted Nazi archives and files on the operation – packed into crates and chests. These were all loaded, with forty-seven of the special prisoners and their meagre camp possessions, into boxcars on a special train. (The rest of the counterfeiting contingent was safely transported out later.) After long night hours, the train halted. A Czech, Morris Gottlieb, looked out through a window and exclaimed when he recognized the 'hundred golden spires' of his native city, Prague. Czechs and Slovaks in the group trembled with joy and the forlorn hope that they would be released in Prague, and allowed to go home.

The train stood still for a few hours. Gottlieb could see his old home from the boxcar. But their hopes were dashed. The train moved out, headed for the death camps in the last territory still controlled by the Nazis.[29]

Their first destination after the stopover in Prague was a site near the notorious Mauthausen camp in northern Austria, which earlier prisoners had called 'Mordhausen' ('The Place of Murder'). The guards shouted '*Raus!*' The team was strip-searched for any scraps of the counterfeit notes, which if found would have meant instant death. They were deloused and marched to Block 20. Mauthausen's previous inmates has been Russian POWs who had risked a mass escape and been massacred, explained the guards when Krüger's men saw the bloodstains on the walls. They soon had to unload the heavy machinery from the train. Solly Smolianoff correctly observed that it would be impossible to continue the counterfeiting operation amid Mauthausen's inadequate facilities.

Sure enough, they had to move again two days later on 23 April 1945 to a secret 'sub-camp' of Mauthausen called Redl-Zipf, between Salzburg and Hitler's birthplace of Linz. They were now on the edge of the Nazis' *Alpenfestung* or 'Alpine Fortress'. It was here that Hitler, by now confined to the underground bunker in embattled Berlin that would within days become his tomb, had hoped his loyalists would make their last stand. As Lawrence Malkin observes, Hitler hoped that a holdout in the *Alpenfestung* 'would split the West from the Russians (assuming, of course, that the West decided to halt Stalin's advance into Western Europe), and allow Hitler to survive by making a separate peace'.[30]

The sub-camp was already a storage site for art, gold, precious stones, currency and other valuables that the Nazis had looted from all of their occupied territories. Burger and his companions feared that it would also become their gravesite now that the war was lost and there was no more need for their skills. Built against the Alps and containing underground caves, Redl-Zipf was the home of the secret production site for the V-2 rockets, which the Nazis had rained down on London and cities like Antwerp captured by the Allies on the Continent. Allied air power had destroyed earlier V-1 'flying bomb' bases at Peenemünde in northern Germany. Here Krüger's men for the first time met fellow prisoners, Spanish Republican exiles arrested by the Vichy government who gave them to the Nazis as part of the French quota of slave labourers.

The counterfeiting machinery was unloaded, but the hour was late: American troops were approaching the *Alpenfestung*. Krüger had been absent from the entire transport operation. SS officer Werner ordered them to burn all banknotes except those of the very best quality. Anyone found neglecting this duty would be shot on the spot. Suddenly Krüger reappeared. He courteously said goodbyes and wished luck to all of the counterfeit team members. He said he had orders to move them all to a 'place of safety' until they were liberated. He would see them there, he claimed. They never saw him again. According to some of the prisoners' accounts, he drove off towards Salzburg with his attractive young secretary and girlfriend, Hilda Moeller, in a car with Swiss licence plates, effectively ending Operation Berhard for the team members.

The next and final destination for the group was Ebensee, another sub-camp of Mauthausen, amid the lakes and mountains of the scenic Salzkammergut region. During the final days and hours before and after the German surrender in May's first week, scores of chests containing counterfeit currency, gold, valuables looted from occupied Europe, and secret documents and archives of the Nazi regime were dumped in nearby Toplitzsee (Lake

Toplitz). Some of the crates were roped to empty rockets, which floated near the surface as markers.

The inmates at Redl-Zipf, who had been told that they should resume production of dollars, awoke on 2 May to the news of Hitler's suicide in the Berlin bunker. The Nazi flag flew at half-mast, and everyone knew the false currency operations were over. This did not stop Willi Schmidt, an SS officer, from killing by lethal injection Karl Sussman, a Viennese member of Krüger's team who had fallen ill. Meanwhile, at Ebensee orders came from Mauthausen to 'liquidate everything'. The 118 prisoners and six SS guards who remained were packed tightly into two closed trucks. Until they arrived outside Ebensee and saw white flags of surrender hoisted by the inmates after the departure of their Nazi tormentors, the men from Redl-Zipf thought final 'liquidation' was at hand. In Ebensee camp, they discovered that troops of the Wehrmacht, the regular German army, had replaced the SS guards, who had fled before the advancing Americans. The Wehrmacht officers could not believe that the relatively healthy and well-clothed counterfeiting team were really KZ inmates. They refused to take over responsibility for their protection until they showed their tattooed numbers on their arms – a scene graphically depicted in *Die Fälscher*.

Next day a contingent of the Third US Army, an armoured cavalry unit commanded by Major Timothy C. Brennan, arrived at Ebensee to be greeted not only by Krüger's former team but also by hundreds of half-starved, skeletal inmates. As Burger says, the Americans could not believe their eyes or comprehend that human beings were capable of such cruelty and inhumanity.

After liberation, inmates formed their own police. They disarmed and held for the Americans the SS and SD personnel at the camp. The survivors of the Sachsenhausen counterfeiting crew managed to make their journey homewards. Many, like Burger, arrived at their former homes to find that neither their houses nor their families existed any more. At his hometown in Slovakia, Burger was told that his mother had been sent to Ravensbrück concentration camp and his father to Sachsenhausen, only four months before the war's end. He never saw either again.

Krüger, Schwend and most of the other Nazi criminals involved in Operation Bernhard managed to save their own lives. After being detained by the Americans on 12 May 1945 and subsequently escaping, Krüger eluded Interpol warrants until the US Secret Service arrested him again on 26 November 1946. He escaped again in May 1949, however, and lived undiscovered for years, working in one of the post-war successor enterprises of the Hahnemühle paper factory. He re-emerged in August 1956 with a formal public declaration of his responsibility, under Himmler's orders, for Operation Bernhard. He did not mention his other crimes, including the murder of sick team members, which is also lacking from the manuscript fragments of his memoirs. He ducked undercover again to pre-empt new prosecution, and lived under an alias in rented quarters in Stuttgart. The investigations and searches for him ended in 1965, and he died later without being convicted of anything.[31]

In addition to working in 2005–6 as a key consultant for Rusowitzky's film, Burger advised some of the fishing expeditions for looted Nazi treasures in Toplitzsee. Austrian residents living nearby, some of whom had been forced by the SS to lend their boats and labour to the 'burial' operations in the lake, described chestfuls of loot stolen from captives in Buchenwald, Auschwitz and Sachsenhausen, as well as the currency and archives remaining from Operation Bernhard. Adolf Eichmann was one of the first to sink stolen Jewish treasures in twenty-two chests in Toplitzsee in early January 1945. (The Nazi butcher was tracked down by the Israelis and finally captured by them in Argentina in 1960. Convicted in 1961, he was executed by Israel on 1 June 1962.) The notorious SS commando leader Otto Skorzeny, who was paid in counterfeit sterling for his spectacular airborne rescue of Benito Mussolini from his Italian partisan captors, personally supervised moving twenty-two chests containing twenty gold bars to the lake in early May 1945.[32]

The attraction of the sunken loot drew hundreds of professional and amateur divers and adventurers from around the world. The lake became a major tourist attraction. Discoveries began in the summer of 1945 when a local fisherman brought up a load of fake £5 notes with a face value of £400,000 and turned them over to local US occupation forces. US Navy divers who had tried earlier that spring were blocked by logs that had fallen down the surrounding mountain slopes and formed a kind of protective mantle about 100 feet below the surface. Two engineers from a nearby abandoned naval research station died mysteriously in the lake in 1946. Another perished trying to slide down underwater limestone cliffs in 1950. The German news magazine *Stern* made an intensive, well-funded search in 1959, aided by Burger. Currency was brought up as well as SS records with precise details about agents, distributors and recipients of the false money. There were copies of orders in Dutch, English, Norwegian and German to attack or sabotage enemy ships, airports and other targets. There were also special passes and many other documents.

Stern's articles raised fears in many business and industrial circles: 'too many careers and firms had been founded with stolen gold and forged currency', Burger wrote.[33] Under pressure, *Stern* cabled the lead reporter on the case to stop all work. On 8 October 1963 Alfred Egner, a nineteen-year-old amateur diver, plunged into Toplitzsee's dark, 350-feet-deep waters and never emerged again. Suspected murderers, never brought to justice, included several right-wing politicians and engineers as well as Georg Freiberger, a spy and associate of master spy Reinhard Gehlen, who turned himself, many of his staff, and most of his archives and records about the Soviet Union over to the CIA after the war.

For the Austrian authorities, this was the last straw. They barred the lake to treasure hunters and sent down their own official investigators with sonar and underwater video cameras, subsequently declaring there was nothing to be found. But this spurred the noted underwater biologist Hans Fricke to explore the bottom for three more years in a miniature submarine. He found more fake pounds, rockets, missiles and assorted experimental Nazi ordnance, as well as discovering an unknown form of worm that lives without oxygen. In 2000, the World Jewish Congress, an Israeli adventurer who said he worked for Israel's Mossad and CBS Television News all teamed up for a month's sonar survey of the lake and a five-weeks dive costing $600,000. This was presented as a search for hidden SS archives. Holocaust survivors and their attorneys still search for archives to back their claims for looted valuables. All that was found was a case of beer caps and more counterfeit £5 notes, the former placed on exhibit at the Simon Wiesenthal Museum of Tolerance in Los Angeles. Later Norman Scott, who dived for the wreck of the US Civil War steamship *Republic* and its cargo of gold off North Carolina, obtained a three-year licence from the Austrian authorities to hunt for gold. As of this writing, nothing has been publicly reported about any finds by Scott.[34]

Tactical Results, Strategic Consequences

Like hordes of past investigators, one might ask: What were the real impacts of the biggest political counterfeiting of all time on the economies and societies it targeted? And what countermeasures were taken to avoid future repetitions?

One of the earliest Nazi distribution efforts was in occupied France in the summer of 1943. In violation of the Reich finance authorities' disapproval of using the notes in occupied territory, some Nazi SD agents sent about 100,000 counterfeit pound notes, mainly fivers, to a French bank, probably hoping to launder them for genuine hard currency or to buy goods and services from the captive French. Almost at once, the German military occupation authorities got wind of the deal. The French banker in question and the Germans involved were promptly jailed. A similar operation was attempted in occupied Greece, where runaway inflation, Nazi looting and general dessication of the economy was wearing down the fierce spirit of the Greek resistance movements.

All this led Funk to issue a formal decree that none of the forged money could be used in any country occupied by Germany, for fear that it might 'upset currencies I am endeavouring to stabilize'. However, following surrender to the Allies and Mussolini's downfall, Italy was already a 'country occupied by Germany'. Funk did not realize that around $100,000 worth of the bogus sterling had already been traded for gold and genuine dollars and Swiss francs. It contributed, if only peripherally, to post-war inflation.

The network operated by Schwend managed to build a large team of distributors and launderers. Most were managers of big hotels in Sweden, Switzerland, Spain and Portugal. Two were bank managers, one Swiss and the other Italian. Millions of the notes went into the pockets or bank accounts of Nazi spies and agents of various sorts in the neutral countries.

The largest amount going to a single spy went to Elyeza Bazna (a.k.a. 'Cicero'), the Albanian valet to British Ambassador to Turkey Sir Hughe Knatchbull-Hugesson, in exchange for documents of great intelligence value. The operation generated one of the most sensational spy stories in history, called the 'Cicero affair'. In 1943–4 Cicero gave the Germans stolen crucial top-secret documents on Allied planning for the war and its aftermath. (Schellenberg, Himmler and the other Nazi spy chiefs, however, did not trust their authenticity and exploit them. More on this in the next chapter.) Unbeknownst to him until later, Cicero was paid in the Nazi's counterfeit sterling. Like the valet, the Nazis involved in the production and distribution of the false notes escaped prosecution and punishment for Operation Bernhard. However, two of the Nazi leaders who instigated it, Reinhard Heydrich and Ernst Kaltenbrunner, paid for their other war crimes with their lives.

Schwend used two neutral ships sailing from Genoa and Trieste to distribute the notes in North Africa, Portugal and Spain after the Allied invasions of November 1943. Schwend's operatives there were warned not to take British pounds in exchange for the notes being laundered. When one broke the rule, they turned out to be first-class samples of the Krüger team's handiwork. In late August of 1943, Count Galeazzo Ciano, Mussolini's son-in-law, freed from imprisonment in Italy and brought to Germany on Hitler's orders, told the SD that he knew all about Operation Bernhard. He asked to distribute the notes in South America, requesting a quarter-million dollars' worth to take with him. Despite efforts of his wife, Edda, in Germany and her safe haven in Switzerland, Ciano never escaped: the pro-Allied Italian government had him shot as a 'conspirator' in Italy in January 1944.[35]

The secretive Bank of England was forced to attribute in a press release issued 18 October 1945 the recall of the old £5 notes and the issue of new ones to 'forgery of high sum Bank of England notes in Germany during the war'. In a later report whose date is missing from the Interpol history written by Fenton Bressler,

Sir Ronald Howe, assistant commissioner at Scotland Yard, complained about the general loss of confidence in paper money after the war and the effect of criminal gangs operating out of the refugee camps spread throughout Europe:

> Financial standards went mad. No one wanted French francs or deutschmarks when they could be paid in kind. Debased currency was further devalued by a flood of counterfeit money, much of which had been produced in German concentration camps.[36]

Allied occupation troops found caches of counterfeit sterling throughout Germany and Austria. US Secret Service Agent George McNally, one of the most expert investigators of Operation Bernhard, discovered a number of crates on a German truck. McNally called British authorities and the Bank of England sent Patrick J. Reeves, head of its printing plant. Reeves reported that on 8 June 1945, he counted £26 million in counterfeit notes and a box of tools to make the plates. After comparing serial numbers and other coded bank data on the bills, he reckoned that more crates with millions more in bogus notes were possibly missing. McNally, quoted by Malkin, describes how Reeves glumly riffled packs of the notes, stopped and stared, then cursed for several seconds. 'Sorry,' he then said, 'but the people who made this have cost us so much.'[37]

Edward Playfair, an academic and Treasury expert working with the British military authorities, feared that the Bank of England might have to pay out good pounds for counterfeits from unspecting foreign banks fooled by the forgeries. (It is unclear from available sources whether it ever did.) The Treasury tightly restricted its exchange of valid sterling notes for non-sterling notes such as dollars, which it wished to hoard as part of its post-war reserves. However, during the post-war years, while the successive diving teams were plumbing the depths of Toplitzsee (where the majority of forgeries were recovered) the counterfeit sterling kept turning up to plague bankers, businessmen and other citizens in Switzerland, Spain and Sweden.[38]

As for the global aim of the Germans to undermine the financial foundations of the British Empire and the Allied war effort, Operation Bernhard was a strategic failure. If the scheme had succeeded, reflects Cornell University professor Jonathan Kirshner in his book *Currency and Coercion*, it could have had ruinous consequences for Britain and the Allies. Moreover, if permanent doubts, as opposed to the kind of episodic disruptions that did occur, had led to universal distrust of sterling's integrity, this would have had international repercussions because there were such large holdings of sterling and US dollars all over the world. Such a crisis of confidence in the pound might indeed have had the real effect on the war's outcome that Hitler's minions hoped for. Kirshner believes that Reich Economic Minister Funk's veto of distribution in German-occupied Europe 'ultimately doomed the entire forging operation'.[39]

A glib and ironic but possibly largely truthful retrospect on Operation Bernhard's impact on the world was written back in 1953 by Murray Teigh Bloom:

> [E]ven if every one of the circulated notes remained undetected in circulation, it probably would not have mattered greatly. Between 1939 and 1956, the [Bank of England's] notes in circulation increased nearly fourfold, from £526 million to £1,913 million. All of which proves that when it comes to inflating the currency, the modern counterfeiter just doesn't stand a chance against the modern central bank issuing bank notes without gold backing.[40]

Bloom may well prove correct in the long run. But the evident truth of his remark has not deterred governments, secret operatives and major and minor criminals in our own time, from Pyongyang to Tehran and Baghdad to Medellin, Colombia, from continuing to practise the black art. How it has especially linked up with espionage and terrorism in the twentieth and twenty-first centuries is our final topic.

Thirteen

Covert Action versus Stabilization: From Vietnam to Iraq

> Clandestine warfare, because it is covert, does not exist as far as treaties and public posture are concerned.
>
> The Pentagon Papers, *1971*

Deep into Europe's terrible post-war winter of 1946–7, the author – then an eighteen-year-old soldier in the US Army assigned as a cryptographer to headquarters, US Forces in Austria (USFA) – shivered in an unheated troop train as it crossed the devastated, winter landscape of defeated Germany towards Vienna. The ruins of central Europe, dramatically apparent from the train's windows in German cities like Frankfurt-am-Main and Munich, rose in their jagged starkness along the route into the mountain scenery of western Austria's American occupation zone – Austria and Vienna, like Germany and Berlin, were divided into American, British, French and Russian zones.

The Viennese variation was that the city's very centre was an International Zone, patrolled and ruled each month by one of the four 'liberating' powers in succession. The military police of each of the Big Four would move in rotation into the district's central police station, or Kommandatura, as the Soviets christened it. When the Russian month rolled around, eastern European refugees and displaced persons (DPs) would move out, fearing seizure and deportation by the Soviet Army or secret police. Vienna was well and truthfully portrayed in the Graham Greene and Carol Reed story *The Third Man*, the Hollywood film version of which earned well-deserved kudos for its producer and stars Orson Welles and Joseph Cotten. People foraged in streets and gutters for stray lumps of coal, pieces of wood to burn or discarded morsels of food in the Gentzgasse neighbourhood, where our 63rd Signal Operations Battalion was quartered quite comfortably in a converted school building.

The once-elegant cafes and sleazy nightspots of the district were hotbeds of black marketeering. There was a constant traffic in counterfeit money, including Austrian schilling notes issued by the Allied authorities and American military scrip for use by US soldiers or authorized US official personnel in PXs, commissaries and other military-sponsored institutions. As payment instruments, there were all manner of substitute currencies such as chocolate, nylon stockings and American cigarettes ('Chesterfields preferred, but Lucky Strikes or Camels will do fine, thank you!'). These were exchangeable for gold coins when available, *objets d'art*, choice seats for the bravura Volksoper performances, an hour or a night with a woman who was possibly quite famished. One could even find precious stones, if one had enough cigarettes, real greenback dollars or other scarce consumables to barter for desired valuables.

In their zones of both Germany and Austria, the Soviet Army had begun to live off the land and to manipulate whatever currencies, real or false, became available. USFA's initial top superior, US Fifth Army Commander General Mark W. Clark, recorded how the Soviets were looting eastern Austria of everything that could be moved. They were showing special interest in getting total control of the Zistersdorf oil fields and other oil installations in the eastern province of Burgenland. They were also grabbing whatever cash they could. When the Red Army first entered Austria and captured Vienna from a stubbornly resisting regiment of the SS, it seized all the German reichsmarks in Austrian banks as war booty. Soon afterwards the Soviet command 'loaned' 400 million of the stolen reichsmarks to the new Austrian government under President Karl Renner, a democrat who had survived the 1938 *Anschluss* and the war. His government had planned to convert this Nazi currency into specially overprinted banknotes and to reissue them as official Austrian currency. This plan had to be dropped after the loan was made. The new post-war, four-power Allied Commission for Austria decreed that the military schillings issued by the four 'liberators' would be used until a new Austrian national schilling currency could be issued and circulated.

The Austrians then tried to return to the Russians the reichsmarks they had 'borrowed'. The Russians made no response. In December of 1945, the new Austrian national schilling was established. In January 1946, the Russians demanded repayment of the 400 million reichsmarks 'loan' – but in the new Austrian currency. The old reichsmarks were by this time worthless, partly as a result of considerable counterfeiting, but chiefly because of the conversion to the new Allied-controlled currency. The Russians sought, successfully, to profit from the change. General Clark then told the Renner government that if the Austrians met the Russian demand, the US would demand payment in the new schilling currency of almost 2 billion Allied military schillings, which the US had advanced for conversion to the new currency. Like the reichsmarks, the military schillings had been legal tender when the advance was paid, but they lost all value after the conversion – they were like outdated counterfeit money. Clark realized that the Austrians would be unable to repay the Russians without also repaying the United States. Their only choice was to refuse both demands.[1] Troops in Vienna were warned that the new schillings, like US military scrip, were much more susceptible to counterfeiting than the now obsolete money, simply because both schillings and scrip had much more purchasing power. They were driving down the black-market values of cigarettes, chocolate, nylons and other barterable goods.

The currency and general economic situations in occupied Germany were even more tangled and chaotic. Millions of Germans, in various stages of hunger or even near starvation, found that the Hitler-era reichsmarks that many had saved and hoarded through the worse war years (and that were still legal tender until the April 1948 US-initiated currency reform) would not buy much at all. In many parts of Europe, some of the middle- and higher-level former Nazi operatives like the Turkish-Albanian spy 'Cicero' were discovering that the fortunes they had thought they were accumulating were worthless counterfeits from

Sachsenhausen's Operation Bernhard. There was a general distrust of almost all paper money and a tendency to hoard old gold and silver coinage and whatever other precious metals were available.

To buy food and other necessities in Germany, one needed ration books and food coupons along with cash. The German author Heinrich Böll, seeing the general misery affecting all classes, wrote about the birth of a 'classless society'. The Roman Catholic Cardinal of Cologne, Joseph Frings, a friend of former Cologne Oberburgermeister and later chancellor Konrad Adenauer, forgave petty robbery of valuables and coal, in desperate shortage during the frigid 1946–7 winter. He called them venal and pardonable sins. In Berlin's Schrebergärten park, the *Schieber*, or black marketeers, and their GI suppliers were getting 20 marks for a package of American cigarettes; 12 million tobacco plants were cultivated there to provided a steady supply for the tobacco-hungry Germans (practically anyone over fourteen at the time). The black-market price of a pound of real coffee was 500 to 800 marks (legally, the exchange rate was 10 reichsmarks to $1, but you had to pay much more if an opportunity to buy real dollars, not scrip, ever came up). A worker earned an average of 250 marks a month; some white-collar workers 450. Kingpins of the *Schieber* could aspire to acquiring a US-made Studebaker or a Maybach German car for 60,000 reichsmarks.[2]

The rise of all sorts of crime in occupied Germany, including counterfeiting of dollars and other hard currencies, led to wide social unrest. Demonstrations by unemployed, often hungry men and women erupted in the Ruhr region. Older people still remembered the bitter years of French occupation and hyperinflation in the 1920s. In Munich a twenty-four-hour general strike produced slogans like 'We want to live, not die a miserable death!' and 'We're Germans and not colonial subjects'. In Hamburg the local trade union chief, Adolf Kummernuss, told an audience of 120,000, 'It's become a matter of life and death.' The head of US Military Government, Lucius D. Clay, cabled to Washington that the situation in occupied Germany was 'really horrible'.[3]

What followed could have, and to some extent actually has, served as a model to the American-led occupation of Iraq from March 2003 on. If the sensible measures taken since then to stabilize the Iraqi currency were followed up and not undone by excessive waste of resources for reconstruction or by organized crime, the lessons of post-1945 Germany and Austria might brighten the future of today's tortured Iraq.

The planners in Washington and a young German economist and future West German chancellor named Ludwig Erhard decided that the first big step towards German recovery and the building of a market economy on the ruins of Hitler's totalitarian structures was drastic currency reform. The Germans had to be given money they could trust and, above all, that would buy them the necessities of life. The main architects of the reform plan (most of which had been drafted back in May 1946 and which was classified as secret under the code-named 'Bird Dog') were American banker Joseph Dodge and two German émigré economists living in the US, Gerhard Colm and Raymond W. Goldsmith. Dodge headed the Finance Division of the Office of Military Government of the United States (OMGUS). A tiny and carefully selected group of German finance officials (and perhaps some law-enforcement officers) were quartered for seven weeks from 23 April 1948 at the Rothwestern Air Base near Kassel. They were allowed to 'consult' with the Americans about the coming currency reform; in fact they were given briefings on what had already been decided in Washington, London and Paris. Young Ludwig Erhard realized that Operation Bird Dog was to be integrated into the giant Marshall Plan for the rehabilitation of Europe. A series of high-level Allied meetings in February and March 1948 decided that the three western occupation zones should take part in the Marshall Plan and, if possible, should be organized into a single federal state.

As a result of these earlier western meetings, on 1 June 1948 a six-power agreement of the three Western powers and the Benelux countries was signed. It called for international control of the Ruhr, German representation in the European Recovery Programme (the name given then to the US-financed, billion-dollar Marshall Plan), closer integration of the three western zones, and drafting of a West German federal constitution. This was a defensive move aimed at Stalin's increasing belligerence in eastern and central Europe. A Soviet decree of 20 March had withdrawn Soviet

Marshal Sokolowski, Moscow's representative on the Four-Power Allied Control Commission in Berlin. This marked the real beginning of the splitting of Germany into what would ultimately become separate western and communist republics. Divided by Churchill's 'Iron Curtain', the basic situation persisted until the fall of the communist German Democratic Republic and Germany's reunification at the start of the 1990s.

On 18 June came the formal announcement and launch of Operation Bird Dog, distributing the stable and in effect US-guaranteed deutschmark. These were originally printed in secret by the American Banknote Company, one of the US Treasury's contractors, in the United States and flown into Germany in time to replace the tired and tattered old reichsmarks. The exchange took place over the weekend of 19 to 20 June. Distribution was handled by the Bank Deutscher Länder (Bank of the German States). The basic exchange rate was to be one new mark for ten old ones. An initial exchange for every citizen and legal resident of the western zones was limited to 40 deutschmarks, extended later to increasingly large amounts.

On the morning of Monday, 21 June, the very first day of the new currency, the shops began miraculously to display goods and offer services hitherto found mainly on the black market. Acting without approval of the occupation powers, Erhard announced the end of price controls, progressive lifting of wage ceilings and other features that eventually led into a free German market.[4] The much-applauded West German *Wirtschaftswunder* ('economic miracle') brought a return of stability and eventually the rise of a prosperous industrial economy in the future Federal Republic of West Germany.

The Soviet reaction to the new currency reform was rejection and the gradual crippling, then the closing on 24 July 1948, of Allied road and rail links to West Berlin through the Soviet Zone: the blockade of Berlin. The US led the other Western powers in a hastily organized but massive and effective airlift to supply the western sectors of Berlin with goods and the new currency. The Soviets were soon to sponsor the 'ostmark', which remained legal tender in the German Democratic Republic until reunification.

Historians, economists and ordinary Europeans old enough to remember it regard the birth and long life of the deutschmark as a singular triumph of Western free-market economics. (It was replaced by the euro, the new European Union currency at the start of the twenty-first century.) For the professional counterfeiters, the desirable new deutschmark naturally became a priority target. National police forces and Interpol found their new anti-counterfeiting missions suddenly more complicated. A proliferation of organized and unorganized crime groups and individuals began to shower their forgeries on Germany and later on other countries (such as the Balkan states in the 1980s and 1990s) where people trusted the dollar and the deutschmark far more than their own currencies. Using every possible method, from the rising colour-copier technology to letterpresses to intaglio printing, the forgers inundated Europe and wider areas with bogus dollars, deutschmarks, Swiss francs and other European currencies.

In one sense, however, law-enforcement efforts in Europe against counterfeiting and other forms of financial fraud became *less* complicated in the second half of the twentieth century. Because – at least until the advent of covert economic warfare from outside Europe, as described early in this book – *governments* were not producing the European forgeries.

It was a far different story in the Far East. There, especially in Indo-China and Korea, counterfeiting of various sorts, often on a huge scale, became an important weapon in the secret arsenals of several countries, notably the United States of America. Although rejected as a weapon by Franklin D. Roosevelt early in the Second World War (FDR rejected a plan for the US Army Air Forces to drop counterfeit currency and forged ration books on enemies with the memorable response: 'Killing is all right, and you can attack religion with impunity, but you were threatening something dearer than life to many people'), forgery has been periodically deployed under all subsequent US administrations, starting with Roosevelt's successor, President Harry S Truman.

CIA and US Army Forgers at Work: South-East Asia

For decades, America's enemies, critics and even rival allies overrated the Central Intelligence Agency's powers. De-mythification of the CIA was accelerated by its failure to detect (or to persuade the Bush administration of the gravity of signals that it *had* analysed) the 11 September 2001 attacks by disciples of Usama bin Laden in New York and Washington. The fading of the CIA's glory began many years earlier with the exposure of the 'family jewels', as some of the CIA's senior men chose to call some of the Agency's darkest and hitherto best-guarded secrets.

The jewel box was opened on 22 December 1974 when the *New York Times* outlined a vast programme of domestic surveillance against anti-Vietnam War activists and other dissidents, expressly violating the CIA charter that limits the Agency to overseas operations. In January of the New Year, President Gerald Ford, sensing the need to avoid another Watergate-type cover-up of the sort that had destroyed President Richard Nixon, named Vice President Nelson Rockefeller to head a special 'blue-ribbon' commission to investigate. Congress quickly opened its agenda to the red-hot issue. Senator Frank Church headed a Senate committee that deeply probed many of the CIA's 'black' activities (though apparently not including counterfeiting), severely damaging the Agency's morale and reputation at home and abroad.[5]

The pre-9/11 judgement failures of the CIA truly began with the Agency's abysmal miscalculations in choosing a mercenary army of extremist Islamists as proxies in the decade-long war to expel the Soviet Union from Afghanistan in 1979–89, and then turning its back on that benighted country. Many in Washington failed to recognize that Usama bin Laden and his spreading Al-Qaeda movement, America's temporary allies in the anti-Soviet war, would soon wield many of the dire weapons that the US had trained them to use in the anti-Soviet war against the US.[6] In all of its massive and often incredibly expensive covert operations, from Indo-China through the Korean War of 1950–2 to Cuba and finally, beginning in the 1990s, to Iraq and Iran, the CIA's secret warriors and those of the US Army's psychological warfare (PSYOPS) units combined counterfeiting with unacknowledged 'black' propaganda actions. From China, North Vietnam and the Pathet Lao Insurgency to Saddam Hussein in Iraq, many of these foes attempted, with significant publicity only in the case of North

Korea, to use the same weapon against the United States. The results differed in each case, but none of the US actions decisively impaired the enemy's war efforts.

'We went all over the world and we did what we wanted,' bragged Al Ulmer, the CIA's Far Eastern division chief in the 1950s. 'God, we had fun.'[7]

Second World War Roots

Like so many covert operations, the roots of the CIA's linked counterfeiting and propaganda offensives began to sprout during the capers of William 'Wild Bill' Donovan's Office of Strategic Sevices (OSS) in the Second World War. Early in the war, the US had little in the way of effective foreign intelligence capabilities. Under the enthusiastic and imaginative projects of President Roosevelt it developed more sophisticated missions of covert warfare. Donovan learned British methods, whereas Winston Churchill's covert warriors, after initial reluctance and some setbacks, borrowed from the Germans, especially after the jarring experience of Operation Bernhard and its aftermath.

In the Pacific War, one of the precedents for the post-bellum efforts of the CIA was the counterfeiting of imperial Japanese paper money. The US Sixth Army and the 'Morale Operations' (MO) branch of the OSS forged various types of Japanese currency – in particular the occupation money used beginning in January 1942 by the Japanese conquerors of the Philippines. (Late in the war, as General Douglas MacArthur prepared to make good his 1942 promise of a return to the islands, a larger tide of the bogus Japanese banknotes began to flow into the Philippines.) The Sixth Army's PSYOPS units also overprinted with propaganda slogans *genuine* Japanese money captured from Japanese forces. One overprinted text mocked Premier Hideki Tojo's propaganda motto for the newly conquered empire, 'The Greater Southeast Asia Co-Prosperity Sphere'. It read: '*THE CO-PROSPERITY SPHERE: WHAT IS IT WORTH?*' The Japanese notes were first overprinted in US-liberated Tacloban, the Philippines, in December 1944. The US Fifth Air Force dropped them over Manila and central Luzon.

One of many official US reports cited by a former American PSYOPS warrior, retired Army Master Sergeant Herbet A. Friedman, said banknotes and messages were intended 'to impress on the Filipino people the worthlessness of Japanese occupation currency, with consequential embarrassment and loss of face to the Japanese'.[8]

'French' Indo-China: Over to the Americans

Covert US action in Vietnam began long before the later massive involvement of US forces during the Eisenhower, Kennedy, Johnson and Nixon administrations. During the final months of the Second World War, OSS Major Archimides Patti worked with a future archenemy, the young guerrilla leader Ho Chi Minh, against the Japanese occupiers. By the early 1950s, with funds and covert operations the US supported the desperate effort of the French, decisively challenged in Algeria from 1954 on, to hang on to their Far Eastern colony and pre-war sphere of influence.

In attempts to demoralize the enemy, France and then the United States (after the French defeat at Dien Bien Phu) used forged currency and linked propaganda messages, either dropped separately or attached to the banknotes. Like the European belligerents in the two World Wars, they relied on the principle described by PSYOPS operator, former Master Sergeant Friedman: 'Even the most law-abiding citizen or soldier who would never think of reading the enemy's [propaganda] poison will stoop to pick up a banknote on the ground. Almost without realizing it, he will read the message and become an unwilling recipient of enemy propaganda.'[9]

The French set the example for their American successors in their futile struggle against the Viet Minh. They counterfeited at least three denominations and overprinted the bogus paper money with at least four propaganda messages. One appealed to Viet Minh fighters to desert and 'return to your homes where your sad old mother, your wife and your weak children have waited a long, long time'. Such messages were dropped with the banknotes around Gia Dinh, near Saigon. The texts were from songs and poems from Vietnamese folklore.[10]

The official directives authorizing the US counterfeiting and leaflet campaigns in Indo-China can be found in the Pentagon Papers, the exhaustive store of official classified documents purloined by Defence Department analyst Daniel Ellsberg. These were first published by the *New York Times* and provoked a celebrated Supreme Court case that the government lost.

In June of 1954 the US began to pick up the burden of the anti-communist struggle abandoned by the defeated French. US Air Force Colonel Edward G. Lonsdale, earlier seconded to the CIA for a largely successful covert warfare campaign against the communist Hukabaluk ('Huk') guerrillas in the post-war Philippines, was assigned to Saigon. Lonsdale headed a team of agents for 'paramilitary operations' and 'political-psychological warfare' against North Vietnam, which was supporting the Viet Cong, as the Americans later dubbed the insurgency in the South. The American covert operations began in October 1954. Lonsdale's team started by sabotaging Hanoi's railways. They contaminated oil supplies for the North Vietnamese capital's city buses. They distributed 'black' propaganda, including defeatist messages of various types, in the form of fake Viet Minh leaflets. Another Lonsdale-directed activity was the recruiting and training of two teams of Vietnamese agents.[11]

US Covert Warriors in Action

At some point in time, there was added to the Pentagon's daily operations record a detailed, 21,000-word report by Lonsdale's team. It covered the early period of US involvement, August 1954 to August 1955. They were ordered to 'undertake paramilitary operations against the enemy and to wage political-psychological warfare'.[12]

The official US narrative was entitled 'provision of assistance to the Army of the Republic of [South] Vietnam (ARVN)'. A 'Studies and Observation Group' (MACV-SOG) was assigned to conduct covert warfare including 'black' propaganda operations. Its six sections were given responsibility for clandestine operations planning, called OPLANS. OP-33 was the PSYOPS section, inspired by the Second World War Morale Operations (MO) branch of the OSS. In 1968 it was renamed OP-39, the Psychological Studies Group. According to Herbert Friedman, 'all black propaganda and currency counterfeiting [originally] emerged from OP-33'.[13]

Small-scale printing of 'black' propaganda leaflets and posters took place in Saigon and lower echelons as far down as battalion and company headquarters. Larger print jobs were handled in Okinawa, from 24 October 1965 until 29 June 1974, by the US Army's Seventh PSYOPS Group. Some printing was also done at the Army Adjutant General's printing plant at Camp Drake in Tokyo, Japan.[14] Friedman records that the specifically banknote portion of the covert offensive appears to have begun in 1968, with the Fourth PSYOPS Group in Saigon. The Pentagon had to approve it, provide funding and order it to begin. Samples of 'parody' currency, with themes satirizing the enemy economy and society, were sent back and forth between Washington and Saigon to work out details of the messages and the Vietnamese dialects used. Defense Secretary Robert McNamara's men in the Pentagon authorized printing to begin at the US Information Agency's (USIA) Regional Service Center in Manila. Leaflets were stored before use at the Machinato Base in Okinawa. Times and sites of the airdrops were determined by units of the Fourth PSYOPS Group in Saigon. Craftsmanship of the bogus notes was of a high quality: when the removable propaganda stub was removed, the notes could pass as genuine – just as their producers intended.

The North's government in Hanoi complained to the US that the counterfeits caused inflation. In congressional debates in Washington, some congressmen objected to using money forgery to fight a war. Massachusetts Senator Edward M. Kennedy's intervention abruptly halted the programme in 1969, about the time of President Richard Nixon's decision to halt the bombing operations against the North.[15]

With meticulous attention to detail, Friedman mentions a possible much earlier date for the programme's onset. The White Plains *Reporter-Dispatch* of 18 November 1966 wrote that 'To cripple Communist savings, counterfeit North Vietnamese banknotes are dropped in the Red River Delta, near Hanoi.' On 9

December 1981 a communist East German newspaper, the *Ostsee Zeitung* in Rostock, ran an article signed by Dr Julius Mader claiming that the first drop of counterfeits was in August 1966. The article asserted that 1.6 million banknotes were then dropped, and that in eight airdrops between August and December 1966 some 16.7 million leaflets were dumped around Vinh, Ha Tinh, Tien Sang, Nghi Loc, Linh Cam, Hanoi, Tran Hoa and Haiphong.[16] Friedman says that remainders were stored in Okinawa until 1973, when President Nixon authorized renewed bombing of the North. Massive amounts of 1, 2 and 5-denomination dong counterfeits with propaganda messages attached were dropped from 25,000 feet. Hanoi reported drops on 19, 21 and 26 October 1972. The *New Republic* magazine of 31 March 1973 said 60 million banknote leaflets were printed in the Okinawa USIA plant between 1965 and 1972. *Covert Action* magazine's July–August 1979 issue mentioned the Regional Service Center (RSC) in Manila as a 'CIA propaganda plant', and the source of airdropped forged Vietnamese money. A Seventh PSYOPS officer confirmed to Friedman that Manila was the main source, and that the Okinawa base 'controlled' printing. A US Embassy official, Friedman says, commented that the forgeries were 'similar' to one used 'several years earlier' during the first full-scale bombing campaign. Vu Thien, director of North Vietnam's state bank, claimed millions of counterfeits were dropped in the North during August and September 1972. He denounced President Nixon as an 'international counterfeiter' seeking to sabotage the North Vietnamese economy.

On the rare occasions when liberal media or commentators in the US challenged the operations as unethical or illegal, CIA and Army PSYOPS officials would reply that the counterfeits attached to propaganda leaflets were not barefaced forgeries of the enemy's money, but simply part of a black propaganda campaign. However, counterfeit notes *not* attached to propaganda messages were prepared by OP-33 units in Okinawa and distributed in the North by OP-34 and OP-35 covert warfare units, Friedman adds. The codename for this operation was 'Benson Silk'. Besides forged money, this programme included insertion of false radio messages into North Vietnamese broadcasts. Airdrops of the 'Benson Silk' banknotes bore the code name 'Stray Goose'. MC-130 Combat Talon aircraft dropped both leaflets and currency over Hanoi and Haiphong, ending in 1969. Friedman affirms that the purpose of the Benson Silk counterfeits was not necessarily to destabilize the North Vietnamese economy, which was already ailing and vulnerable. It was rather to plant the phoney money 'in a camp or on a corpse, large enough [in scope] to create mistrust, engender suspicion and demoralize the soldiers'.

During Operation Benson Silk, the CIA (rather than US Army PSYOPS) sent Vietnamese agents into the North to distribute forged banknotes. Some time in 1961, one South Vietnamese army major refused to carry the notes: he felt the moral stigma attached to debasing the enemy's money would blow his cover if he were detected. In June 1963 a large airdropped container with 4 million counterfeit dong banknotes was accompanied by an infiltration team. The North Vietnamese captured the team and the banknotes. In August 1963, a seaborne team carried another 4 million dong. The North Vietnamese military was tipped off and waited in ambush, successfully seizing the team and the notes.

Perhaps partly because attached propaganda messages were not involved, Benson Silk was classified top secret, which kept mention of the operation out of the official US histories. Several published books confirmed its existence, however. One ex-US official involved, John Plaster, wrote *SOG: The Secret Wars of American Commanders in Vietnam*. Plaster told Herbert Friedman that forging the North's money was easy because the enemy lacked modern anti-counterfeiting safeguards. Still, secrecy was such that Plaster had to sign a 'classified hand receipt' each time that the banknotes were issued to him. In *Hazardous Duty* legendary American Cold Warrior Major General John K. Singlaub identifies the commander of the OP-33 group specialized in counterfeit North Vietnamese currency and other 'ingenious deceptions' as Lieutenant Colonel Tom Bowen, apparently based in Okinawa. *Running Recon* by Frank Greco reports on Benson Silk forgery operations of enemy 'military commodity coupons' for use in the North's military PXs and commissaries.[17] These were apparently similar to the US military scrip that millions of American GIs used in post-war Europe and that were often counterfeited by black marketeers and crooks.

The CIA and the Pathet Lao

An inter-agency task force's report was prepared for President John F. Kennedy and dated 8 May 1961, just as the Kennedy family and the CIA were recovering from the aborted Bay of Pigs invasion of Cuba. Annex 6 of this document, entitled 'Covert Action', recommended infiltration of south-western Laos to locate and attack North Vietnamese bases there. Overflights of the area were also recommended in order to drop materials to undermine enemy morale (counterfeit money was not specifically mentioned).[18]

Meanwhile, the communist Pathet Lao guerrillas targeting the pro-Western royal government in Vientiane issued their own banknotes for use in areas they were gradually conquering. The notes were found in denominations of 10 and 20 dong and 50, 100 and 500 kip. Genuine Pathet Lao 200-kip notes, printed in green and red, portray a Lao temple. When counterfeits first appeared – possibly the work of the royal government in Vientiane, but probably a CIA product – a portrait of Ho Chi Minh replaced the temple. In 1977 the *Bangkok Post* claimed the notes were faked by the royal regime to persuade the Pathet Lao that they were actually fighting for North Vietnam and not for their own cause.

In a Public Broadcasting Service *Nova* programme in March 1992 William Wafford, a pilot of the CIA's well-known 'Air America' airline, showed notes he dropped in 1970 on the Laotian city of Xam Nua, a Pathet Lao headquarters. *Nova* asserted that the CIA produced these notes. Another drop by Wafford from a C7A Caribou aircraft over northern Laos included banknotes weighing 'several hundred pounds'. In *Air America*, Christopher Robbins mentions the CIA drops, saying that 'millions of dollars in forged Pathet Lao currency' were dropped in Laos 'in an attempt to wreck the economy by flooding it with paper money'.[19]

Without much supporting detail Herbert Friedman asserts the plausible thesis that amid their many published complaints against

US counterfeiting (especially under the Nixon administration) the North Vietnamese were doing their best to render tit for tat to the United States. Friedman writes that a captured document dated 12 November 1969 states that a regional Communist Party committee in the North 'orders that individuals named Hao and Co are to continue counterfeiting US currency until further instructions are received because an all-out plan to disrupt the enemy's economy is being formed'.

Plenty of snafus occurred. In one 'blowback' operation, due to adverse winds and probably also some clumsiness on the part of an aircrew, a plane on an airdrop mission over Vietnam landed back at its base with 'thousands of banknotes scattered all over the cargo area'. Airport security at the (unidentified) base thought they had unmasked a currency smuggling operation when the cargo doors opened, revealing the heaps of notes. Security briefly arrested the crew. All was soon smoothed over, but some higher technology was clearly needed for the drops. In *Air America*, Robbins mentions that during an overflight of Laos with CIA-printed banknotes in loose paper bags, the notes burst out of the bags before release. 'We had counterfeit money from one end of the airplane to the other,' pilot Wafford ruefully recalled.[20]

Improving the Distribution Networks

During the Korean War and early stages of the Cold War in Europe, dissemination technology improved. One key to better spreading of 'black' material of all kinds proved to be the use of balloons. Launch sites for balloons in South Korea operated against North Korea; others in Taiwan were deployed against the Communist China mainland in the early 1950s. During one six-month period, a force of 109 South Koreans sent 3,000 pounds of leaflets, possibly including false currency, into the hermit state of Kim Il Sung. This was something Kim doubtless remembered when North Korea began operations against the US dollar with its Swiss-made presses.

In 1953 the CIA–Radio Free Europe (RFE) began a balloon campaign code-named 'Prospero' against Communist-ruled

Czechoslovakia. The balloon launches began at midnight on 13 July 1953 from a Bavarian town safely inside the American occupation zone of Germany. The launches were coordinated with RFE broadcasts beamed into the target country. RFE ridiculed the communist regime's currency reforms and other economic measures. The balloon-borne messages took the form of a counterfeit Czech banknote and an aluminium replica of a new Czech coin, imprinted with the Freedom Bell of Philadelphia and an inscription reading, 'All Czechs and Slovaks for freedom – all the Free World for Czechs and Slovaks'. Printing on the propaganda banknote said in part, 'the other captive peoples are uniting and will join you in your struggle. The free world is with you!'[21] Although a workers' revolt erupted in communist East Germany in 1953, it was quickly smothered by the regime and its Soviet masters. Three years later, Hungary exploded in its historic 1956 anti-Soviet uprising, encouraged by broken promises of US help carried by RFE and Voice of America broadcasts before the Red Army mercilessly crushed it. Balloon campaigns had nothing to do with either.

The Cuban Arena

In 2006, when Fidel Castro's revolutionary Cuba followed the example of its adversary the United States by changing its currency, it was for a good cause. Even before President John F. Kennedy's disastrous mistake in authorizing Allen Dulles' CIA to land a force of anti-Castro mercenaries at the Bay of Pigs in spring 1961, counterfeit Cuban pesos and forged American dollars, printed in both Cuba and the United States by gangs and individuals, had plagued Cuba's economy.

Visiting Cuba in 2006 one found a double standard in currency. Average Cuban citizens use Cuban pesos. The 'convertible pesos' system also exists and, though meant to be used only by foreign visitors, is enjoyed by members of the ruling communist elite. Banknotes and coins are used in both, but standard pesos cannot be converted into foreign hard currency. Still one must pay hard currency to get the pesos when entering Cuba. The convertibility of the second system is the reason counterfeiters in recent years target the convertible pesos rather than the standard coins and banknotes issued by the Cuban Central Bank.

However, by summer of 2007 the 'interim' government of Raúl Castro, brother of the ailing Fidel, reported as recovering from intestinal surgery performed over a year earlier, was replacing the convertible peso currency with newer banknotes dated 2006, which were supposedly more difficult to forge.[22] The fall of the Soviet Union in 1989–90 and the total cutoff of Soviet aid to Castro's economy that followed, the currency wars waged by Cuban exiles in the US, and the CIA and the criminal counterfeiters inside Cuba have all been especially tough on ordinary Cubans. For decades an underground economy fed by US dollars complicated the situation. Individual possession of the dollar was legalized in 1993, when it was worth up to 150 Cuban pesos. The dollar's legalization and other stabilization measures raised the value of the ordinary peso to 20 to the dollar by 2007. The 'convertibles' were pegged 1:1 to the US dollar and are accepted by most people in the island. Many live from remittances abroad, mainly from the US, bringing an estimated $1 billion in hard currency into the economy every year. International banks, notably Canadian ones, cooperate in this by providing easy international currency transfers.

A visitor in 2006 reported in a blogged article that 'Cuba is subject to all kinds of disruptive activity aimed at its economics and politics. This includes inundating Cuba with counterfeit US bills.' As a result, cashing anything higher than a $20 bill requires customers to show their foreign passport or Cuban ID, and to note the number of the document and the banknote's serial number.[23]

One of the American operatives responsible for spreading counterfeit pesos through the Cuban economy around the time of the 1961 Bay of Pigs invasion was Lawrence K. Lunt. In *Leave Me My Spirit*, he described his covert operations for the CIA and the terrible fourteen-year ordeal he endured in Cuban prisons as a result.[24] Larry Lunt had served in both the Second World War and the Korean War. When the Agency recruited him, he was already living on a ranch in western Cuba. Like many other open-minded Americans, he at first welcomed the revolutionary victory of Fidel and his clan over the corrupt regime of dictator General Fulgencio

Batista in 1959. However, following Castro's mass arrests, pro-Soviet pronouncements, expropriations and closing of newspapers, Lunt soon became a believer in the opposition movement encouraged by the militant exiles in Miami, Florida, and the men and women of the CIA.

As a resident covert action officer, Lunt began forming clandestine cells for the CIA among Cubans in all walks of life, from a naval officer and an official of Castro's presidential staff to a luminary of the official communist restaurant syndicate. Later, as quoted in a review of Lunt's book by Steven Emerson, he became involved in 'coordination of airdrops of arms and ammunition and explosives, counterfeit pesos, medicines, and on one memorable occasion, the hysterical *novia* [girlfriend] of an anti-Castro guerrilla chief'.[25] Cuban security apparently had Lunt under surveillance early on, but even during the flood of counterfeit 20-peso notes the CIA dropped before and during the Bay of Pigs operation, they left him at liberty. Until one day in 1965 when they seized him as he was about to board a plane in Havana to attend his parents' golden wedding anniversary celebration in Santa Fe, New Mexico. For the next fourteen years, Lunt experienced the full horrors of the Castro regime's prisons. That he was not executed for espionage was probably due to Castro's fear of US retaliation and a desire to exhibit him before television cameras as an 'imperialist' agent.[26]

Another individual active in trying to undermine the Castro regime during the earlier Nixon era was Mario Garcia Kohly. The son of the Cuban ambassador to Spain in the early 1930s, he later returned to Cuba with his American wife and his father, who subsequently held government posts. During the Cuban Missile Crisis, the 26 October 1962 edition of the *New York Times* reported that Dr Kohly, a former Havana investment banker now living in the US, had been elected president of an anti-Castro movement called the 'Cuban Government in Arms in Exile'. In June 1962, eight anti-Castro groups warned President Kennedy in a telegram not to impose a puppet government following what they predicted would be Castro's overthrow by '300,000 Cubans'. The groups made it clear that they wanted Kohly to be the new post-Castro leader.

On 3 October 1963, shortly before President Kennedy's assassination, the *New York Times* reported that an undercover agent of the Secret Service had arrested Kohly. Its headline was 'Exile Leader Seized Here in Plot to Flood Cuba with Bogus Pesos'. Electronics engineer Robert Morrow and his artist wife Cecily were also arrested. Robert M. Morgenthau, a close friend of Robert Kennedy and later New York City's District Attorney, described the Morrow couple as responsible for the counterfeit plates. A fourth alleged accomplice, Bill Grosch (possibly a false CIA name) was still at large. The *Times* said Kohly had fled Cuba in 1959, was head of the United Organization for the Liberation of Cuba, and lived at 16 South Joyce Street, Arlington, Virginia, with a Washington, DC, office at 1025 Connecticut Avenue.

Kohly and the Morrow couple evidently had not counterfeited any *American* currency. Neither were they up to anything that was not sanctioned by at least some branch of the US government, quite possibly the CIA. However, they were charged with conspiracy, punishable by five years in prison and a $5,000 fine. All were released after arraignment on $5,000 bond. Morrow and wife pleaded 'no contest' at their trial in Baltimore in February 1964 and were given suspended sentences. In spring 1964 Kohly and Bill Grosch (now in custody) were each sentenced to one year in prison. The trial judge specified that the counterfeit pesos found in their possession were for personal use as well as for arming the Cuban underground and for bribes. Kohly and Grosch were freed on $5,000 bail pending appeal. It was disclosed that an effort had been made to induce Secret Service agents, who in a sting operation had posed as money printers, to invest in the scheme.

Not for the first time, inter-agency disharmony about counterfeiting in the Johnson administration became evident in what followed. In court, Kohly affirmed that the Pentagon and the Joint Chiefs of Staff had encouraged him to pursue the forgery of Cuban pesos, then had done nothing to help him during his arrest and trial. In his defence Kohly produced an affidavit signed by US Army Colonel Warren H. Hoover. The colonel recalled that William McCormick on the Pentagon staff discussed the counterfeit plans with Kohly in August 1961, following the Bay of Pigs débâcle. Kohly had proposed using the bogus pesos to purchase weapons for the Cuban insurgents and to weaken Castro's economy. Hoover had spoken favourably about the scheme to General Maxwell Taylor, a key senior commander during the Korean War. However, the court also saw a letter from a General J. Ewell, a former aide to General Taylor. It said Taylor doubted the plan's value and did not think that Kohly had wide appeal among the Cuban people.

Vital to Kohly's defence in court was a letter signed by Richard Nixon. Kohly had allegedly met with Nixon, then still the vice president, at the Burning Tree Golf Club in Washington, DC, in 1960 while Kohly worked as a consulting engineer. According to a book entitled *Betrayal*, written by Robert P. Morrow and purporting to link Kohly and others to President Kennedy's assassination, Nixon allegedly put Kohly in contact with the CIA, two of whose high-ranking officers were also said to be present at the golf meeting with Nixon. In a letter to the court, Nixon asked it to consider a suspended sentence for Kohly who, he said, might have wrongly believed he had US government backing. In the same kind of evasive phraseology he would later use in trying to ward off the Watergate scandal, Nixon claimed he had no knowledge of 'the particular circumstances'.

The *New York Times* did not report the outcome of Kohly's unsuccessful appeal. Evidently, however, Nixon's ambiguous defence did not impress another judge. On 26 March 1966 the *Times* reported that Kohly's one-year sentence was increased to two years after he failed to surrender to prison authorities. However, after Kohly had served nine months, President Johnson pardoned him and he was released. Nixon and his biographers avoid any mention of Kohly in their books.[27]

Like the dark shadows preserved by numerous books and films about the Kennedy assassination, a mist of secrecy and uncertainty still obscures the Cuban peso operation and other covert activities targeting Castro. What appears beyond any doubt is that the CIA, and others working with it, did forge and distribute quantities of false Cuban pesos. They were intended to pay and finance anti-Castro forces and to destabilize the island's economy. It may take many more years to unearth the full truth, especially about the actual impact of the operations on the economy, security and lifestyle of Cuba's people during the long era of Fidel Castro's rule.

Mobsters, from Medallin to Moscow

Early in the 1990s, while $100 Supernotes were flowing in from the Middle East through gateways in Cyprus and points west, the US Secret Service and other global law-enforcement agencies were swamped with forged currencies of every description. In *US News & World Report* magazine of 5 December 1994 Brian Duffy wrote that 'the counterfeiting of money by the use of sophisticated technology is a growing international problem, and may eventually bring about a crisis in the world's currencies. Most of the efforts are being directed toward US currency.'[28]

The Soviet Union's collapse had led to a pandemic of greedy looting of communist treasuries, bank accounts and strongboxes, from Saint Petersburg to Vladivostok. The looters removed and flew out of the former USSR billions of dollars in real US greenback currency. In Cyprus and in European capitals from Vienna and Zurich to London, planeloads of Russians and other ex-Soviet nationals bearing baggage stuffed with real $100 and $50 bills, and smaller quantities of superbly counterfeited specimens, arrived almost daily from 1990 until the middle of the decade. According to European law-enforcement officers, mafias organized in Russia, Chechnya, Kazakhstan and other parts of the ex-USSR were operating veritable airlift operations. They would fly in from Moscow, buy up everything of value in their destination's jewellery and gold and silver marts, return to Moscow, Kiev or Saint Petersburg, and then return on another flight, sometimes as soon as the next day, with empty bags waiting to be filled again. Many private accounts denominated in dollars, sterling, deutschmarks or Swiss francs were opened. Because of its liberal banking laws, Cyprus had to ban the opening of new accounts in the mid-1990s. The island's reputation as an easy place to launder money and other assets was beginning to suffer under the weight of illegal proceeds and counterfeit Supernotes.

The dollar haemorrhages that temporarily impoverished Russia but enriched its new oligarchs (and would-be oligarchs) under the post-Gorbachev regime of President Boris Yeltsin often contained a rich admixture of counterfeit notes. Laundering of the hoards through banks, real estate sales, jewellery shops and gold and silver markets gave mafiosi many ways to launder a dishonest buck.[29]

Before the advent of the European Union's euro currency in 1998, the US dollar in its most sought-after form, the 'C-note' or $100 bill, became a mainstream form of specie throughout the former Soviet Empire and eastern Europe's newly liberated lands. Counterfeit versions of varying quality also proliferated.

Shortly before Christmas 1993, four gunmen attacked a school classroom in Russia's southern city of Rostov. They kidnapped a dozen schoolchildren, a teacher and a bus driver, demanding a ransom of $10 million, to be paid only in US $100 bills. During the four-day drama the Russian Central Bank had to borrow from the often half-empty looted vaults of private banks to collect the ransom, authorized by President Yeltsin. Once the hoard had been sent by air to the bandits, they had one final demand before releasing their hostages: a device to distinguish counterfeit American banknotes from the genuine article.[30]

In 1994, Interpol recorded that US counterfeits accounted for approximately 80 per cent of all the bogus money it was intercepting. US Secret Service data showed an increase in forgeries seized outside the US from $24.9 million in 1992 to $120 million a year later – the period of peak circulation of Iranian and North Korean Supernotes. However, some non-governmental counterfeiting experts believe that, to avoid undermining domestic and international confidence in the dollar, US Treasury estimates tend to be cautiously conservative.

After the visible and non-visible images and security features of US currency were changed from 1996 onwards, the US Treasury in cooperation with other government agencies began to release more snippets of data about counterfeit money reaching the American public. Studies by the Secret Service after 2000 were said to show that 'almost half' of the forged US money found circulating or seized in the US is transported or 'muled' into the country from abroad –

most often from Colombia. The Secret Service traced distribution paths that closely followed drug networks organized by the Medellin and other major cartels in Colombia and its neighbours. A 'mule' is paid a nominal courier's fee. He or she brings the bogus dollars through big cities like Los Angeles, New York or Miami, where there's a wide and receptive drug market. There, US-based 'sleepers' for the sponsoring organization receive the counterfeit dollars and manage their distribution, often parallel with the dope shipments, down to the street level throughout the United States.

The Secret Service focuses on investigations in the large cities and, with US Customs, scrutinizes flights from Latin America. The Bogotá resident office of the US Secret Service works with its Colombian counterparts as best it can, coordinating arrests, raiding clandestine printing plants (which may or may not be near the drug factories) and seizing the hundreds of millions of counterfeit US currency that the drug and organized crime cartels intend to push into the United States.

The Colombian production of counterfeit cash, the Secret Service has affirmed, threatens the worldwide stability of the US dollar. The shakiness of some Third World countries' economies, especially in Latin America, has caused them to 'dollarize' their monetary systems, meaning that they choose to accept the US dollar, officially or (as during the early months of the US occupation of Iraq) unofficially, as legal currency. Ecuador officially dollarized its money in April 2003 to slow down inflation and devaluation of the Ecuadorian currency unit, the sucre. As soon as US dollars became legal tender in Ecuador, the Colombian dollar forgers began to inundate Ecuador with their product. On 17 July 2001 the *Miami Herald* reported the arrest of one of the biggest Colombian forgers. He was held responsible for over $9 million in bogus banknotes passed in the US, and had over $90,000 more when arrested in Quito. The Secret Service says that it received funding from the Clinton and Bush administrations for a 'Plan Colombia'. This was intended to increase US law-enforcement pressure in Colombia and finance operations focused solely on preventing dollar counterfeiting. The Service also moved to expand its field offices to other 'dollarized' countries.

Before the latest US currency issues began circulating in 1996, Colombia was rated as the top producer of forged dollars outside the US. Marino Radillo headed an eight-man Secret Service squad based in Miami. Working with local police from 1992 to 1996, they seized $46,281,980 in fake US banknotes throughout Latin America. Some $20,986,090 came from Colombia, seconded by Argentina with $10,733,400 in counterfeit confiscations. At the same time, the Colombians were faking their own peso currency and that of Venezuela, Peru, Brazil and Cuba. Senior Colombian police officials declared in the 1990s that the Colombian operatives, mostly older men with advanced technical and engineering skills, were the 'best in the world'.

The first step in their production process is to photograph real banknotes, much as the Nazis had done in the 1940s in Operation Bernhard. Images are then transferred to aluminium printing plates. Some of the lesser-grade counterfeits are printed on common bond or other commercial paper. In a throwback to nineteenth-century techniques, real banknotes are bleached, then overprinted, usually in $50 or $100 denominations. Adrian Ramon Gonzalez, a member of the Radillo team, told a *Christian Science Monitor* reporter that the Colombians had learned how to produce the raised impression created by US Treasury intaglio printing on the Swiss-made Giori presses.

The biggest centres of the forgers, especially the most technically advanced ones, were in Bogotá and the southern Colombian city of Cali, a sometime stronghold of the drug cartels. Other groups were detected in the central Colombian city of Ibague and in Cucuta, on the border with Venezuela. False $100 bills sold for as little as $1.75 or as much as $17.50, depending on the quality. The cocaine cartels rarely floated the fake dollars themselves. Drug tycoons in the 1990s did not want to risk retribution and complications to their drug business with counterfeiting.[31]

One of the few widely publicized busts by the US Secret Service and Colombian police was reported in November 2000. Undercover work by the investigators found an underground printing plant, buried in the Andes in western Colombia. They found a press and all the gear needed to turn out high-quality $100, $50 and $20 bills. The plant had a capacity of $3 million a week. Colombian police General Alfonso Orellano estimated that the criminal syndicate had operated for up to ten years and could have produced up to a billion dollars' worth of fakes. Orellano commented ruefully to journalists: 'This, unfortunately is a natural talent, because there are self-trained counterfeiters who produce with a great deal of perfection.'[32]

Counterfeiting and Stability in Iraq

During the welter of misinformation and disinformation about Iraqi dictator Saddam Hussein's supposed weapons of mass destruction (WMDs) in the run-up to the US invasion of Iraq in March 2003, little or nothing was disclosed in Washington about Iraq's pre-1990 counterfeiting operations. Nor did the mainstream media report on the US-led coalition's own covert forging operations during the Desert Storm operation to expel Saddam's forces from Kuwait in 1991.

An Interpol and Western intelligence investigation began in 1994 in Tengen, Germany, which led along the trail of suppliers and wannabe suppliers and buyers of stolen weapons-grade uranium and plutonium using Supernotes in their dealings. A Russian firm called Ostoskotly Ltd in Moscow and the former Bulgarian state firm of Kintex were said to be involved in building up Saddam Hussein's pre-1990 military power. It was conclusively shown by Western and Israeli intelligence and the Vienna-based International Atomic Energy Agency that Saddam and his minions were actively seeking the nuclear weapons capabilities and equipment that the coalition allies and the UN destroyed after the 1991 Kuwait war. German intelligence men seized documents containing such names of Iraqi clients of the operation as Ahmed Abdel Hadi, a businessman and close associate of Jafar Dhia Jafar, Iraq's chief nuclear scientist at that time. Saddam's rogue son Uday, later killed with his brother Qusay by US troops, was almost certainly involved in the counterfeiting and procurement operation as well.[33]

One of the US Army's covert warfare units moving into Saudi Arabia for the Desert Storm campaign was the Fourth PSYOPS

Group so active during the Indo-China wars. It began operations against Iraq by producing what have been identified as four types of counterfeit propaganda notes. They bore Saddam's portrait and a scene of charging cavalry used on genuine Iraqi notes circulated especially in the northern Kurdish areas before the Kuwait war. There were evidently Saudi scruples about issuing high-quality dinar notes that could be taken for the real thing. This led their makers to blur the images somewhat. (According to a currency collectors' Web site, these initial notes were never released and are avidly sought by collectors of rare banknote and counterfeits.) Propaganda messages on the backside varied from, 'Saddam is enjoying wealth while you and your family starve' to 'Do you realize that the value of the money is dropping through the hands of Saddam at a time when he is hoarding lots of gold?'

Another Fourth PSYOPS detachment operating in Turkey printed a series of 25-dinar propaganda notes that *were* apparently disseminated. In 1991, this time as part of an alleged covert CIA operation, five additional types of 25-dinar propaganda banknotes were printed on thin paper. They are especially rare and collectors have paid between $100 and $150 for a single note. One of them shows a line drawing of Saddam with his arm around ragged children. The title reads: 'We can live twenty years . . . But our stores are empty, and your stores are full.'[34]

Iraqi exiles in London made unconfirmed claims that false Iraqi dinar notes (not propaganda forgeries) from Saudi Arabia flooded the region's black markets *after* the 1991 war as part of an ambitious covert operation to destabilize Iraq. These sources claimed the notes were smuggled across the pervious desert boundaries by Bedouin using ewes' bladders, or other equally ridiculous means.[35]

In mid-April of 2003, the second Gulf War was only a month old and already the hunt for the vanished Saddam Hussein had begun. Much of the American (but not European) public was caught up in the euphoria when President George W. Bush, wearing combat gear and standing on the flight deck of the aircraft carrier *Enterprise*, triumphantly proclaimed an illusory victory in May.

Curiosity stirred in the US Treasury building on Pennsylvania

Avenue in Washington, DC. Soldiers had been searching one of Saddam Hussein's presidential palaces in what would soon become the 'Green Zone', a heavily fortified compound sheltering the US Embassy and later the freely elected Iraqi government installed at America's behest. The GIs suddenly came upon a huge stash of hundreds of millions of dollars in boxed bills. A *Los Angeles Times* reporter who had watched one raid observed that each box found in the Baghdad palace contained $4 million in $100 bills. They were marked as Federal Reserve Notes from the Fed branches in Boston, New York or Richmond, Virginia, and dated during the previous four years. (Investigators later accused some of the GIs involved in the quest of yielding to temptation and pocketing some of the trove.) The boxes of cash were airlifted to a secure warehouse in Kuwait. Secret Service agents went over the hoard to determine how much was authentic and how much counterfeit, according to John Gill, a Secret Service spokesman.

Never supported officially because no results of the investigation were published, the early suspicion was that the stash was currency stolen from Kuwait's banks by the Iraqis during the August 1990 to February 1991 occupation. There was no reason to make a thorough check of the hoard unless the money was believed to be derived from criminal activity, according to Jimmy Gurulé, a law professor at the University of Notre Dame who had served as an undersecretary of the Treasury for Enforcement until February 2003. 'What's critical,' he said, 'is for the US government to get a handle on what the criminal activity was.' Mr Gurulé added that Saddam, knowing defeat was imminent and that the coalition would soon control Iraqi banks, had wanted to set aside a stash to continue living comfortably in hiding. (When found hiding in a hole in December 2004, Saddam had $950,000 with him.)

During the same week that over $600 million was found in the palace, $112 million was discovered inside seven dog kennels in an up-market Baghdad residential neighbourhood where top Baath Party and Republican Guard officials lived.[36] The huge dollar finds led to many unconfirmed stories. One was that the money, all originally from looted Kuwait banks, was one-fourth or even one-third counterfeit. Another was that the money was mostly real and intended to finance the nascent insurgency. Still a third theory was that the money was all private loot of Saddam, his family and his supporters, being preserved for a future comeback to power. Or all of the above.

In any case, on 24 September 2003 men and women of the US Army's 812th Military Police Company came upon a cache of counterfeit 250-dinar notes atop large uncut sheets of counterfeit currency. Iraqi detectives, along with investigators from the 812th MPs, counted an estimated 20 billion dinars (equal then to $10 million) in what they called the biggest counterfeiting bust in Iraqi history. The bust led to the phase-out of the old 'Saddam dinar' bearing the deposed dictator's image. Currency reform began on 15 October 2003. Somebody in the Bush administration had actually learned lessons in currency stability from the highly successful 1948 currency reform in occupied Germany, as described earlier in this chapter. It was one of the few successful reforms of the entire Iraq war and occupation, and it was chronicled by the currency printing industry's premier publication, *Currency News*, in its issue of April 2005.

The first aim of the reform, as *Currency News* reported, was to substitute one currency for the two then in general use: the Saddam dinar, first issued in 1992, and the so-called 'Swiss' dinar circulated mainly in the northern Kurdish regions. The second aim was to restore exchange rate stability. In the halcyon days when Western funds poured into Saddam's coffers in the 1980s, a dinar had been worth $3; by 2003 the rate had fallen to 2,300 dinars to the dollar. Security against forgery was the third main reason for the change: as the invasion toppled the regime in spring of 2003, the Central Bank's printing equipment was looted in the general pillage of Baghdad. While removing Saddam's portrait from the national money, Iraqis had to be provided with a more convenient range of denominations. The old currency had only been issued in notes of 250 and 10,000 dinars.

The operation was headed by retired US Army Brigadier General Hugh Tant III, a veteran of thirty years' service. The Civilian Personnel Authority (CPA) publicized the forthcoming new currency in July 2003. Producing it was a consortium headed by the UK's main banknote printer, De la Rue. It would comprise over two billion new notes in denominations of 50, 250, 1,000, 5,000, 10,000 and 25,000 dinars. New designs illustrating monuments and faces of Iraqi history combined with security features including colour shift, security threads, watermarks and raised lettering. The new Iraqi dinars (NIDs) were delivered to the Central Bank and 243 currency exchange points in all of Iraq. The supervising authority, called the Iraqi Currency Exchange (ICE), was to oversee collection and destruction of the old Saddam dinars by the Central Bank – all this against seemingly insuperable obstacles created by mass scepticism about the banking system, the occupation and determined violent opposition by insurgents.

Thousands of personnel took part, including people from the CPA itself, the Iraqi Central Bank, and Bearing Point, a private management consultant. Security was provided by Global Risk Strategies, one of the many private groups profiting from the war and occupation; aircraft, by the firm of Hannover Aviation; and military backup, by US, British and other coalition armies. Temporary banking and exchange personnel at the 243 exchange points were also needed.

Prior to the beginning of the exchange process on 15 October 2003, *Currency News* reported extensive planning and special training for more than 900 Iraqi banking staffers in the exchange points, distribution of equipment like counting and verification gear, and an information campaign to inform the Iraqi public of what was coming. From 15 October 2003 to 15 January 2004, old notes were collected and stored while a continuous flow of new notes went to the exchange points. Payment of government salaries were made in the new currency. In some respects the operations were not unlike those during the monetary reform in Germany of 1948 or the euro's introduction forty years later in Europe. After 15 January 2004 came the destruction of remaining old dinars, the decommissioning of the distribution networks and the final transfer of operations to the Central Bank.

The new paper banknotes weighed altogether 2,300 tons; 2.2 billion notes worth 6.38 *trillion* NIDs (equivalent to about $3.2 billion), replacing 13,000 tons of the old currency. Boeing 747 jets flew a total of twenty-seven charter flights to bring in 90 tons of the paper currency on each flight. Notes were trucked from Baghdad International Airport's well-guarded security precincts to the Central Bank and regional banks, and from there to Mosul in the north and Basra in the south for local distribution points. At each exchange point, tellers counted and verified old notes handed in and marked them indelibly with red ink. Notes were exchanged at one for one for the old Saddam dinars and 150 to one for the 'Swiss' dinars. Bank deposits were automatically converted. The Central Bank then collected the old dinars and took charge of destroying them by burning or burial in waterlogged pits to rot away. The verification process revealed that nearly 1 per cent of the collected old notes were counterfeit, according to *Currency News*, a figure that might seem surprisingly low to some analysts.

The core of the operation was a 700-man private security team including guards and staff for the distribution hubs. They were mainly from the Pacific island republic of Fiji, and included 500 Arabic-speaking Fiji soldiers. Other personnel were from Canada, South Africa, Zimbabwe, Australia, New Zealand and the UK. Some 4,000 Iraqis were recruited by the Central Bank as security guards. Delivering the currency around Iraq were six aircraft and 100 vehicles. US and British Army units of division strength guarded the ground convoys. There was plenty of need for them: there were fifteen direct attacks against surface convoys and seven against banks. In one case cited by Tant, insurgents assaulted two armed convoys on their way from Baghdad to Samarra. Reinforcements quickly appeared in the form of US infantry, ten tanks and an Apache helicopter. In the battle that followed, forty-six insurgents, one ICE team member and five soldiers were wounded. No ICE team members died in the fighting, but one was killed in a later rocket attack on Baghdad International Airport.

Counterfeiting of the new dinars of course continued, but *Currency News* reported that it had moved to Bulgaria (already known for producing quantities of counterfeit euro notes and coins). *Currency News* remarked that this indicated that 'for the first time outside of the country, the Iraqi dinar is seen as a currency worth counterfeiting'. Whoever forged old Saddam dinars was suspected at the time to be printing large quantities in hopes of laundering them during the changeover.[37]

The conservative Heritage Foundation reported in a prescient study in January 2004 on how the evolving insurgency was being financed. To avoid demonetization of their concealed riches, ex-regime elements knew they would have to change their old Saddam dinars for new ones at coalition-controlled banks – which the bank managers would probably feel compelled to report. US General John Abizaid, then commanding coalition troops, told the *Financial Times* that 'very young men have been paid to attack our forces'. The payments were from $150 to $1,000 per attack. The insurgency, the Heritage Foundation report quite accurately predicted, 'will evolve into a mafia-type organization where politically motivated attacks will be supplemented by criminal fundraising activities'. Fighting the insurgency, the report continued, would be 'more like dealing with the mafia tactics of Al Capone than the resistance of the Viet Cong in Indo-China. A national Iraqi police force trained to handle this battle will become the decisive factor.' But even at that early stage of the occupation, erstwhile presidential candidate and retired NATO commander General Wesley Clark declared the campaign to be a '$150 billion mess'.[38]

Such justified fears about the mafia-like development of the insurgency were magnified by the generally lamentable state of Saddam's Iraqi army in 2003. By the time of the US-led invasion in March, the Iraqi currency had been wrecked by over two decades of total mismanagement. The 1980–8 Iran–Iraq war had burned up Baghdad's foreign currency reserves. It laid a huge burden of debt on the country's shoulders. Productive investment dropped precipitously. This lack of investment spending in the 1990s left many scars on the economy, following the 1991 Kuwait war. High inflation (doubtless augmented by widespread counterfeiting) had debased the value of the once-strong Iraqi dinar. The legitimate proceeds and the illegal kickbacks from the UN-supervised oil-for-food sales, intended by the UN to ease the burden of UN and US economic sanctions on ordinary Iraqis, enriched Saddam's ruling Baathist clique, although it also tended to stabilize money supply and hold down price increases. Influx of huge dollar sums under the programme may also have helped to stimulate the presumed Italo-Iraqi counterfeiting operation referred to earlier. Looting, aggravated by the reckless lack of American precautions against it after the invasion began, further impoverished an economy tortured by perennial failure of the occupation authorities to restore electric power, water and other public services.

In May 2003, after Bush's triumphal proclamation that combat had ceased, cash shipments, mostly in $1 and $5 notes, were transferred from the New York Fed to Andrews Air Force base near Washington, DC, and flown to Kuwait. The CPA originally planned to pay Iraqi salaries in dollars, but many Iraqi civil servants preferred their dinars. This avoided official dollarization, as practised in Latin America. It tied Iraqi oil exports close to the US economy, at a time when big oil producers elsewhere, notably Iran and Venezuela, had begun backing away from dollar payments. The Iraqi preference for new, 'clean' dinars over the total dollarization of their economy by the occupation forces was certainly one of the factors spurring the coalition action to introduce the new Iraqi money and destroy the old.

The Strange Saga of Ahmed Chalabi

Some time in the autumn of 1972, I first met Ahmed Chalabi in Beirut. I was the Middle East correspondent of the *Christian Science Monitor*; he was then teaching mathematics at the American University of Beirut (AUB). I wanted to travel to Iraqi Kurdistan, then facing one of its periodic upheavals against Arab power, represented by Baathist rule in Baghdad. Chalabi was reputed to be a good contact with the Kurds. This scion of a big Iraqi Shia banking family proved to be just that. It became clear, as Chalaby arranged my trip to meet the patriarch and senior Kurd of the time, Mullah Mustafa Barzani, on his home territory that Chalabi also enjoyed excellent contacts with the Iranian imperial regime of Shah Muhammad Reza Pahlevi.

It was most certainly a silent man from the Shah's dreaded security and intelligence organization, SAVAK, who accompanied me, first on a grey, early-morning bus ride from Tehran to Tabriz, then in a jeep with two equally mute soldiers to the mountain crossing point that led into the Iraqi Kurdish town of Haji Omran, where Mullah Barzani's men escorted me to a cordial welcome at his headquarters. There, his men were preparing the Kurdish Peshmerga ('They Who Face Death') guerrilla fighers for new battle with the army of the then new Iraqi dictator, Saddam Hussein al-Tikriti.

As he was a Shia, it was not surprising that Chalabi remained a supporter of whatever regime was in power in Tehran. After 1991, Jordan's Petra Bank, founded by Chalabi, collapsed. Jordan filed formal charges and convicted Chalabi *in absentia* for allegedly embezzling over $50 million of Petra Bank assets – a charge he has always vigorously denied, chalking it up to professional jealousy and political rancour against him in King Hussein's realm. Throughout the 1990s, Chalabi plunged into Iraqi opposition politics, founding the well-funded and eventually US-supported Iraqi National Congress (INC). He was bent on ridding his native land of Saddam Hussein and his Sunni Muslim ruling clique.

Gradually, Chalabi worked his way into the confidences of like-minded neo-conservative advisers of President George W. Bush and his Defense Secretary until 2006, Donald Rumsfeld. Chalaby's star rose as the INC received over $40 million in State and Defense Department subsidies. Chalabi was televised sitting close to First Lady Laura Bush during George W. Bush's State of the Union address in January 2004. He turned out to be a main source for articles in the *New York Times* and elsewhere, elaborating exuberantly on Saddam Hussein's legendary WMDs – the main justification, which turned out to be false, for the March 2003 invasion. After the WMD stories began to look dubious, then fraudulent, Vice President Dick Cheney and members of his staff still stuck to their admiration of Chalabi, even after he began losing support at State and Defense – it never was very strong at the CIA.

Chalabi served on the US-appointed Iraqi Governing Council. He was planning to make a serious bid for the presidency or vice presidency following the January 2005 general elections in Iraq. Then lightning struck: Iraqi judge Zuhair al-Maliki issued an arrest warrant for Chalabi in August 2004 while Chalabi was visiting Iran. The charge: fraud and counterfeiting of Iraqi currency. In

Washington, the White House, while admitting foreknowledge of the warrant, claimed that the US was not involved in the case and that it was a purely Iraqi issue. However, unnamed US officials alleged that Chalabi might be guilty of betraying US cryptographic secrets to his Iranian friends. Chalabi denied all the charges and returned to Iraq to defend himself in court.

Before the currency change in 2003–4, counterfeiting of the old Saddam dinars had proliferated. At the time of the change, one raid in Al-Shaab, a Baghdad district, in October yielded about 6 million of the forged dinars, equipment to produce them and three arrested suspects. During the summer's earlier raids, in one against Chalabi's Baghdad residence, US agents found 3,000 counterfeit dinars of the old Saddam variety, mixed in with legitimate ones. One of Chalabi's Baghdad spokesmen confirmed this. In court in September 2004, Chalabi and his defence lawyers convinced Central Bank experts and the judge that he had deliberately retained a quantity of the counterfeit old Saddam dinars in order to show them at a forthcoming conference with banking and law-enforcement officials. Judge Zuhair al-Maliki, who had earlier charged Chalabi, withdrew the counterfeiting and fraud charges 'for lack of evidence'. He added, however, that the file could be reopened after two years if new evidence was presented. It never was. Chalabi was placed in charge of providing needed public services in Baghdad in late 2007.

Al-Qaeda Enters the Scene

The Egyptian Islamists, many of whom were precursors or co-founders of Al-Qaeda, the loosely constructed global terrorist movement spawned during the 1979–89 Afghan war, resorted to counterfeiting and money laundering to raise funds for their campaigns in Egypt. The climactic moment of that campaign was President Anwar al-Sadat's assassination by an Islamist cell in the military in October 1981 in retribution for signing the 1979 Egyptian peace treaty with Israel.

An Egyptian militant named Muhammad Amer and a volunteer associate, Al-Syed Muhammad Ibrahim, conceived with Dr Ayman al-Zawahiri (soon to become Usama bin Laden's main deputy) the idea of printing massive quantities of false US dollars, Saudi riyals and Egyptian pounds. The bogus cash was intended to finance operations in Egypt and abroad. Egyptian intelligence claimed Iranian elements supported them – Iran, in fact, was under heavy suspicion by the US Treasury of counterfeiting and disseminating great quantities of $100 Supernotes. The conspirators smuggled a sophisticated printing press and installed it in the remote village of Bassous, where police attention was thought to be unlikely. However, the Egyptian forensic police managed to turn a known professional counterfeiter and engage his services. The forgers were detected, tracked, brought to trial and imprisoned.

In early 2003, British police and MI5 operatives in Manchester, England, found a training manual on the hard drive of a suspect's computer. It provided instruction on forgeries and counterfeiting. Arrested suspects claimed that this was part of Al-Qaeda training conducted in Afghanistan. During the more recent stages of the Iraqi insurgency, the emergence of 'Al-Qaeda in Iraq' has focused Western intelligence and US Secret Service attention on use of the money-forging weapon in the insurgency. The newer, post-Saddam dinars have not proven all that difficult to duplicate. Counterfeiting, as South African academic analyst Suzanne Wannenberg observes, 'is an attractive option for Al-Qaeda as it serves the dual purpose of raising funds for its operations, as well as waging economic warfare against perceived enemies such as the US'.

This could contribute further to an undermining of public confidence in the US dollar as an international medium of exchange – already under way in 2006 and 2007 with the sharp rise of euro and sterling rates against the US dollar, and the desire of major oil producers such as Iran and the President Hugo Chávez's Venezuela to be paid in currencies other than dollars.

Wannenberg and other analysts have found that distribution of bogus US dollars through drug money-laundering networks by rogue states and groups like Hizbullah and the Chechen insurgents is a main factor compelling the US Treasury to redesign the dollar every few years. Interpol and Europol operatives were deeply concerned about a crime network in the Netherlands arrested in

2003 in possession of $100 Supernotes. They had been produced not on intaglio presses but by a Xerox DocuColor digital press. They had turned out $300 million in Supernotes in only two weeks.

Autonomous Al-Qaeda cells in several parts of the world seem to prefer smaller-scale currency counterfeiting operations. These are appropriate for so-called 'sleeper cells' that provide safe houses, weapons and forged documents for terrorists. Al-Qaeda operatives often work like ordinary white-collar criminals. They fund terrorism by obtaining false identities to obtain bank credit.

This book has sought to dip into history since the ancients, to discover how statesmen, scoundrels, spooks and just plain crooks through history have forged the currency of their adversaries in order to win wars, work the economic ruin of enemies or simply to make themselves rich – often a combination of some or all of the above.

What is clear from these narratives is that no one – the ancient tyrant of Samos, the medieval lords of the Holy Roman Empire, British monarchs and prime ministers combating American or French revolutionaries or Kaiser Wilhelm in the First World War, Napoleon Bonaparte fighting his European foes, the American Union against the Confederacy, Josef Stalin against Herbert Hoover's America, Adolf Hitler against the British Empire and its allies, or the American CIA against the Indo-Chinese communists or Fidel Castro in Cuba – has been able to win wars through the forgery of money alone. Indeed, a majority of the players of false currency games have lost their wars, empires or personal fortunes. A few, like Portugal's Alves Reis, have inadvertently brought about political change, generally for the worse, in their economies and societies.

This is not to say that currency wars will not continue into the world's future. Almost certainly, they will go on indefinitely, human nature and greed being what they are. Understanding the motives, methods and reasons for the successes and failure of the past's leading money forgers may help to limit the damage they work in the future. It is my firm hope that this book will contribute to that end.

"If you've never seen a million pound Swiss franc note, how do you know it's a forgery?"

Cartoon by Keith Waite in the *Daily Mirror*, 18 February 1970. The previous day six men had been sentenced at the Central Criminal Court for their part in a £1m plot to flood Europe with forged 100-franc Swiss notes.

Notes

Introduction

1 Ambler quote from cover of Murray Teigh Bloom, *The Man Who Stole Portugal*, New York, Carroll & Graf, 1958.

Chapter One

1 Bruno Philip 'Macao "l'enfer du jeu" flambé toujours', *Le Monde*, 20 December 2005, p. 17.
2 Quoted by Stephen Mihm in 'No Ordinary Counterfeit', *New York Times*, 23 July 2006.
3 Leong Veng Mei, Sociology Department, University of Hong Kong, 'Gambling and Organized Crime in Macao', lecture at Hong Kong University, 26 June 1999, transcript online.
4 Mihm, op. cit.
5 Mark Sherman, Associated Press, 'Feds Bust Major Counterfeiting Ring', 22 August 2005.
6 Case 1:05-cr-00185, Document 3, US District Court for the District of Columbia filed 19 May 2005, passim, online.
7 See, for example, 'The Rogue Money Printers of Pyongyang', *International Herald Tribune*, 20 October 2005.
8 'US Allegations of North Korean Counterfeiting Emerge', Radio Free Europe/Radio Liberty release, 26 November 2005.
9 Case 1:05-cr-00185, Document 3, op. cit., passim, online; US Department of Justice, press release of 8 October 2005, pp. 1–2; 'IRA Veteran Bailed over US Counterfeiting Charge', *Observer*, London, 9 October 2005, online; 'US Allegations of North Korean Counterfeiting Emerge', op. cit.; John K. Cooley, 'The Rogue Money Printers of Pyongyang', op. cit.; *Independent*, London, 10 December 2005, online.
10 Quoted in a paper by Sheena E. Chestnut, 'The "Sopranos State"?', Centre for International Security Studies, Stanford University, 20 May 2005, p. 82, online.
11 Quoted in Chestnut, ibid., p. 85, from Willie Kealey, 'Worker's Party Boss Linked to Counterfeit "Super Dollars"', *Sunday Independent*, London, 18 August 2002.

12 Kyodo World News Service, Tokyo, 25 January 2006, online.
13 AP Worldstream, 2 February 2006, online.
14 AP Worldstream, 20 April 2006, online.
15 AP Worldstream, 3 May 2006.
16 IISS, 'Strategic Survey 2006', *The IISS Annual Review of World Affairs*, London, 2006, pp. 203–5.
17 Ibid., p. 203.
18 Tony Judt, *Postwar: A History of Europe Since 1945*, New York, Penguin, 2005, pp. 107–8.
19 Jonathan Kirshner, *Currency and Coercion, the Political Economy of International Monetary Power*, Princeton, NJ, Princeton University Press, 1995, p. 156; Judt, op. cit.
20 'The Disappearing Dollar', *Economist*, 2 December 2004, online.
21 Peter G. Peterson, *Running on Empty, How the Democratic and Republican Parties are Bankrupting Our Future and What Americans Can Do About It*, New York, Farrar, Strauss & Giroux, 2004, p. 71.
22 Ibid., Introduction, pp. xi and xiii. Emphasis is mine.
23 Ibid., pp. xiii–xiv.

Chapter Two

1 William Greider, 'Annals of Finance, the Price of Money, III, the Hardest Choice', *New Yorker*, 23 November 1987, p. 102.
2 Ibid., p. 104.
3 ABC News, *World News Tonight*, investigative report, 22 January 1996.
4 Simon Brooke, 'Money to Burn', *Sunday Independent*, 25 April 1995, online.
5 M. C. Jasperson, USIA staff writer, 'Iran, Syria Accused of Counterfeiting US Dollars', USIA release No. 233652, 1 July 1992.
6 Congressional Report, 'Security Threatened by Counterfeit Bills from Iran and Syria', 14 July 1994.
7 Jasperson, op. cit.; Congressional Report, op. cit.
8 ABC News report, op. cit.
9 Author's interviews with Chief Inspector Andreas Nicolaides, Nicosia, 12–15 December 1995.
10 Author's interview with ex-president George Vassiliou, 20 December 1995.
11 Author's interviews with German intelligence sources and ex-East German Stasi operative, Berlin, 1996.
12 Frederic Dannen and Ira Silverman, 'The Supernote', *New Yorker*, 23 October 1995.
13 *Newsday* report, 13 March 1991.
14 Ronnen Bergman, 'Shocking Green', *Haaretz* magazine, Tel Aviv, 17 March 1995; Kurt Royce, 'Mystery of the Missing Money Plate', *Newsday*, 2 November 1996.

15 Author's conversations with Mr Sacavas, 5 March 1992.
16 Transcript of NBC Evening News report, 17 February 1992.
17 Ronnen Bergman, op. cit.; Kurt Royce, op. cit.
18 Ibid.
19 Bergman, op. cit.
20 Ibid.; Wilhelm Dietl, 'Geheimdienststaat Iran', *Terrorismus* newsletter, Hamburg and Wiesbaden, No. 11, April 2006, p. iv.

Chapter Three

1 'Update: Iran, Syria and the Trail of the Counterfeit Money', report by the Task Force on Terrorism and Unconventional Warfare, House Republican Research Committee, US House of Representatives, Washington, DC, 1994; authors listed are Yossef Bodansky and Vaughn S. Forrest, pp. 1–3.
2 Ibid.
3 Ibid.
4 Ibid.
5 Klaus W. Bender, *Moneymakers, the Secret World of Banknote Printing*, Weinheim, Germany, Wiley-VCH Verlag GmbH & Co. KGaA, pp. 57–61.
6 'Whatever Happened to the Commercial Banknote Printers?', in *Currency News*, Shepperton, England, Vol. 1, No. 9, September 2003, p. 13.
7 *Currency News*, Vol. 3, June 2005, p. 8, and Vol. 2, February 2005, p. 8; Bender, op. cit., pp. 68–9.
8 Nathan Adams, *Reader's Digest*, March 1995; Larry Collins, 'Alerte aux faux dollars', *L'Express*, Paris, France, 10 February 1995.
9 Bender, op. cit., pp. 71–2.
10 Interviews with two senior US oil executives in London, 1984 and 1985.
11 Interview with ex-Stasi officer in East Berlin, March 1995.
12 Conversations with Markus Wolf, March 1995.
13 Markus Wolf with Anne McElvoy, *Man without a Face*, New York, Random House, 1997, pp. 120–1; Andreas Herbst, Winfried Ranke, Jürgen Winkler, eds, *So funktionierte die DDR*, Band I, Reinbeck bei Hamburg, Rowohlt Verlag, 1994, pp. 523–9, listing and briefly describing many of KoKo's operations, but failing to mention the supposed Polygraf deal with Iran.
14 Anna Funder, *Stasiland, Stories from Behind the Berlin Wall*, London, Granta Books, 2003, p. 224; Klaus Bender, 'Die Supernote', *Frankfurter Allgemeine Zeitung*, 28 February 2006.
15 Private interviews, United Nations, New York, 1997.
16 Knut Royce, *Newsday*, 13 July 1996, online.
17 ABC News report, 22 January 1996.
18 Christopher Drew and Stephen Engelberg, NY Times Service, 'Flood of Fake $100 Bills Stumps US Investigators', *International Herald Tribune*, 28 February 1996.
19 Private interview, Washington, DC, 1997.

20 *Straits Times*, Singapore, 19 April 1995.
21 'Azeri Paper Points to Negative Impact of Fake Dollars Shipped from Iran', BBC Monitoring Service citing *Ekho* newspaper, Baku, in Russian, 17 January 2002, pp. 1 and 3, online.

Chapter Four

1 Sofia News Agency, 27 September 2006, online.
2 Franc C. Bauer, *Geld & Markt* magazine, Vienna, 24 July 2006.
3 Jonathan Williams, ed., *Money, a History,* London, British Museum Press, 1997, pp. 16–17. This richly illustrated book was published to accompany the British Museum's HSBC Money Gallery in January 1997. See also Bryan Taylor, 'Making Change', *Foreign Policy* magazine, 1 July 2004, online.
4 Williams, op. cit., p. 38.
5 *The Oxford Classical Dictionary*, op. cit., p. 858; Langer, William, ed., *The New Illustrated Encyclopedia of World History*, Vol. 1, New York, Abrams Inc., 1968, pp. 834–5.
6 Saint Clair McElway, 'Annals of Crime, Old Eight-Eighty-I', *New Yorker*, 27 August 1949, p. 10.
7 Williams, op. cit., pp. 87 and 91.
8 Ibid., p. 144.
9 Kirshner, op. cit., p. 3.
10 Langer, op. cit., p. 302.
11 Williams, op. cit., pp. 162–3.
12 Wolfram Bickerich, *Die D-Mark, Eine Biographie*, Berlin, Rowohlt, 1998, pp. 34–6.
13 Jason Goodwin, *Greenback, the Almighty Dollar and the Invention of America*, London, Hamish Hamilton (Penguin Books), 2003, pp. 17–18.
14 McElway, op. cit., p. 31; Lawrence Dwight Smith, *Counterfeiting, Crime Against the People*, New York, W. W. Norton & Co., 1944, pp. 54–7.

Chapter Five

1 Smith, op. cit., pp. 58–60.
2 Williams, op. cit., pp. 177–80.
3 Janet Gleeson, *Millionaire, the Philanderer, Gambler and Duelist Who Invented Modern Finance*, New York, Simon & Schuster, 2000, a lively and colourful account of Law's rise and fall.
4 Smith, op. cit., pp. 57–9; Mark Frankel, review of Gleeson, op. cit., *Business Week*, businessweek.com:/200/00_31, 12 October 2006, online; Lewis J. Walker, 'Easy Money Never Works', *On Wall Street Magazine*, August 1999.
5 Walker, op. cit.
6 Ibid.

7 Quoted in James N. Green and Peter Stallybrass (eds), *Benjamin Franklin, Writer and Printer*, Philadelphia, Oak Knoll Press, 2006, p. 26.
8 Ibid., p. 55.
9 Carl Sifkakis, ed., *The Encyclopedia of American Crime*, New York, Facts on File, Inc., pp. 117–18.
10 Green and Stallybrass, op. cit., p. 56.
11 Langer, op. cit., Vol. I, p. 536.
12 Ibid., p. 537.
13 David McCullough, *1776, America and Britain at War*, London, Penguin Books, 2005, p. 54.
14 Smith, op. cit., pp. 61–2.
15 Goodwin, op. cit., pp. 69–70, citing Charles Bullock, *Essays on the Monetary History of the United States*, New York, 1900.
16 McCullough, op. cit., p. 75.
17 Smith, op. cit., pp. 68–70; Goodwin, op. cit., pp. 71–2.
18 McCullough, op. cit., pp. 207 and 268.
19 David Schoenbrun, *Triumph in Paris*, New York, Harper & Row, 1976, pp. 23–45, passim.
20 John Updike, 'A Critic at Large, Many Bens', *New Yorker*, 22 February 1988, p. 106.
21 Langer, op. cit., p. 541.
22 Ibid., p. 293.
23 Langer, op. cit., pp. 541–2; Schoenbrun, pp. 300–21, passim.
24 Schoenbrun, pp. 389–90.

Chapter Six

1 Jeremy Black, *From Louis XIV to Napoleon: The Fate of a Great Power*, London, University College Press, 1999, pp. 135 and 142.
2 Lecture by Andrew D. White, Cornell University, September 1912, *USAGold* newsletter online, usagold.com/gildedopinion/assignats.html, p. 5.
3 Ibid., pp. 7–30, passim; Langer, op. cit., pp. 410–13.
4 Ibid., p. 33.
5 White, op. cit., p. 34.
6 Ibid., pp. 33–4; David Crystal, ed., *The Cambridge Biographical Encyclopedia*, Cambridge, University Press, p. 911.
7 Ibid., p. 36; Crystal, op. cit., pp. 626–9, passim; Laurent Flechaire and Jacques-Marie Vaslin, 'Et Bonaparte créa la Banque de France', *Le Monde*, 11 September 1999.
8 White, op. cit., pp. 1–2. The text that follows to the chapter's end is a mix of Sargent's ideas with my own conclusions.

Chapter Seven

1 Ernest B. Furgurson, 'The Spy Who Loved Him', *Washington Post*, 31 October 2004, p. W10.
2 John Steele Gordon, *Hamilton's Blessing, the Extraordinary Life and Times of Our National Debt*, New York, Walker, 1997, pp. 11–25; Philip H. Melanson and Peter F. Stevens, *The Secret Service, the Hidden History of an Enigmatic Agency*, New York, Carroll & Graf, 2002, pp. 3–4.
3 Anonymous author, 'Shifty', 'Talk of the Town' column, *New Yorker*, 8 September 1951.
4 Smith, op. cit., pp. 76–8.
5 Langer, op. cit., pp. 762–3.
6 Carl Sandburg, *Abraham Lincoln, the War Years*, New York, Harcourt Brace & Co., 1939, Vol. I, p. 651; Goodwin, op. cit., pp. 220–1.
7 '1861–1865: The Civil War', Tax History Museum, online at http://www.tax.org/Museum/1861-1865.htm, pp. 3–4.
8 Sandburg, op. cit., p. 651.
9 Ibid., p. 653.
10 Ibid., p. 194.
11 Ibid., p. 339; Goodwin, op. cit., p. 224.
12 Anonymous author, 'Wartime Spies', undated, Court TV Crime Library online at www.crimelibrary.com/gangsters_outlaws/cops_others/pinkteron/4.html, pp. 2–10.
13 Anonymous author, 'Southern Comfort: Issues from 1861–1864, 1864, Confederate Currency', online at www.civilwarhistory.com/Confederate%20currency.html, undated, pp. 1–2; anonymous author, 'Crisis in Confederate Currency', online at www.bivouacbooks.com/bbv5i2sl.htm, undated, pp. 1–4.
14 George B. Tremmel, *Counterfeit Currency of the Confederate States of America*, Jefferson, North Carolina and London, 2003, pp. 8–10. Tremmel's book, containing many photos and descriptions of sample bogus Southern notes, seems to be geared to the needs of collectors, and is extremely exhaustive and thorough in its analyses.
15 Ibid., pp. 10–11.
16 Ibid., p. 13.
17 Ibid., p. 13.
18 Ibid., p. 14.
19 Ibid., p. 19.
20 Ibid., p. 48.
21 Ibid., pp. 29–30, 38–41, and 46–53, passim. Direct quotes are all from Tremmel.
22 Goodwin, op. cit., pp. 227–8.
23 Sandburg, op. cit., Vol. I, pp. 418–19; Melanson and Stevens, op. cit., pp. 3–6.
24 Goodwin, op. cit., pp. 228–9.

25 Loreta Janeta Velazquez, authoress, and C. J. Worthington, ed., *The Woman in Battle: A Narrative of the Exploits, Adventures and Travels of Madame Loreta Janeta Velzaquez, Otherwise Known as Lieutenant Harry T. Buford, Confederate States Army, in Which is Given Full Descriptions of the Numerous Battles in which She Participated as a Confederate Officer; of Her Perilous Performances as a Spy, as a Bearer of Dispatches, as a Secret-Service Agent; as a Blockade-Runner; of Her Adventures Behind the Scenes at Washington including the Bond Swindle; of Her Career as a Bounty and Substitute Broker in New York; of Her Travels in Europe and South America; Her Mining Adventures on the Pacific Slope; Her Residence among the Mormons; Her Love Affairs, Courtships, Marriages &c., &c.*, Richmond, Virginia, Dustin, Gulman & Co., 1876, full illustrated book text online at http://docsouth.unc.edu/fpn/velazquez/menu.html.

26 Velazquez, op. cit., pp. 200–19 and 231–44 passim.

27 Sandburg, op. cit., pp. 273–4.

28 Ibid., p. 112.

29 Ibid., p. 429.

30 Velazquez, op. cit., pp. 464–75 passim.

31 Ibid., pp. 476 ff.

32 Quoted in Tremmel, op. cit., p. 69.

33 Ibid., pp. 54–6.

34 Anonymous author, 'Confederate Currency', undated, p. 1, online at http://www.civilwarhistory.com/Confederate%20currency.html; James Wudarczyk, 'Crisis in Confederate Currency', p. 2, online at http://www.bivouacbooks.com/bbv5i2sl.htm.

35 Tremmel, op. cit., p. 57.

36 Melanson and Stevens, op. cit., pp. 5–14.

Chapter Eight

1 Stephen Roskill, *Hankey, Man of Secrets*, Vol. I, London, Collins, 1970, p. 246; Joseph E. Persico, *Roosevelt's Secret War, FDR and World War II Espionage*, New York, Random House, 2001, p. 249; Kirshner, op. cit., p. 11, n. 25.

2 Roskill, op. cit., p. 246.

3 Ibid., p. 246

4 Nigel West, *MI6, British Secret Intelligence Operations 1909–1945*, New York, Random House, 1983, pp. 6–7.

5 H. G. de Fraine, *Servant of This House, Life in the Old Bank of England*, London, Constable, 1960, pp. 173–4.

6 Ibid.

7 Richard Deacon, *The Silent War, a History of Western Naval Intelligence*, London, Grafton Books/Collins, 1988, p. 74.

8 De Fraine, op. cit., pp. 173–4.

9 Ibid.
10 Ibid., p. 176.
11 Murray Teigh Bloom, *The Man Who Stole Portugal*, New York, Carroll & Graf, 1992, pp. 251–2.
12 Ibid.
13 Sergeant-Major Herbert A. Friedman (Ret.), 'British Forgeries of the Stamps and Banknotes of the Central Powers', online at http://www.psywarrior.com/BritishForgeriesWWI.html, pp. 4–5. The reproduction of the false 20-Reichsmarks note appears on page 12. The author interviewed Mr Friedman by telephone in November 2006.
14 Friedman, op. cit., p. 14.
15 Ibid., p. 14; Orhan Pamuk, *My Name is Red*, London, Faber & Faber, 2001, p. 10.
16 German Bundestag Publications, *Fragen an die Deutsche Geschichte*, English edition, *A Historical Exhibition in the Berlin Reichstag Catalogue*, 3rd edition, pp. 238–9.
17 Ibid., pp. 14–16.
18 Quoted in Langer, op. cit., p. 902.
19 J. Orlin Grabbe, *International Financial Markets*, 3rd edition, Englewood Cliffs, NJ, Prentice-Hall, Inc., taken from Chapter 1, 'The Rise and Fall of Bretton Woods', online at www.orlingabbe.com/bretton_woods.htm, p. 4.
20 Kirshner, op. cit., pp. 87–9.

Chapter Nine

1 Levy is also quoted in 'Adam Smith' (George J. W. Goodman), pp. 57–62, found online at www.pbs.org/wgbh/commandingheights/shared/minnito/csgermanhyperinflation.
2 Louis Snyder, *The Weimar Republic, a History of Germany from Ebert to Hitler*, Princeton, NJ, D. Van Nostrand Company, Inc., 1966, pp. 11–16.
3 Niall Ferguson, *The War of the World, History's Age of Hatred*, London, Allen Lane of Penguin Books, 2006, pp. 236–7.
4 Snyder, op. cit., pp. 22–3.
5 Ibid., pp. 53–4.
6 *Deutsche Allgemeine Zeitung*, 14 June 1924.
7 *Der Ostasiatische Lloyd* (Shanghai), 27 July 1930.
8 Sebastian Haffner, *The Ailing Empire, Germany from Bismarck to Hitler*, Munich and New York, Kinder Verlag & Fromm Publishing International Publishing Corporation, 1988, p. 245.
9 Morgan Phillips Pierce, Tamara Rose, eds, *Dispatches from the Weimar Republic, Versailles and German Fascism*, London, Pluto Press, 1999, p. 163.
10 'Loads of Money', *The Economist*, 23 December 1999.
11 Ibid.

12 *Daily Express*, London, 24 February 1923.
13 Leo Lana, *Today We are Brothers*, date and publisher not given, quoted by Snyder, op. cit., pp. 159–60.
14 Snyder, op. cit., pp. 62–5.
15 *The Economist*, 23 December 1999.
16 Georg Kretschmann, *Faszination Fälschung, Kunst, Geld- und andere Fälscher und ihre Schiksäle*, Berlin and Dresden, 2001, p. 9.
17 Karlheinz Walz, *Falschgeld, Spannendes und Kriminalistisches, Ernstes und Amüsantes aus der Welt der Geldfälscher*, Regenstauf, Germany, 1999, H. Gitel Verlag, p. 9.
18 Murray Teigh Bloom, *Money of Their Own, the Stories of the World's Greatest Counterfeiters*, London, Weidenfeld & Nicolson, 1957, pp. 140–57, passim. The German General Staff quotations appear on p. 157. Italics are Bloom's.
19 Bloom, op. cit., p. 166.
20 Langer, op. cit., pp. 947–8.
21 Ibid., p. 1035.

Chapter Ten

1 Langer, op. cit., p. 1100; 'Revolt on the High Seas', *Time*, 3 February 1961.
2 Author's conversations with Delgado in Casablanca, 3 December 1961.
3 Diamantino P. Machado, *The Structure of Portuguese Society: The Failure of Fascism*, New York, 1991, p. 133, online.
4 On Portugal's First World War role in Europe and Africa, see James M. Anderson, *The History of Portugal*, New York, Crescent Press, 2000, pp. 193 ff.
5 Murray Teigh Bloom, *The Man Who Stole Portugal*, pp. 5–10. This and the chapter on Alves Reis in another Bloom book, *Money of Their Own*, are the most complete and authoritative sources for the story of the Alves Reis counterfeiting enterprise. Hereafter they are referred to respectively as Bloom, *The Man*, and Bloom, *Money*.
6 Langer, op. cit., p. 928.
7 Bloom, *The Man*, pp. 10–15; *Money*, pp. 270–2.
8 Bloom, *The Man*, pp. 20–2.
9 Bloom, *Money*, pp. 275–7; Langer, op. cit., p. 928.
10 Bloom, *Money*, pp. 280–2.
11 Bloom, *The Man*, pp. 122–8, passim, and *Money*, pp. 278–85.
12 Sam Burton, 'Break the Bank', *Cabinet* magazine online, Issue 21, Spring 2006, pp. 5–6.
13 Ibid., p. 6; Bloom, *Money*, pp. 284–7 and 289.
14 Bloom, *The Man*, pp. 178–9.
15 Ibid., pp. 176–8.

16 James M. Anderson, ed., *The History of Portugal*, New York, Crescent Press, 2000, p. 144; Langer, op. cit., p. 927.
17 Bloom, *The Man*, pp. 182–7.
18 Langer, op. cit., p. 928; Anderson, op. cit., p. 145.
19 Bloom, *The Man*, p. 224.
20 Langer, op. cit., p. 929.
21 Ibid., p. 929.
22 Bloom, *Money*, pp. 291–7.

Chapter Eleven

1 Walter G. Krivitsky, *I was Stalin's Agent*, London, Right Book Club, 1940, pp. 138–9.
2 Ibid.
3 Langer, op. cit., pp. 955–6.
4 Ibid.
5 Online at http://www.american president.org/history/herbethoover/biography/printable.html, p. 11 of 25.
6 Ronald E. Powaski, *The Cold War, the United States and the Soviet Union 1917–1991*, New York, Oxford University Press, 1998, p. 32.
7 Krivitsky, op. cit., p. 135.
8 Raymond W. Leonard, *Secret Soldiers of the Revolution, Soviet Military Intelligence, 1918–1933*, Westport, Connecticut and London, 1999, p. 9.
9 David Dallin, *Soviet Espionage*, Connecticut, New Haven and London, Yale University Press, p. 389.
10 Ibid., p. 391; Leonard, op. cit., pp. 112–14.
11 Dallin, op. cit., p. 66.
12 Leonard, op. cit., p. 111.
13 Krivitsky, op. cit., p. 8.
14 Donald Rayfield, *Stalin and His Hangmen*, London, Penguin Books, 2005, p. 25.
15 Krivitsky, op. cit., p. 135.
16 Ibid., pp. 143–4.
17 Leonard, op. cit., pp. 38–43.
18 Most likely the same man called 'Alexandrovski', active for Soviet espionage earlier in Weimar, Germany, identified by Dallin, op. cit., pp. 113–14. His first name is mentioned neither by Dallin nor by Krivitsky.
19 Krivitsky, op. cit., pp. 144–7.
20 Leonard, op. cit., p. 113; 'Crane's in Everyone's Pocket', *Hartford Courant*, Hartford, Connecticut, 11 December 1981, p. 1; 'The Company Hat Churns Out Paper for Uncle Sam's Greenbacks', *Christian Science Monitor*, 5 September 1996, online; 'Mass. Firm Gains Allies in Currency Fight', *Boston Globe*, 9 May 1997.

21 Krivitsky, op. cit., pp. 150–7; William R. Corson and Robert T. Crowley, *The New KGB, Engine of Soviet Power*, New York, William Morrow & Company, 1985, pp. 322–6.
22 Gary Kern, *A Death in Washington, Walter G. Krivitsky and the Stalin Terror*, New York, Enigma Books, 1997, pp. xix and 31.
23 Dallin, op. cit., p. 396.
24 Leonard, op. cit., pp. 95–6.
25 Kern, op. cit., p. xiii.
26 Ibid., pp. xv–xviii.
27 Ibid., pp. 250–348, passim.

Chapter Twelve

1 Adolf Burger, *Des Teufels Werkstatt, Die Geldfälscherwerkstatt im KZ Sachsenhausen*, Berlin, Verlag Neues Leben GmbH, 1997. A second edition appeared with the film's release in March 2007: *Die Geldfälscherwerkstatt im KZ Sachsenhausen*, from Elisabeth Sandmann Verlag, Munich. Unless otherwise noted, author's citations and quotes are from the first, Neues Leben, edition, hereafter cited as Burger. Translations from the German by John Cooley, unless otherwise noted.
2 Fenton Bressler, *Interpol*, London, Sinclair-Stevenson, 1992, p. 11.
3 Ibid., pp. 12–13.
4 Ibid., pp. 5–6.
5 Lawrence Malkin, *Krueger's Men, the Secret Waji Counterfeit Plot and the Prisoners of Block 19*, New York, Little Brown & Co., 2006, p. 22.
6 Bloom, *Money*, p. 239.
7 Burger, op. cit., pp. 138–9.
8 Malkin, op. cit., p. 22.
9 Ibid., p. 23.
10 Ibid., pp.23 and p. 23; Burger, op. cit., p. 139.
11 Burger, op. cit., pp. 139–41.
12 Malkin, op. cit., p. 30.
13 Ibid., pp. 31–2.
14 Ibid.
15 Bernhard Krüger, *Operation Bernhard, the Greatest Espionage Operation of All Time*, unpublished manuscript in German with English introduction by Murray Teigh Bloom, pp. 8-1 and 8-2. The manuscript was acquired by Engima Books, and is quoted and cited here with Enigma's permission. The original was deposited with the library of Duke University in North Carolina.
16 Ibid., pp. 3–4.
17 Ibid., pp. 8–9.

18 Evelyn Finger, 'Geld oder Leben', *Die Zeit* weekly newspaper, Hamburg, February 2007; 'Hitler's Lake', *60 Minutes*, Parts I and II, CBS News, online at http://cbsnews.com/now/story/0.1597.2513339-412.00.shtml.
19 Malkin, op. cit., pp. 87–8.
20 Burger, op. cit., p. 119.
21 Malkin, op. cit., p. 107.
22 William Mackenzie, *The Secret History of S.O.E., Special Operations Executive 1940–45*, London, St Ermin's Press, 2002, pp. 113–33.
23 Malkin, op. cit., pp. 9 and 35–6.
24 Ibid., p. 44.
25 Ibid., pp. 118–21.
26 Burger, op. cit., pp. 160–2 and Shraga Elam, *Hitler's Fälscher*, Vienna, Ueberreuter, 2000, passim.
27 Ibid., pp. 128–9.
28 Ibid., pp. 213–17.
29 Ibid., pp. 218–21.
30 Ibid., pp. 224–5; Malkin, op. cit., pp. 171–3.
31 Burger, op. cit., pp. 228–48, passim; Malkin, pp. 167–85, passim.
32 Burger, op. cit., p. 290.
33 Ibid., pp. 254–7.
34 *Guardian*, London, 6 April 2005.
35 Burger, op. cit., p. 253.
36 Bressler, op. cit., p. 83.
37 Malkin, op. cit., pp. 199–200.
38 Ibid., p. 204.
39 Kirshner, op. cit., pp. 100–1.
40 Bloom, *Money*, op. cit., p. 267.

Chapter Thirteen

1 General Mark Clark, *Calculated Risk, His Personal Story of the War in North Africa and Italy*, London, George G. Harrap & Co. Ltd, 1951, pp. 438–9.
2 Wolfram Bickerich, *Die D-Mark, Eine Biographie*, Berlin, Rowohlt, 1998, pp. 104–7.
3 Ibid., p. 107.
4 Ibid., pp. 114–21; Langer, op. cit., p. 1106.
5 Anonymous eds, *Political Scandals and Causes Célèbres Since 1945: An International Reference Compendium*, London, Longman Group UK Ltd, n.d., p. 415.
6 See John K. Cooley, *Unholy Wars, Afghanistan, America and International Terrorism*, 1999, 2001 and 2003. London and Anne Arbor, Michigan, Pluto Press (distributed in the US by University of Michigan Press).

7 Evan Thomas, 'Exposing the Real Face of the CIA', review of Tim Weiner's *Legacy of Ashes, the History of the CIA*, *International Herald Tribune*, 21 July 2007.
8 Millions of other propaganda leaflets – it's not clear whether they were accompanied by bogus money – were dropped by US B-29 bombers over the Japanese main island cities during the summer of 1945 prior to the Hiroshima and Nagasaki nuclear attacks, warning Japanese to evacuate their homes, as bombing would begin 'within 72 hours'. Similar leaflets, also calling on civilians to leave and designated military units to surrender, were dropped during the Korean War and the US campaigns against Iraq in 1991 and beginning in March 2003 (telephone interviews, 2006 and 2007).
9 Sergeant-Major Herbert Friedman (Ret.), 'The United States PSYOP Organization in the Pacific During World War II', p. 10; online at http://www.psywarrior.com/vietnambanknote.html, p. 1.
10 Ibid., p. 38.
11 Neil Shehan, Hedrick Smith, E. W. Kenworthy and Fox Butterfield, *The Pentagon Papers*, Toronto, New York, London, Bantam Books, 1971, p. 3.
12 Ibid., p. 13.
13 Friedman, 'Propaganda Banknote Leaflets of the Vietnam War', online at http://www.psywarrior.com/vietnambanknote.html, p. 2.
14 Ibid., pp. 2–3.
15 Ibid., pp. 18–19.
16 Ibid., p. 20. A possible irony: at this time the Stasi is believed to have been counterfeiting Western currencies.
17 Ibid., pp. 22–3.
18 *The Pentagon Papers*, op. cit., p. 124.
19 Friedman, op. cit., p. 32.
20 Friedman, http://psywarrior.com/dissemination.html, p. 23.
21 Richard Giedroyc, "Cuba Fights Fakers of Tourist Paper Notes,", online at Numistaster.com, Krause Publications, July 11, 2007, p. 1.
22 Ibid.
23 Walter Lippmann, 'Two Months in Cuba, Notes of a Visiting Cuba Solidarity Activist', 11 July 2007; online at http://www.blythe.org/2months.html, pp. 5 and 8.
24 Lawrence K. Lunt, *Leave Me My Spirit*, Tempe, Arizona, Affiliated Writers of America.
25 Steven Emerson, 'Fourteen Years in Castro's Prisons', book review, *New York Times*, 27 January 1991.
26 Ibid.
27 The account of the Kohly affair is from an extract of a book by Peter R. Whitney, *The Morrow–Kohly–Nixon Connection*, online at http://meadams.pose.mu.edu/morrow2.htm.
28 Brian Duffy, 'High-tech Counterfeiting', *US News & World Report*, 5 December 1994.

29 Interviews with Europol, The Hague, in 1997 and personal observations and interviews in Cyprus, Greece, Switzerland, Germany and France, 1991–9.
30 Duffy, op. cit.
31 Stan Yarbro, 'Colombia is Top Foreign Maker of Bogus Dollars, Secret Service Says', *Christian Science Monitor*, 5 September 1996.
32 'Colombia Dollar Forgery Cracked', BBC News Web site, 28 November 2000.
33 Author's private interviews in London, 1998; Europol, The Hague in 1999 and Germany, 2001–3. Sources require strict anonymity.
34 Collectors' Web site: http://currency_den.tripod.com/war_counterfeits/war.html.
35 Private communication, London, 1999.
36 'After Effects: Hidden Millions; Treasury Dept. Studies Possibility Iraqi Horde is Counterfeit', *New York Times*, 25 April 2003.
37 Anonymous, 'Currency Under Attack – the Exchange of the Iraqi Dinar', *Currency News*, Currency Publications Ltd (a Reconnaissance International/Currency Research Company), Shepperton, England and Denver, Colorado, April 2005, pp. 4–5.
38 'Financing an Evolving Insurgency', Heritage Foundation, 15 January 2004, pp. 1–3.

Bibliography

Chapter One

Books

Gertz, Bill, *The China Threat*, New York, Regnery, 1997.

IISS, *Strategic Survey 2006, the IISS Annual Review of World Affairs*, London, International Institute for Strategic Studies, 2006.

Judt, Tony, *Postwar: A History of Europe Since 1945*, New York, Penguin Books, 2005.

Kirshner, Jonathan, *Currency and Coercion, the Political Economy of International Monetary Power*, Princeton, NJ, Princeton University Press, 1995.

Peterson, Peter G., *Running on Empty, How the Democratic and Republican Parties are Bankrupting Our Future and What Americans Can Do About It*, New York, Farrar, Strauss & Giroux, 2004.

Newspapers, Periodicals and Agencies

AP, Mark Sherman, 'Feds Bust Major Counterfeiting Ring', 21 August 2005.

AP Wordstream, 2 February 2006, 20 April 2006; 3 May 2006.

The Economist online, 'The Disappearing Dollar', 2 December 2004.

Independent online, 'North Korean Counterfeiting', 16 December 2005.

Sunday Independent, London, Willie Kealey, 'Worker's Party Boss Linked to Counterfeit "Super Dollars"', 18 August 2002.

International Herald Tribune, John K. Cooley, 'The Rogue Money Printers of Pyongyang', 20 October 2005.

Kyodo News Service online, Tokyo, 25 January 2006.

Le Monde, Bruno Philip, 'Macao, l'enfer du jeu', 20 December 2005.

New York Times Magazine, 'No Ordinary Counterfeit', 23 July 2006.

Observer online, London, 'IRA Veteran Bailed Over US Counterfeiting Charge', 5 October 2005.

Newsletters and Transcripts

Case 1:05-CI-00185, Document 3, US District Court for the District of Columbia, filed 5 September 2005.

Free Republic newsletter, Toronto, Michael Waller, 'Mounties: Clinton Donor a Gangster', 7 April 2000.

Leong Veng Mei, Sociology Dept, University of Hong Kong, *Gambling and Organized Crime in Macao*, lecture at Hong Kong University, 26 June 1999.

Radio Free Europe/Radio Liberty release, 'US Allegations of North Korean Counterfeiting Charge', 26 November 2005.

Stanford University, California, CISS, Sheena E. Chestnut, 'The "Sopranos" State?', published paper, May 2005.

Chapter Two

Newspapers, Periodicals and Agencies

Haaretz magazine, Ronnen Bergman, 'Shocking Green', 17 March 1995.

Independent, Simon Brooke, 'Money to Burn', 25 April 1995.

Newsday, Kurt Royce, 'Mystery of the Missing Money Plate', 2 November 1996.

New Yorker, William Greider, 'Annals of Finance, the Price of Money, III, the Hardest Choice,' 23 November 1987.

— Frederic Dannen and Ira Silverman, 'The Supernotes', 22 October 1995.

USIA (US Information Agency) Release No. 233652, M. S. Jasperson, 'Iran, Syria Accused of Counterfeiting US Dollars', 1 July 1992.

Newsletters and Transcripts

ABC News World News Tonight with Peter Jennings, investigative report, 22 January 1996.

Congressional Report: 'Security Threatened by Counterfeit Bills from Iran and Syria', Washington, DC, 14 July 1994.

NBC Evening News, Fred Francis report, 17 February 1992.

Terrorismus German newsletter, Wilhelm Dietl, 'Geheimdienst Iran', April 2006.

Chapter Three

Books

Bender, Klaus W., *Moneymakers, the Secret World of Banknote Printing*, Weinheim, Germany, Wiley-VCN Verlag GmbH & Co. KGaA.

Newspapers, Periodicals and Agencies

L'Express, Larry Collins, 'Alerte aux faux dollars', 10 February 1995.

Reader's Digest, Pleasantville, NY, Nathan Adams, 'Counterfeits from the Mideast', March 1995.

Newsletters and Transcripts

Currency News, Shepperton, England, anon., 'Whatever Happened to the Commercial Banknote Printers?', Vol. I, No. 9, September 2003.

Report by the Task Force on Terrorism and Unconventional Warfare, 1994, US House of Representatives, Yossef Bodansky and Vaughn S. Forrest, 'Update: Iran, Syria and the Trail of the Counterfeit Money', n.d.

Chapter Four

Books

Bickerich, Wolfram, *Die D-Mark, Eine Biographie*, Berlin, Rowohlt, 1998.

Goodwin, Jason, *Greenback, the Almighty Dollar and the Invention of America*, London, Hamish Hamilton (Penguin Books), 2003.

Hammond, N. G. L. and H. H. Scullard, *The Oxford Classical Dictionary*, second edn, Oxford, Clarendon Press, 1970.

Kirshner, Jonathan, *Currency and Coercion, the Political Economy of International Monetary Power*, Princeton, NJ, Princeton University Press, 1995.

Langer, William L., ed., *The New Illustrated Encyclopedia of World History*, Vol. I, New York, Harry N. Abrams, Inc. (Houghton Mifflin), 1968.

Smith, Lawrence Dwight, *Counterfeiting, Crime Against the People*, New York, W. W. Norton & Co., 1944.

Williams, Jonathan, ed., *Money, a History*, London, British Museum Press, 2002.

Newspapers and Agencies

Sofia News Agency, untitled, 27 September 2006.

Magazines

Foreign Policy, Washington, DC, Brian Taylor, 'Making Change', 1 July 2004.

Geld und Markt magazine, Vienna, Austria, 24 July 2006.

New Yorker, St Clair McElway, 'Annals of Crime', 27 August 1949.

Chapter Five

Books

Gleeson, Janet, *Millionaire, the Philanderer, Gambler and Duelist Who Invented Modern Finance*, New York, Simon & Schuster, 2000.

Green, James N. and Peter Stallybrass, eds, *Benjamin Franklin, Writer and Printer*, Philadelphia, Oak Knoll Press, 2006.

McCullough, David, *1776, America and Britain at War*, Penguin Books, 2005.
Schoenbrun, David, *Triumph in Paris*, New York, Harper & Row, 1976.
Sifkakis, Carl, ed., *The Encyclopedia of American Crime*, New York, Facts on File Inc., n.d.
Smith, Lawrence Dwight, *Counterfeiting, Crime Against the People*, New York, W. W. Norton & Co., 1944.
Williams, Jonathan, ed., *Money, a History*, London, British Museum Press, 2002.

Magazines

New Yorker, John Updike, 'A Critic at Large, Many Bens', 22 February 1988.
On Wall Street magazine, Lewis J. Walker, 'Easy Money Never Works', August 1999.

Chapter Six

Books

Black, Jeremy, *From Louis XIV to Napoleon: The Fate of a Great Power*, London, University College Press, 1999.
Crystal, David, ed., *The Cambridge Biographical Encyclopedia*, second edn, Cambridge, England, Cambridge University Press, 1998.
Langer, William L., ed., *The New Illustrated Encyclopedia of World History*, Vol. I, New York, Harry N. Abrams, Inc. (Houghton Mifflin), 1968.

Newsletters

USA Gold newsletter, New York, Andrew D. White, lecture at Cornell University, September 1912.

Chapter Seven

Books

Goodwin, Jason, *Greenback, the Almighty Dollar and the Invention of America*, London, Hamish Hamilton (Penguin Books), 2003.
Gordon, John Steele, *Hamilton's Blessing, the Extraordinary Life and Times of Our National Debt*, New York, Walker, 1997.
Langer, William L., ed., *The New Illustrated Encyclopedia of World History*, Vol. II, New York, Harry N. Abrams Inc. (Houghton Mifflin), 1968.
Melanson, Philip H. and Peter F. Stevens, *the Secret Service, the Hidden History of an Enigmatic Agency*, New York, Carroll & Graf, 2002.

Sandburg, Carl, *Abraham Lincoln, the War Years*, Vol. I, New York, Harcourt Brace & Co., 1939.

Smith, Lawrence Dwight, *Counterfeiting, Crime Against the People*, New York, W. W. Norton & Co., 1944.

Tremmel, George B., *Counterfeit Currency of the Confederate States of America*, Jefferson, North Carolina and London, McFarland & Co., 2003.

Velazquez, Loreta Janeta (author) and C. J. Worthington, ed., *The Woman in Battle*, Richmond, VA, Dustin Gulman & Co., 1876. Printed mss with engravings, on deposit at the Library of the University of North Carolina, Chapel Hill.

Newspapers

Washington Post, Ernest B. Furgurson, 'The Spy Who Loved Him', 31 October 2004.

Magazines

New Yorker, 'Shifty', in 'Talk of the Town', 8 September 1951.

Transcripts

Civil War History, anon., 'Southern Comfort, Issues from 1861–1864; Confederate Currency', n.d.; online at www.crimelibrary.com/gangstersoutlaws/cops others/pinkerton/4html.

Court TV Crime Library, anon., 'Wartime Spies'; online at www.bivouacbokks.com/bbu5i25/htm, undated.

Chapter Eight

Books

Anon., ed., *Fragen an die Deutsche Geschichte*, English edn, Historical Exhibition in the Berlin Reichstag; Catalogue, third edn, 1998.

Bloom, Murray Teigh, *The Man Who Stole Portugal*, New York, Carroll & Graf, 1992.

Deacon, Richard, *The Silent War: A History of Western Naval Intelligence*, London, Grafton Books/Collins, 1988.

De Fraine, H. G., *Servant of This House, Life in the Old Bank of England*, London, Constable, 1960.

Grabbe, J. Colin, *International Financial Markets*, third edn, Englewood Cliffs, NJ, Prentice Hall (Simon and Schuster), 1999.

Kirshner, Jonathan, *Currency and Coercion, the Political Economy of International Monetary Power*, Princeton, NJ, Princeton University Press, 1995.

Langer, William L., ed., *The New Illustrated Encyclopedia of World History*, Vol. II, New York, Harry N. Abrams (Houghton Mifflin), 1968.
Panmuk, Orhan, *My Name is Red*, London, Faber & Faber, 2006.
Roskill, Stephen, *Hankey, Man of Secrets*, Vol. I, London, Collins, 1970.
West, Nigel, *MI6, British Secret Intelligence Operations 1900–1945*, New York, Random House, 2001.

Transcripts

SGM Herbert A. Friedman (Ret.), 'British Forgeries of the Stamps and Banknotes of the Central Powers', n.d.; online at http://www.psywarrior.com/British ForgeriesWWI.html. Includes images of several forged banknotes, obtained from private collections.

Chapter Nine

Books

Ferguson, Niall, *The War of the World, History's Age of Hatred*, London, Allen Lane (Penguin Books), 2006.
Haffner, Sebastian, *The Ailing Empire, Germany from Bismarck to Hitler*, Munich and New York, Kinder Verlag & Fromm International Publishing Corporation, 1988.
Pierce, Morgan Phillips and Tamara Rose, eds, *Dispatches from the Weimar Republic, Versailles and German Fascism*, London, Pluto Press, 1999.
Snyder, Louis, *The Weimar Republic, a History of Germany from Ebert to Hitler*, Princeton, NJ, D. Van Nostrand Company, Inc., 1966.

Newspapers

Daily Express, London, 24 February 1923.
Deutsche Allgemeine Zeitung, 14 June 1924.
The Economist, 'Loads of Money', 23 December 1989.
Der Ostasiatische Lloyd, Shanghai, 27 July 1930.

Transcripts

'Adam Smith' (George J. W. Gordon), online at www.pbs.org?wgbh/command ingheights/shared/minnito/ssgermanhypoerinflation, 15 February 1997.

Chapter Ten

Books

Anderson, James M., *The History of Portugal*, New York, Crescent Press, 2000.
Bloom, Murray Teigh, *Money of Their Own, the Stories of the World's Greatest Counterfeiters*, London, Weidenfeld & Nicolson, 1957.
— *The Man Who Stole Portugal*, New York, Carroll & Graff, 1992.
Langer, William L., ed., *The New Illustrated Encyclopedia of World History*, Vol. II, New York, Harry N. Abrams, Inc. (Houghton Mifflin), 1968.
Machado, Diamantino P., *The Structure of Portuguese Society: The Failure of Fascism*, New York (publisher not given), 1991.

Magazines

Cabinet, Sam Burton, 'Break the Bank', No. 21, Spring 2006.
TIME, 'Revolt on the High Seas', 3 February 1961.

Chapter Eleven

Books

Corson, William R. and Robert T. Crowley, *The New KGB, Engine of Soviet Power*, New York, William Morrow & Co., 1985.
Dallin, David, *Soviet Espionage*, New Haven, CT and London, Yale University Press, 1955.
Kern, Gary, *A Death in Washington, Walter G. Krivitsky and the Stalin Terror*, New York, Engima Books, 1997.
Krivitsky, Walter G., *I was Stalin's Agent*, London, Right Book Club, 1940.
Langer, William L., ed., *The New Illustrated Encyclopedia of World History*, Vol. II, New York, Harry N. Abrams, Inc. (Houghton Mifflin), 1968.
Leonard, Raymond W., *Secret Soldiers of the Revolution, Soviet Military Intelligence, 1918–1933*, Greenwood Press, Westport, CT and London, 1999.
Powaski, Ronald E., *The Cold War, The United States and the Soviet Union 1917–1991*, New York, Oxford University Press, 1998.
Rayfield, Donald, *Stalin and His Hangmen*, London, Penguin Books, 2005.

Newspapers

Boston Globe, 'Mass. Firm Gains Allies in Currency Fight', 9 May 1997.
Christian Science Monitor, 'The Company That Churns Out Uncle Sam's Greenbacks', 5 September 1996.
Hartford Courant, Hartford, CT, 'Crane's in Everyone's Pocket', 11 December 1981.
New York Times, 20 March 2007.

Transcripts

Anon., 'Herbert Hoover'; online at http://www.american.president.org/history/herberthoover/biography/printable/html.

'Timeline of Russian–American Relations 18th–20th Century'; online at http://moscow.usembassygov./links/printhistory.php.

Chapter Twelve

Books

Bloom, Murray Teigh, *Money of Their Own, the Story of the World's Greatest Counterfeiters*, London, Weidenfeld & Nicolson, 1957.

Bressler, Fenton, *Interpol*, London, Sinclair-Stevenson, 1992.

Burger, Adolph, *Des Teufels Werkstatt, die Geldfälscherwerkstatt im KZ Sachsenhausen*, Berlin and Munich, Verlag Neues Leben, GmbH, 1997.

Kirshner, Jonathan, *The Political Economy of International Monetary Power*, Princeton, NJ, Princeton University Press, 1995.

Krüger, Bernhard, *Operation Bernhard, the Greatest Espionage Operation of All Time* (title in English, text in German), unpublished mss with English introduction by Murray Teigh Bloom. (Publication rights are held by Engima Books, New York. Translations from the German text by John K. Cooley.)

Mackenzie, William, *The Secret History of S.O.E., Special Operations Executive 1940–45*, London, St Ermin's Press, 2002.

Malkin, Lawrence, *Krueger's Men, the Secret Nazi Counterfeit Plot and the Prisoners of Block 19*, New York, Little, Brown & Co., 2006.

Newspapers

Guardian, London, 6 April 2005.

Die Zeit, Hamburg, Evelyn Finger, 'Geld Oder Leben', 9 February 2007.

Transcripts

'Hitler's Lake', on *60 Minutes*, Parts I and II, CBS News; online at http://cbsnews.com/new/story/0.159725339-412.00.shtml.

Chapter Thirteen

Books

Anon., eds, *Political Scandals and Causes Célèbres Since 1945: An International Reference Compendium*, London, Longman Group UK Ltd, n.d.

Bickerich, Wolfram, *Die D-Mark, eine Biographie*, Berlin, Rowohlt, 1998.

Clark, General Mark, *Calculated Risk, His Personal Story of the War in North Africa and Italy*, London, George G. Harrap & Co. Ltd, 1951.

Langer, William L. ed., *The New Illustrated Encyclopedia of World History*, Vol. II, New York, Harry N. Abrams Inc. (Houghton Mifflin), 1968.

Sheehan, Neil, Hedrick Smith, E. W. Kenworthy and Fox Butterfield, *The Pentagon Papers*, London, Bantam Books, 1971.

Newspapers

Christian Science Monitor, Stan Yarbro, 'Colombia is Top Foreign Maker of Bogus Dollars, Secret Service Says', 5 September 1996.

International Herald Tribune, 'Expressing the Real Face of the CIA' (review of Tim Weiner's book *Legacy of Ashes, the History of the CIA*).

Le Monde, 'Arret des pursuites contre Ahmed Chalaby', 29 November 2004.

New York Times, 'Hidden Millions; Treasury Dept. Studies Possibility Iraqi Hoard is Counterfeit', 25 April 2003.

— Steven Emerson, 'Fourteen Years in Castro's Prisons', book review, 27 January 2007.

Magazines and Journals

South African Journal of Political Science, 'Links Between Organized Crime and Al-Qaeda', Vol. 10, No. 2, Spring 2003.

U.S. News and World Report, Brian Duffy, 'High-tech Counterfeiting', 5 December 1994.

Newsletters

Currency News, 'Currency Under Attack – the Exchange of the Iraqi Dinar', Shepperton, England, Currency Publications Ltd (Renasissance International/Currency Research), April 2005.

Heritage Foundation newsletter, 'Financing an Evolving Insurgency', 15 January 2004.

Transcripts

BBC News website, 28 November 2000.

Currency and stamp collectors' website, undated; online at http://currencyden.tripod.com/war_counterfeits/war. html.

SGM (Master Sergeant) Herbert Friedman (Ret.), 'The United States PSYOP Organization in the Pacific During World War II', online at http://www.psywarrior.com/vietnambanknote.html, undated.

— 'Propaganda Banknotes of the Vietnam War', online at same URL as above.

— 'Distribution of Propaganda Banknotes During Asian Wars', online at http://psywarrior.com/dissemination, n.d.

Richard Giedroye, 'Cuba Fights Fakers of Tourist Paper Notes', online at Numistrtel.com, Krause Publications, 11 July 2007.

Walter Lippmann, 'Two Months in Cuba, Notes of a Visiting Cuba Solidarity Activist', online at http://www.blythe.org/2months.html, 11 July 2007.

Suggestions for Further Reading

For more on counterfeiting in America from early colonial times to the twentieth century, two books stand out: Lawrence M. Friedman's *Crime and Punishment in American History*, New York, Basic Books, a Division of HarperCollins, 1993; and Colin Wilson's *The Mammoth Book of True Crime, New Edition*, London, Robinson, 1988.

Stephen Mihm's book *A Nation of Counterfeiters: Capitalists, Con Men and the Making of the United States* (Harvard University Press, 2007), became available too late to be consulted for this book. It deals with the 1790–1860 period in America and is a detailed, well-written and -researched account of maverick banking and promiscuous printing of all types of money in the US during the years between the American Revolution and the Civil War.

Those who read German will appreciate Georg Kretschmann's *Faszination Fälschung, Kunst-, Geld und andere Fälscher und ihre Schicksale*, Berlin, Parthas Verla, 2001, which focuses on the careers of forgers of art and other precious objects, as well as considerable perpetrators and episodes of currency counterfeiting through history.

For one of the most sensationalized consequences of the Nazi Operation Bernhard, Richard Wires' *The Cicero Spy Affair, German Access to British Secrets in World War II*, Westport, CT and London, Praeger, is a thoroughly researched, extremely well-written and analytical approach to the career and repercussions of 'Cicero', the code-name of the British ambassador in Ankara's Albanian-Turkish valet, who in 1943 turned over impressive quantities of highly secret Allied messages and documents to Nazi agents in Turkey – and was paid for his pains in over £50 million in the bogus banknotes produced in Sachsenhausen concentration camp.

This book also contains one of the most exhaustive bibliographies on Second World War espionage and secret operations this author has seen. One of the most important books in English cited by Wires is Ludwig C. Moyzisch, *Operation Cicero* (New York, Coward McCann, 1950), an English-language adaptation of the memoir of the German attaché and intelligence officer in Ankara who received most of the British material from 'Cicero'.

An imaginative German-language novel narrates a tale of European counterfeiters in 1999, during the conversion of the Eurozone currencies to the new euro banknotes, forging euros on a huge, almost industrial scale. Most of the action is set in the Netherlands. Twists in the plot and many of the episodes appear to be based on real events. The Dutch author is Roel Janssen and the book is titled *Die Eurofälscher, Der Wirtschaftskrimi zur neuen Währung*, translated from Dutch into German by Dieter Männer and published by Campus Verlag (Frankfurt, 2000).

'Another thing, Titmouse—when we find £10 million-worth of counterfeit notes, we burn 'em—not stick them in the dustbin'

Cartoon by 'Mac' (Stan McMurtry), published in the *Daily Mail*, 26 July 1973, during a period of high inflation, counterfeiting, and social unrest.

Index